On Top Down Under

By the same authors

Ray Robinson

Between Wickets
From the Boundary
Green Sprigs (The Glad Season)
The Wit of Sir Robert Menzies
Cricket's Fun
The Wildest Tests

Gideon Haigh

The Battle for BHP
The Cricket War
The Border Years
One Summer, Every Summer
Gideon Haigh's Australian Cricket Anecdotes

ON TOP DOWN UNDER

AUSTRALIA'S CRICKET CAPTAINS

Ray Robinson and Gideon Haigh

Foreword by Ian Chappell

ANDRE DEUTSCH

This revised edition first published in Great Britain in 1997 by
André Deutsch Limited
106 Great Russell Street
London WC1B 3LI

First published in Australia in 1975
Revised edition published by Wakefield Press, Australia, in 1996

A catalogue record for this book is available from the British Library

ISBN 0 233 99122 0

Printed and bound by Hyde Park Press, Adelaide, Australia

CONTENTS

For my grandmother
G.H.

FOREWORD

'**B**ertie, you said ...' and with that Ray Robinson would search through his coat pockets and drag out several crumpled bits of newspaper which all looked as though a chook with ink-stained feet had walked across the margins. After peering at his scribbling through fast-fading eyes he'd produce from one particular scrap of paper a quotation of yours which could easily date back to schooldays.

That sums up Australia's best cricket writer. Ray was meticulous when it came to quotations and consequently was a trusted member of the profession. So well-trusted that players didn't baulk when he occasionally used a nickname that was considered 'for team mates' use only'.

In addition to being trusted, Ray Robinson was very popular among the players. Rod Marsh used regularly to take the top off a bottle of beer a couple of hours before stumps, not to make an early start on drowning a thirst, but to accommodate Ray's ulcer. Marsh had discovered that

'Sugar' Ray's angry stomach could be pacified by a flat beer and so he'd have one ready for the gentleman writer, to prolong his stay in the dressing room. For Rod Marsh to deliberately allow a beer to go flat meant he respected Ray.

Ray's entertaining descriptions and thoughtful analysis of Australia's cricket captains have been a great source of amusement and reference over the years. Originally I was seeking more information on my grandfather Vic Richardson, who captained Australia in 1935–36. Having discovered a few things about my mother's father I didn't know, and in the process being amused to discover that we thought along similar lines on the cricket field, I decided to read about some other captains.

That's how I got to know more about characters like handsome Dave Gregory and Herbie Collins the bookmaker. My favourite is the 'Big Ship', Warwick Armstrong. Any man who has a teetotal administrator gunning for him and still downs a few whiskies (medicinal purposes only) before walking on the MCG to belt hell out of the Englishmen is a player I admire. Sadly I didn't meet Armstrong, but because of the quality of Ray Robinson's writing and research I now know more about the 'Big Ship'. I am a fan.

I am delighted Ray Robinson's marvellous work *On Top Down Under* is being updated by Gideon Haigh, another writer with a bent for hunting down facts and quotations. It is good to know that future generations of cricket fans will have the opportunity to get to know better Australia's cricket captains.

IAN CHAPPELL
Sydney 1996

PREFACE

Have Typewriter, Will Travel

Gideon Haigh on Ray Robinson

'We have here a gem of the first water. After reading only the first three chapters already I am deeply fascinated and enthralled by the incredible amount of absorbing detail which you have produced, obviously after long and diligent research. Your book should sell like Woolworths' pantyhose.'

So wrote Sir Donald Bradman to Ray Robinson after perusing an advance copy of *On Top Down Under*, just before its publication in 1975, and the Don was, as ever, right. If ever a cricket book was destined for and deserving of the title 'classic', it is this one.

I can still remember as a twelve-year-old borrowing it from my local library. The style was at once addictive, the subject matter engrossing: it made Australia's cricket captains sound like characters in a sweeping family saga.

Robbie's metaphors and elliptical prose made me buzz with pleasure. There was Bradman 'making others' purple patches look like washed-out lilac', Simpson 'with a mind no easier to change than a 100-pound note', Lawry with a wicket 'as inviolate as a detective's daughter'.

Characters rose from the page as though coming to shake your hand. I can recall without looking it up how the twenty-one-stone ogre Warwick Windridge Armstrong, aka 'The Big Ship', erupted out of Robbie's prose: 'A simple switch of initials could have transformed W.W. Armstrong into the *S.S. Armstrong*, a vessel more noted for tonnage than tact, and one not above a little gunboat diplomacy at times.' I laid the book aside on completion in awe at the staggering scholarship, the minutiae laid bare, and a comprehension of why Bradman called Robinson 'probably the finest cricket writer this country has produced'.

Raymond John Robinson is a figure virtually unique in Australia. Despite cricket's fecundity with books, few Australian writers have aspired to crafting cricket literature of the kind associated with Sir Neville Cardus, R.C. Robertson-Glasgow, Alan Ross, Ronald Mason, E.W. Swanton, J.M. Kilburn and A.A. Thomson.

Australia has been a country where the pronouncements of ex-players – no matter how poorly expressed – have always been viewed as gospel. Among them only Jack Fingleton, Tom Horan and – to a lesser degree perhaps – A.G. Moyes and R.S. Whitington have risen above that ruck to create work that stands scrutiny.

Despite not playing at the top level, Robinson made a reputation in the cricket community too large to ignore. No writer anywhere, I think, has so successfully combined elegance of prose and density of factual detail.

Robinson's is the zeal of the autodidact. He was born in Melbourne on 8 July 1905, the first of three sons for Brighton butcher John Robinson, and attended Brighton State School. He attributed his fascination with sport to a period in his childhood when, because his mother had fallen ill, he lived with his grandmother's family, the Dicks.

The Dicks were a Brighton football dynasty, founded on the exertions of Bob (captain of Footscray), Alec (captain of Essendon for four consecutive premierships in 1891–94) and Alec's son Bill (who captained Carlton 1914–17). Robinson told an interviewer from the National Library of Australia: 'I feel that listening to their conversation, their anecdotes of what was happening every Saturday, greatly stirred my imagination and might have been responsible completely, really, for the interest I later showed in sport myself.'

Robinson's first glimpse of big cricket was watching Australia win the Melbourne Test of 1920–21, and he remembered ever after the image of the country's cumbrous captain. 'As a fourteen-year-old schoolboy watching with older cousins, my first sight of a Test captain had been huge Warwick Armstrong, subjected to barracking as heavy as his own tread.'

Robinson was by then working to support his family in a Flinders Lane warehouse. He later became an office boy at *Punch Weekly* magazine. His uncle by marriage, Ern Bailey, then informed him of a vacancy for a copyboy on Melbourne's afternoon daily the *Herald*, and Robinson started in the telephone room taking copy telephoned in by reporters in the field. He was a general cadet at the *Herald*, then for two years a junior reporter at the *Weekly Times* – which allowed him Saturdays off to play cricket for Brighton.

The first time Robinson's fascination with cricket and interest in writing converged, the publisher was not Australian but English. Sir Pelham Warner was still wanting for an Australian correspondent at his four-year-old *Cricketer* magazine when he received a letter from the twenty-year-old Robinson, deploring its poor coverage of cricket down under.

So began an association that lasted fifty-four years. Scarcely an edition of the magazine appeared without some contribution from Robinson: news, features, match reports, obituaries, spreading his name throughout cricket's kingdom. His last submission appeared alongside his own death notice.

Robinson began writing cricket for Australian audiences at the *Star* in 1930 and, thanks to a kindly and personable manner that swiftly gained him the trust of cricketers, established a reputation for accuracy and for being the first with the latest. A fascinating example of Robinson's *modus operandi*, and an intriguing story of one that got away, emerged in his National Library interview.

Robinson had an understanding with Bill Ponsford that the great Victorian batsmen would keep him appraised by a numerical code of selection news, and was working as a sub-editor at the *Herald* just before the First Test in November 1932 when he received a telegram: 'Three declared unfit, signed Two.'

Robinson's boss, however, refused to believe that Bradman could be unfit. Robinson recalled: 'The editor whom I was working for at the time hadn't been there long and, although a very good editor, he had his doubts about how authentic this could be, so the only thing that happened as a result of the message was that a guarded paragraph was put in the Stop Press ...' Robinson's information was, of course, correct.

Probably no cricket writer before or since has enjoyed such an exceptional rapport with players. Bradman himself said that Robinson 'left

xiii

behind not a single enemy', and the English writer E.W. Swanton observed that his contemporary 'enjoyed the confidence and respect of the players to a degree I have not known equalled by any other cricket writer'.

Despite his work at the *Cricketer*, Robinson found Australian proprietors reluctant to publish him. They preferred to use the talented wordsmith as a sub-editor. There were frustrations even when Jack Waters, editor of the *Star*, induced the managers of the Australian Press Association to attach Robinson to their London office while Australia toured England in 1934.

Geoffrey Tebbutt – an Australian expatriate working in London who had written a book on the 1930 tour – decided that he would again be senior Press Association writer. Allowed to write only weekly, Robinson kicked his heels covering stories at Australia House. It wasn't until late in the tour that he was freed to file more regularly.

The 1934 tour was still an education for the twenty-nine-year-old Australian. He studied for the first time at close quarters the art of cricket literature. 'At the time of my first visit to England I had yet to learn that there was more to cricket writing than accuracy and clarity,' Robinson said. 'Working in London I had for the first time an opportunity to read Neville Cardus with his whimsical charm, and the keener wit of R.C. Robertson-Glasgow.'

Robinson and Cardus became close friends when they found themselves in Sydney during the second world war: the former after accepting an invitation from Cyril Pearl to be foreign editor of the *Sunday Telegraph*, the latter as a refugee from the Blitz slumming it as *Sydney Morning Herald* music critic.

Robinson visited Cardus's residence in King's Cross in 1945, and asked him to peruse the manuscript of a book called *Between Wickets* that he had spent several years of spare time working on. Not only did the Englishman like it, but he offered Robinson an introduction and recommendation to his own publisher Sir William Collins.

Collins, already familiar with Robinson through the *Cricketer* and London's Daily Telegraph, appreciated *Between Wickets* as well. The first of four editions appeared in 1946 to a rapturous response and the book eventually sold 50,000 copies. He bought his house at 11 Wollombi Road, Northbridge, with the proceeds, referring to it ever after as 'Between Wickets'.

On the basis of the reviews, Robinson was rostered to cover the Test matches of 1946–47 by the *Sydney Sun*, and then to report Bradman's valedictory 1948 tour of England. But Australian editors wedded to the idea of player-punditry still did not take to his work. After returning to Australia in November 1948, Robinson was eclipsed at the *Sydney Sun* by an ex-player in R.S. Whitington and put back to work as a sub-editor.

Robinson kept quietly plugging away for his overseas employers – which ranged from English newspapers and magazines to India's *Sportsweek* and the *Times of India* – often filing three or four match reports a day. He sat in press boxes mostly in the company of Bill O'Reilly, watching cricket through field-glasses and covering exercise books in his unintelligible hieroglyphics that recorded every delivery.

Robinson continued to publish books at regular intervals. *From The Boundary* sold 15,000 copies when published in 1951. Then, after Robinson had followed Lindsay Hassett's 1953 Australians round England, *Green Sprigs* emerged in 1954 with a simultaneous British edition called *The Glad Season*.

But the frustrations Robinson suffered in plying his trade in his own country often caused comment. After criticising Australian cricket writing for its sameness and sensationalism in his book on the 1950–51 Ashes series, *Elusive Victory*, E.W. Swanton commented: 'One other thing for which I can scarcely forgive the Australian newspaper proprietors is that, for all their space, they do not allow an outstanding cricket writer like Mr Ray Robinson to write about the game at all.' A visitor during the 1954–55 Ashes series, broadcaster John Arlott, called Robinson 'surely the most underestimated of cricket writers': 'His output was high; his work-rate fast, his reliability monumental, his patience inexhaustible, his good humour unfailing.'

In some respects, Robinson martyred himself to cricket. He followed Australia to the West Indies in 1955 and South Africa in 1957–58, working from then until 1966 as a sub-editor in winter and a cricket writer in summer for the *Sydney Morning Herald*, and the strain of almost constant labour broke Robinson's marriage and his health.

Robinson had married Ellen Gurnin from New Norfolk in Tasmania in 1928 and fathered Brian in 1930 and Audrey Clarice in 1934, but his frequent absences led to their estrangement.

At sixty-one, Robinson suffered detached retinas that required treatment in Boston, Massachusetts. He was too impoverished to afford the trip, and the New South Wales Cricket Association advanced him a loan. When the surgeons there discovered that Robinson had a hereditary stomach complaint, Australian journalists in the US donated fifteen pints of blood for the transfusions.

Loss of sight in Robinson's right eye checked his output, but did not stop it. He was a special writer for *People* magazine and a weekly contributor to the *Sydney Morning Herald* until 1970, while working on a book about cricket matches that had become riotous assemblies, published by Pelham in 1972 as *The Wildest Tests*. He wrote monthly for the *Australian Cricket* magazine founded in 1968, and the local version of *Cricketer* started in 1973.

Robinson had also sought and been granted a six-month Commonwealth Literary Fund Fellowship, worth all of $85 a week, in order to begin *On Top Down Under*. Holed up in his tiny Northbridge home and living on baby food, eggs and black currant juice on account of his diseased stomach, Robinson began what would be his *magnum opus*.

Robinson recounted some of his more spectacular windfalls in the 1977 annual of Australia's *Cricketer*, beginning with a call from a Mr Justice Rae Else-Mitchell.

> The name Else-Mitchell concealed the identity of pioneer captain Dave Gregory's grandson, who had given time to researching the Gregorys' lives for the Australian Dictionary of Biography. The judge gave me the privilege of meeting his mother, only survivor of Dave Gregory's sixteen children. Though nearing ninety, she still had much of the charm she had possessed as Pearl Gregory, a brunette nurse who married a pharmacist ...
>
> 'The Gregorys were too honest really,' she said. 'After walking a mile from Turramurra station with my schoolbag I told father I'd found a shilling on a train. He said to me: "My dear, take that straight back to the railway and give it to the stationmaster."'

Robinson continued:

More luck came from my having been assigned to write about jumbo jets for the Sydney Morning Herald's *educational feature. That article made safe-enough landing for me to be entrusted with a broadsheet full-page about cricket before the arrival of Ray Illingworth's English XI. In this expanse a woman noticed that W.G. Grace had scored 152 against Australia. The woman, Ruth Murdoch, left a message for me that her great-uncle W.L. Murdoch topped Grace by one run.*

A couple of years later, writing about Murdoch, I found her phone number and went to interview her twice at Burwood. She trusted me with relics of her great-uncle, including letters he wrote to his brother, her grandfather, telling of court cases in which he was a Cootamundra solicitor. How would a state react today to a player missing a day against Victoria to appear in a country court, then returning by milk train to resume wicketkeeping next day?

Murdoch was one of the most colourful captains. Newcastle solicitor Paul Trisley lent me an English magazine hinting he jilted a Derbyshire girl to marry a Bendigo gold magnate's heiress.

This fascination for the apparently trifling detail that often brings a character to life was a Robinson hallmark, and stories are legion of his astonishing memory. The English cricket historian James Coldham has recalled starting a correspondence with Robinson in 1970 on business of London's august Cricket Society. Coldham wrote:

In my letter I stated that, although he would not remember me, we had met many years before during an Australian tour of the UK. *In his reply, however, almost by return of post, Ray Robinson insisted that he remembered meeting me one evening in 1948 at Geoffrey Copinger's house and that we had spent a small part of the evening at a local hostelry. Moreover, he was able to recall in passing the district and name and whereabouts of the latter place. In conclusion he recalled that I had bade him farewell at a local railway station, whose name he also knew.*

All this had happened one evening twenty-two years before in the life of a very busy, widely-travelled journalist and, for me, it underlined strongly two of the essential ingredients in the outlook of anyone who wished to become a worthwhile journalist – a keen regard for people and a sharply retentive – indeed, photographic! – memory.

The merits of *On Top Down Under* were recognised at once, and it swiftly sold 17,000 copies in hardback. Never once does Robinson's weight of information stifle the zest of his storytelling. As another stylish scholar, the Anglo-Australian David Frith, has written: 'Robbie's sacred attitude to facts and figures did not lead him – as it has led many another – into regarding himself as the perfect scholar. Far from it. He laid his foundations and then built a house of fun. He was always – always – a good read.'

Robbie isn't, I think, a natural writer. He doesn't flow (and occasionally get lost) like Cardus, he doesn't tweak like Robertson-Glasgow, nor does he crackle like the arch-controversialist Fingleton. His contemporaries speak in respectful incomprehension of Robinson toiling for hours in search of the truly telling phrase, and you can tell: there's nothing effortless about *On Top Down Under* or any of its five predecessors. He's like a batsman who, by endless dedication and perseverance, manages to craft a cover drive as attractive and effectual as that of a born strokeplayer.

Re-reading the book for the umpteenth time, I've found myself admiring again Robbie's trademark zingers. Enjoying word-pictures like his acutely observed description of Richie Benaud's mouth ('If events demanded firm correction, Richie's lower lip jutted farther out, like a tramcar's step ...'), I found myself thinking: 'Ray, that's a ripper. Gee, you must have sweated over that. Bloody well done.'

Many others saw *On Top Down Under* for what it was: the crowning achievement of a lifetime of dedication. Robinson's Melbourne cricket friend Mervyn Shaw brought it to the Cricket Society's attention and, when the book was awarded the society's Silver Jubilee Literary Award in 1976, the writer gave a cheerful and self-deprecating acceptance speech at a London hotel. He mentioned that one buyer had asked him to sign it: 'Not really a sex manual'.

Ian Chappell was among the book's admirers. In lamenting the general feel for the game of most Australian cricket writers in Australia's *Cricketer* magazine, he said: 'I prefer to read the style of writer like Ray Robinson.

I enjoy that type of cricket writing, where it's not only about cricket. My taste is slanted toward humour.'

Contemporary Australian players, likewise, regarded *On Top Down Under* as holy writ. When Kerry O'Keeffe was called upon to captain Australia against Minor Counties during a match on the 1977 tour (because of an injury to Doug Walters), team-mates advised him immediately to press Robinson for inclusion in the updated edition.

That unhappy 1977 tour was Robinson's last to England for, when he damaged his hip in two heavy falls on his return, his health began its final decline. He continued, however, to accompany touring teams round, often taking the train to Perth across the Nullarbor when he could not afford the plane fare.

In an affectionate tribute for the September 1982 edition of the *Cricketer*, the *Sydney Morning Herald*'s Phil Wilkins recalled:

> *Long after the last ball was bowled each day, Robbie would be intently studying his notes, the information squeezed into little, incomprehensible cells in his notebook, his shorthand never failing him, tapping quietly away at his typewriter.*
>
> *He was invariably the last of the correspondents to abandon the press box, his love of the game being as great as his love of the mother tongue. The Queen's English was always a lady to Robbie, one never to be abused or rushed off her feet.*

'It grieved his friends to see him struggling through his last years,' wrote David Frith. 'The major and most ironic disability was his sight. But he never complained. You wanted, more than ever, to help him identify players and read the distant scoreboard. You wanted to thank him again for *Between Wickets*, *From the Boundary* and most of all *On Top Down Under*.'

Robinson updated *On Top Down Under* for a Cassell Australia paperback edition in October 1980, and continued to write for the *Cricketer* in England and its namesake here until the final weeks of his life. But, when Ken Mackay died on 13 June 1982, Robinson began one obituary that he did not finish.

Robbie was admitted to Royal North Shore Hospital a week later with a variety of complaints – he had burned himself on a heater, broken two ribs and punctured a lung in a fall, and was diagnosed also as suffering an intestinal blockage – and died on 6 July. The memorial service a week later at the North Chapel of Northern Suburbs Crematorium was attended by Test players from eighty-seven-year-old 'Stork' Hendry through Bill O'Reilly, Arthur Morris, Alan Davidson, Norm O'Neill, Peter Philpott, Bill Hunt to Brian Taber.

Re-publishing *On Top Down Under* two decades after its first edition, I wonder how Robbie is viewing the scene from his Elysian field. The growing professionalism of cricket and the congestion of its calendars have affected the evolution of our captains, and the next appointee to the position will in all likelihood have done little bar play cricket before his recognition.

Outres temps, outres mores, of course. But *On Top Down Under* does remind us of the extraordinary breadth of the personnel who have occupied Australian cricket's number one seat. I'm not sure that the next generation of our captains will be cut from cloth of the same quality.

It's a pleasure, nonetheless, to be involved in reviving a book of this merit. If you've read Robinson, I hope you don't mind the way I've elongated his saga. If you haven't, prepare yourself for an inspiring story well told, with a lot of fun along the way.

Among a host of tributes to Robinson in the October 1982 edition of Australia's *Cricketer* magazine, Bradman spoke of 'a dedicated cricket lover and writer fit to compare with the best'. He said: 'I think his book *On Top Down Under* ... was his finest work and no cricket library could be complete without it. Ray lived as he wrote: honestly, modestly, sincerely respected a confidence. It was a privilege to have known him.'

Introducing a posthumous Robinson anthology edited by Jack Pollard, Bradman also added: 'Much of his work will give pleasure to a generation unborn.' Yes, Sir Donald, you're right again.

GIDEON HAIGH
Melbourne 1996

Flesh and Blood

The human side of Australia's cricket captains is a fascinating back-drop to the better-known successes that earned them world renown. Romances, family and business interests, unknown to record-books and critics' outpourings, influence Test captains' careers.

Hundreds of books about international cricket, full of facts about bats, balls, runs and wickets, say little about women. Yet women have as much part in the life of cricketers as in the affairs of other males, always excepting film stars and champion prize-fighters. The skippers On Top Down Under have shared the qualities and frailties of the race. They have lived, laughed and loved, sweated and sworn, bled, wed and bred.

Now for the first time the veil is drawn from such relevant questions as whether bachelors make as good captains as married men. With nobody but himself to please, is a bachelor better placed than a husband who has domestic issues in the back of his mind while trying to decide who shall bowl next? If you are thinking 'Behind every successful man stands a . . .' (you know how it goes), it is a help to find what women Australia's Test captains did marry and how they chose them.

Some of the skippers courted girls they met in shipboard romances. One was an amateur actress, the toast of the ship. A socialite from an Italian finishing school toured England to be near the cricketer who made her heartbeat quicken. They became engaged in London. In one team three players timed marriages so that they could take their brides to England on honeymoon, before the Board of Control stepped in to block that sort of thing for years. One of the brides kept the score of runs.

Two captains wed dancers. One of Australia's most honoured captains married a scorer's sister. Another wed a soprano from a church choir. An earlier skipper, a banker, married the general manager's daughter. Two courted receptionists, two florists and one a nurse. Others chose secretaries, girls working in the same offices. Six married twice, one three times.

The demands international cricket makes on players put a strain on marriage. Partings are frequent and can be long – eight months during the 1956 tour of three countries, 7½ months in 1953, seven months in 1964. Resultant stresses were the originating cause of divorces. From 1921 until after the second world war wives were banned from touring teams, prompting one heading in Britannia: 'AUSTRALIA RULES THE WIVES'. By 1938 special permission had to be obtained for them to join their husbands in Britain after the last match. Another conflict of interest occurred when the date of talented all-rounder Gary Gilmour's wedding was arranged one winter for the first Saturday in December. When summer came around the happy day was found to clash with a Shield game. Was Gilmour expected to put marriage to his life partner second to a cricket match? Much clucking went on when he did not. I believe it set back his career at a time when he should have been one of Australia's team touring the West Indies early in 1973. His debut was postponed a year until his selection against New Zealand was a sign that all was forgiven – especially after his match-winning bowling at Auckland in the Test that brought international sport's first streakers into view.

Having been abroad when their second daughter was born, Ian Redpath gave away the 1975 tour of England to be home for his wife Christine's next baby. Ian's successor as vice-captain, Greg Chappell, had been gone three weeks when his wife had their first child.

Allan Border proposed to his fiancee at a gathering before the 1979 World Cup, heard news of his first child after a one-day international at Castries in 1984 and of his second while waiting to bat in the Third Test against India at the SCG twenty months later. His successor Mark Taylor left for his first tour of England having been married three weeks.

Most wives of leading cricketers see enough before marriage to be aware of the vexations of having a husband whose summer weekends and holidays are swallowed by cricket and who at intervals is overseas for months. These wives tolerate the drawbacks, setting them against extra earnings

2

that lift the family's quality of life a little. Not all cricket wives can be as co-operative as Daphne Benaud but even she can hardly rank ahead of Meg Whitfield. Meg is the wife of former all-rounder Harold Whitfield of the Border Cricket Union, South Africa. Disabilities of being married to cricketers were being aired by a group of wives at East London, especially the irritations of having to stow prepared dinners away in the oven until the man comes home. As the chinwag died down Meg spoke up:

> *Sorry girls, but I like cricket. I like Harold playing it. And if rain stops play and the boys get caught up in a bar until all hours I understand how it goes. The only thing I don't like is why does he drop his bag in the hall for me to fall over when I come in?*

A player is seldom entrusted with Test captaincy until at least midway through his twenties. No doubt selectors have heard of a young bachelor skipper's remark to a bowler. Having just taken a wicket with a new ball, the bowler was voraciously eyeing the incoming batsman. Handing him the ball the captain said significantly 'I've taken this chap's sister out three times – and tonight's the night'. The bowler dismissed her brother for 0.

To become captain of the Australian XI has long been regarded as a pinnacle of achievement. American dollars poured into golf purses and professional tennis are enabling Australian stars at these sports to make more money, but I believe the aura still surrounding the Test captaincy owes much of its origin to the skippers having been the first Australians to give Australia an identity. They developed it for twenty years before a straggling set of colonies by the South Seas took shape as an infant nation. For good reasons the captaincy of the Australian XI gained greater prestige than eminence in any other field. While a senior lecturer in history at the Australian National University, William Mandle produced a mass of facts explaining the phenomenon. Booming from the 1850s, cricket was the one game at which the colonials could match themselves against the mother country, with increasing success. By playing it they could dispel fears of white men degenerating in blackfellows' country and showed they could combine in a national sporting side, if Federation was a long way off. Mandle traced the progress of Australian national feelings through cricket from deferential attitudes in the 1860s to self-confident near-arrogance in the 1890s.

3

When Victorian skipper Harry Trott was elected ninth Test captain as the 1800s were running out, a Melbourne newspaper said he 'went on to the highest honour open to an Australian'. More than thirty years later, an unchallenged saying was that millions of Australians knew the line of succession of Test captains while few could recall the prime ministers.

Test captains put in their own money to pioneer Australian team ventures abroad, setting an example for Olympic competitors, tennis champions and others. Their leadership helped keep cricket flourishing despite the collapse of the land boom and despite a world depression. They were prominent in reviving it after two world wars. An ex-captain spared the game from deep wounds just in time by steering official policy away from confrontation with anti-apartheid demonstrators, and enabling Australians to see a multi-racial World XI, the first ever assembled from six countries.

At his peak of popularity in a period of depression Bradman was perhaps the widest-known name in the British Empire. In more than one informal public-opinion poll about the most famous Australian, readers put Don Bradman at the top. In *Farewell to Cricket* Sir Donald comments with characteristic modesty:

I could not help thinking that this knighthood was a sporting example to the world of true democracy ... Born in the country, with no influence whatsoever, I had been able to rise to the Australian XI captaincy and to achieve this distinction. The same opportunity exists for every Australian boy. I believe it was this aspect more than any other which appealed to the vast majority of Australian people who regarded me as a symbol through whom these thoughts were expressed.

The captains' callings have ranged from accountant, solicitor, bank officer, grazier, postman, dentist, clerk, whisky agent, boot salesman and bookmaker to schoolmaster, stockbroker, shopkeeper, pharmacist, crime reporter, investment consultant, plumber, sales-promotion officer and company director.

There has been no governor like Sir Stanley Jackson, no minister of state like Pakistan's Hafeez Kardar, no senator like Trinidad's Jeffrey Stollmeyer, no clergyman like the Rev. David Sheppard who became Bishop of Liverpool. The last Ashes series, however, was the first instance in more than a century of two captains with tertiary qualifications: Mark Taylor (Bachelor of Surveying at the University of NSW) met England's Michael Atherton (Bachelor of Arts, majoring in history, at Cambridge University).

As personalities the captains have been as varied as their jobs or their build. The tiniest, Syd Gregory and Lindsay Hassett, made friends almost as numberless as the sands of Bondi Beach. Mountainous Warwick Armstrong's enemies would have supported anthropology's new theory that man has less in common with the ape than the bear. The keenest fisherman among them built his own boats. Another's hobby is breeding champion racing pigeons. On the family front, who sired the most children? It was a close finish between a Sydney man and one from South Australia. The only Pill known in their day was a 5½ ounce six-stitcher of red leather.

To the shame of a world afflicted by sectarian hostilities and divisions, cricket history contains the example of an Australian XI's only Catholic being elected captain by players of different or no religious faith. One of the best captains, a teetotaller, took his turn buying a round of drinks for his players. An indignant captain took charge of the tea urn so that his players could get a cup instead of being kept waiting by drones. A popular skipper was manoeuvred out of the captaincy by a ruling clique of officials.

In the land to which the Tolpuddle martyrs were transported the set-up used to be more democratic. Cricketers elected their state captains, who picked the Australian XI. On the voyage to England the players chose their skipper. On the first day of the first Test of 1894–95 in Sydney the Australians met in the pavilion just before noon and elected their captain. Jack Blackham walked straight out on to the turf with Andrew Stoddart to toss. When the coin favoured Australia, as any colonial coin should, the English leader accepted his bad luck with a smile and a pleasant word. Today bureaucracy would liken such free-and-easy ways to anarchy.

An unlucky Australian tosser in England offered to wrestle the English skipper for choice of innings at their last meeting. When England asked to borrow a substitute fielder for a hurt man, one captain, forgetful of the dignity of office, went out himself and caught his own side's top-scorer.

The varying fortunes of the skippers prove that a captain with two top-notch bowlers is more than halfway to glory; without them, renown is apt

5

to pass the smartest by. Not all captains had happy endings. Ill-health struck down the jolliest leader. One of the unluckiest had his business ruined by partners. Another's gambling won two fortunes, lost both.

Under the green caps, their forces have been harder to repel than the Spanish Armada. Mostly they have been younger than their opponents and their fieldsmen have out-run, out-thrown and often out-caught opponents. Their batsmen, when cornered, have tried to hit their way out of trouble; as Sir Neville Cardus warned, the kangaroo is a dangerous animal when attacked. It helps that such all-out effort has not squeezed the last drop of relaxed humour out of their game. It was once so evident that A.C. MacLaren said he would give anything to play the game as keenly yet as light-heartedly. With one or two exceptions the captains have not descended to time-wasting gamesmanship and negative field-placings.

We have looked in awe at their names in letters of gold on honour-boards or in black type in lists in booklets. I believe that once you know more of their real selves, their exploits, glories and flops, as characters of flesh and blood, they will not again recede into formal columns of names and figures. Take a deep breath and read on.

Handsome Dave

Silver spoons were scarce in the oddly named colony of New South Wales when Australia's greatest cricketing family was founded. One of the humble portals through which the founder, Edward Gregory, passed as a boy was the drab door of the Male Orphan Institute. His parents had brought him and two infant brothers from London a year before the Battle of Waterloo. After their mother died in 1819 the father returned to England and the three forlorn boys were inmates of the institute until discharged to jobs with tradesmen.

At twenty-two Edward William Gregory became a schoolmaster and played cricket in Hyde Park. At thirty he married Mary Ann Smith, sister of a Melbourne mayor who became a member of the first Parliament. It was a love match. Among thirteen children of this fertile union were seven boys, five of whom grew up to be better cricketers than their father and played for New South Wales.

Governor of the colony in the 1860s was Sir William Denison, whose name is commemorated by Fort Denison, better known as Pinchgut, the once-fortified island that peers respectfully over the waves at the Opera House. Presenting a medal for meritorious conduct at St James's Church of England School in Sydney, Sir William told the boys that if they obtained good passes there would be jobs for them. Among his hearers was David William Gregory, fifteen, who had been born at Fairy Meadow, 80 kilometres south, on 15 April 1845. Awarded the medal in December 1860, young Gregory walked to Government House and told His Excellency 'I've come about that job, sir.' They made him a clerk in the Audit Office at sixteen.

Aboriginals had mia-mias in the trees by the lake in Centennial Park when David and two elder brothers played cricket in the Domain. Governor Denison and veteran cricket-lovers Bill Tunks and Al Park each gave £5 to lay out a pitch as flat as shovels and a spirit-level could make it. This technological aid helped Ned, Walter, Dave, Charlie and Arthur Gregory and their National Club mates develop their game in matches against garrison regiment officers and the Currency Lass Hotel teams of colonial-born youths.

Coaching by William Caffyn, a voluntary exile from Surrey, had so upgraded the colonial cricketers that a crowd of 5000 saw Ned, Dave and Charlie Gregory turn the tables on Victoria's Tom Wills, John Conway and Sam Cosstick, one of whose triumphs had carried a purse of £100. Wills was a founder of the spectacular southern game of football originally designed to keep cricketers fit in winter.

Though less dramatic than Stanley's celebrated meeting with Livingstone in the African jungle later in the same year, the meeting of David Gregory and John Conway has had far-reaching consequences extending to the present day, when cricketers of nine countries criss-cross the globe to play international matches.

When a coach brought Dr W.G. Grace's English team over dusty roads to an up country town in 1873 the publican of a primitive hotel apologised, 'Sorry we can't fix you up like they do in the cities, Doc. No bloody baths, you know!' Grace: 'That's all right, my man. We Graces are no bloody water-spaniels.'

By the time James Lillywhite brought the fourth English side out in 1876 for matches against fifteens and eighteens, an eleven-a-side game was arranged for the All-England team's return from New Zealand.

Finding a captain for the first Australian XI was easier than picking a place for the country's national capital. Without wrangling, string-pulling or a casting vote the players had the captain they wanted, Dave Gregory. His last surviving daughter, Pearl (who lived to ninety-two), told me: 'It always pleased father to recall that his fellow-players elected him captain for the first of all Test matches. Yes, the Victorians elected him, as the match was in Melbourne.' She gave a trill of a laugh, as if inter-city rivalries went back as far as her girlhood.

David Gregory, thirty-one, was a born leader and looked it. His height,

9

187 cm (6 ft 2 in), weight, 90.7 kg (14 st 4 lb), and erect carriage gave him a commanding appearance. 'Handsome Dave', women of Sydney town called him in days when barques' bows jutted over Circular Quay and the cooling nor'-easter was unimpeded by high-rise office buildings.

Nowhere in Australian cities have I noticed whiskers of such masculine grandeur as those that adorned the chin of Australia's first captain. His full beard was more widely known than any other in the antipodes except the one on police posters about outlawed Ned Kelly.

Gregory's brown eyes mingled the gleam of geniality with the glint of authority. His face had the no-nonsense expression of a man versed in the ways of the world who controlled a staff of public servants. Exceptionally keen sight helped his batting and slip-catching. He wrote the batting order in a large flowing hand of a day when the supremacy of penmanship had yet to be challenged by typewriters. His capital M in Murdoch's name trailed a tail curving like a fishhook.

He smoked a pipe, the masculine vogue of the time, and was a sociable drinker. His daughter never saw him the worse for liquor, as the saying used to be. Groups of players often came home and discussed the match. If discussion and the language roamed broader, he would tell Pearl she had better go and read a book.

To cricket devotees 1877 is as venerated a year as, say, 1066 to the English or 1492 to Americans. It was twenty-three years after the Crimean War and twenty-three before the Boer War, tidily spaced by history so that inhabitants of the colonies by the South Seas could give undivided attention to a Combined XI from Sydney and Melbourne playing an all-professional English team. On the Melbourne Cricket Club's ground, amid gumtrees bordering the unpolluted Yarra River, Dave Gregory's toss gained first use of the wicket for his team of six Victorians and five New South Welshmen. Few citizens gave them much chance as Charles Bannerman faced the first ball from Alfred Shaw on a sunny March afternoon. As this Kent-born Sydney batsman headed for the first Test century about 4000 people came from town to watch.

On the second day 12,000 saw Bannerman carry on from 126 to 165. His sorties to disturb the control of the professionals caused Yorkshire lob bowler Thomas Armitage to resort to extremes. Before switching to under-arm grubbers he tried to land lofty full-tosses over Bannerman's head on to the bails. Balls of such pregnant parabola, one reporter estimated, could only have been reached with a clothes-prop. Every backyard had one of these, as science had yet to invent the handle-wound hoist.

Bannerman outlasted seven partners before he retired hurt with a finger split by Yorkshire fast bowler George Ulyett. His 67 per cent of the runs have been approached only by Gordon Greenidge at Manchester in 1976 and Sri Lanka's Asanka Gurusinha in Chandigarh in 1990–91. Admirers subscribed a half-sovereign for each of his runs to reward his astonishing feat. On the rough wickets of the period centuries seemed as scarce as seahorses. Nobody else reached 20, though a stripling of eighteen, Tom Garrett, justified Gregory's judgement in bringing a law student from Sydney University. The youngster coolly made 18 not out toward the total 245. No younger Australian has since played a Test against England. The colonials led by 49 and in the second innings Tom Kendall's left hand bowled them to victory by 45.

Faith in Gregory's capacity to rise above sectional interests was well founded. He gave Melbourne bowlers 159 overs to 42 by Sydney men and they took 17 of the 20 English wickets. The Victorian Cricket Association had gold medals minted for the victors and ordered one slightly larger for the skipper.

News of the unforeseen triumph prompted one Sydney scribe to assume that cricket's sceptre had passed from English hands. With a nib dipped deep in elation he wrote in the *Daily News*:

> *To be defeated in a cricket contest man to man by the natives of an island comparatively lately discovered is too much … It may console them to note that the English race is not degenerating and that in the distant land and where lately the blackfellow hurled his boomerang a generation has arisen which can play the best bowlers of the time.*

Such a tone scarcely made allowance for the Englishmen having entered the field a day after their voyage from New Zealand or for batsmen having to try their hands at keeping wicket. They had left their only wicketkeeper, Edward Pooley, in police custody in NZ on a charge of malicious damage.

11

It all arose from his having tricked a Christchurch man in a hotel bar by betting he could foretell every individual score by the eighteen local players. He wrote down 0 beside each, and when more than half of them failed to score he offered a shilling for each wrong guess and claimed £1 for each correct forecast. Though acquitted of the damage charge, Pooley was fined for having created a disturbance.

The immense interest aroused by the Melbourne match demanded that a second be arranged. Gregory and Conway's judgement and willpower had come through a severe trial before the first game. They had not been stampeded by ace bowler Fred Spofforth's ultimatum that he would play only if Murdoch kept wicket – the only man he believed could cope with his bowling. In bringing Spofforth and Murdoch in for the second Test Dave left out his elder brother Ned but insisted that Jack Blackham continue to keep wicket. Again his appraisal was upheld. Standing up to the stumps in Spofforth's third over, Blackham reined in a rising ball and stumped Shaw in a manner hitherto thought impossible.

Gregory went in first in the second innings and made top score, but the Englishmen won with four wickets to spare.

Lillywhite's professionals were receiving £150 for the trip, expenses paid. The colonials were reimbursed their expenses only, though collections were made for Bannerman, Kendall and Blackham. Half a century later another Test player John Worrall wrote: 'Dave Gregory's team in 1877 created such enthusiasm throughout the Australian continent that its effects have never really abated.' This still applies.

Though unable to interest the Victorian and NSW cricket associations in a tour of England, Gregory and Conway, who managed the side, chose five from NSW (Charles and Alick Bannerman, Garrett, Murdoch and Spofforth), four Victorians (Blackham, Frank Allan, Harry Boyle and Tom Horan) and Tasmanian banker-batsman George Bailey.

Dave's initiative on and off the field stamped him as the man to lead the first representative team on a pilgrimage to England, the Holy Land of cricket. Each contributed £50 toward tour expenses, three times the fare to Britain.

When a storm-tossed steamer was in peril off the NZ coast Charles

Bannerman, an expert swimmer, vowed that if he reached land he would never leave it.

> *Spofforth: 'Suppose we are wrecked. What would you do?'*
> *Bannerman: 'First I'll save Alick, then Murdoch, then you.'*
> *Spofforth: 'What about the Victorians?'*
> *Bannerman: 'Let them drown – do you think I'm going to risk my life for them?'*

The captain, who had married at twenty-one, was the only player over thirty. Most of his men were under twenty-five and all the optimism and resilience of youth were needed for eleven players to tackle 37 matches (15 of them first-class) in Britain. A twelfth man, William Midwinter, joined them for a month until Gloucestershire took him by cab to play at the Oval – a hijack they justified by saying he was still under contract.

In the Australians' opening match Notts had trounced them by an innings on a freezing day. 'What on earth induced us to come to this country?' Gregory groaned. 'I wish I was back in Sydney with the sun shining on me from a blue sky.'

So little was known of them when they entered the field at noon that a Marylebone member exclaimed, 'These can't be Australians; they aren't black!' – a reflected memory of the 1868 Aborigines' tour. Gregory had a deadlier pair of bowlers – Spofforth 10 for 20 and Boyle 9 for 17 – than the MCC's Shaw and Morley. Every chance was caught as Marylebone, 33 and 19, were beaten by nine wickets in 4½ hours.

For the raw colonial boys to overwhelm a strong MCC side was like a war canoe sinking a gunboat. All England took notice. A congratulatory crowd surrounded their hotel. In theatres and music halls actors brought the win into their lines. *Punch* printed a parody on one of Lord Byron's poems:

> *The Australians came down like a wolf on the fold,*
> *The Marylebone stars for a trifle were bowled.*
> *Our Grace before dinner was very soon done*
> *And Grace after dinner did not get a run.*

To see them at railway stations men and women pressed their noses against carriage windows. Players heard such exclamations as 'Which be Demon?', 'Where be stoomper?', 'They beant black at all!', 'Anyway, that 'un in corner be a half-caste' – a reference to Gregory's swarthy complexion.

Home News said their fielding was admired by all who beheld it. They were praised for breaking away from stereotyped positions and adjusting their places in the field to combat each batsman. Only one century was scored against them.

The new approach by Gregory and his men was taken up by the London *Standard*:

> *One of the principal causes of the Australians' success was Mr Gregory's captaincy ... England at present does not possess his equal ... He changes the bowling with promptitude and excellent judgement and varies his field with a quick appreciation of the peculiarities of different batsmen. He realises that his business is to get the other side out as soon as possible and not to prolong innings by a series of useless maiden overs which, while they gratify the bowler's vanity, weary the field and the spectators. As batsman he hits with great power when well set but is somewhat uncertain and does not keep the ball particularly down. He is a marvellous catch.*

With this approach and his oft-expressed statement that 'matches are won by run-getting' Gregory was largely responsible for a new conception of big cricket which won Australia international fame. He was a dealer in instant captaincy.

In days when Australia sends seventeen players to England it seems almost incredible that eleven men, strangers to English wickets and weather, should have got through 37 matches, finished 25 and won 18. The only way Gregory could rest injured, sick or over-tired players was by enlisting outside help to complete the eleven in some minor games. Their play pleased Englishmen in every way, though there was criticism that they failed to accept adverse decisions with good grace.

Although worn thin at times, Gregory's urbanity mostly stood up to the stresses. The world tour yielded them £750 each – more than enough to have bought half a dozen choice home sites on Bellevue Hill.

The team's triumphal return fanned the sparks ignited by the first win in 1877. Cricket held pride of place among the colonies' games and cricketers cornered most schoolboy admiration. Within two years a South Australian

14

XI tackled Victoria and West Australians were sinking a well to water their sandy ground. Within five years Queenslanders played their first match against an English team.

Dislike for Victorian umpires standing in Sydney erupted into the barrackers' riot in 1879, history's blackest mark against an Australian cricket crowd. This is the only instance in the world of a visiting captain (Lord Harris) having been struck on the field.

When Murdoch was adjudged run out for 10 in the colony's follow-on, antagonism flared against umpire George Coulthard, whom the Englishmen had engaged in Melbourne to accompany them. Instead of another batsman coming in Gregory appeared at the gate. He told Lord Harris the NSW XI and he objected to Coulthard on the ground of general incompetence. As a mob was surrounding the fieldsmen by the wicket Lord Harris returned to midfield. In defending Coulthard he was struck by a larrikin with a stick. A.N. Hornby was taking the assailant to the pavilion to be locked up when he was punched by a would-be rescuer.

Hornby's shirt was almost torn off, though he was flanked by a volunteer bodyguard from the pavilion.

The climate was as warm as Captain Cook had originally reported but nobody could say the natives were friendly – especially when they thought Emmett had called them 'sons of convicts'. Lest NSW claim the match on forfeit, Lord Harris held fast in midfield until 6 pm. As NSW would have forfeited if batsmen had not gone in on Monday Gregory resumed play. They lost on a sticky strip.

Gregory was then in the last stage of his third consecutive season in fifteen months, involving about 70 matches in Australia, NZ, England, Canada, USA and Australia again. After a winter's rest he won club batting and bowling averages. He was almost thirty-six when he tied for the fielding prize and he continued to play inter-colonial cricket until he was thirty-seven. For five years he was honorary secretary of the NSW Cricket Association and courageous enough to be sole selector. This coincided with his promotion as Inspector of Accounts at thirty-eight.

His wife, Mary Ann Hitchings, mother of thirteen, died in 1890. He was forty-seven when he married Lilies Leslie MacMillian in 1892. A farmer's daughter, she bore him three children and saw him become Paymaster of the Treasury in 1897. In 1911 he was sixty-seven, a widower of eighteen months, when he married Ellen Hillier, widow of another cricketer.

Though he could be as firm on the field as in the Audit Office, his daughter told me he was a kindly father who insisted on scrupulous honesty. Next to cricket, she said, he was fondest of fishing, a tireless walker, liked playing the flute, bred setters and had a fine garden. He and fellow-players would often land home with loads of fish. He built his own boats, seaworthy enough to go outside the Heads.

After a week at his desk as Paymaster of the Treasury Gregory would go by train to Moss Vale, then walk 50 kilometres through Kangaroo Valley to the coast.

When the States formed the Commonwealth he was offered the post of head of the Federal Treasury, together with a knighthood. He declined. Acceptance would have meant going to live in Melbourne and he could not bear to leave Turramurra. When he retired at sixty Premier Sir Joseph Carruthers complimented him on having served ten governors with distinction and having enjoyed the goodwill of every state minister and officer with whom he had worked.

His hair receded but he never needed spectacles or dentures. He died at seventy-four on 4 August 1919. Near Gore Hill cemetery his true memorial is Channel Two's mast which, until Kerry Packer got his exclusive rights, used to telecast Tests to some two million viewers.

W.L. MURDOCH

3

Law on His Side

The seedling planted by the first Australian XI was too robust a growth to wither easily, even under the windstorm of a riot and the hot breath of acrimony. Its recovery after its Sydney droop, however, owed much to the husbandry and humour of a batsman-wicketkeeper with green fingers, William Lloyd Murdoch. It has since spread branches and continues to put out many a sucker.

Parents Gilbert and Susanna Murdoch had voyaged from Tasmania to Victoria before their second son Will was born at Sandhurst on 18 October 1854. The family moved on to Sydney. On an unfenced paddock in King Street, Balmain, Will Murdoch first played cricket on a rough earth pitch with his brother Gilbert, three years older, and bony-kneed Fred Spofforth.

As a graduate of Sydney University, Will was enrolled as a solicitor, following his brother. Only males were allowed to attend the university. Girls were not admitted until 1881, a year after Premier Sir Henry Parkes, rejecting a plea for co-education, told the New South Wales Parliament: 'We do not propose to teach courtship in these schools.' Seemingly nobody asked 'Why not?'

When thirteen colonials set out on a peace-making tour of Britain in 1880 they had good reasons for electing the young lawyer captain at twenty-five. A topnotch batsman, he was the first Australian to carry his bat throughout an innings. Never moody, he had an outgoing, equable personality that won friends and influenced results long before Dale Carnegie was born. Had Walter Winchell known a quarter as much about the Murdoch type of sportsman as he did about New Yorkers he could scarcely have been so dogmatic that nice guys always run second. Three of

Murdoch's team were older and three only nineteen. Counting in a manager young enough to play several matches, George Alexander, twenty-nine, the average age was only twenty-three and a quarter, three years younger than the average of Ian Chappell's seventeen in 1972.

Because of the 1879 Sydney riot, most leading English clubs cold-shouldered the second side from the colonies. Reaching London in 1880, Murdoch's team felt rather like thirteen actors in search of a stage. No Test was listed and only five first-class games. The under-thirty captain and manager's bearing and diplomacy rescued the tour from disaster. Their 37 games included ten first-class matches.

Lord Harris arranged a Test in September at the Oval. In dismal succession Murdoch lost the toss, missed his injured ace bowler, Spofforth, and saw W.G. Grace make 152 of England's 420. Yet, ever optimistic, he bet Grace he would top his huge score. Will was caught for 0 and his side fell for 149, after rain. Told to follow on, they lost 8 for 187. Defeat by an innings seemed near until the young skipper led one of the great fight-backs of cricket history. In the first Test on English soil the colonials won the crowd's respect when the last two tailenders stayed with their captain while 140 were added. As the solicitor-skipper's last partner was Melbourne barrister William Moule, a judge-to-be, it could have been said that the colonials had the law on their side. When Notts all-rounder William Barnes bowled Moule at 327, Murdoch had moved one run ahead of the world's champion. This strained credulity even more than it did the muscles of England's bowlers but, as proof, the sovereign he won from Grace hung on Will's watch-chain until his dying day.

His biggest batsman, George Bonnor, 198 cm (6 ft 6 in) in his boat-like boots, hit up history's highest catch in the 1880 Test. Known as the Bathurst Giant, Bonnor and his partner ran two and were launched on a third when the ball descended from the heavens. Grace's brother Fred caught it in a corner of the outfield 108 metres from the striker's end. Of all sportsmen, Bonnor had the build and bearded majesty of expression to have served as a model for sculpture of Zeus. Asked to name the world's best batsmen, George replied: 'Grace must be first and Murdoch second.' After a modest pause, 'If you want to know who is third it is not for me to say.'

19

Grace realised that, for all Bonnor's inconsistency, the man who lifted balls right out of English grounds 26 times on this tour could sway a match by knocking the best bowlers off. So he told Bonnor he was just a slogger. Annoyed, the giant vowed he would show Grace he could 'play Murdoch's game'. To counter Grace's ruse, Murdoch would drop the quiescent thumper's name down among the tailenders next time. Bonnor would protest: 'What's the good of putting me in so late?' His skipper would sigh: 'You could hit the ball once, Bon, but now you are only a plodder.' George: 'Put me in early and I'll show you.' He would then spatter the bowling over surrounding buildings.

Murdoch's unbeaten 153 was the only first-class century for the 1880 tourists and Grace's 152 the only hundred off their bowling. England won that Test by five wickets but Murdoch set a new standard for Australian batsmanship on wickets where an individual 50 was regarded with the veneration later given 100.

At twenty-six he moved south to become a successful lawyer at Cootamundra, aided by submitting knotty points to his elder brother, Gilbert, in Phillip Street, Sydney's Latin-quoting quarter. Cootamundra's cricketers proudly installed Australia's captain as their skipper in matches against Grenfell, Temora, Junee and Yass on matting strips.

Grace and Giffen, foe and ally, alike ranked him Australia's undisputed batting champion. In Giffen's words (two of them may make Lawry wince) Murdoch 'had all the attributes that go to make a great batsman – keen eyes (he is a capital pigeon shot), thorough mastery of the science of the game, rare coolness and the patience of Job. He batted as artistically as one could wish and it was an education to watch how he drove and cut the ball along the sward, seldom mistiming . . . He played more great innings than any of us.'

Of medium height, he excelled on the off side and often smiled while batting. If a ball kicked he acknowledged its misbehaviour with a comical snort and round-eyed grimace. He had the quick footwork of a star Wallaroo footballer, noted for drop-kicking goals. An eye for angles made him a consistent winner at billiards.

Giffen, who admired his dauntless courage, enjoyed playing under him, saying, 'His pleasant disposition, in addition to his commanding ability, fitted him admirably for the captaincy. No matter what hole we were in, Billy, with a smile of assurance and a cheering word, would go in himself and often master the bowling.' Whenever frictions occurred in a touring side, he settled them at once and never referred to them again.

First to amass 300 in Australia, Murdoch was twenty-seven when he batted most of two days for 321 against Victoria, helped by a chance at 120. When extra days were added to a match listed for three days, Murdoch missed the fourth day fulfilling a Cootamundra court engagement. Returning by a milk-hours train for the fifth day he resumed wicket-keeping until Victoria lost by an innings. A triple century was a stupendous feat when centuries per year could be counted on the toes of a negligent ice-skater.

Murdoch's 321 stood as the highest score on Sydney Cricket Ground for forty-seven years. It took Bradman to cap it by running up 340 not out against Victoria at twenty, and remains comfortably the highest score by a wicketkeeper.

Murdoch's flexibility of mind was evident. Quick changes of bowling have often brought results but one time he kept his medium-pace opening pair toiling unrelieved for three hours. We have yet to see another Australian skipper do so. At Sydney George Palmer bowled 58 four-ball overs of off-cutters and Ted Evans 57 overs straight. Their captain's humanity might have been open to question but not his judgement: the pair disposed of the Englishmen for 133 and their efforts led to a win by five wickets. Two days before his twenty-first birthday Palmer made himself the youngest Australian ever to take ten wickets in a Test.

As Spofforth and Palmer usually bowled first on good wickets the young Victorian thought it unfair that Boyle partnered Spofforth on rain-affected turf. When he told his approachable skipper so, Murdoch explained:

> I put you on first on good wickets because you are the best bowler in the side on them. If I bowl the other pair on sticky wickets it is because they are more dangerous on those wickets, George. Not each bowler's figures but winning the match is the one thing that concerns me.

Appreciating the point helped Palmer bear his natural yearning resignedly.

In the fourth Test no bowling combination could prevent vigorous Yorkshire all-rounder George Ulyett from making 149, the first Test century for England abroad. The match was unfinished when the Australians had to embark for the 1882 tour of England.

As a team of thirteen committed to 38 matches, the Australians would neither begin play before noon nor continue after 6 pm. In the second game Murdoch's 286 not out against Sussex caused the county to covet such a batsman for years until he settled there to play.

Onlookers crowding the Oval for the only Test, the thirtieth match, saw Peate and Barlow put the side out by 3.20 pm for 63, the lowest score of the tour. England led by 38 and on a rain-soaked ground Australia's second innings of 112 left the Englishmen needing 85 to win. After running a single for Murdoch, Jones walked from his crease to smooth a ballmark on the pitch. From point Grace came to remove the bails. Jones had been careless in leaving sanctuary while the ball was still alive but Spofforth swore he would see to it that England did not win the Test.

Reshuffling his bowling, Murdoch switched Spofforth to the pavilion end. This put its dark background behind the long arm of the vengeful paceman. In the next 17 overs by Spofforth and Boyle the only run was a single for an intentional misfield to bring Lyttelton opposite 'The Demon'. A break-back scattered his bails.

Men noted for coolness were trembling like leaves. Others were shivering, some even fainted. With their last 20 balls Spofforth and Boyle scooped out six wickets for only two scoring shots. Spectators rushed the ground as a dramatic day brought Australia victory by seven runs. Debate in Parliament House, Sydney, was interrupted for news of the triumph. A BBC record of John Snagge reciting poet laureate John Masefield's '85 to Win' describes tense scenes in which a man dropped dead.

The shock of a full-strength team being downed in two days on England's own soil moved a *Sporting Times* writer to publish a mock obituary notice:

In affectionate remembrance

of

ENGLISH CRICKET

which died at the Oval, 29th August, 1882

Deeply lamented by a large circle of sorrowing friends and acquaintances

R.I.P.

N.B. – *The body will be cremated and the ashes taken to Australia*

It was twenty years before any of the subsequent teams touring Britain was considered powerful enough to outshine Murdoch's 1882 band.

When the Hon. Ivo Bligh brought a team to Australia in 1882 Melbourne rain helped Murdoch to become the first captain to make England follow on. Bligh promptly returned the compliment, thanks largely to Yorkshire all-rounder William Bates – first to make a half-century and take ten or more wickets in a Test. By winning two of the three arranged Tests Bligh redeemed his pledge to regain the Ashes.

One critic alleged that Murdoch's men had become stale, gross and careless. Blaming lack of practice, the *Australasian* complained:

> *The captain was perhaps the greatest delinquent. Instead of showing his companions a good example and endeavouring to keep them up to their proper standard, he seemed to prefer shooting, picnics and social parties, which might have been left until the team disbanded. Picnics and champagne are not conducive to good cricket.*

When public interest led to an extra Test, Murdoch lost the toss but Australia won a well-contested match by four wickets. Nothing was said this time about picnics and champagne!

Youngest ever to lead England, Ivo Bligh, twenty-three, was the most handsome Test skipper, unapproached in good looks for generations until Peter May, David Sheppard and Ted Dexter became centres of feminine attention. Heartbeats quickened whenever Ivo appeared, especially within the comely contours of Florence Rose Morphy, daughter of a Beechworth landholder. Florence, twenty-two, led a group of Victorian girls who presented the 190 cm (6 ft 3 in) Adonis with an urn containing cremated ashes of a bail or stump. Marrying a year later, they became the Earl and Countess of Darnley in 1900. After his death in 1927 the Countess sent the urn to Lord's where it is displayed among the treasures of the Long Room.

The 1884 thirteen's 32 games included defeat at Lord's in the first three-Test series in England. Murdoch became the first international captain to catch one of his batsmen (Dr Henry Scott, top score 75) while fielding substitute for an injured Englishman. At the Oval he put together the first Test double-century, 211 in about eight hours. Will was helped by three chances at 46, 171 and 205 off Ulyett, who on such a day found it difficult to live up to his nickname 'Happy Jack'.

On the steamer *Mirzapore's* forty-eight-day return voyage winsome Jemima Watson, an heiress and amateur actress, described as a great favourite on the quarter-deck, shone in all shipboard activities. Australia's thirty-year-old captain found her charms irresistible and a few weeks after the ship berthed, the couple married at Fitzroy on 8 December. Manager George Alexander gave the bride away, causing speculation whether the whirlwind courtship was approved by her father, a Bendigo gold-mining magnate. As Jemima was twenty-one parental sanction was not required. They entrained to Adelaide, arriving three days before a Test match. Gossips commented on Murdoch missing practices.

Failure to settle a dispute about the team's proposed split-up of Adelaide and Melbourne Test profits caused an upheaval that rocked Australian cricket to its boot-sprigs. Taking over the financing of Adelaide's first Test, the SACA guaranteed each side £450, much less than the Englishmen felt they deserved as winners. No terms were reached with manager Alexander for the 1884 team to play in the next Melbourne Test, so a whole new side played.

Murdoch resumed legal practice at Cootamundra. After 16 Tests straight, 13 as captain, he was not seen in the Australian XI for the next 15 Tests, including two tours of England. Spofforth migrated to Derbyshire at thirty-four.

When Murdoch was persuaded to reappear at the age of thirty-six the crowd's rousing reception testified to his immense popularity. His temporary retirement had been a great loss, but Giffen called it a greater calamity when, after opening his cricket bag for the 1890 tour, he flitted off to Sussex.

Murdoch won both his last Test tosses with Grace in England but that was all. In all, Murdoch's seven teams carried off five Tests, lost seven and four were drawn. The wins were gained in the colonials' infancy as international cricketers. Yet he was never subdued by having to tackle more experienced sides directed by famous skippers with the know-how of Lord Harris, Arthur Shrewsbury and W.G. Grace. Over the first 44 Tests England led by 25 wins to 15.

In photographs old books have of him at the wicket in middle-age, Murdoch holds the bat nearer perpendicular than the generations of batsmen I have seen, who have mainly tilted the handle in toward their thighs. His pose appears to have left room between the blade and his knees for a rock-melon to pass through, had one been around, which would have been no surprise, judging by what can be seen of the vegetation on the pitch. His book advised batsmen to stand naturally, without any strain, and to ask the umpire's guidance in making sure their toecaps were not in front of the stumps. This implies that umpires in the 1880s were less lenient to batsmen using pad-play than they have since become.

Two years after his last game for Australia he kept wicket for England against South Africa on Cape Town matting. Sussex enjoyed his captaincy from 1893 to 1899 and Ranjitsinhji joined this county to play under him.

Captains without Murdoch's buoyant personality must have envied the relaxed air of the Australian or Sussex room when this sociable skipper was presiding. Bonhomie entered the door with him. Genial thoughts shaped their own lighthearted phrasing. In *Giants of the Game* C.B. Fry gives us this peep through the doorway at the laugh-making captain:

He does not commit puns nor sputter epigrams; he is simply, genuinely and unaffectedly amusing. Instead of 'It will rain hard today,' he says 'Boys, the sparrows will be washed out.' Instead of 'I'm in good form,' he asks in a concentrated voice: 'Where's Surrey?' How well they know the sound of that cheerful, well-fed voice!

A powerful, well knit figure, as active as most men half his age and every bit as keen; his head of the cut that fits caps; his kind, cheery face tanned and determined; his neat black moustache bristling with vitality; his gait and gestures full of the direct, hard-bitten energy that distinguishes Colonials. His company would help a digger down on his luck no less than an alderman without appetite. No wonder he led the Australians well in the old days – a fit Odysseus to meet our mighty bearded Ajax ...

True, we do not often see that brilliant half-cut half-drive, that marvellous crack past cover-point; but all the other strokes are there, all the watchfulness and patience which at the Oval in the early eighties compiled that famous 211 against England's picked bowling. Not only in batting but in all else our Bill carries a style of his own ... He walks, talks, eats, drinks, smokes and wears a hat distinctively ... A great cricketer and the best possible pal before, during and after a match, wet or fine, sparrows or no sparrows.

After seven years leading Sussex he joined London County and continued making runs until he was forty-nine. The portly veteran's signing-off 140 for Gentlemen against Players at the Oval in 1904 was the twentieth century among the 17,070 runs he amassed in 684 innings in a twenty-nine-year career.

Will and his wife visited Australia in 1911 for the disposal of her father's estate. Watching Australia playing South Africa, old friends clustered around him in the pavilion to hear the discerning comments, always kindly, of a generous old player. The Springboks had won by 38 runs in Adelaide but as they went in to bat this morning, 18 February 1911, he predicted they would lose five wickets before lunch. As Hordern bowled out the fifth man Murdoch rose from his chair. 'I shall never make a prophecy about cricket again,' he said emotionally. 'I've brought bad luck to those boys.'

After lunch he suffered a stroke and sank into a coma. He was fifty-seven. Amid the excitement of the match, solemn whispering in the pavilion and lowering of the flag to half-mast dramatically drew the curtain on a distinguished career. Many in the outer enclosure wondered why the flag was lowered. Long before stumps were drawn at six. the news had spread right around the ground.

His distraught widow and her brothers arranged for the body to be embalmed and shipped to his adopted country. During the funeral at Kensal Green cemetery on 18 May, play on all English county grounds was suspended in an unequalled mark of esteem.

T.P. HORAN

4

Inside, Looking Out

Nobody was pouring oil on troubled waters at the time they called an Irishman to captain Australia on New Year's Day 1885. Judged on outsiders' beliefs about Irish temperament, such an appointment would have seemed more like casting kerosene on the flames.

With a land boom heading for disaster, enough troubles beset Melbourne citizens without an international cricket dispute blowing up. As a sequel to a squabble in England about professionals' higher fees for matches against them, the Australians from the 1884 team would play only if paid half the gate takings of the Melbourne Test. Taking over the selection, the Victorian Cricket Association sacked all the Australians who had lost the Adelaide Test and hit back with a haymaker by disqualifying six Victorians among the dissident internationals.

Amid the resultant uproar Tom Horan had to consider whether he should lead a substitute side – a Scab XI in Trades Hall parlance – while half a dozen of his old tour mates were banned.

Thomas Patrick Horan was born on 8 March 1855 in County Cork. From a hemisphere full of wars and injustice his father James, a building contractor, and mother Ellen chose Melbourne as a better place for their family to grow up in. Among Tommy's playmates at Bell Street School, Fitzroy, was Jack Blackham.

When Horan was named to lead the substitute side Blackham was one of six fellow-players officially banned from the game. Tom put continuation of Test cricket before personal links. It says much for Horan's standing among cricketers that his acceptance did not damage friendships.

The team they gave him contained nine newcomers. Five were appearing in the Australian XI for the only time. With a makeshift attack Horan was unable to prevent Arthur Shrewsbury's English XI scoring 401, in which Lancashire all-rounder Johnny Briggs made 121. Australia's new skipper spread the load among seven bowlers. He batted at No. 3, the position he had been given in the first of all Tests eight years earlier. As captain he made 63 out of 120 for the second wicket. The Australians could not avoid having to follow on.

Australia lost by ten wickets and Horan lost the captaincy, like a fairy gift taken away, to quote an old Dublin ballad. It is hard to see how he could have been blamed for not transforming a pumpkin of a side into a victory coach.

Leading NSW cricketers refused to appear in Sydney until their Victorian comrades' right to play was restored. This link in the chain of Australian mateship resulted in a stronger side tackling England. Only four of the Melbourne stopgaps held their places. Among seven stars who came in the one who mattered most was Spofforth, whose bowling brought a narrow win by six runs.

For the fifth Test a fourth captaincy change hoisted the dismounted Horan back into the saddle in Melbourne but his luck as skipper was still dead out. Though Tom won the toss, Ulyett and Peel had six out before lunch, among them Horan lbw for 0. Seven were down for 67. Tailenders' resistance brought 96 more, in a manner seen again in 1973 when bowlers John Watkins and Bob Massie put on 83 to revive Australia's almost-vanished chance against Pakistan in Sydney.

The scoreless skipper had to watch England's captain patiently make 105 not out. A lead of 223 was enough to bring England victory by an innings. An English reserve, Vernon, fielded for William Bates and Horan lent them Affie Jarvis as substitute for Barnes. The borrowed Australian caught Spofforth. That was accepted as part of the game; yet seventy-six years later, because a Welsh substitute, borrowed for two overs, caught Glamorgan's Gilbert Parkhouse, the Australians' tour contract was stiffened by the Board to require a thirteenth man to be on duty everywhere.

Besides juggling with four captains, outdoing anything in the Moscow Circus, Australia called on twenty-eight players in the series. Little wonder that England, sticking to the same XI, won the rubber, three to two. Half

29

the twenty-eight Australians were given only one match. Such panic has been exceeded only by England's selectors who chose thirty players in five Tests in 1921, and twenty-nine in six in 1989.

For one who could have felt he had been dragged through a drainpipe heels first, Tom Horan came through all reverses without a scratch on his nature deep enough to be visible. Short and thickset, he was somewhat similar to Barry Jarman in build and lively sense of humour. His face was the roundest in the Australian XI. A moustache linked luxuriant mutton-chop whiskers. Entering the Victorian Audit Office as a junior he became one of its chief clerks. Proud to co-operate, the office agreed to his arranging his annual leave so that he could play. On the pioneer tour of Britain, 1878, he was twenty-three when he made the winning hit against Marylebone Cricket Club in the match that put Australia on the cricket map in England.

All-rounder George Giffen esteemed him highly as a solid batsman and tour companion:

> Tommy and I loved to get in together, particularly when there was fast bowling about. We flattered ourselves we could stop all the fast bowlers ... There was something to gain from everything he had to say. He could talk cricket as gracefully as he later wrote about it.

Slow spin bowling, if accurate, tested him most. He was East Melbourne's best batsman when the club had a ground which Victorian Railways overran.

Horan was a full-medium-pace change bowler of round-arm type. In 15 Tests his 27 innings yielded 471 runs, average 18. His 11 Test wickets for 143 took only 33 balls each.

Batsmen were influential enough to have two wickets prepared in Sydney in January 1883 to reduce the toss-winner's advantage over the team batting last. Less wear and tear on the precious pitch, more wear and tear on the perspiring staff, who had no Bill Kelty to ease their lot.

One row about whether Horan's bowling was aided by boot-sprigs cutting up the pitch grew so heated that Spofforth knocked Lancashire all-rounder Dick Barlow backwards over a seat.

Horan's 182 innings in 109 matches totalled 4269 runs. Compared with an average of 21 in games on English tracks, where spin bothered him more, his average rose to 28 in sixty games in Australia. Seven of his eight centuries were made between the ages of twenty-five and twenty-eight. In the first forty-seven years of intercolonial games he was the only Victorian who made three hundreds against NSW bowling; twenty-four more years passed before Armstrong beat that. Horan's highest was 141 not out against Gloucestershire when he was twenty-seven. His last century was 117 not out for Victoria against the English XI when he was thirty-one.

At twenty-four, after his first tour of England, Tom wed Kate Pennefather, a police sergeant's daughter, at Richmond. For much of the fourth year of married life he was touring Britain again but at twenty-nine he declined a third trip. Two of his four sons played for Victoria. James Francis Horan totalled 820 in 20 matches from 1903, his highest 165 against Tasmania. Thomas Ignatius Bernard Horan had ten innings from 1907, with his top score 55.

His playing days over in the early 1890s, Horan continued to arrange his Audit Office leave to coincide with the main matches. Australia now had a Test cricketer turned critic, the country's pioneer player-writer. Horan adopted the pen-name 'Felix'.

Inside that expansive forehead was room for wide-ranging memories and a vocabulary to express them with an easy style. Calling him a friend of everybody, Jack Worrall said Horan's pen was blessed with a silver nib. His contributions helped make the fame of the *Australasian*. His articles made it the most-quoted paper on cricket. Historian Harry Altham was one of the English writers who quoted from his description of the desperate finish at the Oval in 1882:

> One man dropped dead, some fainted, and one man made deep notches with his teeth in the top of his umbrella. One English batsman's lips were ashen and his throat parched as he passed me on the way to the wicket ... The scorer's hands trembled so that he wrote Peate's name like Geese ...

Writing of the Australian XI at sea he told of a fancy-dress ball 'with the colossal Bonnor as a noble Roman – shades of Horace and other departed toga-wearers forgive him for his travesty!'

Players and readers alike appreciated the rare fair-mindedness of a good judge whose writing revealed that he liked to see victory go to the side that played the best cricket, even if the losers were his old team. He often left the pavilion to watch play from the shade of a favourite elm in the outer ground. Old comrades and opponents clustered around him.

Wise editors provided generous space. After Boxing Day and New Year matches they made an annual feature of his Round the Ground pieces, relished by growing numbers of readers, including many who were not cricket followers. His writing did much to cultivate genuine interest in the game and its players, without nearing the scale achieved later by Neville Cardus, the greatest thing that happened to English cricket after Grace.

Looking back, Tom commented: 'The principal sound when Colonials batted against English bowling in 1862 was not the sound of the bat against the ball but of the ball against the stumps.'

Looking behind the news in 1891: 'George Parr himself passed to his account this year at the age of sixty-five. He was a bachelor until sixty-three and in his grand climacteric married the woman who nursed him through a dangerous illness.'

Horan discovered it was harder to be an unerring critic than a successful player. He advised against selection of Hugh Trumble for the 1896 tour, saying, 'Much as I like him personally, I cannot see him a member of the team for England.' Trumble turned out to be the mainstay of Australia's attack.

Tom once suggested that Melbourne fans had rallied in such profitable numbers for nine days of big cricket that the ground should be thrown open free for the remaining district games of the season.

Comparing his match descriptions with post-war reporting, I find that he told much more of the fielding. He was generous in his praise, realistic in discussing errors and their effects. He neither roasted players over mistakes nor glossed over errors. An example: 'McAlister was run out, when if he had been backing up a bit he would have got home.' When East Melbourne selected a young player in his place, Felix referred to himself as 'the veteran Horan'.

Except while playing in England in 1882 he did not miss an issue of the *Australasian* for thirty-seven years. Dropsy caused his heart to fail at sixty-one at his Malvern home on 16 April 1916. News of his death brought a flock of appreciative letters to the editor's desk.

5

Out of the Hat

The name Massie has a way of reverberating around the cricket world for unprecedented deeds. In June 1972 Bob Massie set a new record for a visitor to Britain by snaring 16 English wickets with the most baffling swing bowling Lord's crowds ever saw in a Test match. The West Australian was playing in his first Test at twenty-five.

In May 1882 Hugh Hamon Massie astonished everyone by scorching to 100 before lunch and 206 before tea at Christ Church ground, Oxford, on the opening day of an Australian XI's tour. The daring Sydney strokesman was playing his first innings in England at twenty-eight. The Massie who massacred England's chosen batsmen and the one who mauled the university bowling were both bank officers. These sensation-mongers probably had an ancestral link in the mists of Scotland. Bob's grandfather would have liked him called Hamon, a traditional name in the clan.

Before beginning the 1882 tour the thirteen colonials each put in a hat the name of whichever player they thought would be the failure of the side. For that dubious distinction team-mates gave Hugh Hamon Massie an almost unanimous vote. They felt there were a time and a place for hitting out. So did he: any time, every place.

With rare exceptions the game's freest hitters, from Bonnor to Milburn, have been under-estimated in the scale of values set by fellow players. Batsmen dominated by concern not to get out monotonously mistrust the few who can shake this off and shake up the bowling, taking the risks involved in this enjoyable activity. More, the mistrust tends to stretch beyond hitters to strokeplayers who are willing to go for shots. South Africans gave Durban dasher Roy McLean the ambiguous nickname 'Roaring Roy' but later had to concede that Barry Richards and Graeme

Pollock, taking calculated risks, could win more matches than a trenchful of safety-first players. Queenslander Peter Burge played in parts of nine Test series and was dropped eight times before his right to a regular place was recognised. Keith Stackpole's 104 in two hours between lunch and tea at Cape Town in 1967 failed to keep him in the Australian XI after three more Tests. The brawny Victorian was left out of nine Tests before his recall, a pace-setting batsman most other countries would have liked to own. Those misjudgements are mild misdemeanours alongside England's treatment of Tom Graveney, a batsman out of the world's topmost drawer. Between the ages of twenty-four and thirty-nine this elegant master of batcraft seldom knew what it was to have a place throughout a five-match series. From 1963 to 1966 England laboured through a stretch of 38 Tests without him, to the deepening puzzlement of opposing countries' bowlers. As it is, Tom was the first post-war product to reach 100 centuries and 45,000 runs in first-class games. Given encouragement in his twenties, instead of chastening rebuffs, how much more commanding his delightful batting could have been! In recognising strokeplayers West Indies have erred least, having encouraged them from the time of Headley to Rowe, Walcott to Sobers, Kanhai to Lara.

In next to no time at Oxford Hugh Massie gave his doubters a hatful of second thoughts. Taking strike unacquainted with English conditions – softer pitch, icy wind and all – he warmed to the university bowlers as men seldom do to strangers. He raced to 100 of his side's 145 before lunch. While his companions were adding 12, he smote a second 100 in 50 minutes, causing a fumbling clatter of tin number-plates on the nails of the simple scoreboard. In three hours 206 runs gushed from Massie's bat while partners and extras were contributing 59. For all their youthful agility, students could not close gaps penetrated by his speed of shot. It looked the sort of batting to dismember the bowling and dismantle the scoreboard. Gratefully warm from arm-waving to signal boundary hits, ruddy Yorkshire umpire Luke Greenwood said, 'Ah never see the like of it afore.'

In a day Massie made himself the talk of England. No visitor had ever begun any match with 100 before lunch – a feat thought to be beyond everyone except W.G. Grace. No later visitor accomplished it for twenty years until Victor Trumper's 104 in a Manchester Test in 1902, followed by another at Bristol in 1905. Charles Macartney began the 1926 Leeds Test with a pre-lunch century, Don Bradman at Leeds 1930 and Scarborough 1934, Arthur Morris at Bristol 1948, Colin McDonald at Cambridge 1961, Bob Cowper at Scarborough 1964 and Michael Slater at Oxford 1993. Massie's double-century debut stood alone for forty-four years. With 46 not out in the second innings at Oxford his tally of 252 is still the highest by an Australian in his first match overseas.

In the mud of the only Test of the 1882 tour England led by 38 in a low-scoring game in which runs were almost as scarce as dry raincoats. Rain pattered on hansom cabs taking the disconsolate colonials to the Oval for the second innings. Barlow said the ball was like soap and groundsmen shovelled slush from the footholes before filling them with sawdust. On a pitch where bowlers had grabbed 20 wickets for 8 runs apiece, Massie could not expect to stay long. He had the right game to make every minute tell. His hitting compelled quick changes of bowler. They were wiping the slippery ball but could not stop him wiping off the arrears. One lofty off-drive was dropped near the pavilion as Hugh tore on at a run a minute. He made 55 out of 66 before Bannerman saw Steel get a ball through to his leg stump. Hugh's was the only fifty of the Test, in fact the only innings that passed Grace's 32 in a match of 31 single-figure scores, nine of them ducks.

Massie's stirring 55 created an opening for Spofforth to bowl Australia through to a win by seven runs. His seven wickets in each innings (14 for 90 with 259 balls) stood ninety years as the record by any man against England until Bob Massie's each-way swing at Lord's brought him 16 for 137; they cost Bob the strain of 102 more balls. Excited Londoners carried Spofforth shoulder-high to the pavilion but not even his bowling genius could have prevailed without Massie's valiant part. On merit they deserved to be bracketed as matchwinners.

Only captain Murdoch made more runs on the tour than Massie's 1346 in 29 first-class matches. The man they had written down as inconsistent passed 50 more often than any of them. He tipped the bowler hat on them, you might say. As a fast-running outfield he held every catch he reached.

Hugh Massie was born on 11 April 1854 on a property known as

The Swamp on the Eumeralla River 50 kilometres from the nearest town Belfast (now Port Fairy) on the Southern Ocean. It was a cool birthplace for a man of such personal warmth. The property belonged to Thomas Browne, who as Rolf Boldrewood wrote *Robbery Under Arms*, *Old Melbourne Memories* and other books. Port Fairy historians believe young Hugh's parents were probably a married couple employed on the property, later known as Squattlesea-mere.

Hugh was three when they moved to New South Wales. At twenty-two he entered the NSW XI. At twenty-six he scored 56 and 76 against Alfred Shaw's English XI. That double for a losing state showed Australia's selectors that he had the temperament to hit a side out of trouble.

Awaiting the bowler he was an erect, broad-shouldered figure close to 183 cm (6 ft) tall. Many of his hardest-struck blows were hit from a firm-footed base. Off strokes brought nearly all his runs, especially a bold cover-hit. Balls that others would go back to cut he often met, throwing his front foot across and slamming the ball on the rise. It was risky but often left cover-point looking as mobile as a signpost.

In an 1883 Melbourne Test Massie showed himself above the usual distaste for beginning an innings a quarter-hour before lunch. The sight of fieldsmen crouching close to Alick Bannerman and spreading to the outfield from Hugh caused mirthful barracking. With 43 of the first 56 Massie topped Australia's score. From that point the side could do little with Yorkshire all-rounder William Bates. They followed on and Bates made himself the first with a dozen wickets in the same Test in which he had scored a half-century.

A sequence of eight Tests for Massie ended in 1883. Seven Tests later he was called on to lead the side at Sydney in February after Australia had gone down with a wallop under other skippers in Adelaide and Melbourne. He won the toss but a lunchtime storm covered pitch and ground with hail-stones so thickly it looked like snow. Australia managed only 181. As captain, the one-time opener put himself in seventh, without success – unlike his handling of his bowlers. Promotion of part-time medium-pacer Horan to be Spofforth's main helper caused England to fall 48 short. Massie then promoted his biggest hitter, Bonnor, to go in first with

H.H. MASSIE

Bannerman. A close win, by six runs, halved Australia's leeway in the series. It was Massie's last Test at thirty.

English cricket-goers were sorry that this spectacular batsman and dashing fielder could not accept for another tour. A career in banking was likely to put more golden syrup on his bread than cricket. He applied himself to his position in the Commercial Banking Company of Sydney. Business activity was growing apace. On a sheep station near NSW's border with South Australia young English jackeroo Phillip Charley pricked a chunk of rock with a knife. This led to the world's richest silver find. Four months after Massie's last Test the Broken Hill Proprietary was floated, the greatest company in Australia's history. The initials BHP became better known than lbw.

Relationships between the bank management and staff were remarkably cordial. General manager Sir Thomas Dibbs and Hugh Massie would walk into the banking chamber punctually at 9 am daily. On the general manager's birthday staff would chorus, 'Three cheers for Sir Thomas Dibbs!' The Dibbs lived in quarters behind the bank. Forbidding cigar-smoking indoors, Lady Kitty made the men smoke out the windows into Barrack Street.

Agnes Dibbs, eldest of the general manager's seven daughters, fell in love with the handsome well-built cricketer. Agnes was twenty-two and Hugh thirty-two when they married at St Thomas's Anglican church, North Sydney, in 1887. Within three years they had two sons, followed by a daughter six years later.

On a private trip to Britain at forty Hugh was persuaded by Sir Pelham Warner to play a couple of games at Lord's for Marylebone Cricket Club against Kent and I Zingari. Hugh was not too old at forty to cause a buzz of comment by hitting Test left-hander Frank Martin over extra-cover's head first bounce into the crowd.

Hugh and Agnes made their home in Marilbah on the heights of North Sydney in the idyllic grounds of her parents' elegant stone mansion Graythwaite. Both homes had beautiful harbour views. On the roof of Graythwaite was a lookout fatalistically called a widows' walk, from which women could stare out to sea for the mastheads of their menfolks' ships.

Sir Thomas had sold part of the estate to Shore School (Sydney Church of England Grammar School) and in 1915 gave Graythwaite to the state as a rest home, now run by the Red Cross. Hugh's home is now Robson House in the school which educated his sons before they entered Sydney University. By another link in the chain of events Shore's headmaster is Basil Travers, a 1940 Rhodes Scholar who played for Oxford against Bradman's Australians on the Christ Church ground where Hugh Massie's hitting aroused England's attention sixty-six years earlier.

Touring English cricketers relished Hugh's hospitality. A keen yachtsman and gardener (it's hard to be both) he sailed a nine-metre coach-house boat, *Senga*, his wife's name reversed. His daughter-in-law told me:

> *In those days they didn't take women out sailing; they felt they didn't have the same freedom when women were aboard. He was unfailingly courteous, considerate and tolerant. For all his strength, he was a peace-loving man, though bowlers might not have shared that view.*

When Sir Thomas, eighty-nine, retired Hugh succeeded him as general manager at sixty. Agnes's cousin Eric Dibbs said 'Sydney business was then very much a family affair. Most of the top people were connected in one way or another.' Hugh retired at seventy in 1925. He was eighty-four when he died at Point Piper on 12 October 1938, leaving £57,000. In pre-inflation days that would have built Australia Square's tower, if not the Opera House.

War robbed Hugh of the pleasure of seeing his second son Robert John Allwright Massie follow him into Test cricket. Head prefect and captain of Shore's cricket and rowing, Jack Massie gained colours in rugby and athletics and won a shield for rifle shooting. In his third year in St Paul's College, Sydney University, Massie, twenty-two, played cricket and rugby for NSW and as a forerunner of Davidson's quick left-hand bowling he took 60 wickets in ten first-class games. No other Australian so young has reached this target in his own land.

In the Gallipoli landing Jack Massie tied a scarlet rag to his right arm to keep his left side less conspicuous but a Turkish grenade smashed his left shoulder. He bowled no more, though he wrote an admirable technical text on bowling which the young Bill O'Reilly devoured and swore by as he took 144 Test wickets.

J.M. BLACKHAM

6

The Caged Lion

Keeping wicket ranks close to keeping a secret among things men find hardest to do. Detractors who say a certain player will never make a batsman or never make a bowler have more risk of being disproved than those who say he will never make a wicketkeeper.

Nature endowed a young Victorian with unblinking brown eyes, instant reflexes, a flexible spine, receptive hands and a capacity for day-long concentration. So equipped, Jack Blackham transformed an onerous back-straining adjunct of the game into a new art of its own. It was almost as surprising as a theatre scene-shifter staying on stage and captivating the audience as an impromptu conjurer. Wherever Blackham kept wicket it was a sort of command performance, commanding admiration, that is.

When his father, Fitzroy newsagent Frederick Blackham, registered the birth of his second son, John McCarthy Blackham, on 11 May 1854 the McCarthy was bestowed as the family name of the child's mother. His father, a member of the Press Cricket Club, took Jack with him to a match against a country team in Melbourne. Called in to fill a vacancy, the boy was sent to field in the slips. As if drawn by a magnet, he edged closer to the wicket until he was taking the team's quickest bowlers with his bare hands, while behind him the Press backstop's gloves flapped abortively. Among fieldsmen watching at close quarters was South Melbourne captain John Conway. Hence at sixteen Jack was keeping for Colts against an English XI, at eighteen for Victoria and at twenty-two for Australia in the first of all Test matches.

To take all bowlers he usually stayed at the stumps, catching batsmen off Spofforth the Demon as confidently as he stumped them off Giffen the flighty. Blackham taking Spofforth's range of paces at beard's length from the bails so stirred crowds that years afterwards men said the game had produced no greater spectacle. In one match against Surrey in 1884, however, the ball was flying so erratically that he went back a dozen yards. Barring such exceptional circumstances, nothing could make the intrepid gloveman give an inch.

While Blackham was recovering from a hand injury at Melbourne in his fifth Test Murdoch took over the gloves. Sent in as opening batsman in the next Test in Sydney, Jack fielded skilfully at mid-off. After Murdoch twice missed stumping Ulyett in the second innings the bearded Victorian bank clerk resumed keeping, his hand still tender.

Most of his front teeth were knocked out or broken off. They say that for life he had a cavity in his chest where a fast ball had staved in his ribs.

A modern 'keeper with 3 kg of protective equipment from the ankles up would shy at the sight of the skimpy gloves worn by Blackham – more like light motoring gauntlets. They weighed scarcely one-quarter of the 1 kg creations of leather and rubber in use today.

As fingers and thumbs were so flimsily-protected and leg pads much less bulky than they have become, every captain putting on pace bowlers placed a longstop to back up his hard-pressed wicketkeeper. Though the last traces of turnips had been cleared from most pitches, enough awkward balls careered past wicketkeepers to require the longstop to be a man of tough hands and a brave heart.

People stared when they saw Blackham take pace bowling up at the stumps without a soul behind him. He was an innovator, but he was too honest a man to claim credit for conceiving the idea. He recalled:

> I was keeping for South against East Melbourne on a true Jolimont wicket when Lou Woolf walked up to me and said, 'I'm getting nothing to do, Jack. What say I field at fine leg?' At first I did not like being deprived of the safety valve.

Amid all the frenzied excitement of the Test that created the Ashes he quietly pocketed the ball that bowled England's last man. (Thirty-three years later he gave the ball to help a patriotic fund. It raised £617.)

Jack was 176 cm (5 ft 9½ in), taller than Rodney Marsh but of slighter build. Usually weighing about 70 kilograms (11 stone) he had no need to ration himself to one foaming tankard a day. Among presentations to

42

players at one Sydney Test he was given a service of plate – an oddly chosen present for a bachelor of twenty-seven.

Unable to sleep on a stifling night in Tamworth (years later John Gleeson's home town), Blackham, Giffen and McDonnell were wandering about their hotel in pyjamas. Borrowing silk hats from pegs in the cloakroom they sauntered down the street into Paradise Gardens hall, filled with dancers at a fancy-dress ball. Picking up a bell, one of them rang it for the next dance to start. The master of ceremonies began to hustle the rowdy intruders out when one of the dancers, Charles Bannerman, whispered to him 'Don't you know who they are? They are three of the Australian XI.' Instantly forgiven, the pyjama-clad gatecrashers were lionised.

Knowing Blackham from pitch-length, Giffen said:

During the whole of his first-class career he was peerless as a wicket-keeper. One could not help admiring him as he stood behind the stumps at a critical period of a game. With eyes as keen as a hawk and regardless of knocks, he would take the fastest bowling with marvellous dexterity and woe betide the batsman who lifted the heel of his back foot. To enable the 1884 Australian XI to defeat the Gentlemen of England he stumped the last three batsmen.

When Grace was asked to name the best wicketkeeper he had seen he answered, 'Don't be silly, there has been only one – Jack Blackham.' Players who saw him keep and were still watching cricket up to 1920 said they saw nobody else take the ball so cleverly or with less fuss or make such a study of men batting in front of him.

Jack Worrall told me that at times fieldsmen mischievously tried to catch their wicketkeeper napping by buzzing an unexpected throw to his end when his attention seemed to be elsewhere. Occasionally such a throw would pound against Jarvis's cask-like chest but Blackham was always alert.

Observant wicketkeepers from Blackham to Healy and Lyttelton to Knott have been sources of valuable clues to captains about batsmen's weaknesses. Up at the stumps Blackham probably had more scope for this. Noticing that Frank Iredale's heel screwed around as he turned balls off his toes. Jack spoke to bowler Bob McLeod between overs. Along came a legside yorker which the batsman missed; he was stumped. Iredale walked away believing that it could only have been done so quickly if Blackham, while taking the ball with his left glove, had simultaneously flicked off the bails with his right. Fieldsmen and square-leg umpire knew different.

Blackham's manner of appealing was even less demonstrative than gentlemanly Bert Oldfield's. Sometimes Jack merely raised his hand questioningly to bring the matter up for decision.

A missed chance was always a surprise. In an Adelaide Test he flung up his hands, thinking a ball would bowl Stoddart. Instead, it grazed the bat. Had his hands been down he could have caught and stumped Stoddart off that ball – a dismissal wicketkeepers call a double-bunger.

In front of the stumps Jack's play cut too many corners for him to be classed as a recognised batsman. Yet, valiant in a crisis, he was the first Australian to top 50 in each innings of a Test, 57 and 58 not out at Sydney in his thirteenth Test.

As one of Australia's stopgap skippers in 1885 Blackham lost his first toss. He directed his bowlers well enough to get England out for 269 at Sydney before the first day ended, then sent in bowlers as nightwatchmen. Bonnor's boldly-hit 128 in 115 minutes helped Australia lead by 40. After rain Spofforth and Palmer, unchanged, scuttled England for a win in three days.

Melbourne Cricket Club encouraged the Earl of Sheffield to back a tour with W.G. Grace as skipper. Except for £500 expenses, the club handed the Earl all gate takings from a Melbourne Test. The Earl responded by presenting £150 for a silver Sheffield Shield for competition among the colonies. It is a moot point whether we owe more to the Earl of Sheffield than to an obscure Earl of Sherbrooke who urged discontinuance of transportation of convicts to Australia; the latter cut off sources of initiative and incorrigible audacity.

Blackham played a notable part in this cricket revival as captain of Victoria and Australia, elected by the players of each team. They showed confidence in his judgement, management of bowlers and field placing.

Setting infielders near Grace, Jack called one in so close that England's champion turned to him and asked, 'Do you want a funeral on your side?' Though Blackham had no large margin of runs to play with in the second

44

innings he brought on Harry Trott's slow leg-breaks at 60 instead of a more accurate bowler. Quick wickets and the match rewarded his enterprise.

Though the law still stipulated five balls to an over he and Grace agreed to six-ball overs in that series. Australia won the rubber two to one but, still under Blackham, lost the only Test finished of the three in England in 1893.

Blackham's field tactics were not blamed, except that George Giffen was reported to have shown resentment at being put on too late and bowled too little for his liking. One midfield argument grew so heated that Trumble stepped between them.

One county crowd saw one of the team's two teetotallers, left-hander Arthur Coningham, industriously gather grass cuttings into a heap inside the boundary and set fire to them to warm his hands. Fines as penalties for ill-natured behaviour lost effect because they were not enforced. Members of factions within the team lost tempers on a railway journey into Sussex. When the train reached Brighton porters saw one compartment spattered with blood. Lower profits reduced each player's share to £190 instead of £400 or £500.

Opinion in both lands was that the wizard wicketkeeper was too highly strung for the cares of captaincy. If his batsmen were failing he would pace up and down the room, fists clenched and beard on chest, in a way that caused tour mates to call him 'The Caged Lion'. During one Victorian slump against NSW he rebuked batsmen for chasing off-balls. Then he bustled to the crease, one hand swinging the bat angrily. The other hand was in his pocket – a habit when going in. He pulled the innings around with his highest score in twenty-one years of first-class cricket, 109. On return to the room he looked at the unmasked batsmen with savage satisfaction. One of them piped up defensively, 'But you chased the off-stuff, Jack.' Blackham: 'From now on I hope you'll know *how* to do it.'

In the second innings of an Adelaide Test players thought him almost hysterical when Giffen went in to bat. He hid deep in the room and told Harry Moses and Frank Iredale that if they went outside the luck would change and Giff would get out.

To their dismay Giffen returned. Rushing to him Blackham asked 'What's up?' Giffen replied, 'Wrong hat.'

45

Blackham was so upset he insisted on Moses and Iredale staying with him until the day's end. Australia won by 72 runs.

Blackham's last Test, his eighth as skipper, was in turn filled with pleasure, pain and gnawing tension. Making his highest Test score, 74, he and Syd Gregory clapped on 154 in 73 minutes for the ninth wicket at Sydney in 1894. His team piled up 586. A ball from Lyons forced a thumb back, injuring the top joint and ripping open an old wound.

As England fell 261 short, Blackham told Andrew Stoddart to follow on. Fighting back, the Englishmen kept the Australians in the field from Saturday afternoon until Wednesday, making 437, for a lead of 176. On the sixth morning Australia had eight wickets left to score 64 more runs. Blackham had insisted that all the Australian XI live together in a Coogee hotel. Several of them slept through the noise of rain on the roofs but not Jack. It had often been said that, when captain, he seldom slept until a match ended. This time, nursing his throbbing thumb, he paced the hotel balcony all night, cursing the falling rain. The pearly sluice-gates jammed open for hours.

Tortured by his aching hand, Blackham watched the left-hander Bobby Peel make the ball do everything except dry-retch. When he became Peel's sixth victim England snatched victory by ten runs – the first of two occasions when a Test team following on has won. Captaincy worries in that series caused to him to lose six kilograms (about a stone).

The injury closed his seventeen-year Test career at thirty-nine. In his 35 Tests, all against England, he stumped 24 of his 60 wickets. He made a couple of his 36 catches while fielding elsewhere. In 277 first-class matches his total was 449 (269 caught, 180 stumped) and his 6394 runs included 27 scores past 50. The only keeper who toured England eight times, he stumped four batsmen there for every six he caught. The comparative infrequency of stumpings today illustrates a vast change in the nature of the game. When I asked his much-younger brother Fred had Jack given him any hints about wicketkeeping he replied, 'Only one – to give it up and take on bowling.'

The one-time bank clerk's friends were saddened when his main investments failed. He accepted the blow as he had accepted umpires' decisions.

Arranging a testimonial which yielded £1359 for him at fifty-seven, the VCA provided an annuity for the State's finest cricketer of the period.

Blackham was the first Australian XI captain who never married. Friends subscribed to send him to Sydney for Tests until his death on 28 December 1932.

H.J.H. SCOTT

7

Going for the Doctor

The name Scott was linked with adventure long before Captain Robert Scott lost his life in Antarctica and Charles Scott, with Campbell Black, won the Melbourne Centenary Air Race from Britain in 1934. An earlier Charles, a pioneering captain of the Royal Marines, sailed his cutter from England to Port Phillip Bay and took up land now traversed by Little Collins Street. Frequent raids by Aborigines drove him elsewhere. His son John grew up to be secretary of the Melbourne Gas and Coke Company and married Elizabeth Miller. The Scotts could afford fees for the boys at Wesley College and Melbourne University, where three of them graduated in medicine.

Born the day after Christmas 1858, Henry James Herbert Scott was playing in a college match at thirteen when professional bowler Sam Cosstick remarked, 'That little nipper will make a good 'un!' Henry won the St Kilda Club's batting average while still at school. At nineteen he was awarded a cup for best bowling when Victoria narrowly lost in Sydney.

When Scott gained selection at twenty-five for the fourth Australian XI's tour of England in 1884 he was about average build, 175 cm and 73.6 kg (5 ft 9 in and 11 st 8 lb). As a newcomer to English turf he was mostly sent in sixth or seventh until in the Lord's Test he topped the score in both innings. Promoted to fourth in the Oval Test he was one of three century-makers after a let-off at 60. He batted 3½ hours for 102 out of 207 while he was in. Finding him the hardest man in the team to bowl, the Englishmen disturbed his sticks only ten times in 51 innings. His 69 stand with Boyle was Australia's last-wicket record at Lord's until equalled by Lillee and Mallett in 1975.

Fascinated by vistas unrolled to the gaze of an upstairs bus passenger – still the best way to see London – Henry could never get too much topdeck travel. Mates joked about his fondness for riding in twopenny buses. They nicknamed him Tuppence, then shortened it to Tup.

While completing the third year of his Melbourne medical course at twenty-seven Henry scored 111 against NSW. The fifth overseas tour was arranged by Melbourne Cricket Club with Scott as captain. It was 1886, when cabhorses in four-wheelers were looking at intruding cable-trams as men now look at automation.

His batting was noted for grit rather than gaiety. Yet at times an adventurous globule inherited from his marine grandsire bubbled through. One ionospheric drive landed a ball from A.G. Steel on the Oval pavilion roof, as if to chase the clouds away from the sky as well as from Australia's prospects. Scott's 22 off a four-ball over from Yorkshire off-spinner Saul Wade set a record.

Wisden editor Sydney Pardon said Scott led the team with sincerity of purpose but lacked the necessary authority and experience. Every shelf of *Wisden*s bears cumulative evidence of its editors' fair-mindedness, yet I know it is difficult for a man surveying a season as a whole to keep close enough to the touring side to judge how much captaincy could have influenced the tide of events.

A loss in the first match and several injuries robbed the side of confidence. In the sixth match Spofforth dislocated his right middle finger. Bonnor's hitting was lost after an injury in July. To fill his team in some matches the hard-pressed skipper had to borrow players, in addition to calling on forty-four-year-old manager Ben Wardill for one game and team doctor Roland Pope for four.

Cares weighed heavily on him. Yet qualities, revealed elsewhere, make me wonder whether a combination of Caesar, Monash and Churchill could have lifted his losing side from a marsh of misadventures. Tup Scott mostly batted third in the early games but undertook opening the innings in 16 matches, including the Manchester and Lord's Tests. In the Oval Test fieldsmen dropped Grace four times in the first 100 of his 170; rain softened the pitch enough for Lohmann and Briggs to make Australia follow on and lose by an innings. Unsparing to himself, Scott rested only once and finished third on the tour run list.

Amid the stresses, quarrels were reported in a discouraged side. His captaincy was more open to question than his cricket. When the bowling is not incisive critics become more so.

Doubtless it all left Scott hoping distant fans Down Under would not fear his was a case for lobotomy. His second tour brought his total in England to 2244 runs in 67 innings, including two hundreds and 12 half-centuries; he held 33 catches.

When his team sailed home Tup stayed on to complete medical degrees. By June 1888 he was surgeon to the Cordillera mines. He married Mary Minnie Mickle, twenty-seven, pretty daughter of grazier Thomas Mickle and Mary Syme, on 31 July 1888 at St Kilda. The twenty-nine-year-old bridegroom took her to central NSW before moving to Scone.

Tup Scott undertook the life of a pioneer country doctor with a spirit of service that won him even greater esteem than such Test deeds as a century at the Oval and the honour of having captained Australia. Calls took him over primitive roads often too rough for a buggy. He rode long distances to lonely farmhouses and sawmills to save lives. The saddle-sore Samaritan bought a motor-buggy steered by a tiller. Townsfolk came from their cottages to watch this technological marvel go by. Relatives said he disposed of unpaid accounts by simply ruling them out of his books. As the town's outstanding personality, he was three years mayor of Scone. Test cricket and the main races attracted him periodically to Sydney.

Typhoid ended Dr Scott's ministrations on 23 September 1910 when he was fifty-one. Many cities are sprinkled with streets and parks called after sportsmen. Not content with that, the grateful townspeople of Scone named their new hospital the Scott Memorial Hospital.

P.S. McDONNELL

8

Percy Greatheart

To the under-twenty crowd Percy McDonnell was the most enviable young man in the land: good-looking, well-built, gracefully athletic, gracious in manner, son of a prominent barrister ... all this and a brain too.

Though powered by a broad chest's lungs his voice was more velvety than those of players descended from the currency lads and lasses of Port Jackson. His birthplace on 13 November 1860 had been the Kensington district of London's West End. When his barrister father brought him to Victoria he was four; he had to stand on a pile of *Wisden*s to reach the honey jar. As the Hon. Morgan Augustine McDonnell, his father held the office of Attorney-General in two short-lived state Cabinets.

Enrolled at St Patrick's College, Melbourne, and Xavier College, Kew, Percy Stanislaus McDonnell gratified his tutors by emerging as a successful Greek scholar and mathematician. Credits and distinctions made the Education Department eager to have him on the State's teaching strength. When he left Xavier for such a post he had appeared in the Melbourne Cricket Club's first XI at sixteen. Victoria sent him to Sydney at seventeen for his intercolonial debut. When you're seventeen or eighteen your name in the batting order is like a season ticket to paradise.

Pleasure at being chosen at nineteen to tour England was modified by the Education Department's reluctance to give him leave. McDonnell and George Palmer stepping on to the Oval in 1880 for the first Test on English soil was the only occasion Britons have seen two teenagers in the Australian XI. Percy headed the tour averages. Even the wan orb Englishmen call the sun seemed to have a golden glow!

Of all Australia's batsmen in the first fifty years of international cricket few captured public fancy to such a fond degree as McDonnell, combining a hitter's power with a stylist's symmetry. Jack Worrall's list of Australia's four greatest hitters on all wickets names McDonnell first, ahead of Jack Lyons whose drive once bent an iron rail at Adelaide Oval, Hugh Massie and George Bonnor. Since their day Australia has seen Joe Darling, Jack Ryder, Keith Miller and Mark Waugh make the field appear to shrink.

Giffen commented on Lyons's and McDonnell's ability to stand firm footed and straight-drive balls, even some that pitched a trifle short. Percy's hardest strokes were hit from a base as solidly steady as a statue's plinth. He was recognised as a batsman whose audacity could turn the fortunes of a game. Paderewski's music teacher Leschetizsky once said a good pianist should be able to play on a ludo board. Applying the gist of this to cricket, McDonnell was a more gallant player on bad pitches than most of the others. Giffen suggested that a more appropriate name for Mac would have been Percy Greatheart McDonnell, for when things were going wrong he was seen at his best. When no desperate crisis called for remedial hitting he could reveal the poetry of batting.

Already a big-occasion player at twenty-one, Percy made his first century in first-class cricket in a Test match – 147 in a side-saving innings that included two chances and a drive over the corner of a Sydney stand.

At twenty-three he opened the Oval Test in 1884 like a forerunner of Colin Milburn, Bob Barber, Keith Stackpole and Michael Slater. Of 130 before lunch his eager bat whipped up 86 – the nearest anyone approached to 100 before lunch until Trumper achieved this breathless target in 1902. When caught for 103, McDonnell had made two-thirds of the total. He shook up the bowling so severely that Lord Harris called on every one of England's XI to bowl.

In an Adelaide Test the way an early boundary shot sped to the pickets told Percy the pitch was inviting rapid mastery of England's bowlers. His mixture of long-handled vigour, dainty cuts and precise placements non-plussed the fieldsmen. After one dropped him near the long-off boundary at 79, there was no stopping the first Test 100 seen on Adelaide Oval. Fourth out, Mac made 124 of the first 190 by mid-afternoon on a day when all other batsmen except Blackham failed. Two days later reporters were preparing to hail Percy as the first man to make 100 in each innings of a Test when he was run out for 83.

Bureaucrats had yet to realise that a Test star's prestige could be valuable to the Education Department. Refused leave to go on tour, he resigned from his post. Moving to Sydney in his mid-twenties he made 239 out of 310 against his old comrades in 1886. He was presented with a time-piece which, although called a watch, was too big to wear. Behind its informative dial, mechanism whirred to chime not only the hours but each quarter.

Percy was eleven weeks past twenty-six when after 13 Tests he was pro-moted captain to give directions to his elders. Australia's only younger skipper against England has been Murdoch, seventeen weeks younger at his first toss. McDonnell's team contained seven men ranging up to eight years older than himself and four of them had experience in more Tests. When John Cottam joined Jack Ferris in the side for a Sydney Test onlookers in Australia had their only sight of two nineteen-year-olds representing their country.

For the second time in ten years Australia was being led by a player born overseas. This has not happened since, though at least eight captains of England have been born abroad: Lord Harris and Sir Pelham Warner in the West Indies, Douglas Jardine and Colin Cowdrey in India, G.O. Allen in Sydney, Freddie Brown in Peru, Ted Dexter in Italy and Tony Greig in South Africa. No opposing captain had dared put England in to bat first until McDonnell, winning his first toss, put the hard word on Arthur Shrewsbury's team. He tried this strategy twice in low-scoring games on rain-softened wickets, but his Australians batted worse. No other skipper has been able to take from McDonnell the credit for having directed the bowlers who put the Englishmen out for their poorest score, 45 (Turner and Ferris unchanged for 36 four-ball overs at Sydney in 1887).

England's main matchwinner in that January Test, Notts all-rounder William Barnes, was missing from the February Test because of injury. English writer Ralph Barker stated that in a hasty moment Barnes had swung a punch at McDonnell, missed and bruised his hand on a bar wall. Barnes's eight wickets in the January Test included the Australian captain in

55

each innings, the second time lbw for 0. History is silent on what led to the telegraphed punch that failed to find its addressee.

For light-hearted Percy Mac to be involved in unpleasantness was as out-of-character as Harry Secombe wearing a scowl. Other actions were more in keeping with his magnanimity. He agreed to one of the English XI, William Gunn, umpiring for part of a Test in the absence of an appointed man. McDonnell raised no difficulty about England bringing into Barnes's place migrant ex-Lancashire left-hander Reg Wood who had settled for two years in Melbourne and played for Victoria against the Englishmen earlier in the same season. When a fieldsman was hurt, Percy lent as substitute fieldsman one of his bowlers, Turner, who caught his team-mate Reg Allen.

Yet to be equalled as a captain's innings was McDonnell's 82 out of 86 in an hour against the North of England on a bowler's wicket at Old Trafford in 1888; a match-winning wonder. Over the fence in England counted four runs in those days. At three separate changes of bowling, Percy Mac lifted the first ball from each new bowler into the crowd.

McDonnell was the only Australian captain who could read the Greek philosophers and playwrights in their own lettering. He could appreciate Aristotle's logic, chuckle at Lysistrata. Intellect and personal charm, however, could not assure success in a period marked by so many muddy wickets and illnesses that his touring thirteen, tackling 40 matches, had difficulty fielding a fit eleven.

Hard pressed, McDonnell called in a twenty-year-old Cambridge under-graduate for the three Tests, Sam Woods from Sydney, who was reputed to bowl fastest after hearty lobster breakfast parties.

Five losses to one win under McDonnell's captaincy formed part of Australia's longest losing sequence: seven consecutive Tests. The win gained by Turner's off-cutters and Ferris's left-hand spin at Lord's in 1888 was the only interruption to a stretch of 11 victories by powerful English teams. Superficial opinion labels a losing skipper as a bad skipper but Grace said McDonnell captained with fine judgement and it was no disgrace that his team had to concede victory.

In Sydney Percy had met Grace McDonald socially. On his tour of Britain as captain their friendship ripened. Grace, a pretty blue-eyed blonde, and Percy announced their engagement in London, about the time he played the last of his 19 Tests at the age of twenty-seven. Each was thirty when they married at Randwick in 1891, an eye-catching couple; the bride, about 167 cm (5 ft 6 in), was a few inches taller than the average Australian girl and the handsome groom stood 185 cm (6 ft 1 in).

Xavier old boys took pride in the only Catholic in the 1888 touring thirteen being elected captain – a notable illustration of Australian XI's freedom from sectarian issues. The McDonnells moved north to Brisbane, where he became a stockbroker. Queenslanders were delighted to have a man of Percy Mac's fame and personality as their third captain in eleven-a-side matches.

Heart disease began striking at him before he reached his mid-thirties. Yet a season before his death he captained a Combined XI against the 1896 Australian XI and could still pillage 65 in less than an hour for Queensland against NSW. Two months short of thirty-six his heart failed on 24 September 1896. He totalled 6460 runs in about 280 first-class matches. Though in his side's interests he risked his wicket with alacrity, he was topscorer more than fifty times. At his death he and English captain Arthur Shrewsbury were the only men with three centuries in Anglo–Australian Tests.

G. GIFFEN

9

Early Riser No. 1

Nothing on two legs could outdo George Giffen for stamina, not even an Olympic runner from Kenya. Giffen alone has taken 1000 wickets and scored 10,000 runs in first-class matches for Australian and state teams. On one of his five tours of Britain this robust South Australian topped both the bowling and batting averages – another feat yet to be equalled. On a voyage to England at twenty-five for an earlier tour he and others went down to the stokehold day after day and shovelled coal into the furnace to keep fit.

Phrases in use about him at the time were that he was as strong as a scrub bull, worked like a horse and developed a thirst like a camel. After bowling for hours in the nets at Adelaide Oval George would run around the field and finish with a 100-metre sprint. He would walk right across the city to the Giffen home on the corner of South Terrace (a home demolished in about 1970 to be the site for an office block). On the walk he passed the General Post Office where he worked in the letter-sorting section. On match days, the walk to and from the Oval added about four kilometres to the day's exertions.

A carpenter's third son, George was born on 27 March 1859. He and his younger brother Walter were similar in build to Ian Chappell, 180 cm tall (5 ft 11 in) but their 85 kg (13 st 5 lb) frames looked more muscular, rather like the great Melbourne footballer Ron Barassi. Both brothers could throw cricket balls 108 yards (98.5 metres) in competitions. Before SA was strong enough to play others with even sides he was chosen at seventeen and twenty against English teams. When a telegram from Melbourne invited him to play in a Test match Giffen, twenty-two, almost feared to ask for leave, as he had just joined the postal service; it was readily granted.

At twenty-four he was the first bowler outside England to get a whole side out. His 10 for 66 for an Australian XI against The Rest in Sydney was viewed with wonderment for fifty-one years before another man, fast bowler Tim Wall, collected ten for SA against NSW in Sydney in 1933. Since the war Queensland fast bowler Peter Allan in Melbourne and West Australian swinger Ian Brayshaw in Perth have each dismissed all ten Victorians, leaving Giffen the only off-spinner among the four.

Season after season the untiring all-rounder brought off double-barrelled performances still unequalled in cricket anywhere. His deeds would strain belief today if they were not authenticated by well-balanced old books and described by pressbox witnesses. It's all there in black and white, even if some of the white is going yellow.

His unique double of 271 runs in seven hours and 16 wickets against Victoria in Adelaide in 1891 looks like standing 100 years unapproached, maybe 200. A year earlier it was 237 and 12 wickets in Melbourne. No other player in any country has coupled a double-century with a dozen or more wickets. At twenty-six he was the first to take 17 wickets in a match (against Victoria in Adelaide). He is the only man anywhere to have lowered 16 wickets or more five times. Among Australians since the second world war only Terry Alderman – 14 for 87 for Western Australia against NSW in Perth in 1981–82 – has taken more than 13 wickets in a match on home Australian soil. In his 113 and six wickets against Lancashire in 1884 George made himself the first to couple a century with a hat-trick. No Australian has done so since.

In one twelve-year period he took five-eighths of the wickets and scored one-third of the runs for South Australia.

He measured eight paces, then began his approach by swinging both arms to the rear. Assiduous practice perfected balance, rhythm and the art of running at varying speeds yet keeping control of the ball's line and length. Just before delivery his side-on body completely hid his arm. Batsmen could never tell whether a quicker stride heralded a quicker or slower ball from his hairy arm and big hand. His slow-to-medium bowling was built on off-breaks yet he always said variety in pace and flight meant more than turn.

Mastery of at least four main types of balls kept up the pressure. Hidden among off-breaks would come a similar-paced ball, with overspin which Peel admiringly called his masterpiece. A higher, slower ball, wicketkeepers said, behaved as if tied to a string. Drawn forward by expectation that it would pitch further up, batsmen seeing it dip suddenly felt dismay of the sort caused in recent years by Lance Gibbs. Without change of action, a straight one's pace from the earth trapped many a man playing back. Giffen the guileful even varied the expression on his face, bronzed by exposure to the sun longer than other bowlers. A determined look might accompany one of his flightiest balls, followed by a relaxed smile to camouflage his quickest one. With a sardonic grin he could make a batsman feel the end was near. He was the Olivier of off-spinners as well as the Gibbs of his time. He was an over-the-wicket bowler except when some English conditions induced him to switch to around-the-wicket with a Laker-like field of up to four short-legs.

Reward came with 103 English wickets in 31 Tests. Flight brought him six stumpings, ten catches to his own horny hands and many of the other 45 catches off his bowling. He hit the stumps of 36 men and had six lbw. He was the second of ten bowlers who have taken 100 English wickets in Tests – Turner 101, Giffen 103, Trumble 141, Noble 115, Grimmett 106, O'Reilly 102, Lindwall 114, Lillee 167, Alderman 100, Thomson 100.

Worth a place for bowling alone, Giffen also made 1238 runs, mostly batting as high as third in the Test side. Noble is the only other Australian with 100 wickets and 1000 runs against England. Armstrong was grouped with them to make the three best all-rounders up to 1920 – a line that led on to Jack Gregory, Keith Miller, Richie Benaud and Alan Davidson, with more to come.

Players envied the way he always appeared to bring the full face of his high-gripped bat to the ball. Steel-wristed drives to either side were his chief strokes. His cutting was praised and glides to leg added hundreds to his totals.

After a wicketless first game in Adelaide, Victorian all-rounder Albert Trott put a box in front of the stumps as he practised in Melbourne. When his elder brother Harry asked what the box was for, Albert replied, 'Oh, that's George Giffen.' Harry: 'Easier to get past than George's bat, isn't it?' Saying, 'That's just it,' Albert proceeded to perfect a breakback around the box to hit the stumps.

As mainstay of the 1886 team in England Giffen headed both bowling and batting averages with 159 wickets at 17 runs apiece and 1453 runs at 26 an innings. It was the first of his three 100 and 1000 doubles in Britain. No touring Test player has achieved one of these doubles since Indian left-hander Vinoo Mankad in 1946.

George's 203 for SA in 1888 was the first Adelaide double-century against English bowling.

He was willing to put his own position at stake, as when he told the selectors 'You can strike my name out if Syd Gregory is not picked' and gave his reasons. Denying a charge that he declined to join the 1893 team unless brother Walter was chosen, he pointed out that a man with form good enough to be in the Australian XI in the last two Tests was not out of place in a touring XIV.

In his book *With Bat and Ball* he deeply regrets having brought a black mark against his name by refusing to go out when adjudged to have hit his wicket at Adelaide Oval. Victoria's captain Blackham played on under protest.

George was a bit stubborn on the field, said Worrall, though there was no truer and more open-handed man off it.

As players staked money to finance tours, his chief explanation for staying home in 1888 and 1890 was that loss of stars left Australia unable to muster a team with a reasonable hope of success.

On tours he was no dancer or singer but his realistic mimicry of a dog's bark at well-timed moments was a source of team merriment.

When a catch was dropped off him in a Sydney Test in December 1894 Giffen accepted loss of the wicket without a turn or a look. A deputy wicketkeeper who replaced the injured Blackham fumbled a stumping chance. 'Giffen kept plugging away as calmly as if he were at the practice nets,' the *Sydney Morning Herald* reported

The nearest approach to 100 wickets and 1000 runs in an Australian season has been Giffen's 93 wickets and 902 runs in 11 matches in 1894–95.

Next comes Sobers's 51 wickets and 1006 runs in ten games for SA in 1962–63.

At his first toss for Australia Giffen put the other side in at Melbourne in 1894. Before the toss he and Andrew Stoddart agreed that the soaked Melbourne pitch would be rolled for fifteen minutes at the day's end to flatten out dents. Before that happened, both sides were out, England 75 and Australia 123. The rolling created a batsman's wicket for the other four days and England won by 94 to be two up. Heat and flawless catching enabled the Australians to peg one back in Adelaide, where the shade temperature ranged from 39 to 41°C. Though Giffen lost the toss in Sydney and Stoddart sent the Australians in, more rain gave England the worst of the wicket. It was the only time a whole English XI were out twice in one day.

With the series two all, trains and steamers swelled the Melbourne attendances to the first 100,000 crowd. Giffen's right little finger was hurt as he was making 57 of Australia's 414. He dropped return catches twice early in MacLaren's 120 and blamed this for England's ultimate win. The match was in the balance until John Brown, 50 in 28 minutes, tore gaping holes in Australia's bowling. The first 50 of Brown's 140 still stands as the fastest half-century in Tests.

Besides landing most wickets (34) in that series Giffen was the only batsman in either side who exceeded 450 runs. No other all-rounder has since been the most penetrating bowler and heaviest scorer. Gifts from the public filled a purse with 400 sovereigns for George.

Though as skipper in four Tests he had led a fightback to break even he was not asked to captain Australia again. His habitual role as lock-stock-and-barrel bowler had a side-effect that counted against him as skipper. Sir Pelham Warner summed it up with, 'He bowled himself too much.'

The first time he had the say in a Test, he had bowled 78.2 six-ball overs in England's 333 at Melbourne – 23 overs more than anyone else. Other players at last persuaded vice-captain Hugh Trumble to ask George to take himself off. Giffen: 'Yes, I think I'll go on at the other end.' Telling the story against himself later, Trumble grinned: 'He did – and finished with six wickets.'

Blamed for keeping himself on too long in England's last innings in

Melbourne (one for 106 off 31 six-ball overs), Giffen said more than once he wanted to go off but Trott had said, 'No Giff, you are bowling better than any of us and had better stay on.' He made the heaviest payout in any innings against English batsmen, 309 off 522 balls in Adelaide. He was not skipper when he bowled his greatest number of balls in a Test, 708 in two innings in Sydney.

On a fiery Essex pitch when he was thirty-seven a high-speed ball from Kortright hit the peak of Giffen's cap and spun it around. He was well clear to leg when the next one ripped through and it was the only time he was glad to get out. To suggestions that it had broken his nerve he gave a visible answer in a Manchester Test by driving Tom Richardson harder than Australians ever saw the great fast bowler hit in England. Richardson was among the bowlers in a Sydney Test in 1894 when Giffen made 161 before a slip-catch ended the innings he believed was his best.

When his turn came for a week off it was understood that he was going to Paris. Next day George reappeared to watch the game, puffing his pipe.

Twelve of Giffen's 18 centuries in first-class matches were made in Australia and he carried four on past 200. He coupled a century with one of his three hat-tricks.

After two years of voluntary retirement he was close to forty-four when he was recalled against the Victorians. By scoring 178 for once out and taking 15 wickets George had his last laugh on the calendar.

Giffen's career totals stand cliff-like: 1022 wickets and 11,757 runs in 248 first-class matches spread over twenty-three years. In the decades since his last game the closest to his totals has been Australia's busiest post-war cricketer, Richie Benaud, with 945 wickets and 11,801 runs. As one sign of how the game has changed, Richie played 11 more matches in a career three years shorter. While Giffen was wheeling along 46,355 balls for his wickets his moustache was the only thing that drooped.

In retirement he channelled his fondness for the game into coaching boys on South Parkland from 6 am to 7.30 am on Mondays, Wednesdays and Fridays. Visiting a class, Lancashire Test players Cecil Parkin and Harry Makepeace were astonished by George's bowling and batting at sixty-one. The boys formed a team known as The Early Risers.

At a postal Sunday picnic one of the contests was bowling at one stump. Somebody put the old champion's name down. Some competitors hit the stump once. One hit it twice. Everybody had bowled when they called George out of the liquor booth. He walked to the pitch, took his coat off and began the old familiar run-up. To the crowd's astonishment he hit the stump nine times before a ball missed.

After forty-three years in the GPO he retired at sixty-five, two years after his benefit match, South Australia v. Victoria, had yielded £2020, invested with trustees.

When Giffen died at sixty-six in Adelaide on 29 November 1927 two captains, Joe Darling and Clem Hill, eulogised him for the willing hours he had given bowling to them and other young players to bring their batting up to international standard.

G.H.S. TROTT

10

Postman's Knock

If a boy with a talent for sport asked which job would most help fit him for international rank what would you suggest? Vocational guidance could scarcely recommend an occupation more favourable than postman. Delivering letters gives leg-strengthening exercise while the lungs gratefully breathe air as fresh as the locality permits. One of cricket's most-admired captains, Harry Trott, was a postman. His leather bag held letters stamped with names of places which his skill as a player and gifts as a skipper would take him to see.

Born in the Melbourne inner suburb of Collingwood on 5 August 1866, George Henry Stevens Trott was the third of eight children of Adolphus Trott. Stevens was his mother's maiden name. Scouts who saw Harry at seventeen playing with park juniors recruited him to South Melbourne in 1885. In his first match for Victoria he was as cool as the underside of a cucumber. It was the first time a youth making his debut at Adelaide Oval had hit George Giffen over onlookers outside the chain that then marked the leg boundary.

Rapidly developing into Victoria's most attractive batsman, he scored mainly in front of the wicket, yet his late-cuts were close to perfection. Bowlers grew to fear a swinging on-drive that he was not afraid to lift. 'Let his side be under the whip and you see him at his best,' said Giffen. 'He wields a wide blade and no matter how he may stonewall he never loses his elegance of style.' Harry folded his shirtsleeves as formally as banquet serviettes around elbows that knew how to bend after a hot day's play.

A man of middle height, 175 cm (5 ft 9 in), he weighed 70 kg (11 st) when he made 0 on his Test debut at twenty-one. At twenty-two he set Sydney talking by scoring 172 for the 1888 Australian XI against NSW. At twenty-three he married buxom Violet Hodson at Fitzroy in February 1890 before his second successful tour of England and New Zealand. By his mid-twenties he was one of those fuller figures in flannels, like Queensland all-rounder Tom Veivers in the 1960s and Victorian fast bowler Merv Hughes in the 1990s.

His wide well-nourished moustache could never mask his good-natured smile but batsmen had no right to expect Australia's best leg-spinner to be friendly to them at the wicket. Like later spinners Mailey and Fleetwood-Smith, he put wicket-taking before economy. It was hard to get much turn from Sydney tracks as shiny as the marble pillars of the GPO but, varying pace and flight, he obtained whip from the pitch. At Leicester on his third tour, 1893, he made 100 in 130 minutes and took 11 wickets.

Driving at Lancashire spinner Johnny Briggs, Trott was stumped while scrambling back but umpire West ruled him not out. Harry repeated the shot next ball and walked to the pavilion. Tackled about having thrown his wicket away he replied, 'Little Briggsy had bowled himself inside out trying to trap me. Why should he be robbed because West was out late last night?'

Trott's fielding at point caused the position to be called strong-point. His interceptions earned the imprecations of square-cutting forerunners of Barnes, Burge, Stackpole, Walters and Boon.

In days when few grounds had shower facilities, tired cricketers soaked in baths. When Trott climbed out and towelled himself the first thing he put on was his felt hat. Harry was instantly recognisable by this habit regardless of other unveiled means of identification.

Trott captained Victoria with striking success and not always with the best sides to handle. He was twenty-eight when he sent an English XI in and won by seven wickets. His eight wickets for 63 in 1895 still form the best average for Victoria against an English Test side.

When some other public servants complained about the frequent absence of Trott the postal chief replied, 'Harry Trott is a national institution.'

On four tours of England from 1888 to 1896 he exceeded 1000 runs on each visit and totalled 145 wickets. Six of his ten centuries were made there. Yet it is as captain that he is best remembered, an understanding judge of human nature. Studying players' whims and fancies, he got the best out of his men. They grew fond of this genial man and were resolved never to let him down.

The seemingly drowsy top lids of Harry's grey eyes deceived nobody. The more intense the battle the more flexible his mind became. He gave the impression of being a more intuitive captain than the others. Intuition impelled him to act promptly without waiting for confirmation. Dumping the textbook, some called it. If he did act on hunches they were the sort of hunches endorsed by his teams, beneficiaries of his quick perception and subtlety of strategy.

We have the word of fellow players that, himself a regular bowler, he had a fuller knowledge than batsman-captains of his bowlers' powers and limitations. He changed them more frequently, knowing the value of nursing them to keep them at their best. Players thought him an uncanny judge of who was likeliest to get most out of the pitch – not only which wicket but which end. Far from being an egotist, he gave himself an average of a dozen overs a Test innings. When his tossed leg-breaks separated pairs who had frustrated other bowlers he would promptly bring on someone else. He took 29 wickets and 21 catches in 24 Tests, in addition to making 921 runs.

By direction of an Australian Cricket Council the selectors chose the 1896 team early before the season's main games. One result was the staggering omission of Albert Trott, who at twenty-one had made a match-winning debut in the 1895 Adelaide Test when Harry was twenty-eight. Middlesex snapped up Albert, recognised as one of the world's best all-rounders.

Though not eager to undertake the captaincy Harry Trott accepted election by the players. Several of his team came from higher up the social scale and had the advantage of better education. Among them were three college boys, an engineer, a solicitor, a secretary and a bank officer. As usual, there was no room for class distinction when they elected this cricket-wise postman their skipper, a man of personality and homespun humour. One of the college boys, Clem Hill, said:

> As a captain Harry Trott was in a class by himself – the best I ever played under. Harry was quick to grasp a situation. He saw an

69

opponent's weakness in a second. He knew in a moment when a crack bowler was having an off day. Time and again he got a champion batsman's wicket by putting on a bowler whom he knew the batsman did not like.

When he became captain at twenty-nine Australian enthusiasm for international cricket had waned from its early fervour under Gregory and Murdoch. England had won 19 to seven of the preceding 30 Tests. To tour Britain with a team of fourteen containing nine players new to English conditions was called ridiculous.

When Hill dropped Grace at 40 off Trott's bowling he shamefacedly told his skipper he was sorry. Trott: 'Don't let that upset you, son. Every one on this field has dropped catches. Better luck next time!' He spilt few himself – and never missed a chance for a practical joke. Nothing seemed to upset him. Going to bat in a game at Lord's he put a lighted cigar aside. When Harry returned, out first ball, he calmly walked to the cigar, saying, 'Glad it hasn't gone out.' Mostly he smoked a pipe with a bowl like an embryo incinerator.

On the eve of a Test Harry remarked to Jones that critics were saying he was losing some of his pace, leaving England's Tom Richardson the fastest bowler of the year. Jones replied, 'I'll show them tomorrow that they are a bit out in their reckoning.'

Against Richardson's phenomenal bowling at Lord's on the fastest wicket for weeks, Harry was one of five out for blobs in Australia's calamitous 53. The second innings was slumping until Trott and Syd Gregory astonished all by the effrontery of their batting. In the face of impending defeat on a pitch where 13 Australian wickets had gone for 120 they clapped on 90 in 65 minutes. Bowlers who had been on top saw the ball faring no better than a watchdog's nose against a postman's boot. The intransigent pair carried on to 221 at almost 80 an hour. Their fourth-wicket stand could not win the Test but batting of such valiant quality set the series aglow, assuring success for the tour. The new skipper hit 24 fours in 143, his highest in Tests.

A notoriously nervous starter, tall Frank Iredale was depressed by low scores. One morning at Trent Bridge Trott told this teetotaller, 'Look here,

Noss, what you need is a tonic. I'll mix you one.' Harry brought him an unidentified drink. Repeats of the prescription brought more successes, including 108 in an Old Trafford Test. Not until long afterwards did Trott let anyone know it was brandy and soda.

Grace's footwork at forty-eight was becoming laboured and Stoddart, thirty-six, had not played leg-breaks well. In the second innings of a Manchester Test, Harry went on opposite Jones for the first over against the breeze. While others started at a leg-spinner sharing a new ball, Jim Kelly stumped both in Trott's first two overs.

When seven batsmen's failures at Old Trafford left wicketkeeper Kelly to help Trumble get 27 runs to win against the dreaded Richardson, Trott could watch no longer. Boarding a cab outside the ground, he told the cabby to drive anywhere. It was the only time the team knew Trott had nerves.

Trott's team adopted a couple of music-hall ditties. One from The Country Girl was 'Peace, peace, let us have peace!' When a wicket fell, a group of fielders awaiting the next batsman would sing a parody:

Peace, peace, two innings apiece,
But nobody stayed very long.

MacLaren told them he would give anything to play the game as keenly yet as light-heartedly as they did. Not even a collapse for 18 depressed Harry. The slump caused Spofforth to come to the Oval to commiserate. 'Terrible isn't it?' Trott agreed. 'Things could hardly be worse. But tell me, Spoff, are there any decent leg shows on at the theatres?'

As originator of a sly slander about Sheffield chimneys' smoke, how he would have laughed at the general credence it received, even to a supposed quote! 'Stoke up laads, Aussies be batting.'

On a fiery track Jones was so alarming that Yorkshire batsmen unashamedly declined singles that would have made them face his next over. Seeing Moorhouse struck on the thigh, the crowd began chorusing 'Tek 'im off, Trott!' As if heeding them, Harry threw the ball to Charles Eady. On so unfriendly a pitch the Tasmanian giant was almost as dangerous. The crowd protested anew. Moorhouse, waving his bat at Trott objected, 'Tha tek off wonn and put on 'nother fasst as t'other.'

71

Wisden felt that even in a season of ill-fortune he would have earned just as great a reputation: 'Blessed with a humour that nothing could ruffle, he was always master both of himself and his team, whatever the position of the game.'

Under Trott's benign captaincy and theatre director Harry Musgrove's management, the 1896 team regained prestige that Australian cricket in England had not enjoyed for a dozen years. Their play in a well-contested rubber proved that a tour could be an over-all success without being boosted by triumph (England won two Tests to one, though Grace said luckily). They finished 25 of their 34 first-class matches in Britain where their skipper allowed himself only one game off. On their way home a reporter in Philadelphia asked the captain had the Australians ever heard of baseball. Trott: 'Of course we have.' Reporter: 'Then why don't you play it?' Trott: 'Running around in circles makes us giddy.'

His players had admired his natural ease of manner as he chatted in London with the Prince of Wales (later Edward VII) who wound up a long talk by handing him a cigar. Asked what he had done with this, Harry replied, 'I smoked it,' to the surprise of some who thought it should have been preserved as a souvenir. This led to a practical joke on his return to Melbourne. He handed a friend a butt of a cigar which he said had been smoked by the Prince. Others were given similar butts, each being begged not to mention it in case it aroused jealousy. When that request was broken, it came out that he had collected the souvenirs from ashtrays the night before the ship berthed.

Harry Trott was Australia's Man of the 90s. With the deference of worshippers at a shrine, men taking their families to the beach would pause outside his double-fronted weatherboard house, 40 Phillipson Street, Albert Park.

Players who had brought a revival of interest were still being paid only £15 a match despite a leap in profits. Parleys with the Melbourne and Sydney ground trustees lifted pay to £25 a Test. (There it stood for twenty-three years until after the first world war when it was raised to £30 a Test.)

Called a 'team of all the talents', Stoddart's side was regarded as unbeatable. Yet Trott led Australia to win four Tests out of five. His tactics

72

included rapid changes of bowling to prevent batsmen settling down and new field settings. Ranji called him the finest tactician ever to skipper a side.

Editors castigated the public for showing no interest in a convention of fifty politicians discussing federation of the colonies. Another editorial defended the people for preferring the cricket, saying, 'Our cricketing eleven forms the best example of federation yet achieved ... We believe Harry Trott and his ten good men and true have done more for the federation of Australian hearts than all the big delegates put together.'

Fielding with cheetah-like speed, the side stirred the crowds to roars of admiration. Horan described Trott's team as 'the finest combination of players I have ever seen in action. They played as if the eleven had one mind and that a master-mind of cricket.' Trott is the only skipper who has ordered England to follow-on in three consecutive Tests.

Wicketkeeper in five tests against him, William Storer gave reasons why English professionals did not think much of Trott's captaincy: 'I like a captain to have a settled plan. He just seemed to do whatever he thought of at the moment. Some of our chaps found it rather upsetting.' Very likely. With all due disrespect to orthodox strategy every one of his eight Tests as skipper was finished, with a winning ratio of five to three.

The eupeptic skipper's girth grew until at 102 kg (16 st) he was likened to Falstaff in bulk as well as humour. Sunstroke at Sydney cost the sight of one eye before his last Test innings, 18, at the age of thirty-two. An ailment that baffled doctors unhinged his reason. That such a warm-hearted member of the brotherhood of man should be so afflicted – with pitiless cruelties soon to rend the Trott family – strained orthodox beliefs.

Love of cricket helped him fight back to sanity. In 1902 he strolled on to Bendigo United Cricket Club's ground and asked could he join in practice. After six years out of first-class cricket Trott reappeared as Victoria's captain against the English XI in 1904. In his last big match for his state against another English side in 1908 at the age of forty-one he took five for 116. At forty-four he headed both South Melbourne's averages, for the fifth time as batsman and third as bowler. No all-rounder has since approached this.

A few days before Trott turned forty-eight came the shock of the pistol-in-mouth suicide of Albert, forty-one, mistakenly believing he had cancer. A week later the first world war began carnage in which younger relatives and friends were dying. The man who was everybody's friend died gauntly at fifty-one on 9 November 1917. As the cortege moved toward Brighton cemetery it became greater at every part of the journey.

J. Darling

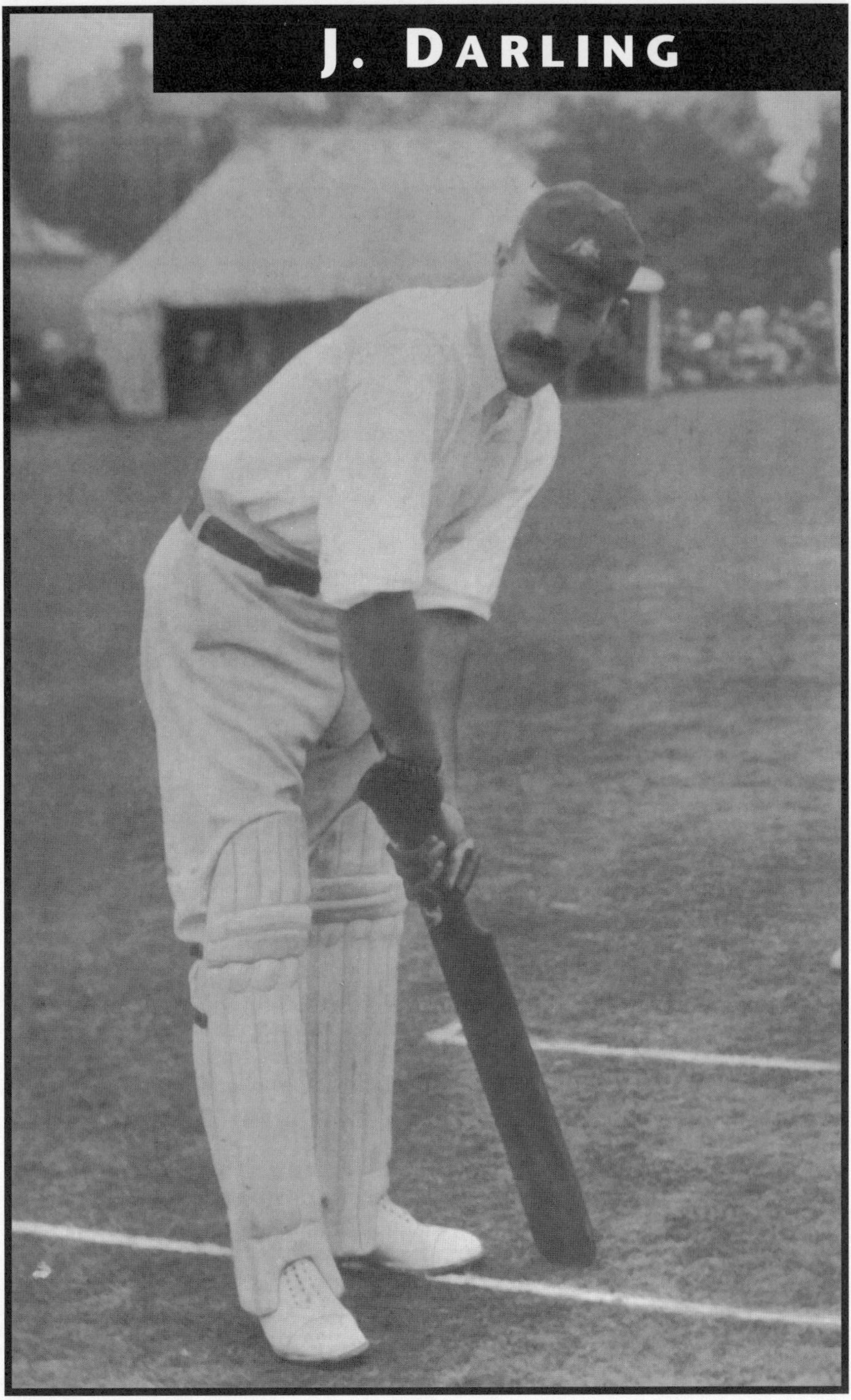

11

Wrestler's Grip

Uncanny powers of observation enabled Sherlock Holmes to deduce a man's occupation from his appearance – and give the reasons why. I wonder what Conan Doyle's omniscient detective would have made of the head of Joseph Darling? Photographs of Darling as captain of Australia on three of his four visits to England show a striking likeness to boxer Paddy Slavin. Unretreating dark hair, similar moustaches that never grew limp, blue eyes that did not know how to waver. The jawline denoted the kind of determination needed to withstand the menaces of heavy punching or dangerous bowling. Two years before Darling's first Test match Slavin stood up to heavyweight Peter Jackson at the National Sporting Club through torrid rounds that were talked about for years. In the Australian dressing-room Joe was inescapably nicknamed Paddy.

Every contour of Darling's face reveals strength of character. It fits the qualities described by people who knew him well: strong personality ... independent outlook ... unwavering determination ... purposeful concentration ... one who would countenance no frivolity ... a good judge of his fellows ... destined to be a leader in whatever he undertook.

No glance to right or left detracted from the resolution of his tread to the wicket. He held his bat full-face to the bowler. Joe could defend as dourly as a later left-hander of Scottish descent, Ken Mackay. When in revolt against his inherited trait he could drive even further than a bigger man, Alan Davidson. Fellow-players thought he tended to stonewall unnecessarily and was at his best playing a hard-driving game. Giffen described how Joe jumped in to make well-up balls half-volleys; he knew no Australian whose cuts travelled past point at greater speed.

On one tour of Britain, Rhodes was worrying Darling with a ball the

Yorkshire left-hander swung with his arm. Instead of natural spin turning it in to left-handed batsmen this ball drifted out. When Darling mentioned his difficulty Victor Trumper promised, 'I'll find his arm-ball for you, Paddy.' Before long Trumper described how Rhodes held this ball for delivery. Darling: 'I'll hit him out of the ground next time.' He on-drove it so far out of Old Trafford across Warwick Road that a porter fielded the ball at the railway station. This is the locality where Johnny Douglas resolved to score as many runs an hour as trains passed through Warwick Road; John Arlott says the trains won by 11.

Fearing a collapse on a fiery Lord's wicket Darling batted as if the ball was stitched with cordite. His mulish obstinacy almost sent the crowd up the wall of the clocktower. Knowing he could do better, they joined in with a man whistling the Dixie lament 'Poor Old Joe'. Next the head whistler led them into 'We Won't Get Home Till Morning'. Then they changed key and tempo to the 'Dead March in Saul'. Such a repertoire showed that cricket and culture could mix but it was not music to the serenaded stonewaller's ears. The shrill sarcasm upset him – one of the rare occasions when his even temperament was disturbed.

His men were content to follow his directions unquestioningly, believing that his deep understanding of the game and his thorough knowledge of its laws made him as near as could be to having all the answers. Confidence in him was reinforced by his showing no sign of worry in a crisis.

Evidence suggests that of all Australian skippers he came closest to being a disciplinarian. Yet the players, choosing their own captain, never looked past him. They were aware of his plain man's aversion to any foppish or showy player. Of staunch Presbyterian parentage, he shunned strong drink as well as tobacco and found over-indulgence in liquor hard to tolerate.

Sixth son of a wheat exporter, Joe was as Australian as pure Scottish parents could make him. In Parliament his father put through an Act permitting fencing-in of Adelaide Oval. Cricket had no place in his plans for Joseph. Prince Alfred College, however, has a way of producing cricketers, as witness the three Chappell brothers generations later. Joe Darling at fifteen made 252 against St Peter's College, batting on although both hands were tender with blood-blisters from friction with the cordbound handle. In the South Australia's XI at the age of sixteen he shaped well against the 1880 Australian XI's bowlers. As Joe also played Australian Rules football in his teens, sport was occupying so much time that his schoolwork suffered.

So John Darling, chieftain of the Caledonian Society, sent his seventeen-year-old son to work on wheat farms and learn agricultural management. Burying him in the backblocks, Giffen called it. South Australia chose Joe at nineteen but his father would not give him leave from the wheatbelt. Hard labour from dawn to dusk built up a farmhand's muscles on Joe's frame, already stocky and athletic. Within months of marrying a Mundoora farmer's fair daughter, Alice Minna Francis, at twenty-two he could no longer resist the call of cricket on Adelaide's turf, so returned to open a sports shop in Rundle Street.

Compact as John Edrich, Joe stood 172 cm (5 ft 8 in), weighed almost 82 kg (12 st 12 lb) and could handle a bag of cement, a sack of wheat or the most difficult bowling around. Ernie Jones, an ex-miner from Broken Hill, had a high-spirited habit of coming from a shower to wrestle other players naked. Like the champion of a college dormitory, Jonah downed everyone until the day he seized Joe. Locked together, they stumbled around the room until the ex-farmer dumped the ex-miner on his bare buttocks.

The first time he faced English bowling he scored 117 and 37 not out against Stoddart's team in 1894 but fast bowler Tom Richardson spoilt his Test debut by bowling him for 0. In the fifth Test at Melbourne his 74 and 50 won him a bat for most runs for Australia, a beaten side. If the cricket world was waiting for a left-hander who could control the desire to swing the ball to leg Joe Darling was that man. His play on his first tour of England at twenty-five caused *Wisden* to comment: 'With his upright style and a good straight bat he plays as orthodox a game as a right-handed man.' In fact, Joe was right-handed in everything except batting stance. Crowds had to wait until the 53rd Test to see a left-hander make a century, his 101 at Sydney.

His 1555 in 32 matches on the 1896 tour set a record for a newcomer to English wickets. They were a reward for farseeing originality in his preparation. For weeks before each of Joe's visits to England the Adelaide Oval groundsman watered a wicket in the nets for him to have long practices as the turf dried. As a result, while Clem Hill was honoured as Australia's foremost left-hander on true turf, fellow-players rated Darling best on all wickets because of his resource on sticky tracks. He had the confidence and skill to pick balls he could hit with a kick like one of the horses he left on the farm.

As Joe approached 100 in an Adelaide Test a leg-hit off Johnny Briggs sailed over the eastern gate into the park. This is the only time a man has raised 100 in Anglo–Australian Tests with a hit right out of the ground. The ball crashed along an ice-cream stall. At twenty-seven Darling was the only one before 1900 who topped 500 runs in a series and made three centuries in a rubber. The runaway farmer's batting in the final Sydney Test lifted Australia from a losing position by stopping Richardson bowling so fast and so well. The left-hander's drives had the force to loosen tight bowling like a heavyweight's right cross loosens teeth. He caused MacLaren to place three outfielders for the fast bowler, yet several shots over mid-off and cover sent the ball scrapping up an asphalt cycle-track around the boundary. Darling's 100 is still Australia's fastest Test century against England's bowling, 91 minutes.

Fifteen years after the startling victory at the Oval in 1882 Lord Northcliffe suddenly awakened Fleet Street to the fact that international cricket had become one of the most newsworthy sports. Instead of a few lines newspapers printed columns, despite high cable costs.

As the 1899 team sailed to Britain the players elected Darling captain at twenty-eight. He was the first Australian cricketer in Tussaud's Waxworks. Joe was capable of flexibility rare in a man of such definite opinions. After Victor Trumper had missed selection Darling saw him make 76 for The Rest against Australia's chosen bowlers in Adelaide. Realising it would be a mistake to go without a twenty-one-year-old batsman of such potential, Joe called a team meeting. They added Trumper to the side as fourteenth man on halfshare (£200). In the twelfth match on tour Victor's 135 not out in the Lord's Test bore such a stamp of quality that another meeting promptly voted him to a full share of tour profits.

Seeing Algy Gehrs out lbw in another game Darling told his men, 'If anyone except Vic and Clem attempts to glance a ball I'll drop them.'

79

On a morning so wet that play was reported improbable before lunch, half the team went to see through Player's Nottingham tobacco factory. Soon after each had accepted six cigars word came that the match had begun. Hurrying back, they saw Darling, who had lost the toss, fielding with five Australians and five substitutes. A team meeting called by Darling fined the culprits £5 each for breach of a tour rule requiring them to be at grounds at appointed times.

After the eleven and emergency fieldsman were named for each match on tour the two spare men were freed for three days' sightseeing. Because one player had a fast bowler's thirst, the skipper feared he might impair his fitness for a coming Test. To shield him from liquor's lure, captain and vice-captain switched him from the freed list to twelfth man. While the Australians fielded, the bowler left the ground. Asked why, he said he was going to have his three days off whether they liked it or not. Given a chance to explain, the rebel said they could all go to hell. Two players then proposed and seconded that he be sent back to Australia by the next ship. Before a vote, Darling took the man aside, advising him to apologise to the team; once the motion was carried he would see it was carried out. The mutineer apologised and never transgressed again. That prompt and firm action had a lasting effect on teams' discipline throughout Darling's seven-year reign.

Yet he was nothing like so rigid a martinet as some assumed. On a Worcester wicket favouring batsmen the Australians unexpectedly lost four wickets early, so the scorer was sent to hunt several late sleepers out of their hotel beds. He got them to the cathedral on time.

At a dinner where Surrey's president deplored riskless batting making the game tedious, Darling urged the English authorities to give six runs for every hit over the boundary fence (only hits right out of the ground were sixes). He was prime mover in SA setting a lead in this.

Visitors usually regard the general standard of umpiring in first-class matches in England as the best. Yet Darling and his players thought two run-out decisions at Trent Bridge showed that a retired international was emotionally influenced by desire to see his old side win. As Tyldesley was throwing Hill out they were disturbed to see umpire Barlow jumping with both arms uplifted jubilantly before fieldsmen appealed. On the last afternoon Laver's underhand flick from short-leg to wicketkeeper Kelly so clearly ran Ranji out for 30 that the Indian prince jogged on toward the pavilion until Barlow called after him, 'You're not out!' Ranji returned to make 93 not out, enabling England, seven for 155, to escape with a draw. After the Australians reported the incidents to the MCC Lord Harris told Darling: 'It is evident that this man is unsuitable. He will not umpire any more of your matches.'

When Tom Hayward suffered sunstroke in freakish heat at Old Trafford in 1899 he was replaced in the field by Johnny Tyldesley instead of the listed twelfth man Wilfred Rhodes, who lacked the dash of the Lancashire out-fielder. After one over Darling walked on to tell MacLaren he thought the departure from the list was wrong. Agreeing, MacLaren called Rhodes on. The sight of a local hero being sent off caused an angry demonstration. At last the Australians were 150 ahead with little more than two hours left. Longing for an exciting finish that would give England a chance, Lancashire secretary A.N. Hornby jokingly offered £250 if Australia would declare the innings closed. Darling said, 'Make it £500 and we'll consider it.' When he did declare with seven out – first visitor to close a Test innings in England – the Englishmen had no hope of making 171 in 65 minutes.

Player-manager Frank Laver wrote that on some grounds dressing rooms so lacked privacy that 'ladies in the reserves were now and then able to see us putting on our flannels. This was, however, quite interesting to a number of them, if we may judge by the close attention with which they watched us.'

No Australian captain since has allowed himself so little rest as Darling. His 1941 runs in 35 games at an average of 41 set a record for an Australian touring England.

The wheatgrower's deeds as batsman and captain reconciled John Darling to his son's preference for a cricket career, but the wealthy farmer thought it infra dig for a Darling to run a sports shop. Buying a 4000-hectare (10,000-acre) sheep station in Tasmania's midlands, he told Joseph to take up the property – or be left out of his will. Then twenty-nine and a father of four, Joe took his family to live on the lonely station, 34 kilometres by rough-track from the nearest doctor at Oatlands. The year 1901 opened with a 101-gun salutation to the new Commonwealth. Cricketers who had brought their country so much to Britons' notice at last had a legally constituted Australia to represent. Instead of blue and white their colours became green and gold.

After two years at grass – as much as the rabbits left – Darling was persuaded by Melbourne Cricket Club to return to the mainland long enough to lead the team in the first three of five Tests. The first match, Joe's first game of the season, was lost by an innings. Unawed by the green caps, captain Archie MacLaren scored the only century of this Sydney Test and made the Australians follow on.

Darling's sharpest battle of wits with this clever skipper came as 25 wickets tumbled for 221 on the most sensational day a Melbourne crowd had ever watched. Within three hours of MacLaren's sending Australia in on a rain-softened pitch both sides were out, Australia 51 runs ahead. Realising that mortal wounds could be suffered in the last two hours, Darling rejigged his batting order. With a cool-headed tailender, Trumble, he held out for an hour and a half and thought his 32 one of his best innings. Yet Barnes and Blythe spun five out in the last 20 minutes. Next day on a good wicket held-back batting stars piled up a lead that left England no chance. In winning a Test by 229 after having been sent in, Darling refused to bow to what looked like Fate and responded to quick-changing situations so resourcefully that the captaincy was his for as long as he cared to hold it.

Fate sided with Darling in Adelaide when Barnes's knee gave way in the first hour. The world's outstanding bowler played no more in the series. Darling and Hill led Australia's six-hour struggle to 315 – the first 300 in the fourth innings by any team to win a Test.

All Darling's stimulating qualities were needed when his well-balanced second team in England ran into a bitterly cold and wet season in 1902. At practice before the first match a drive by Hill broke off-spin bowler Trumble's right thumb. Five of the fourteen went down with flu. More than once some left beds to play. Soaked wickets and grounds caused the omission of Jones from three Tests. As Darling, reading out the names, would near the end, the fast bowler would call 'Jonah twelfth . . . Haven't you got anybody else for twelfth man?'

Inspired batting put the side in a winning vein. With an hour to bat on a rain-ruined Sheffield wicket on the second evening, Darling called for volunteers. The first hand up was Trumper's. Joe said: 'I don't want you, Vic. I don't want to lose good wickets on this gluepot.' Blows on the chest knocked Trumper down three times as he made 62 in 50 minutes. Next day Hill ensured a win with 119. First to make 100 before lunch in a Test, Victor began the Old Trafford match with a stand of 135 in 78 minutes with Reg Duff, on a damp day in which 15 wickets fell. At lunch on the last day England needed only 87 more runs with all wickets standing. MacLaren looked in the Australians' door and said, 'I think we've got you this time, Joe!' Darling: 'We've only got to shift a few of you and the rest will shiver with fright.'

In the closest finish of his Tests abroad, eight more runs were needed when the last Englishman, Fred Tate, came in. Asking Trumble to prevent Rhodes scoring off the last three balls of the over, Darling called the fieldsmen in close. That saved any single, so the last man had to face left-hander Jack Saunders. The fourth ball knocked his off stump out, giving Australia victory by three runs. Packing up in the dressing room, wicket-keeper Jim Kelly was walking about hunting for his gloves. They were still on his hands.

Players climbing on to their shooting-brake had been accustomed to hearing Darling check that all fourteen were aboard before telling the driver he could shake up the reins. As Trumper shone in match after match Joe was content to ask, 'Is Vic aboard?'

By scoring 2570 runs, studded with 11 centuries (highest 128), Trumper enriched the game with records that it took a Bradman to challenge or surpass twenty-eight years later. Companions knew Victor had one superstition. As he was unbuckling his pads one day he said: 'I knew I wouldn't make runs today with all those parsons around.' Had MacLaren only known this, even such an admirable sportsman might have been tempted to station a cluster of curates by the pavilion gate.

In Darling's twenty-fourth Test Braund caught him off Barnes at Sheffield for 0 in each innings – first Test captain out for a pair. Players heard Joe's bat bang down in the room, followed by a loud clump as a boot came off.

83

Looking around a corner, off-spinner Bill Howell asked innocently: 'What's wrong, Paddy? What are you worrying about? It's nothing.' Flinging a boot at him, Joe growled: 'You go to Hong-Kong!'; coarse language for him at a time when damn was a four-letter word.

Otherwise a stickler for fair play, Darling saw nothing wrong in one legside tactic against Ranji which would be branded today as gamesmanship: 'After Ranji looked to see where we stood we would move as the bowler delivered the ball, sometimes shifting one way, sometimes another. Once it resulted in a glance a few inches above ground being caught. From that day Ranji was never the same batsman. This worried him and eventually led to England leaving him out.'

In England's last innings on an Oval wicket responding to spin a stumping chance failed to deter Gilbert Jessop from springing along the track to pound Saunders and Trumble in the most challenging Test innings ever played on turf, 104 in 75 minutes. I have come across only one instance of Darling's players having felt their Napoleon was persisting with a Moscow-like mistake. He kept Trumble on from the pavilion end, where the Oval outfield is shorter. They believed that, had Joe switched Hugh to the city end and Jessop continued to make similar lusty drives, hits that scattered members in the reserve would have come down inside the longer boundary.

That win by one wicket was the second loss on the tour. They won 23 of 38 matches, ten by innings margins. *Wisden's* summing-up: 'In the all-important matter of physical well-being they undoubtedly owed much to the precept and example of their captain ... He has the rare power of being able to keep a whole team up to something approaching his own standard.' Players noticed that such a glutton for work had a tendency common among batsman-captains: to work bowlers harder than would have been likely with Trott and other all-rounder skippers.

From the time his players thawed out Darling believed his team the strongest ever to leave Australia – an honour held until then by Murdoch's 1882 band. The 1902 team was widely recognised as such not only on its own batting, bowling and fielding merits but because it met England at top strength. That could not be said of the opposition crushed by the two most powerful sides since the first world war, Armstrong's in 1921 and Bradman's invincible 1948 team. An all-rounder of twenty-three in 1902, and captain at forty-one in 1921, Armstrong told a questioner, 'The 1902 side could play twenty-two of my chaps and give them a beating.'

Under Darling's captaincy Australia won series in two consecutive tours of England, a feat equalled only by Woodfull's teams in 1930 and 1934 and Border's teams in 1989 and 1993.

On the way back to Australia, he was the fielding captain at Cape Town when South African all-rounder Jim Sinclair hit six sixes in storming to 100 in 80 minutes. Jessop's and Sinclair's hundreds are the two fastest ever made off Australian Test bowling.

Having seen three fieldsmen standing waiting for officials and guests to finish eating before they could have lunch at Sydney Cricket Ground, Darling never shirked making a stand for players' rights. Finding the tea urn hemmed in by non-players at a tea interval, Joe walked through and took control of the urn, to give players priority for drinks before they returned to the field. Another time he demanded posting of a doorkeeper to prevent outsiders from usurping the players' balcony seats.

After two years improving his sheep station without handling a bat, Darling reappeared for South Australia.

At thirty-four, Darling was the 1905 side's surest batsman in the Tests but his tactics suffered because most of his bowlers were not sharing wine's secret of getting better with age. Unfinished games, 19, exceeded wins, 16. To deny England quick runs in three Tests Darling had Armstrong bowling leg-breaks and top-spinners down the leg-side, with up to seven leg-fielders.

These back-slidings from the direct principles espoused by Dave Gregory were the worst debits in Darling's captaincy account. He defended them by saying the hooting and jeering surprised him, as Armstrong copied the leg-theory from Somerset leg-spinner Len Braund, who had bowled it without English crowds' disapproval.

In twenty-seven years since the first Australian visit the game had become more sophisticated. Up to this time five in every six Tests had been finished but the ratio of games left undecided was growing. For the first time in England players were leaving the field for a tea interval.

One down, Darling pressed for a win in the fourth Test at all costs. Apart from four sixes he hit in his 73, Australia's all-or-nothing policy scarcely got off the ground and England won by an innings.

When Lilley split a finger in the Oval Test Joe took no mean-spirited stand but allowed the substitute fieldsman, A.O. Jones, to keep wicket. In this drawn Test England's captain had difficulty avoiding blows from two chest-high bouncers in one over from fast bowler Albert Cotter. Jackson objected to Cotter bowling at him. Darling's view on intimidation was:

I would never allow Cotter to have more than two men on the leg-side. I purposely did this to make Tibby bowl at the wicket or the off-stump. I consider that if I had allowed Cotter to bowl the same theory as Larwood did later with a packed leg-field my 1905 Australian XI would have been hooted out of England and deservedly so.

Having lost all six tosses to Jackson (five Tests and a Marylebone Cricket Club game) Darling was stripped to the waist at the Scarborough Festival when his team suggested a wrestle for choice of innings. Stanley Jackson, less muscular, with the political finesse of a future knighted Governor of Bengal, hinted that he would depute George Hirst to act as captain for the purpose. Assessing the Yorkshire all-rounder's bulk with his eye, Joe concluded that Australia's chance of batting first would be as good with a coin as a cross-buttock. As both captains were born on 21 November 1870, this must be one of the worst setbacks astrology has suffered.

More than half the 1657 runs the ex-farmer harvested in 34 Tests against England and South Africa were made opening the innings. He held 27 catches, dropped few. Playing 333 innings in 202 first-class games, he totalled 10,637 runs at an average of 34. He made 21 centuries (two fewer than Ken Mackay). Though he lost two-thirds of his tosses, his teams won seven Tests, lost four, drew ten. Of his 18 Tests as captain against the Englishmen 15 were in England, the most by any visiting skipper before Allan Border.

Darling became a South Australian representative on the Board of Control. Quitting big cricket at thirty-six, he gave his next thirteen years to his sheep station.

He proposed testimonial matches for old players and headed the donation lists. Between the wars he drafted a plan to use part of mounting Test profits for a long-service fund to reward retiring Test men. The plan dwelt in a pigeon-hole more than forty years before a reconstituted Board launched a retirement benefit scheme.

As a father of fifteen, Darling ranks second in virility to Dave Gregory, sire of sixteen.

Elected to the Legislative Council at fifty, he was re-elected through the last twenty-five years of his life. After surgery for a ruptured gall bladder he died on 2 January 1946, a day after Bradman's first post-war century, 112 for South Australia against the Services XI. As he had given his properties to his sons years before, the probate value of his will, £7000, was a modest residue alongside the £1,700,000 left by his eldest brother John, managing director of BHP from 1907 to 1914.

H. TRUMBLE

12

Length Tells

Look down the list of Test cricketers and you see some names that sound as if they ought to belong to bowlers. We notice Loader, Sharp, Shutter and Warr of England, Lance of South Africa, Archer, Hawke, Hunt and Trumble of Australia. Besides spelling trouble close at hand for batsmen, Trumble somehow suggests the rumble of distant thunder.

'Never trouble trouble till Trumble troubles you' could have been a useful motto for batsmen opposed to the bowler whose total of English Test wickets is second only to Dennis Lillee's. Hugh Trumble is the only one who has brought off hat-tricks in two separate Tests. Only 21 hat-tricks have been performed in more than 1300 Tests, compared with more than twice as many scores of more than 250.

El Greco, with his lengthening touch, would have liked to draw Trumble. Hugh's lantern-shaped head set on a column of a neck would have given the Spaniard a halfway start. Length of face was Nature's gift for a cricketer whose humour ran deep, a seemingly innocent practical joker given to leg-pulling as if he wanted everyone to have a pair as long as his own trousered stilts. Standing 193 cm (6 ft 4 in), he was 2.5 cm taller than Ashley Mallett. Fry called him a most cunning and longheaded adversary and said batsmen opposing him were up against a brain as well as an arm.

Born in the Melbourne suburb of Abbotsford on 19 May 1867, Hugh was the third son of a migrant from Northern Ireland, William Trumble, who bowled leg-breaks for South Melbourne. Marrying Elizabeth Clark, William laid out a turf wicket in Kew on which their four sons could practise. Putting down a feather for a length ball and urging them to bowl at it, their father aided Hugh to gain command of pitch. As a young bank clerk, Hugh could land the ball on a length that batsmen often found not negotiable. The eldest brother, John William, was a capable all-rounder. When Hugh, twenty, joined him in the Victorian XI, J.W. was twenty-four. He preceded the rising bowler into Test cricket before concentrating on his profession as a solicitor.

At twenty-two a wicketless opening stretch against NSW left Hugh feeling his chance for a tour of Britain had faded. To revive his spirits at lunch a friend suggested a glass of beer, his first taste of it. Liking it, he drank more, only to wonder was his step steady as he re-entered the field. With his earlier over-anxiety relaxed, he took a succession of wickets that clinched a place on the 1890 tour. At twenty-three he had his first Test at Lord's, a full medium-pace bowler. With Turner and Ferris dominating the bowling he was given only 22 five-ball overs in two Tests.

Touring New Zealand he blinked twice when he saw an Auckland advertisement 'Come and see Hugh Trumble, greatest bowler in the world'. Awed by such propaganda, batsmen facing him blinked more than twice – or so he implied by crediting the advertisement with many of his wickets.

Newcomers to deck sports were flattered when the famous Test cricketer volunteered to coach them. Innocently accepting his guidance, they swayed and twisted into attitudes that caused gales of laughter among onlookers. As Frank Laver recalled it: 'Some even described circles and semi-circles before tossing the quoit, because Hugh told them that was the way to get a proper sight.' To carry out the joke thoroughly the arch-fiend himself, in his own games, assumed the stand and peculiarities he advocated.

Partly because his mast-like height made him too conspicuous for some practical jokes he often stayed in the background while others carried through larks he thought up. News that Egyptian passengers would join the ship at Ismailia caused him to devise a prank involving the empty bunk of a four-berth cabin he shared with all-rounder Charles McLeod and wicketkeeper Alf Johns. About 2.30 am a stranger entered the cabin, got under the bedclothes without removing his clothes or hat and began coughing, and gasping for breath. With a well-timed murmur 'What have we struck?' Hugh deepened the concern of his companions, wakened by the graveyard cough. Getting no satisfaction from the cabin steward next day McLeod and Johns protested to the purser about having to share the cabin with a man suspected of having an infectious disease. When the truth came out, Trumble's accomplice was umpire Jim Phillips.

For a bowler of Hugh's mentality, fielding at slip for Giffen and Turner was like a post-graduate course. Especially he absorbed Giffen's secret of launching the ball to make batsmen think of a forward stroke, then wish they hadn't. Noble described his approach as 'sidelong and insinuating, with his neck craned like a gigantic bird'. From an arm like a flagpole, coming right over the top, his sinuous fingers made the ball bounce higher than other off-spinners. After pushing his well-concealed slower ball back for three or four catches, one of England's top batsmen, Jackson, said 'You old devil Hughie! You get me caught-and-bowled whenever you like but I'll pick that slow one sooner or later.'

Trumble's third visit to Britain, in 1896, yielded him most wickets, 148. Naming him one of the Five Cricketers of the Year, *Wisden* added to its praise of his achievements: 'Always the same, whether on the winning side or losing, Hugh Trumble is one of the most popular of Australian cricketers.'

Trumble said he hardly met an English pitch on which he could not get some turn and in the temperate weather he could 'bowl all day' without tiring. He spun along more balls there than any other visiting bowler – one short of 24,000. His 587 wickets in 139 games in Britain cost 15 runs apiece. While not so penetrating as Turner the Terror (610 victims in England) or Spofforth the Demon (589) he was classed by fellow-players as Australia's most reliable bowler on all wickets.

He had to pay more for wickets in Australia. Subtle pace-changes enabled him to profit by a lot of forward play on hard turf – batsmen playing at, rather than to, the length of the ball. Loose ones from the loftiest off-spinner's hand were as rare as rust spots on royal plate. He believed he could land the ball on a saucer 17 metres away five times out of six. When I wondered how Trumble could have coaxed the ball to turn on pitches as true and unyielding as Caesar's wife, Ernest Baillie gave me this explanation: by continually pitching ball after ball on the one place Hugh wore a spot powdery enough to allow off-spin to grip. A help-yourself off-break. Bowling longer than an hour on the trot in Australian heat tired him, although overs longer than six balls were an affliction saved up for later generations until late in 1979. He could bear occasional punishment, as he was as hard to rattle as two grapes in a wineglass.

Sir Pelham Warner, victim of one of his hat-tricks, said he had seen Trumble make the ball jump so abruptly from a sticky wicket in Australia and break back so much that he had to bowl around-the-wicket and place eight fielders on the leg-side.

As a fieldsman with long, prehensile fingers he was the first to hold 20 catches in an Australian season. England's Johnny Douglas once protested 'Trumble should not be allowed on a cricket field – his natural place would be up trees in the bush.'

To spare Victoria's bowlers longer hours in the field he bowled two wides which fieldsmen allowed to roll to the boundary to save SA having to follow on, compulsory at that time. Melbourne members questioned the sportsmanship of Trumble's unprecedented action. To a remonstrating friend the twenty-nine-year-old bowler said, 'I had to do it, old chap, but I wonder what my father will think of it?' When William Trumble heard of the incident he scorned the suggestion that the wides were intentional, saying, 'Hughie was not brought up in that way.'

At full stretch as an all-rounder, Trumble scored 1183 runs as well as taking 142 wickets in England in 1899. Before him only Giffen had brought off such doubles for touring Test teams in England and only five have done so for Test teams since – Armstrong, Jack Gregory, Aubrey Faulkner (South Africa), Learie Constantine (West Indies) and Vinoo Mankad (India). Having to put his best powers into bowling, Trumble did not have the edge necessary for consistent high scoring.

Hugh brought off his first Test hat-trick in January 1902. He took over captaincy from Darling for the last two Tests – tallest skipper ever to lead the Australian XI. His side held every chance in Sydney while the losers turfed several. Only two Englishmen topped 50 against the bowling he directed in those victories and in one innings he kept Noble and Saunders on unchanged. It was Hugh's most successful series, 28 wickets.

On the 1899 team's voyage to England Hugh, thirty-one, fell in love with tiny Florence Christian, nineteen, and they became engaged. The couple timed the marriage to make a honeymoon trip of the Australians' 1902 tour of England.

Broken at practice, his right thumb kept him out for the first month of the 1902 tour, yet he took 26 wickets in three Tests, a feat no other visiting bowler has repeated. Six of the wickets were taken on a tense last afternoon at Old Trafford when Australia had to get England out under 123. At the climax Trumble had to pin Rhodes to one end so that the Yorkshireman could not save the last man having to face left-hander Jack Saunders's next over. Hugh recalled 'With the ball greasy and my boots unable to get a proper foothold on slippery turf, it was the most trying over I ever bowled.' Saunders bowled Fred Tate to bring a breathless win by three runs.

Darling had such faith in Hugh that in the final Test at the Oval he kept him going unchanged from the pavilion end – more than three hours in each innings. With 389 balls, Trumble took 12 wickets (as at the Oval in 1896) but England won by one wicket. He shares with Spofforth the distinction of 12 wickets twice in Anglo–Australian Tests. Trumble and O'Reilly are the only Australians who have landed at least 25 wickets in a five-Test series in each country – a feat Alec Bedser alone has accomplished for England with 30 in 1950–51 and 39 in 1953. (Lillee's 25 in 1974–75 and McDermott's 30 in 1985 came in six Tests.)

The first English XI consigned by the MCC began with a clear-cut win in Sydney, so Trumble, nearing thirty-six, was persuaded to emerge from retirement in 1904. Though Warner's side won the series, Hugh was the out-standing bowler, 24 wickets in four Tests. On the last day his offbreaks were almost unplayable on rain-softened Merri Creek turf as he took 7 for 28. He finished with a hat-trick with his last three balls.

Two of his Australian fielding records still stand: 207 catches in England and the only fieldsman, except wicketkeepers, who reached 50 catches on one tour there. Those figures are almost bewildering when we reflect that Jack Gregory brought off 37 catches on a tour, Bob Simpson 36 and Alan Davidson (The Claw) 27. Trumble held 45 catches in 32 Tests. Bowling 34 batsmen, catching 15 off his own slower one and trapping 16 lbw, he obtained 65 of his Test wickets unaided, except by fieldsmen's appeals. Fielders caught 73 for him and Kelly stumped three. In 213 first-class games 44,170 balls brought 929 wickets at an average of 18.

On return from each of his five tours of Britain Hugh found junior bank officers had advanced ahead of him. Four years after his last Test the National Bank appointed him a manager but at the urging of fellow committeemen of Melbourne Cricket Club he took over the secretaryship in 1911. Amid lunch-hour throngs on Collins Street his sombrero-like felt hat stood out like a mushroom among toadstools.

As Jack Ryder was leading the Victorian XI back into the field on Christmas Day 1929 he had ample reason to be confident. They had scored 376 and had nine of NSW for 113. Seeing Trumble by the gate Ryder asked, 'What would you do, Hughie? Put 'em in again?' The cautious oracle replied, 'Well Jack, I think I'd just get 'em out first.' They did get 'em out – on the following day after Alan Kippax (260 not out) and Hal Hooker put on 307 for the last wicket.

In his twenty-seven years as a secretary, 1911 to 1938, the ground changed beyond recognition. The stand was completed eighteen months before Trumble died at seventy-one on 14 August 1938.

M.A. NOBLE

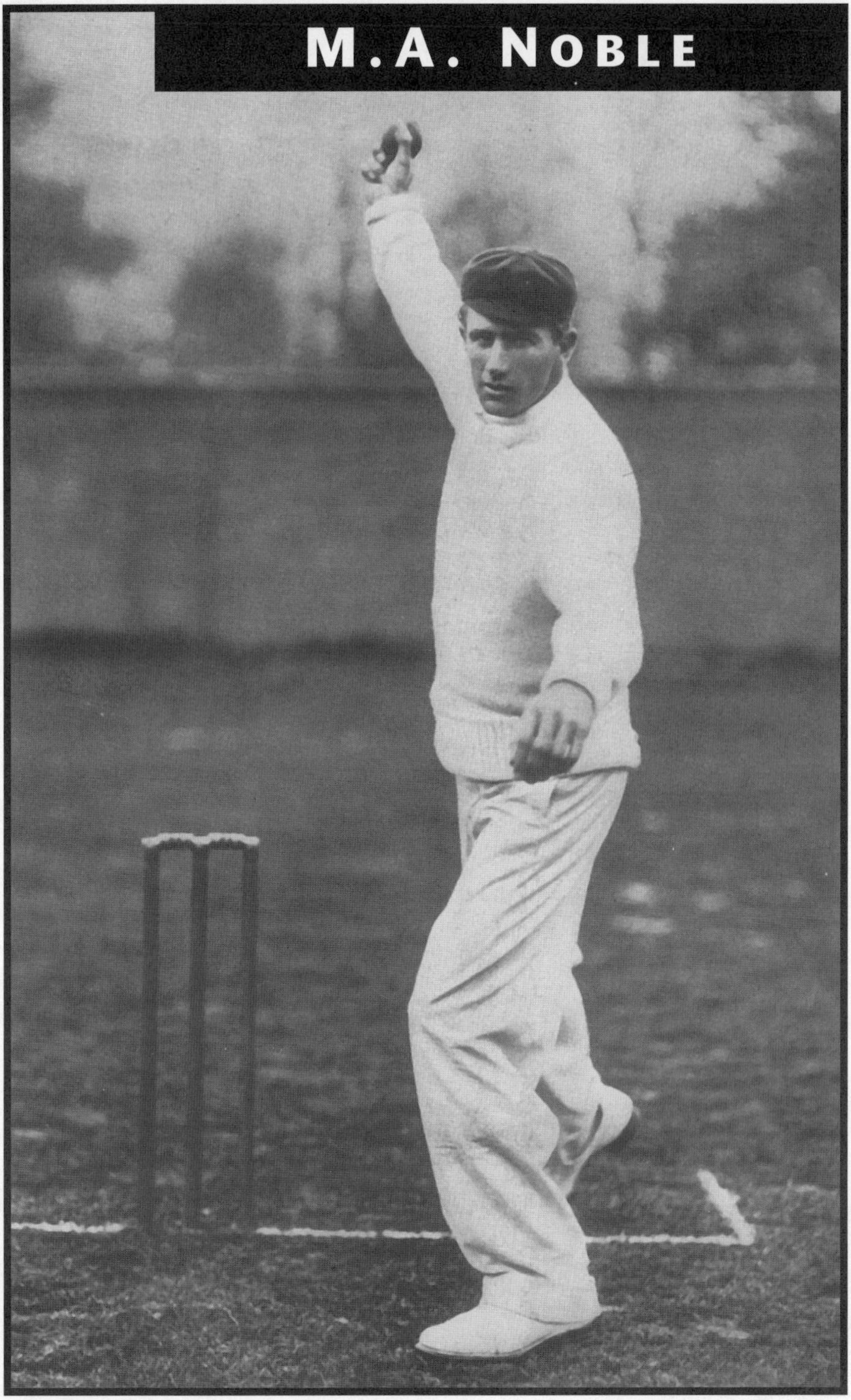

13

Boots and All

History remembers the third Emperor of Rome by his nickname Caligula (Little Boot) rather than his proper name Gaius Caesar Augustus. In the annals of Australia an emperor among cricketers, M.A. Noble, was called Monty by some, Alf by others. With raucous irreverence barrackers pretended his initials stood for Mary Ann. He was big enough not to mind. In circles closer to him players used another nickname, Boots.

Like his deeds in international cricket Noble's feet were of heroic pro-portions. His boots were outstanding, you might say. Cartoonists made great play with them. One caricaturist depicted Noble's footwear the size of skateboards. He was probably exaggerating. Noble's daughter says their size was 'only 10½' and his son remembers that as a schoolboy he was paid sixpence a week to clean them.

Noble took great care of the feet that filled them. To ensure comfortable fitting all his boots were specially made. His feet were to carry him through twenty-seven years as one of the top all-rounders. They brought him to the crease to deliver 33,000 medium-pace balls in first-class matches. At home his daily keep-fit exercises included push-ups. Though a big man, 185 cm (6 ft 1 in) and weighing 80 to 83 kg (13 st), he won praise for agile fielding at point. Playing a lot of beach cricket in a swimsuit gave him strenuous running in sand. On voyages to and from England Noble was one of the team's best at tandem skipping, in which each player held a giggling girl by the elbows as the pair cleared a twirling rope.

Noble was a first-generation Australian, youngest of eight sons of a couple from Egham, Surrey. The ship in which they migrated to Sydney had a cow aboard to supply milk for Maria Noble's first baby. Montague Alfred was born on 28 January 1873 at home in Dixon Street, a quarter now redolent of Peking duck. He was delivered with musical honours. Hearing a military band passing, Maria prophesied 'My son will be famous.' They laughed ... but time proved it a clairvoyant accouchement. The father, Joseph, a grocer, became a hotel manager.

Grasping a chance at twenty-one when eighteen NSW Colts played the 1894 English XI he made 152 not out. He was then rather gawkily long. After two years in interstate games he came into the Australian XI at twenty-four. A breakback from Richardson in Melbourne made a mess of his stumps at 17. After a similar fate in Adelaide he said to an older player, 'I suppose after such a silly display they'll never pick me for Australia again.' In between, however, the young all-rounder had taken six English wickets for 49 in an innings with a type of medium-pace spin-swerve new to batsmen in 1898. Just as right-handed batsmen shaped for a ball to land in line with the leg stump it swerved to pitch by the off stick, then turned in to knock the middle and leg pegs. After changing his stroke twice and being out before he could try a third, Archie MacLaren exclaimed 'Hang it, a man can't play jugglery.'

The innovator acquired the swerve from baseball. Instead of pressing two or three fingers on the ball's seam, like a spinner, Noble held it between his thumb and his strong corn-studded forefinger. On the truest of tracks all he needed was some sort of headwind for this spin-swerve to be difficult. Five wickets in the second innings at Adelaide made his tally 15 victims in his first two Tests. This deceitful ball, plus a well-concealed quick one and a penetrating off-cutting from a moist pitch, were reasons why England's Indian batting genius Ranjitsinhji rated him among the six best medium-pacers he ever faced. Ability to sort them out helped Albert Trott to drive one over Lord's Pavilion.

When it was clear that the selectors would want Noble to tour England in 1899 he gave up a bank job to study dentistry. In his first innings on English turf he made 116 not out in 3½ hours against South of England at Crystal Palace – the first in seventeen years since Hugh Massie to have led off with a century. His resolution and concentration showed out in mid-tour after the ignominy of two ducks in a Leeds Test. When caught for the second 0 as a victim of Hearne's hat-trick he was so upset that he walked

97

away in the wrong direction. It was the only time team-mates saw his self-control fail. He was given a little silver duck five centimetres long. Though too rational to be superstitious, he put the duck in his pocket before going in to bat. In the next Test he stood between England's bowlers and victory. He resisted them more than three hours for 60 not out, then went in to open the follow-on, calmly saying 'You won't see me back here for some time.' For more than five hours he stuck tighter than a whisky cork, making 89.

Some of the Manchester crowd began intoning 'The Dead March'. One yelled 'Put the rawp around bounder's neck and drag him ote.'

After 8½ hours of unblinking defiance which denied England time to win, an anonymous donor posted a leather medal inscribed: 'To M.A. Noble, the greatest Australian cricketer. 1000 runs in 1000 years.' Revisiting Manchester years later the offender apologised. Those 17½ runs an hour that made Manchester miserable were a contrast to 46 an hour in his 230 against SA on Sydney's Bulli soil in 1904.

Comfortably erect at the crease, Noble looked cut out for strokeplay – rather than having his bat hanging around eavesdropping on his boots' squeaks. Statisticians noted that he topped Australian seasons' batting averages four times – a record until Bradman did so eleven times in fourteen full seasons. Playing down the line in orthodox style, Monty's high grip on a long handle gave full effect to his reach in driving. He showed least assurance against leg-spinners. On softer English turf he could not play forward with the same vigour and safety, so became largely a back-foot player. *Wisden* was impressed by his ability to alter his play in England without setback to his scoring.

Watching him lead NSW into the field, his mother heard this conversation: 'There's Mary Ann.' 'Where?' 'Out in front.' Maria Noble told her son that night, 'My boy, had I known they would call you that name I'd have given you different initials.'

His seven for 17 with 45 balls, unchanged with Trumble on a Melbourne sticky, were part of the most destructive Test day Australians have seen: 25 wickets on New Year's Day 1902. Drilling more cavities in England's batting he made his match tally 13 and went on to 32 in the series. Only Giffen had taken more English wickets in a series. For his 121 wickets in 42

Tests on open pitches he averaged a victim every 59 balls, a ball sooner than Lindwall's striking-rate.

By giving Jim Kelly opportunities for 14 wickets (11 caught, 3 stumped) he was the best friend a Test wicketkeeper had until Oldfield combined with Grimmett for 28, Evans with Bedser for 25, Grout with Davidson for 44 and Benaud for 26. Marsh caught 95 for Lillee and 36 each for Walker and Thomson, Dujon 71 for Marshall, and Taylor 60 for Botham. The most prosperous extant collaboration is that of 'c Healy b McDermott', which has appeared 55 times in test scoreboards.

Two years after a judge established a basic wage of 42 shillings a week for an unskilled labourer, a testimonial match brought this skilled cricketer £2000. Here are lines S.J. Coy wrote in the *Sydney Mail* for the occasion:

When old England's at the creases
And our bowling's gone to pieces
And we fancy all the records will be broken by our foes,
Then the eyes of all observers
Are just fixed on Noble's swervers
As he sends along a beauty and a batsman homeward goes . . .
When the wicket's sticky
And treacherous and tricky
And we want a bat who'll stay there till the evening shadows fall,
You're glad the strain has ended
And you go home feeling splendid
When you've witnessed Monty Noble with his back against the wall.

In his ever-alert fielding at point he stood close, though not as intimately as Ian Botham. His accuracy with longer throws was evident as the team's ship passed through the Suez Canal. Objectionable gestures by a canal-side Arab were disgusting many passengers until an apple flung by Noble hit the performer behind the ear.

Noble had experience in 22 Tests before his first toss as Australia's captain in 1903. Sir Pelham Warner had asked travelling Bishop Welldon would it be wrong to pray to beat the Australians. The bishop replied, 'Anything that tends to the prestige of England is worth praying for.' Plum said he would do so. As Noble was a bellringer at St Mark's, Darling

99

Point, and his voice was welcomed in the choir, when available, the Almighty must have been confronted with no easy choice.

Noble was the first captain to face an English skipper who had the professionals staying in the same hotel as the amateurs. Warner broke through the snob barrier 'to encourage unity and good fellowship'. It could be argued whether this or his prayers enabled him to win the rubber, three to two, but there was no gainsaying professional spinner Wilfred Rhodes's 31 wickets in five Tests and amateur Reginald Foster's 500 runs.

Appointed captain on the morning of the first Test, Noble made a chanceless 133 to rescue Australia from a disastrous start in Sydney. In the field he was credited with knowing all the answers – except how to get Foster out or stop him hitting 38 fours in 7¼ hours. Foster's 287 still stands as the highest Test innings for any other country in Australia, even surviving the challenge posed at the start of 1993 by Brian Lara.

At the height of an impassioned outcry against Clem Hill being adjudged run out, Noble expressed regret as they waited, sitting by the pitch, and persuaded Warner to go on with the match.

On the voyage to England in 1905 cabins were subjected to skylarking night raids and reprisal swoops; to repel invaders Noble and cabin-mate Frank Laver bought water pistols.

Before sailing for his fourth tour of England, the 1909 captain told them:

You won't find me snooping around while you're off the field. Do what you like with your spare time but take your cricket as seriously as I do. You are all potential Australian captains so make sure you turn out as such for the Tests.

This approach set the pattern generally followed by Australia's skippers since.

At Lord's Monty became the first visiting skipper to send England in to bat. Deploying his bowlers cleverly to exploit changing moods of the pitch he won by nine wickets.

Each player given two games off was due to rejoin the team the night before the next match. Warwick Armstrong did not show up until just as cabs were leaving for the ground. Noble told the unshaven offender to go in first. Armstrong batted most of the day for a century.

He often wanted century-makers to make way for others needing match practice. Once he told Bardsley: 'Let's see how you go hitting sixes.'

With his strength of character, he seldom had to put his foot down because his magnetic personality assured him of popularity. He could change bowlers and demote batsmen without hurting their feelings. In a county game he asked Laver: 'What sort of stuff do you think you are sending down?' Laver: 'I'm working out a little plan.' Noble: 'It had better get us wickets or off you come.' He soon replaced him.

In getting a lot out of bowlers he seemed to inspire them with his own determination. He was one of the first to leave a gap to invite cover-drives at balls that could yield catches in the gully. Demands of the moment did not cause him to overwork bowlers because he aimed to keep a couple fresh in readiness to attempt a breakthrough late in the day.

As a disciplinarian – some say martinet – he saw Macartney speak over the fence to a girl. Stopping play, he called Charlie to midfield and placed him in the slips. Fry nominated him for captaincy of an Earth XI to play Mars. The evening after Hendry said 'No' to a second run he said in a bar-side chat: 'When I say two I mean two.' Noble would not agree to allow a substitute fielder unless the absent man was injured or ill.

On Edmund Dwyer's first trip to Melbourne Noble stayed with the youth on Saturday night instead of accompanying the others out on the town. Dwyer said: 'Noble was doing the right thing by me, though I'd have liked to be in it with them.'

So that Jim Mackay could follow up 105 for NSW with a second innings century against SA Monty limited himself to 37 while Jim scored 102.

Any member of his side who made an unjustified appeal would be given a reproving look, sometimes a spoken rebuke. To save an umpire uncertainty about a supposed catch he would roll the ball slowly to the bowler.

He was the first visitor to call all five right in a rubber in England. He correctly judged gravity's pull on the coin in both hemispheres by winning 11 out of 15 tosses. The first 13 of his Tests as captain were finished – eight wins, five losses.

I believe he must have been the most accomplished cricketer Australia produced as bowler, batsman, captain and fieldsman, at least in the pre-1954 era of all-weather wickets. He reached 1000 runs and 100 wickets in 27 Tests: the swiftest ascent an Australian had achieved and, while slower to the landmark than Ian Botham and Kapil Dev, swifter than Sir Garfield Sobers, Sir Richard Hadlee and Imran Khan.

In 245 matches Noble's 378 innings totalled 14,000 runs (average 49) and he took 628 wickets (average 23). Of his 37 hundreds, seven passed 200. His highest was 284 against Sussex in 1902 in a 428 partnership with Armstrong – still the highest sixth wicket stand by Australians. His prestige was so great that for a while NSW made him sole selector.

He was a health faddist in choice of food yet smoked a pipe. The night before a match he ceased smoking and drinking alcoholic beverages, advising players to do likewise.

Absences overseas and interstate made it impracticable to continue dental practice so he became an agent for manufacturers. One dental patient, William Ferguson, confessed to having gone to Noble in order to obtain his recommendation for the post of baggage-master and scorer in 1905. Monty launched Fergie into a globe-trotting career as the Ulysses of handymen. One good turn deserved a better, so Fergie sent his sister to him to have her teeth fixed.

At forty Monty married Ellen Ferguson, twenty-four, a 164.5 cm (5 ft 5 in) brunette. Of their four children the two longest-surviving recalled a happy household.

Noble's baritone was heard in the Sydney Choral Society chorus. After his brother Arthur began singing professionally Monty would no longer sing at functions, only home parties.

To help get cricket moving again after the first world war Noble reappeared at forty-six. In his farewell match at Brisbane, Ted Adams, later Town Clerk of Sydney, recalled:

> After making 37 Noble strained a leg. To allow him to try to wind up his career with 100, I was sent in to run for him. When Noble played a firm cover-drive the other batsman and I started to run. A smart interception caused hesitation and a swift throw beat me back. Through no fault of his own, the veteran had to limp out of first-class cricket.

On the Sydney Cricket Ground Trust he was the driving force behind the building of a fine stand (later to bear his name).

As a writer on the 1926 tour he saw Britain in the throes of a general strike and poverty resulting from unemployment. Hotel maids were working for ten shillings a week. Noble always ordered a full breakfast and told the maids to have it. On the way to the ground he had coffee at a snack-bar.

When the second world war began he became a volunteer dentist in the Army Dental Corps at Liverpool camp. He died on 22 June 1940, a week after suffering a heart attack while playing in a social game at sixty-seven.

ERNEST BEAN

14

The 1912 Overture

Anyone who has thrown away a winning ticket can understand the feelings of office-bearers who turned down an invitation to run international cricket tours. The cold shoulder ached with remorse. Cricketers risking their own money proved it to be a profitable enterprise. Once exchanges of visits made it unmistakably clear that tours were here to stay, and to pay, the idea emerged of a take-over to channel profits back to state cricket associations composed of hard-up clubs.

A short-lived Cricket Council faded fruitlessly, little remembered except for leaving Test players without faith in officials' capacity to run their affairs satisfactorily and provide a manager as good as those they had chosen for eleven of their twelve tours of England.

Moving in again, a Melbourne conference of two delegates each from the NSW, Victorian and SA cricket associations drew up a constitution for a Board of Control in May 1905. A draft provided that each should appoint two representatives in addition to the Australian XI cricketers selecting one and interstate players one. This broad-based framework gave some recognition to the players' inherent right to have a say in decisions about their creation's growing profits.

The constitution's Clause 9 preserved another right and made the players parties to the principle of having a Board: 'The appointment of Manager of any Australian Team visiting England or elsewhere shall be made by the players interested and submitted to the Board for confirmation.' If you think that means what it says, you are making the same mistake as those who believed the last seven words set out routine procedure for endorsement. Seven years later those seven words were used as a tail to wag the dog out of existence.

Among four men who held the first Board meeting in 1905 the prime movers were the Victorian Cricket Association's thorough honorary secretary, E.E. Bean, of the Government Printing Office, and Alderman W.P. McElhone, a solicitor being toughened by the hurly-burly of Sydney municipal politics. On his way to finishing on top as Lord Mayor in 1922, William McElhone was chairman, or it seems ruler, of the NSW cricket executive and of the Board. A compulsive decision-maker, he was an acknowledged master at controlling debates.

The constitution the four adopted dropped the draft provision for players to be represented. South Australia declined to join a Board denying players representation and objected to any interference with the finances of Australian XIs. Promising a Test for Brisbane, the founders gained the allegiance of Queensland a few weeks later. They stepped in with an invitation to the MCC to send a team to Australia. As the Board was limited to three States and there was no sign of the Melbourne Cricket Club (with which the Englishmen were used to dealing) the Club replied that no team would go until the Board was representative of Australian cricket.

Away in England the 1905 Australian XI were doubly pleased at having asked East Melbourne bowler Frank Laver to manage their tour, though he had not sought the position. He was a favourite of fellow-players as well as of fortune. Frank had been sent to Melbourne University at a time when only well-off parents could afford that (his musician brother William became Ormond Professor of Music there in 1916). For his secretaryship of the ocean liner's amusement committee in 1905, Lady Gormanstown presented Frank with a turquoise stone set in diamonds.

Besides fulfilling managerial duties in Britain admirably, he played the five Tests and took 115 wickets on the tour. He bowled more balls than anyone except leg-spinner Armstrong, though at thirty-six he often had to use an elastic bandage on one leg. Laver was equally at ease fielding at short leg or chatting with the Prince of Wales. He frequently followed English custom by wearing a top-hat and frock-coat.

Plotting to make Laver's old-fashioned bat look more antique, the Australians forged on it the names of old-time heroes, added their own signatures and inscribed it 'Presented to Frank Laver on the eve of his departure for England with the first Australian XI 1878'. Then they varnished it. Frank enjoyed the joke and would not part with the bat.

At the request of the MCC committee, the immediate future of exchanging tours was discussed at Lord's. Australia's four representatives were captain Darling, vice-captain Noble, co-selector Hill and player-manager Laver. It was agreed that the Australian Board as then constituted did not represent the true interests of all parties concerned.

Until it did, the MCC felt they could not recognise it and spokesmen said they would not send a team to Australia in 1906 or until the existing trouble had ended. They had no wish to interfere with the management of cricket in Australia but would welcome Australian teams to England under existing conditions if the teams were representative. By frankly reporting this in *An Australian Cricketer on Tour*, Laver hardly endeared himself to the thwarted founders of the mini-Board.

Fears that an English visit due in 1907 would fall through caused leading players to turn to the Melbourne Cricket Club. Darling called a meeting of South Australian and Victorian stars who were playing in Adelaide. They decided that, if leading NSW players were also willing to sign a letter asking the MCC to bring out an English team, they would bind themselves to play for Australia, if selected.

Piqued, NSW officials disqualified all the senior State players who signed the letter. With this bludgeon of authority officials inflicted a slow-to-fade bruise on relationships in the game. Darling and Hill, saying they would not play in Sydney until their victimised Test mates were reinstated, caused a hurried back-down by officials, gulping hard.

When England's rejection compelled the Board to widen its structure. officials sought a formula to induce SA to join. They worked out a definition of the meaning of finance in Clause I of the constitution: 'The objects of the Board shall be to arrange, control, regulate and finance the visits of Australian teams to England and elsewhere.' A definition containing two assurances was dictated by Alderman McElhone: 'The Board shall see that all profits of the tour be distributed equally between the members of the team. The Board has no intention of interfering in any way with the profits earned by the players on the tour.'

Accepting this, the SA Cricket Association rejoined the Board, letting other objections lapse. With them lapsed the original 1905 conference provision for players to have delegates on the Board. South Australia's appointment of Darling as a delegate gave the ex-captain a close-up view of the Board founders' methods. 'I was disgusted with the underhand way the Board conducted its dealings,' he said, alleging that minutes of one meeting had been faked.

> *Everything on the agenda for meetings was discussed privately at a prior meeting of five delegates from Victoria and New South Wales and two from Queensland, who in that period sold their votes for a secret promise of a Test match. Western Australia was denied even one delegate, as the ruling clique were afraid he might vote against them. Some Board delegates, particularly Bean and McElhone, openly boasted that they would drive out of the game all players who signed the letter making themselves available if the Melbourne Cricket Club brought a team from England ... We signatories felt we were acting in the best interests of Australian cricket, as the Marylebone Cricket Club had definitely declined the partly-formed Board's invitation. In approaching the Melbourne Cricket Club, we were only asking the same body which had been financing these tours in the past.*

As the team's choice, Laver was manager of the 1909 Australian XI in Britain, played four Tests and headed the tour bowling averages. However, instead of the state captains choosing the players to tour, the Board appointed two lesser lights. One was former Test batsman Frank Iredale, an official of the NSW Cricket Association subservient to McElhone, and the other Victorian batsman Peter McAlister, of Melbourne's Metropolitan Board of Works, who played eight Tests without reaching 50 in an innings. With a smouldering eye and a mouth that knew no curve, Peter had all the determination and dour intensity of a Covenanter in the Scotland of his ancestors. Evidence more than hints that he was devoured by a man-eating grievance from not having been selected for the 1905 tour when he was not yet thirty. By appointing McAlister a selector, the Board put him in a position to rectify that omission. On choosing himself, nearing forty years and a newcomer to England, Peter was appointed vice-captain over Trumper,

Armstrong and three others with English experience. Already it was clear that he was as fervent a supporter of Board policies as the rest of the team were sceptical.

Besides elevating McAlister to vice-captain, the Board created a new post by naming him treasurer of the tour. Two people to look after the money, but no cash or credit advanced for the period in England before matches brought in revenue! In writing from the liner *Orontes* to secretary McElhone about that oversight, Laver mentioned other mistakes, especially unpleasantness caused by McElhone's arbitrary allotting of ship berths without asking players their wishes about cabinmates. By finding such faults, on top of having been one of the guilty signatories, Laver was laying his head on the block, though his executioners took a couple more years to bring their axe down.

Unblushingly going back on its financial definition, the Board decided to take 5 per cent of the first £6000 earned by the 1909 team in England and 12.5 per cent of any profits over that. Board delegates who opposed that as a breach of faith were overruled. After the Board's cut, it would divide the remainder among the fifteen players; any player had the option of accepting £400 lump sum plus his tour expenses.

After the 1909 team's return, Board men could not get all they wanted from Treasurer McAlister's book. Their stool-pigeon had come home to roost without full financial details but with feathers ruffled. Laver was asked for his books. When he said they contained many private entries of his own and other players' affairs, Board secretary Colin Sinclair replied in April 1910 that in those circumstances he could not expect Laver to hand them over.

Twenty months later new Board secretary Sydney Smith renewed the demand. Laver repeated his explanation about his books' private contents and offered to attend a Board meeting to answer any questions about receipts and expenditure. Some members wanted this but the cabal majority opposed it and accused Laver of disloyalty and neglect.

The 1912 Overture was full of discords that would have pained Tchaikovsky's ear. After sitting in private (then, as now) the Board announced on 30 December 1911: 'The only matter of importance was the appointment of the selection committee to act in England. The Board decided to leave this work in the hands of the captain, vice-captain and a third member nominated by the captain.' Secrecy failed to bottle up the news that G. Mostyn Evan (SA) moved that the players appoint a manager on the same financial terms as themselves. Victorian treasurer Henry Rush moved an amendment: 'As the Board has already decided to send a representative with the team, the players be informed, as soon as the team is selected, that it will be unnecessary for them to appoint a manager.'

When chairman McElhone would not accept several amendments passed up by Queensland soldier-lawyer Colonel J.F.G. Foxton, Justin Foxton remarked: 'But under Regulation 9 the players have the right to appoint a manager.' Harry Rush: 'Oh, we swept Regulation 9 away last night.'

Rush's amendment was carried by seven votes to four. In a last-minute plea for a creditable solution, Dr Ramsay Mailer (Melbourne Cricket Club) suggested respecting the players' right to appoint their own manager and that the Board then bind the manager by agreement to carry out its wishes. When the majority turned this down, Dr Mailer and the three South Australians asked that the minutes record their refusal to take part in an illegal appointment of a Board representative. Only the ruling junta took part in a ballot to appoint the representative. McAlister received only two votes (from fellow-Victorians Bean and Rush) because chairman McElhone's view had switched. He now realised that personal antipathies between Peter and leading Test players would create an intolerable position – a probability not weighed when McAlister was made treasurer in 1909. In retaliation for the dumping of loyal Peter, the two Victorian delegates would not support McElhone's nominee (Ernest Hume of Sydney) and their votes swung the appointment to a Queenslander, G.S. Crouch, a batsman who played five interstate games before 1906. (Denial of his reward did not dim Peter's outlook on cricket. He found solace in marriage at fifty-eight and his interest kept keen through the remaining ten years of his life.)

The second double-cross alerted Test players to the realisation that the last of the assurances they had been given was being circumvented and was in danger of being dishonoured. Men able to outwit England's best batsmen and vie with the cleverest English bowlers were no match for bureaucratic backroom boys. Novices at negotiation, they had inactively seen their original rights gradually whittled away, leaving them little platform on which to make a belated stand. In return for the meat, they had been left with a bone, as they thought, only to have that taken away.

Six of them sent a letter beginning 'We beg respectfully to approach the Board of Control ...' They said they had been advised that a decision to send a representative to England, clothed with the powers of a manager, and to charge his expenses against tour takings, was clearly illegal. If the players were not allowed to select their own manager, as Board rules provided, a breach of faith with them would be committed. The letter suggested repeating the 1909 method of selecting fourteen players who should then select a player-manager on equal pay. If so, 'such of us as shall be selected will be prepared and glad to make the trip but, failing compliance with our requests, we have to inform you with much regret none of us will be available for selection or to play if selected ...'

The six who signed the letter were among the world's finest cricketers: captain Clem Hill, batting idol Victor Trumper, leading all-rounder Warwick Armstrong, left-handed batsman and star outfielder Vernon Ransford, fast bowler Albert Cotter and wicketkeeper Hanson Carter. Australia had no other six to match them, any more than the Chappell brothers, Lillee, Massie, Marsh, and Stackpole could be matched in 1972, or Border, Taylor, the Waughs, Healy and Warne in 1993.

Three weeks after Harry Rush's triumphant assertion that the Board had swept away Regulation 9, its honorary secretary was assuring the players it had not been abrogated. Well, for perfidy's sake! In replying to the letter, the secretary pointed out what he said were errors in it. Then he went on:

> In the first place, the team which is being sent to England by the Board as the governing body of cricket in Australia, in accordance with the agreement entered into with the Marylebone Cricket Club, has nothing whatever to do with the arrangements, the Board taking the whole of the responsibility. Certain terms, which will be communicated to each individual member on selection, have been decided on by the Board, and each member will then have the opportunity of declining the Board's invitation if he is not satisfied.

In the next place, the Board has in no sense abrogated Clause 9 of the constitution but has only expressed its opinion that, as a representative of the Board will accompany the team, the appointment of a manager is unnecessary; so that it follows that, if this opinion is not voiced by a majority of members of the team, they can still nominate a manager for confirmation by the Board.

Personally I do not see why the positions could not be carried out by one person acceptable to the Board as well as to the members of the team.

While the Board is anxious at all times to send the best team possible, still, at the same time, I am sure it will not permit any number of cricketers to dictate the terms and conditions on which a visit is to be made, or if a manager is appointed the terms and nature of his engagement.

Yours faithfully,

SYDNEY SMITH, Jnr.

Double-talk reinforced half-truth. A special meeting of the Board on 2 February received the players' letter and the majority endorsed the secretary's reply. The star cricketers' defence of their promised right was labelled as defiance of constituted authority and could not be tolerated.

Board chiefs had no difficulty getting their course of action approved by delegates of clubs struggling to pay their way. No dividend had come to Victorian clubs for twelve years but calls had been made on them. If things got much worse they'd have to pawn the tea urn and use the minutes of previous meetings to stoke the fire. A VCA vote on 8 January was 21 to two. Dominant boardmen took it as a signal to lash the helm on a collision course.

Public feeling, divided in Sydney, was running so high in Melbourne and Adelaide that protest meetings were crowded. So the VCA issued a 24-page pamphlet to justify Board actions. Taking inequalities, flaws and discontents in the players' running of their tours, the pamphlet presented them as a chapter of avaricious deals and misdeals. It implied that one unnamed player had bought a place by paying a premium of £200. It alleged that management of the game had descended into the shady regions of cliquism and favouritism. Parts of the 24 pages looked as genuine as a film star's eye-lashes. The pamphleteers sought to make out a case for action 'to wrest control of international cricket from the hands of men who had unequivocally shown that their chief and almost their only desire was individual aggrandisement'.

Enough red herrings to restock the North Sea were brought in. The basic issue was simple, but the splashing of the herrings confused the picture sufficiently for the inner group to get away with their stratagem. By overstating their case and spicing it with see-through half-truths and worse, the compilers of the pamphlet defeated their own object. The recoil was devastating. Answering pamphlets shot holes through the obsessed opus. Enough pamphlets were around to paper the Melbourne Cricket Club office. Too much was known about the maligned sportsmen for the public to accept besmirching of national heroes who had won personal distinction in bringing their young country Empire-wide prestige through a field of sport.

In no walk of life in Australia could be found celebrities of higher standing as citizens than Gregory, Murdoch, Massie, Scott, McDonnell, Darling, Noble and others prominent in touring ventures. Noble in particular was esteemed everywhere as an exemplar of the finest qualities an Australian could possess. Mud would not stick to their names.

A Citizens' Committee pamphlet found that the ruling spirits on the Board, in conflict with leading players, had missed an opportunity to show a conciliatory spirit; certain Board actions created a feeling of mistrust; unjustifiably, the Board repeatedly passed over cricketers of great experience holding the confidence of the public and appointed as selectors players of less note, known to be out of sympathy with the players and prepared to do as the Board directed; these appointments had been responsible for a great deal of the trouble.

The six stars were missing from the steamer that sailed for England with a makeshift team. In Port Phillip Bay its screws churned water thick with seaweed and broken promises. Inferior, the side lost money (£1286). Down went the country's standing in world cricket, depressed by an avoidable crisis. Those who contrived the crisis risked setting cricket's house on fire to roast a plucked chicken to their liking. Far from looping a lei around the

113

game, as they might have fancied, they hung a millstone of mistrust around the neck of Australian cricket. The machinations doomed it to the most bitter and prolonged row that has racked any Australian sport.

Those guilty of the double-cross showed no sense of shame. It was an unexplained paradox of human nature. They were men of probity, self-righteous in their rectitude, as upright souls as could be found in any church pew. With such moral certitude, the meanest means were justified by the end.

Conspiring hatchet-men in the 1912 dispute were otherwise mostly respected and esteemed for honourable labours for the game. They were best remembered for uncounted unpaid hours of diligent organising and administrative duties. Power-hungry some of these men might have been but I have never come across the faintest suggestion that they sought personal financial gain from diverting Test profits into the near-dry channels of their clubs. The reverse, in fact. Once when funds were wanted quickly, McElhone advanced them from his own account. Toward the end of his twenty years of Boardom, Bean waged a last-ditch fight against a decision recommending players a bonus of £10 a Test. Embossed in silver, Ernest gazes from the E.E. Bean Shield, for which Victoria's senior clubs play.

The 1912 row takes beating as an instance of authoritarianism which playwright David Williamson sees as still one of the major factors in Australian life today. One who felt its weight, Sir Donald Bradman, was long conscious of the Board of Control's public image. When he became chairman he sought a different title, untainted by ponderous shows of authority. As ex-chairman he was sixty-five when the States agreed to give it an updated constitution and rename it simply the Australian Cricket Board.

C. HILL

15

Dates with Destiny

A son born in the year his father made the first century on Adelaide Oval was clearly destined to go places. The stars in their courses were charting more distant travel for the infant than the dusty journeys John Hill's coaches were making over South Australian roads. Any fortune-teller worth her fee could have named some of these places – Lord's of London, Manchester, Sheffield, Johannesburg – where Clem Hill would hold the attention of thousands. Tall dark-haired men who would cross his path, and short fair men with rounded vowels, too, would have cause to remember the blue-eyed boy before he attained full manhood. He was eagerly on time for each date with destiny. Before he turned twenty-one, players classed Clem as the best left-handed batsman in the world and one of the most dashing fielders.

The third son and only left-hander, Clement, born 18 March 1877, was nicknamed Kruger after the Boer leader. Six of the brothers played for the state, three of them in the side together. Clem was one of three who also played interstate football.

While at Prince Alfred College, Clem was nine days past sixteen when SA chose him against WA. Keeping wicket to Ernie Jones's blistering speed, his hands suffered. After he piled up 360 (retired) for his school against St Peter's College, he heeded advice to quit the dangerous post behind the sticks. Even after that huge score beat Darling's record, a sportsmaster threatened to leave Clem out of the College XI if he persisted in hooking. He had a penchant for quick-stepping across to short off balls and carting them around to the leg paddock.

He entered Sheffield Shield cricket at seventeen-and-a-half. The way he made 21 on his debut against Victoria so impressed wicketkeeper Jack Blackham that he announced the discovery of another great batsman.

Having made 150 not out for South Australia against the Englishmen in 1895, Clem was disappointed at missing selection in the thirteen to tour England in 1896. His response: 206 not out against NSW at Sydney, where he astonished veterans with his resourceful control of the strike in making 154 of his side's last 197. The opposing skipper Tom Garrett, who tried vainly to slow him down with leg theory and five on-side fielders, was a Test selector. Widespread public demand for adding Hill to the team was gratified, so at nineteen he was off for his first trip, seasick if not homesick. In team photos Clem was sitting on the ground in front of seated seniors; photographers as well as bowlers used to separate the men from the boys.

He was mostly an on-side scorer until his first venture on English wickets widened his repertoire, developing his cutting and well-placed cover-driving. Already he was so expert that the only improvement Giffen could suggest was more discretion in using the hook; it brought him hundreds of runs, but often got him out on wickets where the ball's bounce was inconsistent.

'A Youth of 20 saves Australia' a newspaper heading ran after a Test began with Hearne and Richardson lowering six wickets for 58 on a fresh two-paced Melbourne pitch. As first-drop batsman playing his seventh Test, Hill was a close witness of the downfall of his seniors until Hugh Trumble stuck with him. When the youthful left-hander reached his first Test 100, he had made all except 42 of his side's score. A barracker called to England's captain, 'Archie, the kangaroo's still hopping!' A shower at tea interval and a change into dry flannels so refreshed Clem that as he re-entered the field he told his partner, 'I think I'll have a go at them now.' Trumble, ten years older: 'You young devil, you have to stop there. Go along as you have been doing.' Trumble's supporting 46 enabled their seventh-wicket stand to put on 165, which still stands as an Ashes record and has been surpassed only against New Zealand and Pakistan. Almost five hours brought Hill 182 not out by stumps – still the highest first-day innings against England in Australia. Records take on deeper meaning when the runs are made for a side down on its knees.

Except for a wide semi-chance at 65, the bowling bothered him less than photographers. Coming off 182 not out, Hill dodged behind fieldsmen who shielded him from a battery of cameras. 'My luck's been queered that

117

way before this season,' he said. He was referring to having been photographed on 200 not out for SA against the Englishmen, only to go quickly next day. After a Sunday's rest, camera-shy Clem added only six more. His 188 is the highest score in Anglo–Australian Tests by a player under twenty-one. His batting inspired Horan to write, 'Hill's innings will be talked of when the smallest boy who saw it will be white with the snows of time.' The rally he led excited such interest that a funeral paused in Swanston Street so mourners could read scores posted outside a hotel. Though 44 other hundreds came from his unresting bat, his 188 ranked as the innings of his career. Bushfire smoke wreathed the ground, causing Ranji to say Australians must be the only people who would set fire to their country to win a cricket match.

At twenty the left-handed wonder totalled 1186 in 19 innings – the first Australian to score 1000 in a home season and the only one until 1908. Bowlers feared Hill's scores were becoming mountainous.

Clem was one of those gifted batsmen who from the moment they take strike make the game full of life. Every team should have one. It was not simply that he often scored quickly, but that his batting was always animated. He was constantly on the move, playing attractive shots. Fieldsmen intercepting his strokes might keep him to a maiden over or two but he would continue to hold crowds all the time he was in.

As the only low-grip batsman in international cricket at the time, he was the exception to the adage 'Lower the grip, lessen the command'. His grip's limitation of forward reach and power prevented him from being one of the great drivers, but the compensation of quick footwork gave his enterprising spirit scope. 'He was never at home,' Bill Whitty told me. Clem excelled his countrymen in lynx-eyed placing of the ball through the leg field, turning it off his middle peg with Ranji-like confidence. He looked as if he could have made 100 with a jockey's whip. Yet in keeping out the most intrusive bowling his bat seemed as wide as North Terrace. While he was in, the end he occupied held more than a corner of Adelaide's heart – and Australia's.

His hook was made of courage and power in equal parts. He was one of the rare men who always had a preference for bowling of a speed that others disliked, many secretly, some openly. England's greatest paceman of the period, Tom Richardson, once said, 'You make me feel I took up fast bowling for your benefit.'

The scourge of fast bowlers was of medium height and solidly built, about 175 cm (5 ft 9 in) and 76 kg (12 stone). Among post-war players Arthur Morris, another left-hander noted for footwork, resembles him most in build.

Surgery to remove a growth from his nose roughly halved Clem's second tour of England when twenty-two, yet he headed the Australians' Test averages (60) with batting that won him a place among *Wisden*'s Five Cricketers of the Year. Except for that surgery and severe influenza at thirty, he enjoyed good health.

Able to concentrate on ball and bowlers without the tautness that stiffens many players, Clem liked to hear bands playing at grounds. At twenty-three he batted 8 hours 35 minutes for 365 against NSW at Adelaide Oval. In averaging 43 an hour, he hit 35 fours and overthrows swelled another stroke to eight. As a Shield record, his 365 stood twenty-seven years until Bill Ponsford's 437 against Queensland.

In the only Test ever played at Bramall Lane, Sheffield, Hill hustled to 100 in under two hours. He gave two chances in the seventies, but nobody else in the match got as far as that on a poor wicket which none of them wanted to see again. Though he was not regularly as rapid a scorer as Trumper or Woolley (career average 40 an hour), Jessop or Bonnor, 110 runs spouted from Hill's bat before lunch on the third morning of a Test at Johannesburg in 1902, when he was twenty-four.

He was the first man out for 99 in a Test and six of his 87 Test dismissals were in the nineties. As he was the first man outside England to make 45 centuries in first-class games, many an opposing skipper wished it were true that he dropped his bundle nearing 100. However, his father offered him £5 – which would have bought him a tailor-made suit – for every run over 100.

Clem's 1060 in 12 Tests in 1902 made him the first Australian to score 1000 in a calendar year.

In a Sydney Test in 1903 Trumper drove spinner Len Braund and ran four with Hill. In finishing the fourth, Hill ran several yards past the wicket. When an overthrow went 18 metres past mid-on, Hill, already short of breath, had to run about 24 metres to the crease at the wicketkeeper's end. Amid a crescendo of excitement, Relf threw to wicketkeeper Lilley and, as Hill sprinted past the stumps, umpire Bob Crockett signalled him out. Lilley's body blocked the view of onlookers in the pavilion, but many of those on the outer slopes angrily shouted that Hill was not out. One of the worst demonstrations witnessed at the ground followed as Hill turned from his run-past. Obviously he thought that, as Relf's throw passed behind him, it was inconceivable that it could have reached the stumps before his bat slid over the line. Barrackers hooted and kept up a chant of 'Crock! Crock!' Bottles were thrown on a cycle-track encircling the field. Fielding captain Pelham Warner tried to tell the crowd he would take England's team off unless the booing ceased. At the end two detectives escorted Crockett away.

Romance as well as runs filled players' minds as they prepared for the 1905 tour of England, Hill's fourth, Trumper's third and SA wicket-keeper Phillip Newland's first. Trumper had gone to Melbourne to marry Mrs Jim Kelly's younger sister, Ann Briggs, in St Patrick's Cathedral. From SA's game in Sydney, Clem, twenty-seven, travelled 800 kilometres by train and 480 kilometres by storm-tossed Bass Strait steamer to Tasmania to wed tiny brunette Florence Hart, twenty-six, on 17 January.

Phil Newland, twenty-nine, married Josephine Ferguson, twenty-six, at St David's Church, Burnside, in February and they joined the team in NZ. It was the only time three brides travelled all around with an Australian XI. They had laced-in waists Spofforth's arm would have gone around twice. Grey-eyed Florrie Hill was so keen on the cricket that she kept the score. Scorer Bill Ferguson would have rather she had other hobbies. He said, 'At the end of each day's play she invariably badgered her husband with the complaint that there had been scoring mistakes – just because my books did not agree with the one she kept for amusement. Clem would look at his wife indulgently and then appeal to me, "For heaven's sake Fergie, check my wife's book. She insists you're wrong but I can't be bothered with it."'

Comparing ways, Clem said more players smoked and drank than those he observed after the first world war and they went to bed later. One custom had already become a tradition: the evening chat in the dressing-room before the team broke up. Lolling around with pipes smouldering, glasses emptying and refilling and tensions easing, players ruminated the meaningful lessons of the day.

When nightwatchman Kelly fell in the morning's first over against Surrey, Hill joined all-rounder Charles McLeod, warning him they must hang on at all costs because no other players had arrived, only manager Laver. Along came a short ball, but Hill muzzled his usual hook. This precaution saved him from being bowled when the ball shot through low. After a while the batsmen could see reinforcements had arrived.

The Englishmen were well on the way toward victory in Adelaide in 1908 when Hill – too ill to field in the match – came wanly in ninth to join Queensland auctioneer Roger Hartigan. Willpower and a spilt chance at 22 kept Clem going. He vomited on the grass and had to run off the field more than once. Hartigan's leave expired on the fourth day, when the pair were not out. He was under orders to leave Adelaide for hide sales in Brisbane: the Australians were relieved when a telegram arrived: 'Stay as long as you are making runs.' The Mac Taggart brothers had cancelled a repudiation. Hartigan batted into the fifth day for 116 of a record eighth-wicket stand of 243. After 5 hours 19 minutes of fortitude for 160, Hill was near collapse, but his side won.

Clem's fame as a team-rescuing batsman and a creator of Australian records – he hardly missed a page – was matched by his popularity as a personality. Sir Pelham Warner commented on his pleasant manner. Robert Trumble recalls him as a playful, alert and kindly spirit, direct, honest and without guile. He treated the obscure as he did the famous.

Late one sun-scorched afternoon at Adelaide Oval Hill hit a low shot into outfield shadows and ran one. He asked the umpire at the bowler's end had the ball been caught. The umpire: 'I couldn't tell – couldn't see in that shadow.' Hill called to outfielder Bardsley, 'Did you catch it, Warren?' Bardsley: 'Yes, Clem.' Hill instantly walked away.

After two series against England in his first three years of married life, Clem did not accept an invitation to go to Britain again in 1909. His next Test series was as captain against visiting South Africans in 1910–11, followed by the Englishmen in 1911–12.

Before he led Australia into the field for the first time in 1910, his 39th

Test, Hill presided over a council of war. They decided to counter South Africa's novel cluster of googly bowlers by knocking the spinners off their length. Hill showed the way by hastening to 100 in 98 minutes – since equalled only once in Tests in Australia, by Bradman.

Clem and Bardsley slapped on 224 in only two hours in a second-wicket left-hand stand. Hill's 191 in 200 minutes, his highest Test score, helped regale a Sydney crowd with 494 for six wickets on the first day at a team rate almost 100 runs an hour, close to five runs an over. In winning the Adelaide Test by 38, the Springboks averaged 51 runs each 100 balls and the losers 69 – the fastest over-all run rate by both sides in any Test.

Twice when Hill lost tosses, Percy Sherwell sent the Australians in on rain-affected turf, only to see them win, reaffirming their fighting spirit and adding to their skipper's laurels.

Twelve English wickets to dentist Herbert Hordern's googlies in his first Test carried this heady note into the 1911–12 series but not for long. Coupling of Sid Barnes and left-hander Frank Foster gave England an attack to startle the Antipodes out of their slumbers. In action against each batsman they were like a couple of thrush cornering a witchetty grub.

Practising on the Melbourne ground on a December morning fast bowler Tibby Cotter said, 'Clem, I hope you lose the toss today – it's the same sort of humid heat as when I bowled the Vics out a few days ago. If the Englishmen bat first with the ball swinging like that again, half of them will be out by lunch.' Putting the other side in had never won a Test in Australia but had lost six, so Hill failed to profit by Cotter's tip. Instead four Australians were out before lunch for 32 as Barnes made the ball veer and turn past their bats and rise past their gloves. Hill lasted long enough at one end to show involuntary amusement at the way Barnes had his partners' bats prodding empty air. Between overs Kelleway walked to him and said, 'You'll lose your laugh when you get to the other end, Clem.' He did, and with it his middle peg. Barnes's sharpest turn jagged the ball the width of the stumps until a weather change calmed the pitch down. Foster's long-fingered left hand swung fast-medium balls into right-handers, stinging their thighs and hips and having them caught in a packed leg field. 'If the atmosphere had stayed as it was,' Hill said, 'the eleven best batsmen in the world could not have totalled 100.' Australia made 184 and England won by eight wickets.

As if the English bowlers' superiority were not enough, Hill had to contend with backstairs machinations, a sniping co-selector and trade unions' threat to ban the main Test ground. Queensland fast bowler John William McLaren was alleged to have been a special constable. Melbourne Trades Hall Council threatened to put a black ban on the ground unless McLaren gave certain assurances (presumably that he would dissociate himself from a force used for strike-breaking).

McLaren was made twelfth man, Hill lost the toss and Johnny Douglas sent Australia in on a drying pitch, where Barnes and Foster shot them out for 191. Hobbs's and Rhodes's first-wicket 323, still a record, helped Douglas to be the first skipper to win by fielding first in Australia. Playing in the next Test McLaren, twenty-four, took one wicket.

The Englishmen allowed only one century in the five Tests (Trumper 113). Barnes and Foster grabbed 70 per cent of the wickets (66 out of 95). For the first time England won four consecutive Tests in a series but Hill's players put no blame on him. Iredale wrote that he was a cheery skipper whose men were happy under his leadership.

Australia's captain must have felt he was walking in a minefield since the inner group running the early Board of Control laid the first boobytrap. South Australia's delegates urged that vice-captain Victor Trumper ought to be one of the selectors but the Board majority appointed Peter McAlister and Frank Iredale. McAlister was as friendly as a bull ant, nursing resentment from his non-selection on earlier tours. The captain received limited support in team-choosing because Iredale was inhibited by a conflict of interest as a pre-1900 Test batsman holding office in the NSW Cricket Association on his way to becoming its paid secretary two years later.

Ill-feeling about the Board's manoeuvring to dispossess the players of their favoured tour manager caused rumblings during the first Test. Disagreement between the selectors flared before the third Test in Adelaide over Charles Macartney, twenty-five, who had wound up the preceding season with three consecutive centuries: a foretaste of a glorious career lying ahead of a superb all-rounder. When Hill wired McAlister urging the inclusion of Macartney, the Victorian's reply, in effect, was, 'If you must have Macartney, leave yourself out.'

When the captain objected to the nature of that, the inner group had the numbers to hold that this act by one of its selectors had nothing to do with the Board. That night when the selectors met in Sydney to pick the fourth Test side, McAlister severely criticised Hill's captaincy. It stung the skipper into replying, 'In England Armstrong wouldn't play under you. Did you ever win any except second-rate games?'

McAlister: 'I'm a better captain than Trumper, Armstrong and yourself put together. You are the worst captain I have ever seen.'

Hill: 'If you keep on insulting me, I'll pull your nose.'

McAlister repeated: 'You are the worst captain I have ever seen.'

Hill's self-control snapped. Saying, 'You've been looking for a bloody punch in the jaw all night,' he struck his tormentor in the face.

McAlister: 'You hit me when my hands were down.'

Hill (putting his hands behind his back): 'My hands are down now.'

Rushing around the table, McAlister grappled with Hill. Locked together, they swayed around the room, crashing against the table and walls. McAlister, a wiry build of 183 cm (6 ft), had longer reach but his shorter adversary was eight years younger and more powerful, though he had once appeared in a fancy-dress ball as a Japanese. Blood stained their clothes and splashed on Iredale and secretary Sydney Smith. Fearing the grapplers would plunge out a window into the street, Smith hauled on Hill's coat tails. Ten minutes' fighting ended with McAlister on his back on the floor, with Hill standing over him, unmarked. When the captain left the room, Peter rose, called out 'Coward!' and made to follow, but Iredale and Smith stood against the locked door.

When Hill told Smith he could no longer act as a selector with McAlister, the secretary asked him to put his resignation in writing. A hurriedly-called meeting of available Board members accepted it that night. The two remaining selectors then chose the team for the Fourth Test – Macartney still out – and, by official request, named a preliminary ten for the tour of England.

Six days later Melbourne onlookers' usual welcome to a popular player swelled into three cheers for Clem as he reached the wicket. A fortnight later the Sydney crowd also cheered Hill in what was to be his last Test. Deprived of the chance to lead Australia in a triangular Test tournament in England, Hill dropped out of big cricket at thirty-five. Yet much of his batting skill was still evident at forty-three when he reappeared to help get the game going after the first world war. Clem bet his wife he would top the score in one innings and won his bet with 66.

To add interest to a fund match for Giffen he reappeared against Victoria in Adelaide at forty-five. Hill's last re-appearance when forty-seven was to score 40 for an Australian XI against NSW in a benefit match for off-spinner Bill Howell in 1924. His career spanned thirty-two years.

Hill was the only Aussie who topped 17,000 runs before they began sheltering wickets from rain in Australia around 1926. In seventy years since, among Australians who played most of their cricket at home, only Bradman, Border, Harvey, Simpson, Greg and Ian Chappell and Lawry have piled up higher career totals than his 17,213 in 416 innings in 252 games. His 8027 in 160 innings stood as the state record until Les Favell passed it in 1967 in his 205th innings.

Clem was not one to gloat over records, and often could not remember them. When Hobbs passed 60 against Australia in the Leeds Test, 1926, he waved his bat toward a stand where his wife was sitting in front of a group of Australians. One of them, Hill, asked, 'Ada, why is Jack waving his bat like that?' Mrs Hobbs, 'You should know if anybody does – he has beaten your record of most runs in Test matches.' Hill's total was 3412 in 49 Tests. When Sir Jack went on to 5410 in 61 Tests, how could anyone have foreseen that an Indian named Gavaskar would climb past 10,000 runs?

South Australian Jockey Club and Adelaide Racing Club made Clem a stipendiary steward and a handicapper. Appointment by Victorian Amateur Turf Club at Caulfield in 1937 made him one of Australia's top three hand-icappers at sixty. He moved to Toorak with Florrie and their two daughters. Under weights he allotted, Buzalong, Rivette, Beaulivre, Velocity and Tranquil Star won Caulfield Cups in a period when Ajax was winning 18 races on end, mostly at weight-for-age.

After ill-health caused him to resign at sixty-six, Geelong Racing Club appointed him handicapper, a less-demanding post. He was sixty-eight when he was thrown from a tram in a traffic accident in Collins Street. He died in Royal Melbourne Hospital on 5 September 1945, survived by his daughters Lesley and Brenda. The body of South Australia's greatest home-bred batsman was taken to Adelaide for burial at North Road cemetery.

S.E. GREGORY

16

Little Tich

Syd Gregory was one off being the 13th captain of Australia but fate treated him at if he were number 13. Anyone sufficiently superstitious to believe in the power of the devil's number might regard what befell Syd as a spillover from the cauldron that scalded Clem Hill.

Standing 165 cm (5 ft 5 in) at full stretch Syd was the tiniest cricketer ever to play for Australia. We have since seen Sonny Ramadhin, Roy Fredericks and Alvin Kallicharran, 161 cm, play for the West Indies and Indian batsmen. Sunil Gavaskar and Gundappa Viswanath, 163 cm. Holding a World XI together against Bob Massie's swing in Sydney, Sunil made me think of a faultless office-boy carrying on after failures by the firm's senior partners.

Syd's father, known as Ned the Lionheart, laid out Sydney Cricket Ground. He built a score board with 100 openings to show name-plates and figures on calico on 400 rollers. From the farthest corner of the ground figures 18 inches by 15 could be clearly seen, except perhaps from the most hard-worked frontage of the members' bar. His design inspired the rise of tell-all scoreboards on all Test grounds in Australia, West Indies and South Africa.

Sydney Edward Gregory was born on 14 April 1870 in a cottage on the site of the ground which his father built and tended until he died there at 60. Before Syd turned seven, his father played in the first Australian XI, captained by his brother Dave. As a teenage midget Syd played for Sydney club and for Waverley. He was 19 when NSW first chose him. At 20 he toured England – a habit he found hard to break – and played his first Test. A moustache took some of the boyishness from his appearance. C.B. Fry called him 'this blackberry-eyed slip of accomplishment'.

When the midget entered the Australian XI thirteen years after his dad it was the only Australian instance of son following father into Test cricket. Among 30 cases in other countries have been Sir Leonard and Richard Hutton and Mickey Stewart and Alec Stewart for England, six pairs of Indians, George and Ronald Headley (West Indies), Jehangir and Majid Khan then Hanif and Shoaib Mohammed (Pakistan), Walter, Dayle and Sir Richard Hadlee then Lance and Chris Cairns (NZ).

In London vaudeville shows tiny Kent clown Harry Relph was making his name with dwarfish pranks as Little Tich. This gave the Australians a ready-made nickname for their diminutive cricketer. The French made Little Tich an officer of the Academie Francaise, honouring him as an artist showing human nature as seen through the wrong end of a telescope. Through the wrong end of a telescope at the wicket, bowling seemed to look easier to Syd Gregory than to most bigger players.

W.G. Grace told Gregory that if he kept up his agile fielding, it would keep him in Test cricket twenty years. When Syd told his family this they smiled, but cricket's Colossus was right; he could have said twenty-two years. With a lone 57 an exception, Gregory had a stretch of ten Test innings without reaching double figures. Cricketers today could marvel at the selectors' judgement but his fellow-players knew his capabilities. England had seen no overseas fielder so outstanding. Close-to-the-ground balance helped Gregory scuttle to fame as the best cover-point his country produced, at least up to the first world war. By some marvel of co-ordination, the team's smallest man could throw 110 metres, nearly 11 metres farther than powerful George Giffen.

Syd had a kind eye. His moustache did not protrude beyond his lip line but it was fuller than the toothbrush style. His manliness contained nothing assertive. He was so modest that, if conversation brought in his own deeds, he minimised them and courteously changed the subject. Geniality was matched by conviviality. Nestling in his grasp, a glass looked completely at home.

He usually wore open-slat pads, Nature's air-conditioning for quick-moving legs. He used a wrap-around glove with sausage-type fingers on the right hand only, unless a pitch permitting murderous bounce caused him to unearth its companion from his bag.

129

After paying all expenses on his first tour of England, Syd cleared about £400 – the equivalent of four years' pay as a postal clerk. He resigned from the Post Office before his second trip, 1893, but made nothing from that disappointing tour.

Though venturesome starts were often bad for his career average, he upset predictions that lack of height would be against him in playing fast bowling. His high grip on his bat's long cord handle allowed an erect stance to give him a steady head. He was grouped among the four best hookers of his time. Bill Whitty told me Syd did not sweep but moved quickly to play more upright shots, especially his distinctive flick leg-shot.

No Australian crowd had seen an individual Test 200 until Gregory's 201 in 1894. As Syd used a bat made in Sydney, it was a genuine colonial effort. Joining Giffen with four out for 192, he unfolded superb back-foot strokes. His second shot, a hook, was so sure that it travelled forward of square-leg. He unleashed shots that astonished his team-mates as well as the Englishmen trying to cut them off. On a true pitch he sometimes came across confidently for what were known as front-foot cuts past point's groping right hand. A Saturday crowd of 24,000 saw their favourite complete 100. They were relieved when his only chance escaped Gay's gloves at 131. After he had to run his hardest in a perilous single for Blackham's cut, barrackers shouted warnings to be more careful. The pace was telling on Blackham (playing his last Test at forty-one, though he did not know it), and the captain-keeper signalled for a drink before continuing to help twenty-four-year-old Syd add 154 for the ninth wicket in 73 busy minutes. This is still Australia's ninth-wicket record. Peel had to sprint around the leg boundary to catch Syd off the seventh bowler, Stoddart. Grateful cheers for his 201 in only 4½ hours of rapture followed Syd all the way off.

By the day's end at 6 pm admirers had collected £103 to recognise the size and quality of Gregory's innings. Handing over the money, president George Reid said:

> If we had left the list open a week, I believe we would have got enough to set him up for life, but it was thought better to crown this performance with a spontaneous expression of admiration. When I say no grander innings was ever played on the ground, I feel glad for the

sake of the Old Country that our friend is no taller, for if he had been a Bonnor he would have got into millions. (Laughter)

Syd was a little bundle of batsmanship wrapped so tight that strokes stuck out the edges. Any batsman today would feel gratified if one of his most knowledgeable opponents could write of his play in terms similar to those used by Ranji after Syd's 171 for NSW against the English XI before he reached his mid-twenties:

> *Every imaginable stroke: behind the wicket, in front of point, drives past the bowler, glances and hooks, all were executed to a nicety. Pulls were indulged in, high drives were shown, cutting of every description. Risks of all sorts were taken by him with comparative ease, and much safety. No other Australian, to my mind, showed such resource and variety of strokes during our tour.*

The collection provided capital toward opening a shop. At twenty-five Syd married Maria Sullivan in February 1896 before leaving on his third trip. At twenty-six Australia's gem of a batsman topped the averages – first outsider to average better than 30 an innings on English wickets as they were before 1900. At the worst point of the tour, after Tom Richardson had shunted Australia out for 53 at Lord's, Gregory became captain Harry Trott's partner in a second-innings rally as exciting as it was unexpected. Upsetting preconceptions of how a fightback should proceed, the pair brazenly scored about 80 runs an hour. They kept it up for 2¾ hours and their fourth-wicket 221 stand lifted the side toward a total that called for good batting for England to win. Gregory's chanceless 103 contained 17 fours. Team-mates classed the rousing partnership as the greatest achievement of the tour. Crowds flocked to see a side that could play such cricket.

Fellow-players honoured him as invariably playing for his side, aiming at a good scoring rate and scorning to go carefully to build up his own averages. He produced some of his most glorious innings when his side was in difficulties. He was one of the ablest and most courageous bad-wicket batsmen in a period before pitch-covers made such challenges to batsmanship rare. On a Cheltenham pitch drying after rain, Gloucestershire had six Australians down for 54 but Gregory made 71 not out, then fielded while Trumble and McKibbin spun Grace and his team out for 17.

To relieve the tedium of a train journey across America, the team matched their tallest and shortest players in a boxing bout near a wayside station. Wondering at the incongruity of the match-making as Little Tich shaped up to 193 cm (6 ft 4 in) Hugh Trumble, some townspeople thought it a shame that other players stood by callously taking snapshots. Though giving away 28 cm (11 in) in height and probably more in reach, the light-weight made it willing and emerged without a scratch.

More than £400, his share of tour profits, enabled him to buy a cottage for £280 in Grafton Street, a couple of blocks west of Bondi Junction.

Syd's bold running sometimes disorganised the fielding side. Arthur Gregory, a young uncle, said the most daring occurred when Hill's bat stunned a ball from Richardson inside the crease. Syd dashed up for a single before a slip-fielder or wicketkeeper Storer could get to it.

Of all the talented Gregory clan, Syd was the finest batsman, though his brother Charles, eight years younger and not much taller, was the first Australian to score a triple-century in a day, 318 of his 383 for NSW against Queensland at Brisbane in November 1906. Their young cousin Jack added lustre to the family name as the world's best all-rounder.

On the way to England for his fourth tour, 1899, news came of his father's death. After fast-scoring Englishmen piled up 576 at the Oval, leaving 10½ hours to get Australia out twice, Gregory again rose to the occasion by making 117. When play resumed after one dark stoppage his rare courage against Bradley and Lockwood's fast bowling in poor light did much towards avoiding defeat.

He lost his shop on a corner of Pitt Street and Imperial Arcade through having been too trusting to a succession of partners while his tour shares were £700 in 1900 and £800 from England and South Africa in 1902. Sent bankrupt, he had to make a fresh start at 33 with a batting average, a wife and two children to provide for. He found a clerical job in the Water Board, where he was soon one of the most popular employees.

Warner's English XI had Australia two down in 1903–4 before Syd helped peg one back in Adelaide. When he came in fifth in the second innings Warner posted six slip-fielders to catch him. Nothing like a chance went near the slips or any other fielders as Gregory's vivacity raised 100 in 127 minutes. He hit 15 fours in his 112.

Whatever the reason for his batting late in Sydney, for two failures, 2 and 0, the selectors stood him down in Melbourne, amid protests. Missing his first Test in twelve years ended a sequence of 39 in succession. At thirty-five years he still had enough dash to whip up 100 in 75 minutes in his 134 against Hampshire in 1905.

New South Wales passed him by in 1906. Given a testimonial match a year later he scored 94 in a manner that changed selectors' minds. At 37 he equalled his top score by making 201 against Victoria. He played his way at 39 to his seventh trip.

No other seasonal visitor left so many footprints on English cricket grounds as Syd's neat boots patrolling cover-point's territory. Opening the innings in the last three Tests of 1909, Syd was out to a too-risky run for 74 at the Oval after he and Bardsley made 180. That stood as Australia's first-wicket record against England for fifty-five years until Simpson and Lawry lifted it past 200.

When a Board majority carried a point which made terms for the 1912 tour unacceptable to six leading internationals, the victors in the row had to find a captain for the weakest side Australia ever sent to England. In desperation their selectors recalled the veteran, banking on his knowledge of English conditions. They saddled this likeable player with the most mis-guidedly hopeless assignment since the biblical Tower of Babel, maybe. Of 37 matches only nine were won in a rainy season. Two were Tests against South Africa in the first triangular tournament. Eight losses included two to counties, Surrey and Hampshire.

Kind-heartedness showed up in Syd's captaincy at times when he allowed unsuccessful bowlers extra overs in the hope that their luck would change. With the traits that made him popular, easy-going Syd did not combine the faculty of command. He led his side with every care, setting an example in the field, but was let down by several players. They lacked the self-discipline which has been a cementing element in most Australian touring sides. No whisky was wasted on massage this time.

Nemesis must have grinned sardonically, seeing Board committeemen sitting in judgement on events their actions had set in motion – a forlorn mission with a scratch team that failed to attract crowds. Losing money as well as matches it left Anglo–Australian Test cricket the nearest it ever came to being wrecked. Outwardly officials let the matter drop after reprimands but Sydney Smith told me years afterward that on the return voyage South Australian batsman Edgar Mayne had refused to share a cabin with another. Smith added, 'At my instance, acting on the manager's report, we decided the Board must have power to say whether, for reasons other than cricket ability, a cricketer is fit to represent Australia.'

By retirement at forty-two Gregory had totalled 15,303 runs in 592 innings, including 25 centuries. He died at fifty-nine on 31 July 1929 at his home in Hendy Avenue, Kensington, and was buried in Randwick cemetery. His son Leo showed pleasing strokes for Randwick but was discouraged by everyone expecting him to be another Syd.

There could never be another. His total of 58 Tests was the highest by an Australian for forty-four years until Ray Lindwall passed it. No player of any country has approached Syd's 52 Tests as the most-chosen cricketer against England. As the first man to pass 50 Tests he had been presented by Australia's High Commissioner in London, Sir George Reid, with a silver cup containing a purse of 200 sovereigns. The Syd Gregory Cup continues to help his country's cricket as NSW and Queensland Colts compete for it. The annual game has been a stepping stone for such players as Stan McCabe, Alan Fairfax, Colin McCool, Ernie Toshack, Ron Saggers, Richie Benaud, Alan Davidson, Les Favell, Peter Burge, Jim Burke, Graeme Hole, Pat Crawford, Norman O'Neill, Peter Philpott, Johnny Martin, Bill Watson, Gordon Rorke, Grahame Thomas, Tom Veivers, Sam Trimble, Doug Walters, Kerry O'Keeffe, David Colley, Gary Gilmour, Ian Davis, Jeff Thomson, Steve Rixon, Trevor Hohns, Len Pascoe, Graham Whyte, David Ogilvie, John Dyson, Martin Kent and Allan Border.

W.W. ARMSTRONG

17

The Big Ship

We are still waiting for the rise of another Test captain as overpoweringly successful as Warwick Armstrong. Neither before nor since has a victorious international cricket skipper come through his campaigns with the proud record of never having lost a Test match.

The leviathan of Australian cricket in the first quarter of the twentieth century was a man to be looked up to and a man used to being looked up to. Unless they were as tall as Jack Gregory all men had to raise their eyes to look at him, a commanding 190 cm (6 ft 3 in). His teams called him 'The Big Ship'.

In youth Armstrong was tall and slender, like the mast of *Gipsy Moth IV*, but in maturity his shape made you think of a hull rather than a mast – a hull as capacious as one of those tankers too enormous to pass through the Suez Canal. A simple switch of initials could have transformed W.W. Armstrong into the *S.S. Armstrong*, a vessel more noted for tonnage than tact, and one not above a little gunboat diplomacy at times. In displacement, 125 kg gradually built up to 133 kg (21 st). His bills of lading showed more than 16,000 runs, 45 hundreds and some 830 wickets in 269 first-class matches. His career from 1899 to 1921 yielded him averages of 46 runs an innings and 19 runs a wicket.

Warwick Windridge Armstrong was born on 22 May 1897, at Kyneton, 80 kilometres north-west of Melbourne. He was educated at Cumloden School, Alma Road, and the University College, Armadale. In the Victorian XI at 20 he made 118 in his first match. New Year's Day 1902 brought his first Test at 22 – on a Melbourne gluepot. Sent in ninth, Armstrong made a few without losing his wicket in either innings.

In the Melbourne pavilion Armstrong's shirt and boots dwarf other relics. The tent-like shirt, unstitched, would make a headsail for Jim Hardy. Before the first of his four Test tours of Britain he was being presented with a travelling case when jockey Percy Kennedy called out, 'Will he be able to get his boots into it?'

Legends fastened on to him, as barnacles have a way of doing to big ships. In confidence, dominance, willpower and ability to get his own way Armstrong is the nearest Down Under approach to W.G. Grace.

June was at its sunniest when the Australians played Hampshire in 1921 and a Southampton newspaper reported that Armstrong, strolling around the ground while Bardsley and Macartney made centuries, became aware of a little boy dogging his heels. He thought it a manifestation of hero worship, but the boy's persistency at last made him say, 'Here, give me your autograph book and I'll sign it.' The boy: 'I ain't got one.' Armstrong: 'Then what do you want?' The boy: 'Please, sir, you are the only bit of decent shade in the place.' Warwick's shade was not only long and wide but cool, real cool.

On his first tour, 1902, *Wisden* predicted a great future for the twenty-three-year-old Australian, playing two matches a week for the first time in his life. On his second visit, 1905, he headed the bowling with 122 wickets and made 303 not out against Somerset, his tallest score. Only three Australian visitors have exceeded it – Macartney 345 against Notts, Bradman 334 and 304 in Leeds Tests and Simpson 311 in the Manchester Test, 1964. On Armstrong's third tour, 1909, his six wickets for 35 in England's second innings at Lord's brought his captain, Noble, the first win in Anglo–Australian Tests by a skipper who put the other side in.

No ball that Armstrong drove, and no deckchair he sat on, was ever the same again. Edmund Blunden said he made the bat look like a teaspoon and bowling like weak tea. His 248 not out at Lord's in 1905 was a 4¼-hour ordeal for the Gentlemen. Four men posted in a long-field cordon were unable to prevent many drives reaching the boundary. Armstrong knew how to plant his big boots wide apart to magnify the arc of the bat's swing. The massive Victorian's square-cut had stunning force. Pace bowling suited him best. One of his six Test centuries. 132 at Melbourne, was against South Africa's puzzling googly bowlers, a year after they had perfected Bosanquet's invention to take a rubber from England. As Armstrong grew bulkier, his difficulties with spin increased and arch-flighter Mailey tormented him in a way that bordered on bear-baiting.

Troubled by malaria after a wartime visit to New Guinea, he was 88 in one Test in the last over before tea and doubted whether he could continue after the interval. Three fours off Fender in that over took him to 100. Being so gross did not prevent his stealing runs, or rather the first run, aided by a flying start. When he got under way it behoved his partner to give 'The Big Ship' a wide berth. If he fell in the field he looked like a beached white whale.

Despite his weight he seemed tireless as a slow bowler who could land the ball almost as he liked for hours on end. His twisting hand imparted as much over-spin as leg-spin, causing batsmen trouble in detecting which were his 'straight breaks'. As England moved into a winning position at Trent Bridge in 1905, Darling used Armstrong to put a brake on scoring. The hefty all-rounder wheeled along 35 overs wide of the leg stump for 50 runs. In all, his 52 overs (24 maidens) yielded only 67 runs for one wicket. Such negative tactics must have been hard on Nottingham people who paid to see cricket.

On an average Armstrong had to bowl 92 balls for each Test wicket, compared with Benaud's 79 balls. No other Australian has totalled 10 wickets and 100 runs in a match in England, as Armstrong did with 11 for 70 and scores of 55 and 50 not out against Middlesex in 1905. No taker of 100 wickets on a tour has got as close to 2000 runs on the same trip, 98 short.

Through the second half of his career he had to ride out storms. He was one of six leading players England missed seeing in 1912 because of the stormiest row Australian sport has endured.

In addition to making runs Armstrong made enemies in positions where they could do him harm. Three times Victoria's selectors tried to push him off his pedestal. Armstrong treated them with utter disdain. The first world war raged while he was ageing from thirty-five to forty, well beyond the age at which leading Australians now quit cricket for business.

In 1920 he scored his best batting double, 157 not out and 245 for Victoria against SA, first man to total 400 with two century innings in a match. Coming just before the selection for the first post-war Test against England, it clinched the claim of Australia's senior player to the captaincy, but the fact that he was the last of the disobedient six was not forgotten.

He was the star of the first Test in Sydney. Nobody knows why he gave medium-pacer Kelleway the first over instead of fast bowler Gregory. It was a surprise, as Hobbs had been expecting first ball at the other end. The sight of Russell's bails flying first ball satisfied most people that a tactical genius was in command. In the second innings Armstrong, padded up, had whisky with his mates at the members' bar. He went out to make the highest score of the match, 158, with the most terrific driving most of the watchers ever saw. It forced even that master cover, Hobbs, back almost into the outfield and left several fieldsmen with sore hands. Most of his 17 fours were drives, enabling him to score 45 runs an hour and leave the Englishmen 659 to get. To make sure they didn't, he dismissed Hobbs lbw for 59. His main contribution to the second Test victory was to take six wickets. In the Adelaide Test England led by 447 to 354 but Armstrong hit hard for 121. By regaining the Ashes with three wins straight, he established himself as a national hero but his leg had been severely bruised.

He went to Sydney to captain Victoria against NSW but did not practise and, minutes before the game, withdrew from the team. One day he was reported to have been seen a mile or two beyond Sydney Cricket Ground at Randwick Racecourse – and with a man of his dimensions the odds were against mistaken identity. Back in Melbourne the state selectors wasted no time asking questions. They dropped him from the Victorian XI to play the English XI on the following Friday.

Besieged for an explanation, administrator Ernest Bean refused to give any reasons. He was mistaken if he fancied such a big ship could be sunk without trace. To a protest meeting convenor H.D. Westley said the most dastardly outrage in the history of cricket was the culmination of a series of oppressive acts against players. He moved, 'This meeting of lovers of sport expresses condemnation of the treatment meted out to Australia's greatest cricketer Mr W. Armstrong, who has been omitted from the Victorian XI without even an opportunity to make an explanation.'

The lovers of sport decided on a monster indignation meeting at 3 pm on

139

Saturday outside the Melbourne Cricket Ground, inside which the bereft Victorian XI would be playing the Englishmen. By refusing to issue the usual pass-out checks, the VCA required all protesters who left the match to pay again to re-enter. Despite a partial boycott, 17,000 watched play until 3 pm, when about 8000 dragged themselves away from Patsy Hendren's batting. Those who could not make such a sacrifice heard the outside crowd cheer the speakers. Those outside, in turn, heard the insiders cheer Hendren's approach to 200. Before the protesters carried the same resolution, Westley said:

> I desire to apologise to the English cricketers for the indignity placed on them by the holding of an indignation meeting outside the ground where they are playing. But the Englishmen are true sports and I am sure they are in sympathy with the objects of the meeting.

Inside, barrackers bawled, 'Put Armstrong on!' and, 'Why don't you give Ernie Bean a bowl?' As the day closed with Hendren 262 not out and Marylebone Cricket Club 445 for five wickets, a disconsolate wail crossed the field, 'Oh, where's Warwick?'

On the third night of the match, a full meeting of the VCA heard facts which the uncomfortable selectors failed to ascertain. Falling back on the old stand-by of beleaguered officialdom, suppression, the VCA issued a limited statement but it came to be known that vice-captain Mayne and Dr R.L. Park (player-physician) had agreed that Armstrong's bruised leg had been unfit for play.

His appearance in the fourth Test set off a unique demonstration. First, the thousands in one stand gave him a standing ovation. As that subsided the crowd in the next stand took it up, in the manner of a choral round. Because of a recurrence of malaria he lowered himself in the order, hoping for a weekend's rest before batting, and sent for a couple of stiff whiskies. But loss of five wickets for 153 obliged him to go in. As a youngster who had no right to be listening, I heard later that, as Warwick walked in to bat, he saw among the sea of faces the countenance of Bean, wearing an expression that seemed to say 'I've got him now!' The sight of the teetotaller, seemingly gloating, sobered Armstrong if he needed sobering. He pulled the innings round to give Australia a lead of 105 and after 3½ hours walked off amid the plaudits of the crowd for his 123 not out.

In the second Test the guileful giant had trapped Hobbs lbw by following a number of leg-breaks with a top-spinner delivered with seemingly the same action. As the great opening batsmen walked out, he said good-naturedly, 'Never again, Warwick!' In the fourth Test, googly bowler Arthur Mailey took his wicket the same way. As Hobbs walked past, Armstrong remarked, 'Got you again, Jack!' He had instructed Mailey to try the same ruse.

Though they backed him against official injustice and were subscribing to a fund for him, Melbourne barrackers were not always respectful. If he failed to reach an edged ball, they would yell, 'You big jellyfish' and coarser terms of endearment.

A clean sweep of five Test victories might have been expected to assure the triumphant general of the captaincy for the first post-war tour of Britain. The selectors' choice was announced as unanimous, yet A.G. Moyes, who was a state office-bearer close to inner circles, probably had good reasons for saying that in the Board vote Armstrong scraped in by the narrowest possible margin.

If a captain can be no better than the side he has to handle, as every losing skipper knows, Armstrong had a long start. The Australian Imperial Forces' successful 1919 tour of England bequeathed him the nucleus of a powerful side, imbued with fine team-spirit. Possession of Gregory and McDonald enabled him to show England his new method of opening a Test attack with express bowlers at both ends – the most far-reaching strategical change of his period. In a cartoon Tom Webster said things looked bright for England until play began at 11.30 am and Armstrong handed the ball to Gregory. In addition to the two fastest bowlers, Australia had the two most effective slow bowlers. Bowlers went into action happy in the knowledge that they had the two finest slipsmen, Gregory and Hendry, the two best outfielders, Bardsley and Taylor, two of the best covers, Andrews and Pellew, and wicketkeepers as good as any, Carter or Oldfield. Hardly an error was made in the field. Armstrong could write down his batting order from men who were to make 37 hundreds on the tour while only eight centuries could be raised against them. It would be superficial to say he had it easy – no Test tour is ever that – but no captain ever had it so good, unless it was Sir Donald Bradman after the next world war.

As eleven of Armstrong's fifteen players had captained their own state or district teams their knowledge of strategy and general tactics enabled them to take their places in the field for different opponents with a minimum of direction. Armstrong's captaincy came through this expert surveillance well, although from what I have heard his players did not rank him as a tactician with Noble, Trott or Collins. Unlike vice-captain Collins, Armstrong seldom bothered to take part in discussion groups in the team's hotel to cook up plans to dismiss leading opponents. Mailey regarded him as a tenacious and relentless fighter, full of courage and determination, who bluffed rather than cajoled the opposition out.

Other members of his team looked to him as a strong character who would not allow an opposing skipper to score a point at his own or his team's expense. He was an indomitable fighter in his team's interest. All-rounder Hunter Hendry told me that many rights and privileges of players today derived from stands made by Armstrong.

After difficulties about hours and travel, Armstrong called a meeting of his players and proposed a stand to alter arrangements that would adversely affect their play. The program which the Australian Board had approved allowed no rest days before Tests. The captain said it was intolerable that they should be expected to finish late against a strong country, travel overnight to a Test city and, if he lost the toss, find themselves in the field with a hard day ahead of tired fast bowlers. Three opponents consented to dropping the third day to save the Australians overnight journeys to the Nottingham, Lord's and Leeds Tests and a fourth compromised by finishing at 4, enabling the Australians to reach Manchester by 7 pm.

Suggesting that Test umpires be not appointed until the day, Armstrong said, 'The umpires are paid little for their services and, as there is a lot of betting on Tests, it would be wise to remove them from temptation.' Next day Lord Harris said, 'people don't bet on cricket' and Armstrong replied, 'If you'd like £500 on the next Test, My Lord, I can get it on for you.'

His team won the first Test in two days, the second Test by 1.35 pm on the third day and had the Ashes settled by 5 pm on the third day at Leeds.

Armstrong called total abstainers in his side 'the lemonade crowd'. Though he might have looked condescendingly on their way of life, he did not underestimate their cricketing ability. They formed two-thirds of his touring side. The batting depended chiefly on the clear eyes of Macartney, Bardsley, Andrews, Taylor, Ryder and Mayne, the wicketkeeping on Carter and Oldfield, and at that time googly bowler Mailey was a total abstainer too. If there was drinking to be done for sociability's sake, the duty was carried through – and carried through well – by the minority, Armstrong, McDonald, Gregory, Hendry and Pellew.

Providence was on the side of big ships, as well as big battalions. The dry 1921 summer reproduced almost Australian conditions. Loss of Hobbs because of illness worsened a panic which resulted in England calling on thirty players in the series, an all-time low in selectorship. Only Douglas and Woolley played in all five Tests.

Several times crowds objected to the frequency of Gregory's bouncers especially when Ernest Tyldesley was hit in the face in the Nottingham and Oval Tests, trying to hook. The first time, the ball cannoned from the bat's handle to Tyldesley's chin, knocking him over his stumps. No more than three fieldsmen were on the leg side. Bouncing was not entirely one way, as in a match against Marylebone Cricket Club both captains retired hurt: P.R. Johnson with a hand damaged by Gregory, and Armstrong with a gash over the eye from Durston.

By contrast with tour frictions, the Australian manager saw a few thousand standing outside in Bramall Lane, unable to afford entry. After cries of 'Can't we go in to see the last hour?', Smith suggested letting them in free at 5 pm. On his urging the Lancashire committee issued rain-checks on a Saturday so that frustrated onlookers could attend the Test on Monday.

After a washed-out opening day, Tennyson closed England's innings at about 5.40 pm on the first playing day. He had the advice of half a dozen ex-captains in the pavilion but wicketkeeper Carter produced a rule book to show Armstrong that it was illegal to close an innings later than 100 minutes before the end of the first day of a two-day match (as the Test had become). Arguing the point out gave Australia's bowlers and fielders a 20-minute rest. They emerged to the most hostile demonstration an English crowd ever gave Australians. Knowing nothing of the rule, the crowd blamed them for the infuriating stoppage. Tennyson crossed the ground and, with umpire Street, tried to explain that it was England's mistake. But when Armstrong began to bowl, hooting gave him an excuse to sit down until the noise subsided. In the commotion he overlooked that he had bowled the last over – if it was an oversight, not a ruse to take time if the umpires intervened. So one rule was upheld and another, forbidding overs in succession, was broken.

In the opening innings of the Oval Test he told his three main bowlers, 'I won't ask you not to get a man out, but as long as Mead remains at the wicket we cannot be beaten.' The left-hander batted five hours for 182 not out before Tennyson closed, 403 for 8, at 3.50 pm on the middle day.

As a carry-over from misunderstandings and irritations Armstrong was guilty of actions that antagonised English cricket fans by making the last three hours of the three-day final Test a farce when there was no chance of a finish. Not content with putting batsmen Taylor and Pellew on to bowl, he lumbered away to the longfield. It was one thing to take a catch there, light-footed as a performing elephant, but another to pick up a wind-blown piece of newspaper and read it. In telling batsmen to bowl, he was determined not to put further strain on his best bowlers, who had six more matches to play.

His team gave an object lesson of positive cricket by scoring 66 runs an hour to the losers' 59 an hour and bowling 118 balls hourly to England's 116 – rather more activity than Test crowds have seen in recent decades.

After 34 matches without loss, they went down to MacLaren's all-amateur side at Eastbourne by 28 runs. At Hastings four days later, as Arthur Gilligan was about to throw the ball to the wicketkeeper to run out Andrews, his arm was struck by Armstrong's bat as the captain bustled in at the bowler's end. Warwick said, 'You don't think I did that on purpose, do you?' Gilligan's next ball to Armstrong knocked his cap off. In their last match the Australians lost and had to be content with equalling the 1902 team's record of only two defeats.

In addition to heading the bowling averages with 100 wickets on his last tour at the age of forty-two he was one of the four fastest scorers, 43 an hour, in totalling 1213 runs. On 26 tours from 1878 to 1972 only four Australians have taken 100 wickets as well as scoring 1000 runs – Giffen and

144

Armstrong each three times, Trumble in 1899 and Gregory in 1921. Because of many blows on the leg in England Armstrong was unable to play in South Africa. On his four visits to England he took 409 wickets in 125 matches at close to 17 runs a wicket and totalled 5650 runs at 40 an innings.

Armstrong was the first Australian all-rounder to play 50 Tests, on the heels of England's Wilfred Rhodes. He made six Test centuries (top score 159 not out) and eight 50s in 84 innings for 2863 runs (average 38) and bowled 8000 balls for 87 Test wickets (average 33). Forty-four catches sank into his fleshy hands.

Always unequivocal and sometimes gruff, Armstrong to some people typified not so much the kangaroo as the wombat. Respect for their outsize captain's ability enabled his players to put up with such incidents as the night he ordered them to be in bed by 11 pm, yet did not get back to the hotel until 1 am himself.

Armstrong's salary as Melbourne pavilion clerk (it was £228 in 1911) sounds meagre today. To the fund begun by the 1921 protest meetings, sympathisers subscribed £2500.

On appointment as general manager for James Buchanan's whisky in 1935 'The Big Ship' changed register to Sydney. At thirty-four he had married Aileen O'Donnell, twenty-one, a grazier's daughter. Armstrong was a widower when he died at sixty-eight on 13 July 1947, leaving £90,000, the richest Test captain Australia has had, except one.

18

Holding the Cards

Shocks on the cricket field no more changed Herbert Collins's expression than reversals of racecourse form – events with which he was equally familiar. The only bookmaker who ever captained Australia was noted for the composure with which he won or lost matches and fortunes. His eyelids would not flicker nor his mouth twitch, no matter what happened when he had 100 runs or £1000 at stake.

By card-table habit, his face revealed no more than the sphinx's inscrutable smile tells camels. It was once said that no judge could be as wise as Sir Frederick Darley looked. No captain could be as shrewd as Herbert Leslie Collins looked. Nerveless as a city window-cleaner, Sydney's sphinx accepted a full-toss as impenetrably as a full hand. He enjoyed poker sessions lasting hours after midnight. Friends knew him to open Australia's batting after only 4½ hours' sleep.

To the public he was 'Lucky' Collins for two reasons. Getting away with slip-chances from his none-too-straight bat was matched later by winning toss after toss against England and South Africa. At Collins's third winning toss in a row English captain Arthur Gilligan knelt on Adelaide Oval, pretending to verify that the coin had a head as well as a tail. Gilligan's dumb-play delighted barrackers who believed a legend that Collins perfected his tossing skills at army two-up schools in France and had carried his winnings around in a sugar bag.

An accountant's son, born on 21 January 1889 in the Darlinghurst area of Sydney, Herby was a Trumper admirer when he began playing for Paddington as a left-handed spin bowler who batted the other way around. In his first season in the state XI at twenty-four he scored 282 against Tasmania at Hobart. That brought him an invitation to tour Canada and the USA with Edgar Mayne's XI in 1914, the year the first world war began. Collins was one of 417,000 Australians who enlisted. He left Australia in 1915 as Trooper H.L. Collins, Light Horse reinforcements, but in France for once he had to turn his back on horseflesh for the perilous job of driving truck-loads of shells up to guns bombarding the German lines.

After a dispute about the list of games in 1919 ended Charles Kelleway's six-match control of the AIF XI in England a players' meeting at the Oval elected Lance-Corporal Collins captain. They included Major Cyril Docker, Captains Clarence Pellew, Carl Willis and William Trenerry and Lieutenant Jack Gregory. His election was a sign of the loyal support his considerate handling always won from his teams. The quiet little corporal's capacity for leadership soon wove assorted elements into a side that beat MCC at Lord's and lost only four out of 28 matches. All profits went to a Sports Board. The players lived on their army pay. The skipper was on 'six bob' a day plus what he could win at two-up.

At Portsmouth Collins wanted to beat South of England in time to catch an earlier train to London but Gregory's speed had slackened. Collins asked wicketkeeper Bert Oldfield to come up to the stumps as the fast bowler walked back. Oldfield protested, 'If I do he'll knock my head off,' but Collins insisted; 'Don't worry, it will be for only one ball.' When Gregory saw Oldfield up at the sticks he glared at Collins, stormed up and soon took six wickets. A win put the team on the desired train.

They enjoyed a house match as guests of furniture magnate Sir Julien Cahn. After champagne flowed freely in a prolonged lunch interval the umpiring of the butler and under-gardener became fallible. Seeing Sir Julien come into bat, Herby told Docker, 'Throw a few outside his legs and let him have a few runs.' As one ball went from his pad as a leg-bye the knight ran to the under-gardener's end. Purely in devilment Docker called out 'How's that?' The reply 'Out' astonished Sir Julien, who asked 'What for?' The under-gardener: 'For the rest of the bluddy afternoon.'

A dapper man no more than 173 cm (5 ft 8 in) Collins was an inconspicuous figure of almost self-effacing mien – an asset when placing commissions in the betting ring. Though muscular companions on the field made him look almost frail, he had the staying power of a Melbourne

Cup lightweight. Besides making 1615 runs, including five centuries, for the AIF XI he bowled more than 700 overs of spin in taking 106 wickets. As a contribution to Australian cricket nothing else in his career rivalled his nurturing and development of this side. His AIF team injected rich new blood to help make the 1920–21 Australian XI the best-balanced side any country ever possessed.

He was only five weeks short of thirty-two when he played his first Test. Aided by a couple of chances he made 70 (run out) and 104 and went on to top 550 in the series against England.

Armstrong's 1921 team had not been in the Savoy Hotel long before Collins located a baccarat school opposite. In a team chorus refined from a ribald first world war ditty, 'Mademoiselle from Armentieres', a verse about the vice-captain ran:

> Collins is just as often missed, parlez-vous,
> As mademoiselle has never been kissed, parlez-vous.
> It's good safe betting to put your shirt
> On Fortune's odds-on favourite Bert,
> Inky-pinky parlez-vous.

In the Trent Bridge Test his right thumb was broken catching Ernest Tyldesley at silly-point. The injury put him out for six weeks. But for that damage, just imagine what later opposing captains would have thought of his touch as a tosser! As it was, he won seven out of 11 Test tosses.

Collins's bat never knew it was in the hands of a gambler. It was never urged to take a risk. Any ball pitching near a length was watched mistrustfully from earth to blade or allowed to pass. Instead of an array of strokes which a Test average of 45 would imply, a lot of his runs came from anonymous nudges and unidentifiable dabs made at the last moment. He brought off some of the best-placed pushes and prods in the game. An over-the-shoulder hook was the one bold shot in his deft onside range of taps and glances. His typical attitude was to finish standing on his right foot with his left boot six inches above ground. Bowlers kept him quietest by pitching well up to a man deficient in driving power.

He had an implacable trench-warfare style that in difficult times earned admiration from his own side, put bowlers on the road to exasperation and

149

sent onlookers through the doors of bars. In this respect, his game ascended to its zenith when drying turf at Old Trafford made it possible that defeat for Australia was just around the corner. Collins kept it around the corner. His first six partners were spun out quickly, causing anxiety in the Australian room. When at last he was lbw, appropriately, his vigil of four hours 49 minutes left too little time for England to order a follow-on and get Australia out again. It was hard to remember how 40 runs accrued to him while he concentrated on keeping his side safe.

Collins was nearing thirty-three when he succeeded Armstrong as captain in his ninth Test. At his second go as skipper his hook ran hot on Johannesburg's matting, the pitch that suited him down to the ground. Unearthing shots as never before, he made 203. He gave no chance in 244 minutes and profited by Gregory tearing South Africa's bowling to tatters for 119 in 85 minutes in a third-wicket partnership, 209. Collins's 203 is still the record output for an Australian captain in a day, though Bradman drew near with 201 in a day against India at Adelaide in 1948.

When South African opening batsman John Zulch questioned him about McDonald's speed, Collins casually replied, 'Medium fast until he warms up.' But at Johannesburg Ted simultaneously ended Zulch's curiosity and his innings with a ball that broke a shoulder off his bat and knocked it against the stumps.

After watching Gregory, McDonald and Hendry run up over the turfless red-soil ground, a Transvaaler was fascinated to see Collins deliver his slow spinners from two lazy steps. 'Collins is getting weary,' he yelled. 'Why don't you carry him up to the wicket?'

Herby preferred batting without mitts on easy wickets, which were increasing. Sometimes he promoted Gregory up the list, even opening with him, to give the big all-rounder a rest before he had to bowl fast.

In Sydney's sun Gilligan's pink face was reddening as he bowled to Collins, opening for New South Wales. As Arthur walked back toward the Hill, barrackers called 'Change the bowling!' and 'You'll never get him out!' After such a shout when Collins was 32, Gilligan held up the ball to them and called 'This time!' before he ran up. Herby snicked it into Strudwick's gloves.

Collins was the first Australian to reach 1000 runs in 12 Tests, his 18th innings. He had the confidence to shelter Ponsford from Tate's baffling swing before the great Victorian settled in for 110 in his first Test. None of his ruses worked when England's champion pair, Sir Jack Hobbs and Herbert Sutcliffe, batted through a whole Saturday in a Melbourne Test for 283 off 83 eight-ball overs in five hours. Before Monday's resumption former interstate batsman Frank Buckle and googly bowler Arthur Mailey were breakfasting when Collins came to the table and said to Mailey, 'You're going straight on to get Hobbs if we're to have a chance.' Arthur opened with a full-toss, fielders were moved to leave an offside gap before the next ball, another full toss. Trying to steer through the gap, Hobbs was left standing when an in-ducking ball struck well up the leg peg.

In that Test England had seven wickets to score 159 more to win when a broken bat and tea interval gave Collins a tactical opening. Frank Woolley was rubbishing the bowling when his bat broke at 40. With the new bat came a message cautioning the shot-playing left-hander against taking risks when England had ample time. Collins responded by bringing his wide-spread fieldsmen in and putting off-spinner Arthur Richardson on without an outfield. The reined-in Woolley's goose game (an hour adding ten) ended in Richardson getting him lbw. Collins then switched leg-spinner Mailey on opposite Gregory and England were goosed. For the first time a Test attracted 200,000 people in a series watched by half a million.

Hobbs was 66 in a Melbourne Test when he moved into position to turn a fast-medium ball which Ryder pitched a foot outside his leg stump. Wicketkeeper Oldfield stepped to cover the line of the ball. When it jumped higher than expected he took it in front of his forehead and his right glove whipped it to the bails to stump Hobbs. Walking across, Collins slapped Oldfield on the shoulder and said, 'How the bloody hell did you do it?'

I can picture him standing at mid off or short leg, his face like one in a trance as he hitched his trousers with his forearms as if his hands would soil their creaminess. To obviate calling or clapping to get fieldsmen's attention, he had every man look to him after each ball. No arm-waving, just slight hand movements to adjust a fielder's position. Sometimes a bent finger was enough. In the evening, players chatting, drinking and dressing often noticed their laconic skipper sitting silently in a corner with his togs on. They assumed that he was replaying the game in his mind, studying the lessons of the day and applying them to the probabilities of the morrow. Everyone else would be dressed before he had a shower.

One of his nicknames was 'The Squirrel'; Mailey said this was because his eyes were brightest at night. His brain was equally alert day or night. To his players he was chiefly 'Nutty' Collins; it's an even-money guess whether this was because he used his nut or because he was a hard nut to crack. Gilligan called him 'Horseshoe' Collins. I never knew Herby to wear a horseshoe pin or any other lucky charm, unless it was the kookaburra feather in the band of his felt hat, which he wore at a Digger slant.

Next to a day at the races or a session at poker or baccarat, bohemian Collins enjoyed a night at the opera. An appreciative listener at Covent Garden, he was sometimes induced to sing at a party, a light tenor. He had no taste for liquor, beyond a glass of champagne to honour a toast or a friend's birthday at a nightclub. From his army days he was a chain smoker throughout his cricket career.

His men liked their quietly-spoken, cagey skipper. Their faith in his captaincy caused most of them to say he was the best they knew. Oldfield told me:

> Herby had the human touch and got to know his fellow men. He was just as close to a religious boy, Johnny Taylor, son of a clergyman, as he was to Nip Pellew, a lad of the village. He studied every player's temperament and acted accordingly.

Mailey said:

> I learnt more of the psychology of cricket from Collins than all the hundreds of cricketers I met. Without being perceptibly diplomatic, he could carry the burden of responsibility yet transfer the credit to those he thought deserved it most.

He countered tendencies to envy, which in the minds of certain types can result in a small group becoming a discontented faction. He had an encouraging way of showing faith in players. Swing bowler Halford Hooker, who had taken a few wickets in his first state game, had to strap pads on quickly because of a rattle of wickets. Collins gave no instructions, but clapped him on the shoulder, saying, 'It's your match – good on you!' Tailender Hooker stayed in two hours.

At a time when Victoria had several notorious runners between wickets Dr Roy Park was making one of his three centuries against NSW in a big stand on a greasy-top Melbourne pitch. Unable to grip the ball properly, the bowlers were not eager to come up for more punishment. At last Park was caught for 111 and all the bowlers ran up, offering to get back into the game. 'Hold your horses,' Collins told them. 'Don't worry about trying to bowl them out. From now on we're going to run them out.'

On the field he played the game hard yet all his cricket was not unsmiling. When Victorian medium-pacer Arthur Liddicut was checking scoring by bowling well clear of the off stick Herby signalled for a change of bat. Three were brought out. He rejected them all and said, 'Bring me the long jigger.' In an inter-district game in Sydney his slow-bowler, Oswald Asher was clumped for half a dozen sixes in a few overs and pleaded to be taken off. 'No fear,' replied Collins, 'I haven't enjoyed anything like this for years.'

Hooker recalled:

He would bet on anything – perhaps he was the original of the saying about flies crawling up the window. Waiting on a railway platform he would bet on how many trains would pass through the opposite platform, how many carriages would be on the next one, how many carriage windows would be open. In a train he would produce a brass top stamped Put and Take – he paid out or collected according to which way it fell when it stopped spinning. The players would take turn, clockwise, to spin the top as banker, who usually fared luckiest. Once a bowler out of work was too sensitive to say he couldn't afford to gamble with it. As the top came around Herby would leave the compartment to hasten the bowler's turn to be banker. He was supposed to have gone to the toilet but he would simply yarn to players in another compartment before returning.

Unlike many other cricketers over the years he did not play cards in the room while a game was going on. Even on wet days, Pellew told me, he was unlikely to play with members of his team. For a good poker player who got

153

pleasure out of taking on other experts it was no fun beating players no match for him.

Collins was one of nine bachelors in his 1926 team of sixteen. On the voyage to England he combined with bookmaker passengers to lay odds about girls in the liner's ribbon-snipping championship. In heats Nancy, a grazier's daughter, out-snipped all along five yards of ribbon. On the day of the final Hendry asked, 'How are you going, Nutty?' Collins, in a deep, confidential voice replied: 'If Nancy wins I'll have to jump overboard.' Fussing around Nancy, telling her she was going to win £300 for them, her supporters made her nervous. She dropped her scissors and lost her chance. As Hendry put it: 'Lucky Collins wins again.'

For a man who made precious few mistakes Collins dropped a resounding clanger when he did err. The Englishmen, 22 behind on the first innings, were caught on a sticky Oval wicket on the third day. Yet Hobbs and Sutcliffe batted through 2½ hours before lunch without even giving a chance and England scored a great triumph. Members of England's brains-trust admitted having been on tenterhooks during the crucial 1½ hours from noon when the wicket was worst, dreading that Collins might bring Gregory's speed on when he saw Richardson make some medium-pace off-breaks kick. Hobbs never confirmed having pretended to be in difficulty to encourage continuance of the tactics – Richardson pitching on the stumps, turning into the batsmen's pads, or outside them, in the hope that a catch might be popped to four or five short-leg fieldsmen.

At fifty-one he married Marjorie Paine, twenty-four, a race steward's daughter. She did not defend his divorce petition seven years before his death at seventy on 28 May 1939.

W. Bardsley

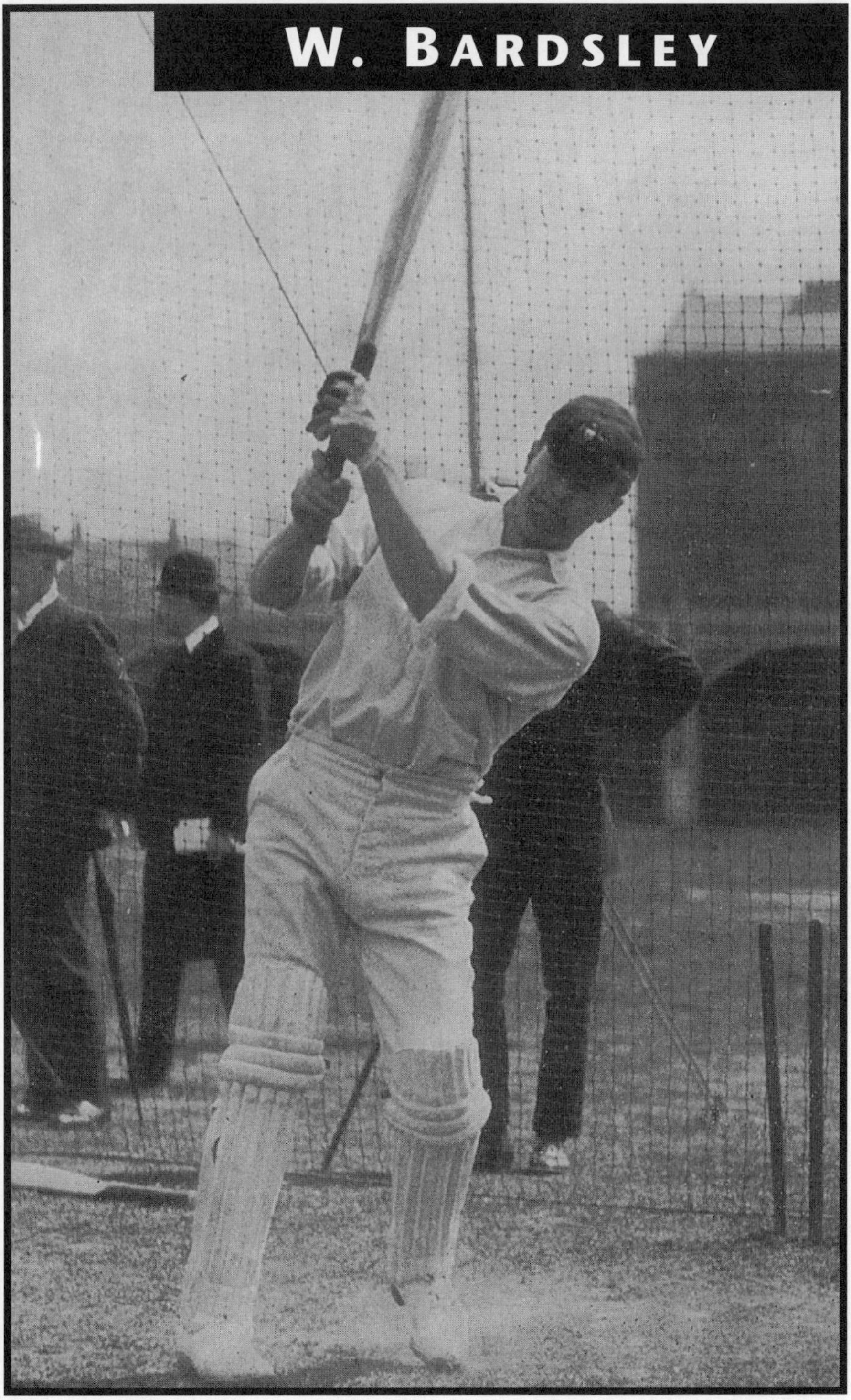

19

Fighting Fit at 43

Thick curving eyebrows, Nature's gift to comedians and politicians, were wasted on Warren Bardsley. The Australian left-hander's London stage friend George Robey switched his pair up and down to enhance laugh-making expressions. Bardsley's brows were archways under which pale blue eyes peered pessimistically. He never underestimated the menace of the bowling. He always overestimated the difficulties of the pitch. Between the two he produced batting that made him master of both.

Bardsley's round face looked happiest when he was watching George Robey, who took pride in wearing a gift Australian blazer from Warren to practise at Lord's.

Australia's vice-captain sometimes looked so glum that captain Herbert Collins once said, 'Cheer up Bards – it can't be that bad.' Bardsley: 'Can't it Nutty? Wait till we get out there. You may wish you hadn't chosen to bat first on such a mudheap.' Out he would walk to make more runs and centuries than any visitor to England until Bradman arrived.

Bardsley made the most of his height, 175 cm (5 ft 9 in). No opening batsman stood more erect, hands at the top of his long handle 2 lb 8 oz bat. Only the lower hand had a glove protecting the fingers, with an elastic band tethered to the thumb. *Wisden* editor Sydney Pardon once wrote, 'No left-handed batsmen in my time has possessed greater skill in scoring all around the wicket.' Warren did not attempt bold shots like Hill but in back-play he kept his top elbow well up above a bat so straight that purists nodded approval.

Eldest son of a schoolmaster, Bardsley was born on 7 December 1882. They named the boy Warren after the town where his birth was registered but his birthplace, Nevertire, signified the energy he would put into playing cricket. Warren never tired of methodically striving to perfect his defence and develop safe strokes. He carried a ball to squeeze to strengthen hand and wrist, boxed to improve wind and footwork. He did not smoke, shunned liquor, and as a vegetarian used to eat out if the family had a meat or chicken meal.

Warren was a leading figure in 6 am practice at Jubilee Oval, Glebe. Four of the group became Test players – Cotter, Kelleway, Bardsley, Oldfield – and Warren's youngest brother Ray, a right-hander, toured NZ in 1924. Warren would walk two miles into the city to the Crown Law Office. Jubilee Oval turf at 6 am was apt to be dewy. It was batting on it, I believe, that Bardsley developed the art of middling the ball that made him Australia's most consistently successful batsman in England before Bradman.

At twenty-one he played for NSW at Brisbane and at twenty-five made 108 for his state against the English XI. An innings of 264 for Australia against The Rest carried him on to his first tour of England at twenty-six. It was the highest of his career and he headed the Australian averages on the tour, 1909.

He was first man to score a century in each innings of a Test match, 136 and 130 at the Oval, fulfilling a confident prediction to scorer Bill Ferguson. In the second innings his 180 partnership with Syd Gregory stood as Australia's best opening against England for fifty-six years until Simpson and Lawry passed it with 244 at Adelaide.

Before team-mates were ready to leave the hotel after breakfast Warren would go ahead, walk the field and talk to the groundsmen. He would notice which end had worse visibility, which were the farthest boundaries and whether they were favoured by slopes; casing the joint for stealing runs. One morning he went early to Trent Bridge but could see no pitch rolled out. When he asked where was the pitch for that day, the groundsman replied, 'I'll pick one out in a minute and go to work on it.' In the first innings Notts made 239 and the Australians 389. Teased about the thoroughness of his preparations he would reprove the others for insufficient keenness. Leaving the room to open a Test innings, his last words would be in this strain: 'You fellows don't take the game seriously enough. If I happen to miss the bus you'll all be out before lunch.'

At his Collaroy home later he told me how on his first tour his batting hero, Trumper, taught him a lesson in team spirit. In his third game his third partner, Vernon Ransford, was caught for 174 after the two left-handers had put on 355 against Essex.

> *While I was resting on the grass I thought that, being near 200 with almost three hours to go, I might have the luck to go well past Warwick Armstrong's 303 and set a new record for an Australian in England. On 219, I pushed a ball into the covers, called Trumper and ran. By the time I noticed Vic was not running I was too far to get back. When Vic came in I asked him why he had left me stranded when it was my call. Vic said, 'How many more did you want, Curly? Remember there are others in the side who'd like an innings.'*

His 219 remained his top score in England. (More than sixty years later English captain Ray Illingworth persuaded Geoffrey Boycott at lunchtime to retire on 124 against Queensland so that another batsman could have a hand on the Brisbane wicket before the first Test.)

He was so hungry for runs that he always wanted to play. A blow made his finger swell like a sausage, yet when he was rested he objected so much that the team executive fined him.

Asked which innings was his best, he named none of his seven double-centuries but his 124 against Victoria in 1910.

> *After four days' rain the Melbourne groundsman said the whole side would not total 50 on the glue-pot. Losing the toss, Trumper said to me, 'Come on Curly, put them on. Stay there half an hour and I'll always remember you.' We got to lunch without losing a wicket.*

His average against English bowling in Australia was 20 less than his average in Britain but two great bowlers were the chief reason for that, fast left-hander Frank Foster and fast-medium genius Maurice Tate. Foster usually left him black and blue from ribs to ankle; pads were lighter and shorter then. The limping left-hander took Australia's quickest left-armer, Bill Whitty, to give him extra practice, but Foster hit his stumps four times, bowling him out of the Australian XI. Knowing he could reach peak form in England, the selectors restored him for the 1912 tour. In a rainy season he totalled 2441 runs and became the first Australian to average 50 an innings there.

Warren had a term as sole selector in New South Wales. He was thirty-eight when Tests were resumed after the first world war. His third trip to England, 1921, brought him 2000 for the third time. He was an efficient outfield with safe hands and a reliable left-hand throw.

Whereas others played tennis or golf for relaxation and billiards or snooker at night, he never joined in. He gave cricket everything.

Bardsley was still fit enough at forty-three to become the oldest player Australia ever sent to England, his fourth tour, in 1926. In the Lord's Test he made his highest Test score, 193 not out, batting right through the innings, 6½ hours, while nobody else got more than 39. The veteran survived four chances and once retired hurt for first-aid to a hand damaged by Larwood. He was the third batsman and first left-hander to carry his bat through a Test innings.

Bardsley was captain in the Oxford game when Ponsford threw down the stumps to run out J.S. Stephenson for 13. The umpire signalled out, but the Australians told him Stephenson had been inadvertently obstructed by the bowler's run-through. Bardsley withdrew the appeal.

Though he had never yearned after the responsibility he was pleased to take over leading his country's team for two Tests while Collins was in hospital for treatment for neuritis. Losing his first toss to Carr, who sent Australia in on a damp Leeds pitch, Warren was caught low off Tate's first ball. He was relieved to see Macartney survive a difficult chance off the fifth ball and make 151.

Oldest of all Australia's skippers, Bardsley was the first to have two googly spinners in a Test in England, guileful Mailey and Grimmett. Warner praised his handling of them, Macartney's left-hand spin and Richardson's off-spin. Warren emerged as the first captain whose side had the better of an unfinished Test after having been sent in.

After Bardsley called correctly at Manchester, Carr's tonsillitis on the first night resulted in Warren being confronted by Hobbs, first professional to captain England in a Test in Britain. Hobbs set up to seven leg-fielders for Fred Root's inswing. Rain left no time for a finish, so after two draws Bardsley handed the side back to Collins.

He was one of five dismissed by Robertson-Glasgow's swing bowling at

Taunton in 1926. Putting his hand on Crusoe's shoulder he said, 'Some of our fellows say you bowled me with a straight ball. But you and I know different, don't we?'

Bardsley's 7866 runs on four trips, average 49, were the most by a visitor to England until Bradman on his fourth tour hoisted his total to 9837. It took Bradman to eclipse the consistent left-hander's 27 centuries there. Bardsley shares with Bradman the record of having made them on 18 grounds. Allan Border has come closest since, with 23 centuries at 16 English arenas. The run-rich left-hander's deeds won him such fame that dozens of boys were christened Warren after him. Among them was Warren Saunders, who scored 1700 runs in 35 games for NSW and opened the innings for the Prime Minister's XI against Peter May's Englishmen in 1959.

In 41 Tests Bardsley totalled 2469 runs, including six centuries. At forty-three he became the first cricketer outside England to make 50 centuries. He had 53 hundreds in his career total, 17,025 runs in 250 first-class games at an average of 50.

After fourteen years in the Crown Law Office he became an indent agent for English cricket material and a headache cure which he never needed himself. The evergreen left-hander's straight-bat technique and footwork enabled his Sydney club career to span thirty-four years. His positive opinions were spoken louder after he was deafened by a blow on the head when he tried to hook Ted McDonald, then playing for Lancashire.

After tours as team-mates Mailey floated a number of balls outside the left-hander's off stump in a club game at Birchgrove Oval. Bardsley remarked to close fieldsmen, 'Does Arthur think I'm silly enough to nibble out there? He'll have to bring them in a lot for me to play at them.' Between overs Mailey asked the fielders, 'What's old Grumps saying?' They told him. When the first ball of Mailey's next over went by outside the off peg, Bardsley turned to wicketkeeper Bob Andrews, saying, 'He must think I'm a fool. I know every ball he bowls.' As the next ball came along on the off, Bardsley stepped across and again lifted his bat over his shoulder. The ball broke back sharply and hit his stumps. As he walked out Mailey, with his characteristic half-smile, said, 'If you thought you knew all about my bowling you'll never learn, Warren.'

Before Bardsley's last innings at the age of fifty on Sydney Cricket Ground the fielding Mosman captain, Hampden Love, told his team, 'We must do the right thing. Whatever happens Bards must make double figures.' As the veteran came in about 5 pm the sun was sinking, causing long shadows across the field. A ball jumping unexpectedly flew from a corner of Warren's bat to point, fielding with his back to the shadows. There the sure Bill Hunt raised his hands as if shading his eyes and the ball dropped to the grass. After Hunt stammered an apology to his skipper Bardsley walked across to the embarrassed fieldsman and said, 'You were wrong to have done that. You might be sorry you did. Thanks all the same. One can always learn, but this is the first time I've ever known the sun to set in the east.'

Bardsley was sixty-two when he married Gertrude Cope, forty-five, a stockbroker's clerk, at Strathfield in 1945.

Not long after he retired, Bardsley and Macartney were sitting in the Sydney pavilion when a shower stopped play. They saw groundsmen take covers out to shelter the pitch. Up went the eyebrows as Warren turned to his companion and said, 'Charlie, we were born a generation too soon.'

A week before his death at seventy-one on 20 January 1954 he was one of a lunch group when, as if by some premonition, Prime Minister Menzies said across the table, 'Warren, your name will go down in history and be remembered by people when poor politicians are forgotten.'

J. RYDER

20

King of the
Long Handle

For better or worse, city skyscrapers took longer to rear their heads in Melbourne than Sydney. One reason is that only a light layer of soil covers Sydney's rocky heart. The southern city above Port Phillip Bay's high-tide mark mostly has sandy subsoil, as well as unsurpassed golf courses and high-leaping footballers. But those who understand the town know there is something solid about Melbourne if you dig deep enough.

Bowlers and fieldsmen never had to wait long to find that Jack Ryder's drive had the force of a slamming gate. Gripping a long handle high gave the tall Victorian maximum leverage and his 2 lb 6 oz bat swung through a long arc. It had a thicker bulge at the back than the general run of 2 lb 3 oz bats in use until Sobers, the Pollocks, Richards, Marsh, the Chappell brothers and Turner led a return to heavier weapons. Lloyd outdid all with 3 lb 5 oz.

With an upright stance, the 185 cm (6 ft 1 in) right-hander was credited with more sixes around Melbourne than anybody else. Ryder rampant was a sight to bring the best out of barrackers, if not bowlers. No bowler could dictate to him. Not even Harold Larwood.

Born on 8 August 1889 at Collingwood, John Ryder was the third native of this sport-mad suburb to become captain of Australia. He was the second son of a carpenter who became a leading umpire. When district cricket began in Melbourne in 1906 a hansom-cab was sent to bring Jack, seventeen, to play in Collingwood's first team. For twenty-five years from 1917 players did not bother to hold a vote for club captaincy. All Melbourne knew him as the sporting King of Collingwood.

In the Victorian XI at twenty-two Jack discovered that first-class cricket tried the nerves more. As he walked in to bat English skipper Johnny

Douglas, lying on the grass, rose to call loudly as Ryder passed, 'We want another wicket, chaps!' Early in his first double-century, 242, South Australians were sure he snicked left-handed Bill Whitty to the wicket-keeper but a Melbourne umpire ruled 'Not out'. Late in the afternoon Ryder safely padded away a ball outside his off stump. Whitty shouted 'How's that?' and the umpire replied, 'Oh Bill, how can you ask for a thing like that?' Whitty: 'I just thought you might make two bloody mistakes in the one afternoon.'

At twenty-six Ryder married Fan Smith, a tiny brunette confectioner. They had a two-year-old son, John Thomas, when Jack played in Australia's first post-war Test. Batting ninth and eighth, he was run out each time but he kept his place as a supporting all-rounder to Gregory.

His running between wickets was too open to second and third thoughts, in contrast to his otherwise positive play. His habit of following a drive several paces caused some partners to run, thinking he was on the way, only to see him turn back if a fielder intercepted the shot. Confidence was lacking in much of the Victorians' running, as other states thought captain Edgar Mayne, wicketkeeper Jack Ellis and all-rounder Arthur Liddicut potential victims to be run out. 'Yes' 'No' 'Come on!' and 'Go back!' echoed around the ground. When the Melbourne Cricket Club brought Stork Hendry from Sydney to succeed Armstrong as pavilion clerk, the new-comer to the Victorian XI made up his mind not to lose his wicket through misunderstandings. In the room he told them, 'If you don't mind, I'm doing the calling.' They accepted this and saw Stork made 325 not out for Victoria against New Zealand.

At top pace before the war, Ryder's fast-medium swing bowling took 13 SA wickets in one game. He was in his thirties for all his Tests, yet he continued to use a fast bowler's length of approach after years had reduced his speed. A stopwatch timed him to take one-third of a minute on his walk-back and run-up for each ball. As fieldsman, he had safe hands.

In a Perth match before the 1921 team embarked for Britain, Ryder's 102 was the only century against WA but on English turf Armstrong did not need him in Tests. Mainly a forward player, he was below his best on England's softer turf during both his visits. South Africa's dry matting wickets suited his strong on-side play, especially his forcing shots between mid-on and square-leg.

Recovering from having strained his back bowling for Victoria at thirty-five, Ryder re-entered Tests in Adelaide in 1925. Five were out for 118, so he was less vigorous in rebuilding the innings, favoured by injuries to Tate and Gilligan. One pulverising on-drive made leg-spinner Freeman faint with pain. That chance at 145 was Ryder's only error in 6½ hours. Following 201 not out with 88, Ryder was the first batsman to score a double-yolk century and a 50 in one Test.

At thirty-seven Ryder was still young enough to begin his highest score against NSW at Melbourne just after Christmas in 1926. With 100 in 115 minutes, he then began chasing the ball. From 100 to 200 took merely 74 minutes. In two hours between lunch and tea his score leapt by 147. Grateful for 295 in four hours containing six sixes and 33 fours, onlookers carried him off, no easy task as he weighed almost 89 kg (14 stone). Nothing so spectacular was seen in a Sheffield Shield match until Colin Milburn's 242 before tea for WA at Brisbane in 1968.

Nobody else has hit six sixes in a first-class match at Melbourne. Only two members of the brotherhood of bash have landed more sixes at any of Australia's main grounds. In his volcanic 80 for NSW at Brisbane in 1939 Cecil Pepper lifted seven sixes, six off leg-spinner Bill Tallon and one off left-hander Charles Christ. Some of his drives cleared a wooden structure since replaced by the Clem Jones Stand.

Fair-haired left-hander David Hookes thumped seven sixes in his 163 against Victoria at Adelaide in 1977, including four from five balls in an over that cost leg-spinner Colin Thwaites 29 runs. Hookes also holds the current record for sixes in an innings on Australian soil: 10 in 243 at home for South Australia against NSW in 1985–86.

As state captain Ryder acted promptly to end an angry scene when a Melbourne crowd demonstrated against the world's fastest bowler, Larwood, being brought on against the world's worst bat, last man Bert Ironmonger. Larwood was lying on the grass until the noise ceased when Jack hurried through the gate and closed the innings.

Though a ruddy-hued commercial traveller selling boots, Ryder was

165

the first of a line of three non-smoking teetotallers who captained against England in the eleven years before the second world war.

Honest John Ryder was thirty-nine when he took charge of the team at its lowest ebb for sixteen years, opposed to one of England's greatest sides, led by Percy Chapman. No other skipper has had such a dismaying initiation. Losing the toss Ryder saw England pile up 521 on the Brisbane showground. After Larwood and Tate rattled his side out for 122, England, though 399 ahead, did not order a follow-on. They still batted on after the Australians were down to nine fit men and had substitutes fielding for Gregory (broken-down knee) and Kelleway (ill). On a sticky wicket the nine slumped for 66 and lost by 675, a record deficit. It was enough to discourage anybody except a man nothing could dishearten.

As the only Australian skipper who lost his first four Tests, Jack was the man in the middle making do with odd selections.

After England's record win and the dropping of Bradman, 58,456 people packed Sydney Cricket Ground on the Saturday of the second Test. Bardsley said he opposed omitting Don but was outvoted (on a committee of four, that meant three to one). Commenting years later, Bradman said, 'I heard the selectors, unable to decide who should be twelfth man, asked the captain and he said, "Well, the Little Fella has a lot of time ahead of him."' Jack heard this with a non-committal grin. When I asked him was Don's belief correct, he replied, 'Well, Rob, the only thing I ever said to the selectors was "Give me some pace."' He was kept waiting until the last Test for a fast bowler, Tim Wall.

Melbourne had the excitement of seeing Larwood's speed take two for six before Kippax and Ryder broke his spell. A sliced hook by Ryder for six brought the cost of two overs to 23 and Jack went on to 112, his third Test century. When the Australians failed to rout England on a desperately sticky Melbourne wicket, Ryder was widely blamed for allowing Hobbs and Sutcliffe to get away with a repeat performance of their 1926 Oval triumph which he had witnessed from the team's balcony. A good catcher's dropped chance at 10 enabled the brave partners to score 105. Ryder had neither a fast bowler nor a left-handed spinner. Australia's off-spinner Don Blackie repeated the Oval tactics of pitching on the sticks angling for leg-trap

166

catches. Ryder told me he tried to get his men to bowl the right stuff but they could not alter their dry-turf habits enough to suit the conditions.

In a close finish in Adelaide Jack said to Bradman, 'Play your own game. I think you can pull this off for us.' Don: 'I think so too.' Neither guessed that Bradman would be run out off Oldfield's call for a cover-drive to the unerring Hobbs.

Through it all Jack Ryder carried his red head high, gripped his bat high and courageously sailed into the strong English bowling. In a Sydney Test where the losing margin looked like being an innings he uncorked 50 in 36 minutes on his way to 79. At last the selectors gave Ryder more adequate bowling for an eight-day struggle in the fifth Test. Ryder was carried off, 57 not out, after his side's only success. It was the first time Australia battled through to win after England led off by exceeding 500.

A year later he was one of the three selectors choosing fifteen players to tour England in 1930. In preliminary talks Ryder was on all lists but his name was missing at the end, jockeyed out.

Ryder's forceful 100 not out against NSW that day contained chances but that innings and 168 in Brisbane were quoted as more instances of indomitable fighting spirit.

Unexpected dumping of the Australian captain caused public meetings showing how deeply people were stirred. Indignation penetrated Pentridge Jail. Chief Secretary Tom Tunnecliff received a letter stating that outside their own faults the inmates had more sense than the selectors.

Ryder took the blow without yelp or whimper. He declined all interviews, despite offers tempting to a man of modest means. Next season the Victorian Cricket Association arranged a benefit match which yielded £2463.

His seventeen years a state player would have been twenty-one, except for the suspension of district premierships for the first world war, which cancelled a tour of South Africa in 1914–15. He was a Victorian selector when he ended his state career at forty-two. When Aboriginal fast bowler Eddie Gilbert bowled him for 71 at Brisbane he had totalled 5064 runs for Victoria (average 45) and 150 wickets (average 29).

At forty-six he captained a team financed by the Maharaja of Patiala to

167

give Indians their first sight of Australian cricketers. To protect his greying head from the sun's sting Jack was given a felt hat with a double crown. He scored the only century in the unofficial Tests.

For 1394 runs in 20 Tests, his average, 51, was much higher than his career average for first-class games, 44. His 10,494 runs included 24 centuries. Against five English teams in Australia he totalled 1482 at 43 an innings. He played club cricket until his fifty-fourth year.

Sixteen years after his ordeal as national selector the Board reappointed Ryder a Test selector with Don Bradman and Edmund Dwyer to choose the team for Australia's first post-war Test in New Zealand. A world record of its sort was set when he carried on for twenty-three years until he was eighty. When his efforts to get Leslie Joslin in a team of fourteen to tour NZ failed, Board secretary Alan Barnes asked, 'What will you have to drink, Jack?' Ryder: 'Poison.' Barnes: 'Have a bitter lemon and stay alive.'

Selectorship was such a part of his life that nobody would nominate against Jack. When his reappointment at eighty caused criticism elsewhere, friends pointed out that having a national selector of eighty was not good for the image of the game. Accepting this as he had done the ups and downs of his career, he continued his close interest, though by eighty-four he was using binoculars to give his blue eyes a satisfactory view of play.

For unprecedented services to cricket for sixty-eight years he was decorated with an MBE in 1958. Victoria's annual award to the District Cricketer of the Year is the Jack Ryder Medal.

Few enjoyed meeting old fellow-players as much as Jack at the Centennial Test. Scarcely three weeks later he died of heart failure at eighty-seven on 5 April 1977.

Ryder had foreseen that bouncers would be a telling element in England's attack in 1970–71. He arranged for bowlers to pitch short to Stackpole in the nets to tone up his hooking. Midway through Stackpole's prosperous series he asked Keith, 'Will you be practising tomorrow?' Stackpole: 'Yes.' Ryder, reassuringly: 'I'll put you right.' Hearing this, a bystander commented, 'Not a bad touch of humour for an old fella in the eighties!'

W.M. WOODFULL

21

Old Steadfast

Radio was emerging from its crystal-set cat's-whisker infancy in Australia when W.M. Woodfull was coming to the fore in cricket. Nobody ever thought Bill Woodfull the cat's whiskers as a strokeplayer but his many qualities made him a pre-eminent leader of men. He first faced English bowlers a year before 2BL and 2FC pioneered Australian broadcasting in 1923. He had scored four centuries for Victoria when 3AR began Melbourne broadcasts on Australia Day 1924. At that time he did not imagine he would lead a team whose Tests would give radio in his homeland the greatest lift it ever received.

William Maldon Woodfull was born on 22 August 1897, third of the four sons of the Rev. T.S.B. Woodfull. After his transfer from Maldon to Collingwood Methodist Mission the cricket-loving parson had a backyard pitch made. Practising with older players, Bill developed the tenacity and application that shaped his career.

While teaching at Williamstown High School he studied at night for a Bachelor of Arts degree. A lack of freedom in his movements was ascribed to after-affects of rheumatic fever in boyhood. On his Sheffield Shield debut the twenty-four-year-old batsman was sent in eighth, where he made 22 not out against South Australia. Captain Edgar Mayne was not always well briefed about newcomers to the Victorian XI. As Edgar walked into the field another time with right-handed batsman Bryan Cosgrave, he said, 'You bat left-handed, don't you son?' Cosgrave: 'No, but I'll try.'

Promoted one place in his second match, Woodfull scored 153 run out, chanceless top score in Victoria's 485 against WA at Perth. Next season Mayne lost no time taking him in first. Consistent success on all-weather wickets sentenced Woodfull to be an opening batsman for life. His defence was so near impenetrable that a burst of applause rewarded a bowler in a South Melbourne club game when he uprooted Bill's off stump. It was the first time a ball had reached those well-guarded sticks in two seasons. The advance of 'The Unbowlable' into international cricket was so rapid that a wag said it almost created a draught.

The first time he batted in a first-class match in England the twenty-eight-year-old run-stalker adjusted to moist conditions for 201 against Essex – at 48 an hour! Next his 118 amid sawdust against Surrey contained only one four. Watching the ball closer than any 1926 colleague, he scored most runs and topped the averages with 57, first newcomer to average 50 on English tracks. *Wisden* listed him first of its Five Cricketers of the Year. Home crowds watched him battle for three centuries against Chapman's English bowlers in 1928–29. It was the first time they had seen that for a losing Australian side. Making the highest score for Australia against NZ, 284 at Auckland in 1928, Woodfull gave two chances in averaging 50 runs an hour. His tallest against English bowling was 275 not out for Victoria in 1929 at 35 an hour. Four times (twice in Tests and twice for Victoria) he opened innings against England and was still unconquered when the last man was out.

From the moment his sailor-like gait carried him in to take block on the leg peg it looked as if his motto were 'They shall not pass' (including shooters). Once he moved behind the ball bowlers saw no more of his stumps than his stumps saw of the ball. Warner said bowling to Woodfull was like throwing stones at Gibraltar. English bowlers called him 'The Wormkiller'. Depending on shoulder power and strong hands he could drive with a full follow-through, cut, glance and hook hard, when he thought it wise. His standby was a straight-bat push, with the blade often angled to place the ball, keeping mid-on and square leg on the run. The way he made a yard along the track to deal with spinners did not support a belief that he was a slow mover.

Amid the stir when co-selectors ditched Ryder, W.L. Kelly, while managing the Victorian XI in Sydney, persuaded a reluctant Bill to agree to being nominated for a Board ballot. Woodfull was the Carlton club's skipper. He had skippered a side touring New Zealand. When appointed captain at thirty-two Woodfull was teaching mathematics at Melbourne High School.

World-wide depression was putting thousands of the workforce on the dole but Oswald Anderson of 2UW reasoned that radio could divert people from their worries. He arranged for skeletonised messages over by over to be sent from English Test grounds to Australia via Beam Wireless, which had opened in 1927. In radio studios pencil taps and other sound-effects simulated Test atmosphere. Historian Philip Geeves says cricket gave commercial radio its greatest lift. It brought about the first commercial network when the Tests were described over ten stations, headed by 2UW Sydney, with Alf Noble commenting, and 3DB Melbourne, with comments by Jack Ryder and Keith Rigg. In a month the number of listeners' licences jumped by 10,000. Advertisers saw that hitherto-neglected radio could reach captive mass audiences.

A suggestion that 3DB's transmission would end at midnight, with the last sponsored advertisement, swamped the switchboard with pleas for continuation, nay demands. So broadcasts continued until 3.30 am (stumps drawn). Electric power stations' generating hours had to be extended to meet after-midnight demand. In flats ablaze with lights occupants held rounds of Test parties. Australia's taste for bottled beer deepened with the fall of each English wicket. The life expectancy of stock shortened as extra tons of cocktail sausages were needed for the beer to wash down at supper (coinciding with tea interval at English grounds).

A skipper in the democratic Trott tradition, Woodfull was indistinguishable from his players on ship or train. He was usually in a bridge four. A man without a vice, he did not touch alcohol even for a toast. Yet in a prelunch group he would buy a round of drinks for his players. His unseasoned fifteen, called Woodfull's kindergarten or Kelly's creche, formed one of the youngest sides ever to go abroad. Only four knew English conditions.

The Black Boy Hotel was close to Nottingham Town Hall which boomed the hours all night until Woodfull asked to have the chimes silenced between 11 pm and 7 am so his team could sleep during the first Test. They still lost. Defeat failed to halt their progress as their purposeful skipper moulded them into an attractive team, even if overmuch dependent on Grimmett to get England out. Woodfull and Ponsford were two solid Bills for England's bowlers to meet. Mates called them Mutt and Jeff after a movie pair, rather more slapstick. Fast-medium bowler Alan Fairfax intoned, 'Confucius say Australia do best with Chinese opening pair Willy Wo and Willy Po.' The dark-haired brown-eyed Victorians were the first pair to give Australia three century openings in a series, 162, 106 and 159 – in two cases followed by double centuries by the next man, Bradman.

Woodfull's organising made baggage-master Bill Ferguson's life easier, with everything running like clockwork. Fergie called him a model for the exacting art of cricket captaincy. Woodfull was King George V's favourite cricketer. In their informal talks the King used to ask Bill to settle cricketing arguments for him. Yet in the Lord's Test, a Woodfull/Ponsford partnership was halted about 160 by the King's arrival for the teams to be presented. On resumption Hammond caught Ponsford for 81 off White, and the King said, 'I shall have to come again and get some more wickets.' Woodfull went on to 155, his second partner Bradman followed up superbly with 254 and Australia won by seven wickets, levelling the series.

Bradman's 309 in a day at Leeds caused such enthusiasm among listeners that as an Alice Springs party under the stars broke up an Aboriginal stock-man was asked, 'What do you think of that, Jackie?' After a pause the stockman said, 'Plurry wonder, boss – but what sort of score he make in day-light?' A win at the Oval regained the Ashes on the skipper's 33rd birthday.

The kernel of Woodfull's captaincy was the way he got the utmost from each man. Their esteem was their response to his personal qualities of common sense, straightforwardness, tolerance, consideration and unselfish service to his side. Bill was so truthful he could not utter even an off-white lie. More than any predecessor, he showed interest in their personal welfare, as well as their field performances – all about their families, problems and hopes. From a hundred instances I mention one because Methodism seems to be on the farthest edge of the Christian spectrum from Catholicism. Before bedtime on the Australians' first Saturday outside London the Methodist parson's son quietly told St Joseph's Old Collegian Stan McCabe, nineteen, the whereabouts of the nearest church for Mass in the morning.

I know of no other national captain who held players' trust and loyalty to such a degree, though cricketers who played for Sir Frank Worrell and Richie Benaud would scarcely think they could be outdone. In a game

173

of delicate balance between individual aims and team needs, Woodfull's unrivalled selflessness won fidelity bordering on devotion.

In matches he gave few commands. He knew that unsought advice was more likely to unsettle than help an entering batsman. His way was more to tell his team the course he plotted and have faith in the good sense of each to use his own methods in the best way to bring the desired result. When Australia's first three wickets tumbled cheaply at Lord's he greeted incoming McCabe reassuringly: 'Play your own game, Napper. There's nothing in this pitch.'

As he led his team out the door Woodfull invariably uttered an old Australian football exhortation: 'Come on, youse! Straight up the centre – no short passes – boots and all!' A player dropping a chance would get a consoling word. He made a point of being supplied with the day's bowling figures, which he read loudly enough for all to hear as they were showering and dressing. None of his players could follow his example of not reading newspaper comments during a match. After the Adelaide bodyline Test Noble rebuked him on the radio for not having curbed Bradman's recklessness.

Before each interstate match gambling all-rounder Sid Hird used to lay a book about the runs opposing batsmen would score. When NSW played Victoria Sid shied off how many runs Woodfull and Ponsford would make and switched to how long their opening partnership would last. The highest price bowlers had to pay for their first wicket was 375 runs by NSW, the foundation on which Victoria built 1107 in 1926.

Another time a ball with damaged stitches was shown to Woodfull and an umpire. 'Let the bowler have a look,' he said. Tossing the ball to Ernie McCormick he asked, 'What do you think about this?' The fast bowler inspected the frayed stitches and replied, 'Short at the back and sides and a little bit off the top.'

About 180 cm tall (within an inch of six feet), Woodfull had the broadest shoulders of any Australian captain in the last seventy years. Just as well.

When bodyline was ripping strips off his team he suffered by far the cruellest punishment. He tried to create an atmosphere of confidence in the room, not easy when a player might be walking up and down agitatedly calling out, 'Did you see that? Look at that!'

Like a storm-lashed headland in rough seas, he took the brunt of the bodyline onslaught and tried to manage without anti-bodyline chest padding until Adelaide brought a second blow over the heart from Larwood.

Woodfull was lying on a massage table receiving treatment for a livid bruise on the breast when Marylebone Cricket Club manager Pelham Warner walked in to express sympathy. Woodfull said, 'I do not wish to discuss it, Mr Warner.' Warner: 'Why, what is the matter?' Woodfull: 'There are two sides out there. One is playing cricket and the other is not. The game is too good to be spoilt. It is time some people got out of the game. Good afternoon.'

For an under-manned bowling side, further reduced by a bowler's strain, O'Reilly's hard labour under Brisbane's February sun left him too fatigued to take off his sweat-stained flannels. His left-handed spin partner Bert Ironmonger, aged forty-nine, slumped in even worse shape. Their skipper sent a request for champagne. It was refused under a standing instruction. Hunting out Queensland president J. Hutcheon, Woodfull told him, 'Something must be done to lift my exhausted bowlers off the floor. I want champagne. Please see that it is in the room straight away.' It was.

Selectors divided about bodyline policy sounded him out. Woodfull told them, 'If I am again chosen I will try to do my duty but while I am captain there will be no retaliation.' Dismissing all suggestions for a counter-offensive, he never ceased trying to beat bodyline by doggedly wearing down the bowlers exploiting it, though this only once got near succeeding. He stuck it out for 1145 minutes (more than 19 hours) in the five Tests, facing 107 more balls from the three bodyliners than any other batsman. His 305 runs were the slowest of his career, 16 an hour, but each innings survival held priority over scoring.

When Larwood in the last bodyline Test broke a bone in his left foot, Jardine told him to complete the over, five more balls. Harold said:

> All I could do was stand against the crease and swing my arm over. 'Here's five fours,' I murmured to myself. Bill Woodfull just patted the balls back to me. He knew I was hurt. That's the kind of sportsman he was.

Oldfield believed that 'but for Bill the situation might have severely interrupted relations between England and Australia'. MCC committeemen's

175

vote to invite a 1934 team was eight to five. Several Boardmen opposed sending a team without a clear undertaking that no more bodyline would be used.

Like over-stretched elastic, Woodfull's batting could not recover fully from bodyline's trauma. Dissatisfied with his form before the first Test, he suggested standing down. His co-selectors, Bradman and Kippax, would not hear of it. He averaged better than 50 for the third time in England.

A close team secret – until you read it here – was immediate steps taken at Nottingham after Voce's flagrant breach of the so-called 'gentlemen's agreement' by bouncing bodyline balls at batsmen's heads with up to seven leg-side fielders. Woodfull authorised an official protest. During rain stoppages on Monday afternoon the indignant Australians said they would not resume their second innings if Voce played. To avoid an explosive climax, umpires Bill Hitch and Walter Buswell agreed not to resume the match for the last half-hour. Woodfull resolved that if Voce bowled again he would instantly close the innings. Notts's chiefs conceded that the attack had been intimidatory and withdrew Voce from the last day on a pretext of shin-soreness.

Critics called his captaincy stereotyped because of the way he harped away with his chief bowlers. He did seem to overplay his trump cards, O'Reilly and Grimmett, yet when either was given a spell you could almost hear the batsmen sigh with relief.

I noticed only two drawbacks in Woodfull's unostentatious leadership that were likely to cost the chance to win a match. He would go into a Test with only three real bowlers, sacrificing one so he could strengthen the middle of the batting list. It was a hard-to-rid fear of collapse, a carryover from having seen bodyline flatten Australia's batting.

Over-caution led him to delay closing Australia's innings on the last morning of the first Test in 1934. (Foreseeing this I sent him a congratulatory message the previous night. It was presumptuously designed to egg him on but unsurprisingly failed; the Australians batted 90 minutes into the last day.) He left the Englishmen a target of 380 at 80 runs an hour, but his bowlers had only 4¾ hours to get them out. O'Reilly and Grimmett managed it, when Tiger took his seventh wicket ten minutes before time.

The decision to promote O'Reilly to opening bowler in a Melbourne Test and repeat it at Adelaide was the reverse of stereotyped. So was his taking Grimmett off after only three overs on a drying Sydney pitch in the West Indies' second innings. Woodfull was the only captain who did not give Grimmett a bowl through a whole Test; it was another sticky wicket at Melbourne against South Africa in 1932.

A clue to his effectiveness as a tactician handling bowlers and fieldsmen was contained in Hammond's scoring when he was at his peak in pre-war Tests: 908 runs in 26 innings when Woodfull was the opposing skipper and 1776 in the other 24 innings against Australia.

Crossed bats had been among church decorations when Bill, twenty-nine, married Gwen King, twenty-one, soprano in the choir of his father's Albert Park church. At the time of the bodyline Battle of Adelaide she was at home in Melbourne with her sons, aged three and one. Asked about a published report that she feared for his life, she said,

> It was a great worry. I felt it was detrimental to Bill's health. He was deeply concerned about the damage being done to the game he loved. I would have been quite happy if he had got out of the game. I personally think going back to England with his team was the most wonderful thing. It took a lot of courage to go back as a leader of a misunderstood side. It was obvious English people had little idea of what the trouble was really about. If he hadn't gone back there I don't think international cricket would have carried on in the way it has.

No player won higher esteem from a top English critic than Woodfull from R.C. Robertson-Glasgow:

> The most calm-browed cricketer I have seen. He reminded me of a master who gets the whole school to and from a picnic without losing his reason or a boy. Of all the protagonists in that fiercest controversy, I should say that he alone came out of it with reputation heightened and personal friendships increased. He neither concealed nor exaggerated a difficulty ... He remains the only man who has twice come here as challenger and twice carried off the victory ...

Bowlers he directed brought about the cheapest downfall of any Test side by dismissing South Africa twice for 81 on rain-softened Melbourne turf in

1932. Leading Australia through five consecutive rubbers, he was his country's first skipper against the West Indies and the first of any nation to be captain in 25 Tests.

Quitting cricket at thirty-seven, he shared a £2084 benefit match with Ponsford. In 35 Tests his 2300 runs included seven centuries and his average was 46. In 174 first-class games he scored 49 hundreds and his career average for 13,388 runs was 65 an innings.

O'Reilly said his admiring team-mates all held imperishable memories of his personal touch and his courage, for which they affectionately named him 'Old Steadfast'. Oldfield called him skipper, psychologist and humanitarian all in one.

Woodfull retired after six years as Melbourne High School's principal. At sixty-seven he was on holiday from his Mount Eliza home when his heart failed as he golfed at Tweed Heads on 11 August 1965. Gwen Woodfull kept Bill's study the way he left it – the cricket photographs around the walls and the portrait by W.B. McInnes, the outcome of a bob-in fund from admirers.

V.Y. RICHARDSON

22

Verve and Nerve

The way he walked told a lot about Victor Richardson. Each brisk step into the field was that of a well-built athletic man taking pleasure in what he was doing, eager to get on with the enjoyment. Each stride implied confidence to meet whatever challenge the day might bring – and for a skipper opposed to stronger forces challenges were almost as numerous as seagulls fossicking in the outfield. Alf Marlow and companions in the Giffen Stand used to say Richardson walked onto Adelaide Oval as if he owned the place. At least it was a home away from home, belonging to him as the most versatile and popular sportsman South Australia has produced.

Close-up impressions of Vic Richardson confirmed that he had personality plus. Rather handsome, he was more likely to be taken for a dare-devil than a deacon. The wrinkles at the corners of his eyes were laugh-lines. Frequently half-veiled in merriment, the blue irises could at times be steely but never stealthy. At the drop of an eyelid his mouth would widen in a grin. A tilt showing more teeth at one side gave a slightly mocking air to his laconic levity. He could tackle a steak, a speech, a schooner or a speedball with gusto.

Beside dual captaincy of his state at cricket and football (Australian Rules), he represented SA at baseball. When he was thirty the Helms award put him in the American Hall of Fame as best Australian athlete in 1925. He golfed off 12 handicap but much preferred team games, choosing cricket as his favourite because of 'team spirit that puts success of the side before personal glory'.

Victor York Richardson was born in unsuspecting Unley on September 1894, second son of a house decorator from Kyre College, Unley Park (now Scotch College). His first job was in the Produce Department, Victoria Square. At eighteen he began a thirty-year association with Sturt.

Standing 181 cm (5 ft 11½ in) and weighing 76 kg (12 stone), he was a dozen years a Sturt footballer. Six nights a week he practised or played football, baseball, basketball, lacrosse, cricket, tennis or trained at a gymnasium. Nature had given him muscles so flexible that he never bothered to climb on a massage table.

The first world war delayed Victor's entry into first-class cricket until he was twenty-four. In the same summer he married Vida Knapman, a publican's daughter. Fielding in Melbourne, he made a baseball slide to catch Vernon Ransford. As he rose brushing grass-stained flannels, captain Clem Hill patted his shoulder saying, 'After a catch like that young fella, it doesn't matter if you make a duck.' In his third match he hit 18 fours making 134. In three years he was captain, remembering the benefits of leading rather than driving, encouraging rather than chiding. He led SA from 1921 to 1935, a record period. Opening for Australia in NZ at twenty-seven he made 112 vigorously in an unofficial Test at Auckland.

He soon earned a name for producing his best when nothing less would save his side. He was batting No. 4 when he became the first South Australian to make a century in each innings of a Shield match. Two were out for 10 when he came in to score 100. In the second innings two were gone for two when he began in fading light and went on to 123. Leg-spinner Hugh Chilvers's quick four-step run-up was liable to surprise batsmen. After a couple of balls from him Vic stepped back from the stumps saying, 'Just a minute, son – we've got four days to finish this match.'

Given out by a great umpire, George Hele, Richardson was slapping his bat against his pad as he walked upstairs to the team room. A voice: 'A bad decision?' Vic: 'If you can get away with anything with Hele you're pretty smart.' Talking after the game, he told Hele, 'I was mad at the time, until I thought of all the wonderful decisions you had given.'

Richardson had a hooker and square-cutter's grip and liked angling drives past mid-on. His short-arm hook was a pivoting model of its kind but all his technique was not up to the standard of his temperament. Spinners making him play forward could curb him. In Adelaide Oval members' dining-room a photograph shows his stance, the right knee bent and his low grip hunching his shoulders a little. To friends teasing him about his stance,

Vic explained, 'The fact is, I didn't know whether they were going to do me in oils – like a sardine. At the finish they only had a small frame, so they had to squeeze me down a bit.'

If his style gave bowlers hope, he often took heavy toll before that hope was realised. Once Vic and Arthur Richardson (no relation) travelled by overnight express to a Melbourne Test. Arthur asked, 'How did you sleep?' Vic: 'Like a top – how about you?' Arthur: 'Couldn't get a wink – thinking of Tate all night.'

In his second Test Victor gave a forward-leg chance at 67 on his way to a three-hour 100. It was dropped by Johnny Douglas, a colonel whose vocabulary went far beyond barrack-room ballads. When Douglas came on with the second new ball Vic greeted it with 4, 4, 4, 4, 2, 3. His 21 off a six-ball over equalled the Melbourne Test record by Hanson Carter off Wilfred Rhodes in 1908. The Anglo-Saxon terms with which Douglas relieved his exasperation caused Pat Hendren to double up with mirth. After a misfield, Richardson was attempting a fourth run when Chapman's underhand throw pegged the stumps to run him out, 138.

Richardson made a hundred against every English team in Australia from 1920 to 1932 except the first, when he was 59 not out for SA on a rain-affected track. His first clash with Larwood was as SA opening batsman in October 1928. Making 231 in about five hours, he delighted the crowd by hooking the world's fastest bowler for six. His 231 is still the tallest innings for SA against a touring English Test side, though Barry Richards drew near, 224 in 1970.

Son of a man who had been secretary of the Victorian Temperance Alliance for some years, Vic avoided alcoholic drinks until he was twenty-seven. Thereafter overseas and interstate visitors found him a centre of group conviviality. A variation from exploits on foot came at a late supper at a kerbside Cafe de Wheels. The chef's temporary absence tempted Richardson to mount the piecart horse and ride it around to another street. It was like a scene from *Ben Hur*, Chaplin style.

His fielding stole the show from batsmen and bowlers at Sydney in 1928 when he was thirty-four. Hammond was driving at his imposing best, with Hendren stroking well, but Richardson intercepted shot after shot, as if his size-eight boots had Mercury's wings. At the day's end the players stood back for him to leave the field first amid an ovation. A *Sydney Morning Herald* editorial expressing wonderment was headed 'Is Richardson Human?'

Years of leading SA teams which were outgunned by NSW and Victoria sharpened his alertness for ruses to steal wins which his side was unlikely to get if matches went along in orthodox manner. Any team led by Vic Richardson was as chockful of camaraderie as he was of courage. He combined determination with buoyancy. To quote Sydney Downer, in *100 Not Out*: 'For romantic minds he turned Adelaide Oval centre pitch into King Arthur's Round Table.'

Richardson's teams always fielded as if they were winning – or thought they had a chance. He never asked another to do anything he would not tackle himself. If fading light made batting more difficult he believed conditions called for a proficient batsman, not a tailender promoted to be nightwatchman. He never shirked dungeon-like gloom, no doubt hoping there'd be a glow-worm or two about.

On the way to open an innings in poor light in Sydney he muttered to partner Gordon Harris, 'Do as I do.' Instead of heading for the pitch they detoured toward the Hill stand near the Showground. From cover NSW captain Tom Andrews called, 'Vic, where do you think you're going?' Richardson: 'Call out again, Tommy. I can hear you but I can't see you.' When he reached the wicket an appeal against light was promptly upheld.

Leading a weaker side is no way to fame for a captain. The fact that he achieved it as a skipper is its own hall-mark. At thirty-three he led Australia in NZ, with Woodfull his vice-captain and a heavy runmaker. In dumping Ryder from the 1930 England tour Charles Dolling aimed to have Richardson as captain but the Board appointed Woodfull, with Vic as his deputy.

To avoid the risk of injuries by fast left-hander Bill Voce's bumper-spiced attack, the Australians left their four key players – Woodfull Bradman, Grimmett and Oldfield – out of the Notts game before the third Test. Richardson led the other XI. Watching Voce disconcert early batsmen, he exclaimed, 'Somebody's got to crack this fella.' As he left the room to join McCabe he said, 'One of us is for it.' The valorous pair's hooking

183

counter-attack and Voce's second innings figures (one for 112) misled England's selectors into leaving the menacing left-hander out of the series. No team he captained in NZ, England, Canada, USA and South Africa lost a match, but it was a close thing at Bristol in 1930; Australia's only tie in Britain.

Richardson led Arthur Mailey's Australians through Canada and USA, where three of their toughest games were against Harlem – mostly migrants from the West Indies – on a rough gravel track. Negro barrackers were clamouring to see 'Massa Don' so Vic turned to Bradman, saying, 'Put the pads on, Massa Don, it's your show.' Don got through without wounds.

In the stormy Adelaide bodyline Test Richardson stood guard 45 cm outside his leg stump but the ball kept flying at or about his head. Yet he was one of the least daunted by bodyline. In the first opening stand to pass 40 against it he took no risks until the total neared 100. Then he unchained his hook, causing two of the short-leg fielders to be moved back to safer distance. Woodfull walked along to remind him that, above all, they must deny Larwood the encouragement of a wicket. Richardson's epic reply: 'I'll show the bugger he can't bowl!' Several times he fell cheaply – once out for 0 and 0 – and one critic said his eyesight was failing. Sir Robert Menzies characteristically disposed of this at a dinner: 'I am sorry to have to agree. Watch Vic snapping up catches at silly-point! Every match, obviously because of failing sight, he has been standing closer and closer to the bat.'

Of those consulted, Richardson was the only player who opposed the Board's cabled protest to Lord's about bodyline. His appraisal of its likely effect was borne out. Years later I heard Larwood tell him, 'I only bowled it against the good players. It was a compliment really.' Richardson: 'If you lived to appreciate it!'

At forty he made the last of his 27 centuries, 185 in a 255 opening stand with H.C. ('Slinger') Nitschke against Queensland in Adelaide.

A sequence of seven clean-shaven skippers was broken when the Australian XI followed a leader whose clipped moustache was grown for adornment not use (his upper lip required no buttressing). Vic was third skipper from Sturt after Darling and Hill. Cricketers who played under him ranked Richardson among the highest as an enterprising tactician, notable for a gift of quick decision. With his flair for fun Vic proved that the ring-master on the field could be a ringleader in pranks – a fusion many had thought would mix no better than oil and water.

As a debonair captain on the first full Australian tour of South Africa, 1935–36, he led an unbeaten side though the Springboks had won their preceding series against England. He was ever-conscious of giving Test crowds a fair run for their money. When a gale continually blew bails off the stumps in a Durban Test he talked the umpires into sticking them on with chewing gum. As thunderclouds darkened a Johannesburg Test he told his batsmen not to appeal, as he felt they could reach about 400 to win. When McCabe was 189 and Australia needed 124 more, the fielding side appealed, saying Stan's cuts were endangering slip-fielders in the gloom.

When leg-spinner Bill O'Reilly showed his opinion of a placid pitch by simply rolling his arm over, his skipper's insight into human nature found a solution. Taking him off, he acted as if Bill were unworthy of another bowl. Allies kept needling the neglected bowler, asking 'Aren't you playing, Tiger?' Richardson gave him only a few overs on the last morning. He purposely lunched away from the team, then chose the psychological moment to throw Bill the ball. O'Reilly soon wrapped up an innings win.

The sophisticated adventurer who never side-stepped a challenge sent up no distress flare while keeping afloat on South Africans' submerging hospitality. At breakfast in Durban all-rounder Arthur Chipperfield reported to his skipper, doubting that he felt well enough to play. Richardson asked, 'Have you a feeling of nausea and does your tongue feel furry? Have you an ache here' (holding his forehead) 'and a pain here?' (feeling the back of his head). The sufferer nodded each time. Vic: 'I think you can play – I feel like that *every* morning.'

Baggage-master Bill Ferguson complimented Richardson on achieving the perfect blend between fun off the field and seriousness on it. Fergie likened Vic to Noble in being in the good books of every one of his players.

In return for his trust, all would work like slaves for the skipper. They were able to paint Durban, Johannesburg or Cape Town the rosiest of reds yet not forget for an instant that the man who helped them to it was captain of Australia.

V.Y. RICHARDSON ◼◼◼◼◼◼◼◼◼◼◼◼◼◼◼◼◼

Jack Fingleton, a star cover and infielder, ranked Richardson the greatest close fieldsman he knew. Fingleton recalls how on a cool Johannesburg day he asked couldn't he be given more to do. Vic replied, 'Would you like to join me?' So was born the double legtrap for O'Reilly, Richardson silly short leg and Fingleton silly square leg. Their effect on South African batting justified the physical risks when the Springboks tried to dislodge them.

At forty-one his sight seemed as sharp as that of players half his age. The Springboks were battling to avoid an innings defeat at Durban when his five catches off Grimmett and O'Reilly saved Australia from having to bat again. His undefeated side's 13 wins included three consecutive Tests with an innings to spare.

The hands that seized 211 cricket catches were little larger than average but fleshy fingers must have helped. In Tests he held 24 of 25 chances.

Through nineteen years of first-class cricket and thirty years of club play he was never off the field through injury or illness, either as fieldsman or batsman. He totalled 10,727 runs in 297 innings in first-class games.

Joining the Royal Australian Air Force in 1942 he was posted to duty in India. When I was surprised to see a man of such exceptional sight wearing spectacles he explained that poring over maps in India had affected his vision.

For twelve years he was Radio 5AD's sports editor. He was awarded the OBE for services to sport. Noted broadcaster Alan McGilvray ranked Vic tops for humour-spiced discernment of what really mattered in the middle.

Two years after completing *The Vic Richardson Story* he died at seventy-five on 29 October 1969. A road named after him leads to the Victor Richardson Gates at the oval that echoed with acclamation for his deeds.

SIR D.G. BRADMAN

23

The Knight

Don Bradman had at least one great advantage over other Test captains: himself batting for his own cause. None of the others could go in knowing he could score more runs than anybody else. Not only could but probably would. He could make whatever demand he wished on his own incomparable powers. The presence of his name in his neatly written batting order notified opposing skippers that they could not match him.

Bradman's position at the top of batting averages was as changeless as alphabetic order. He topped Australia's score in 24 Tests, close to half his international appearances.

In the memory of many bowlers 27 August 1908 is a date comparable with the Ides of March for Caesar. Donald George Bradman's birthday at Cootamundra was at once an augury of pleasure for countless onlookers and a day of ill-omen for opponents. The carpenter's son who developed ball-sense by playing alone with a golf ball, hitting and catching, grew to be the boy from Bowral, bound for fame and fortune, fame on the scoreboard and a fortune in his blockhole. Gapfinding shots hurried him along the trail, leaving barrackers howling for more, bowlers gasping for air and turnstiles squeaking for oil.

Nobody else got so close to 1000 runs in one series of five Tests. Nobody else clocked 300 in a Test day (309, his overnight stopover on his way to 334 at Leeds). Nobody equalled his 29 centuries in only 52 Tests. Nobody got near Don's Test career average of 99.94 for each dismissal.

In first-class games he is the only visitor to have twice tallied 1000 in England before June (1930 and 1938). His first-tour total 2960 is the highest by any tourist there. His average of 115 an innings on his third tour reigns as the highest by any batsman in an English year, an average above avarice. No other player has made 13 hundreds on one visit, or should I say visitation? He alone has run up eight 100s in an Australian season. His season's total of 1690 when he was twenty still awaits eclipse. He alone averaged a century every third time he went in. Almost two-thirds of his 100s were chanceless. Among Don's 117 hundreds in 338 first-class games he carried 37 on past 200, and six of these past 300, one of them past 450.

On his debut at nineteen for NSW at Adelaide Oval his 118 was like the first rim of the sun above the horizon. From a land agent's office he became a Mick Simmons sportsgoods salesman. Five 100s in his first nine games ushered him into his first Test at twenty. Omission from the second Test – an historic howler – made him cautious in the third, longer than four hours for his first Test hundred.

When a medium-pace ball from Alec Hurwood hit Bradman's stumps at 80 in Sydney in 1930 no bail fell – costliest piece of inertia in the annals of the game. He was 205 that Saturday evening ... 105 before Monday's lunch ... acceleration to 142 more before his captain's closure at tea stopped the slaughter of Queensland's bowlers, off whom he hit 49 fours making 452 not out in 415 minutes.

Four runs an over were devoured by his insatiable bat, so masterly at farming the bowling that reporters said he often received six balls an over. His enormous score lifted notable records from Bill Ponsford (437) – the world's highest in a first-class game, most fours in a Sheffield Shield match, fastest and youngest scorer of 400 (11 months younger than Ponsford had been in his 429 against Tasmania).

The rising runsman introduced himself to Britons in 1930 with 236 at Worcester, a handshake with English turf. Relishing the ball's slower pace from English wickets, he had ample reason for confidence, to a degree that impressed room-mates. Some mornings he would say, 'If I get a start today I'll make some runs.' A clean-living non-smoker, he soon made record-books burst their bindings.

When Australia faced 425 in the Lord's Test he felt his blue-ribbon 254 was technically his best innings. Lord's scoreboard could not cope with Australia reaching 700, so a loose 7 was hung on a nail. A barracker below kept chipping at Walter Robins, whose one wicket cost 172 runs. When the

7 plate fell off, it landed on the heckler's head. 'My only happy memory of the Test,' said Robins, after Australia won by seven wickets, levelling the series.

People felt Don looked the right type to be a batting hero, a fair-haired, blue-eyed, agile, shot-playing young chap. The animated enjoyment in his cricket, batting or fielding, came across to crowds. A wisp above 168 cm (5 ft 6¾ in), he had several centimetres less reach than big hitters and he used a short-handle bat. Weighing about 65 kg (10 st 4 lb) he had at least 12 kilograms less weight. Normally, sixes scarcely figured in his along-the-grass technique. Yet one off googly left-hander Leslie Fleetwood-Smith sailed to the upper deck of the Sydney pavilion. Such was the superb mechanism commanded by this lightweight athlete in size-six boots.

Watching Bradman's footwork, sudden hooks and daring pulls, I used to think his reflexes must be exceptional. Yet electrical tests at Adelaide University showed his reaction slightly slower than the average student's. His secret lay in peerless co-ordination of eyes, mind, feet and hands. Urged on by his mind, his muscles did not wait for loose balls. He set out to loosen the bowling, as a stonemason uses wedges to crack rock. His bat was not always as straight as the veranda posts on Cootamundra railway station. Bowlers had most to fear when it moved at less-conventional angles for hooks, pulls, sweeps, on-drives, cuts that kept slip-fielders pessimistic and cover-drives through spaces. His top hand's grip, farther back than normal, helped keep on-shots down. Though I reckon three-fifths of Don's runs came from back-foot shots, often deeper within the crease than anyone goes now, only Neil Harvey could leave the crease farther behind to pounce on a spinning ball. Don's hands lifted his 2¼-lb bat back towards second slip. From there he could hook or quickly line the blade up in the orthodox way coaches advise. One or two English judges had mistaken his originality for unsoundness. When they hinted he couldn't bat for nuts they must have meant for peanuts.

Advertising agencies hummed with ideas to exploit the renown of the young man monopolising headlines. His name on bats yielded royalties. Knowing his presence would attract crowds, organisers offered him appearance fees, such as £100 to be introduced from the stage. Off-field activities left Bradman less leisure than the other fourteen team members. Some saw so little of him away from grounds that they thought him not much more pally than a hermit crab. Being regarded as a loner was a price to be paid while he was so busy making himself a self-made man. Those who said he was chasing money were inaccurate. He was overhauling it.

In the third Test at Headingley Don sped to 105 before lunch, 220 by tea and a triple-century in the day (309 not out in 5¾ hours). Next day he was caught for 334. This grand score became the best-rewarded Test innings when Australian soap magnate A.E. Whitelaw telegraphed he was making a gift of £1000.

A player's request to stay on for experience at his employers' British headquarters failed when manager William Kelly pointed to the tour contract requiring the Australians to return as a team. While the liner was crossing the Indian Ocean a radio message brought a Board-sanctioned project for Bradman to leave the ship at Adelaide, two stops before his home port, and be flown on ahead. Thousands flocked to give the lone conqueror a hero's welcome. They were part of an advertising stunt in which a motor company, not his employers, presented him with a sports car. Manager Kelly deplored a breach of team spirit. As the radio message had come through Don's employers the blame lay at doors other than his. Too late he realised that being singled out caused an unfortunate impression. Some misconstrued it as an attempt to steal the limelight, as he says, but others felt it too much like Hollywood-style ballyhoo publicising a star, leaving his fellow players as anonymous as a bunch of extras. Factors over which he had little or no control were adding strands to a pattern that was no help to a future team leader.

If in his twenties he was more often on the fringe of a group than in the centre it could also partly have been a sensitive carry-over from excesses of practical joking on his first trip to Adelaide. They had him playing a piano without a shirt and brought guests from the lounge to give opinions on whether his side muscles were developed more by cricket or music. When a youth of nineteen in a strange city was sent through the night to a distant suburb on a fool's errand in response to a supposed SOS, it carried japemanship to a heartless extreme unlikely to be forgotten.

Offering £1500, three times the ruling rate, in 1931 Accrington tried to lure Bradman into the Lancashire League. Bradman was saved for Australia when he entered a three-tier contract to write for the *Sun*, broadcast over 2UE and sell sportsgoods for Palmer's store in Pitt Street.

A quarter-way through his career larger stumps made the wicket an inch wider and higher (9 in by 28 in). His scores refused to contract in proportion. Not one for stretching waking hours past midnight, he never batted on an empty wallet. His average was trying to keep ahead of his tax assessment. If there was bowling to be whipped, a single to be stolen, a cheque to be written, he was the one with the lash, dash and cash to do it ... a record to be broken, he would smash it. The chosen of the gods was making others' purple patches look like washed-out lilac.

The mainline runmaker's 226 at Brisbane in 1931 was his luckiest Test venture. It was a king-size filter knock, the biggest against South Africa while three chances filtered through the fielders. After that Bradman never seemed bursting to face left-arm swinger Neville Quinn with a new ball, yet he made hundreds in six consecutive games against the Springboks, topping his own record with 299 not out. His total 1190 still stands as a season's record against any touring side anywhere. That's cricket. On a sticky Melbourne pitch in the final Test, Quinn and Sandy Bell were rubbing retributive hands in anticipation of humiliating the record-breaker but in jumping from a bench in the team room he strained an ankle ligament and did not bat. 'Not cricket!' groaned Bell and Quinn.

Bowlers might have taken as their theme song Bruce George's catchy refrain *The World is Made for Somebody but Not for Us*. But the vast majority felt that with Don at the wicket and God in his Heaven all was well with the world.

To quote British historian C.E.M. Young, history is influenced less by actual happenings than by what people believe is happening (as was borne out by a record majority re-electing President Nixon before Watergate truths were tapped). A schoolboy day-dreaming of a career as glittering as Bradman's knows only half of it. The other half is full of strain on mind and muscle ... of unsparing determination to make every post a winner ... stresses of antagonism ... inescapable clashes of personality ... keeping a level head amid hero-worship.

192

As in other walks of life, especially business and politics, swift ascent of the ladder of success is apt to have perils. Fingers on rungs have a way of getting in the path of ambitious boots.

Just as post-war cricketers discuss Richards and Sobers, I remember Don being the most bowled-to and talked-about figure. Criticism tended to make the bulk of Australians close ranks behind their national hero. In allowing no shadow to settle on Bradman's image, a couple of his most devoted admirers showed less concern about casting shadows elsewhere. They disposed of fault-finding by simply blaming other players' jealousy. With a few exceptions that was a slur on a bunch of team-men of oft-proved sportsmanship. Arrows from the untiring bows of a couple of ex-player writers caused defenders to lean far the other way, as if all Don's attributes were akin to those of a saint. Did Bradman have flaws? You bet he did!

Film star Raquel Welch was once quoted as saying, 'All I want out of life is everything.' Fair enough, for one who has a lot to give. Accepted as almost essential in individualist sports, the me-first principle needs modification to fit into a team game without a rub somewhere. Nineteen times out of 20 – as he saw it, every time – what was best for Don Bradman was best for his side, a shared benefit, and fellow players were better off for it. The odd occasion lacking that ratio could not escape their notice. Don could bat like nobody's business, except his own. How the other half lived was their affair. Occasionally his single-mindedness affected members of his own side.

To millions of people the dazzling feat of making 299 not out against South Africa – then the highest Test score in Australia – was the all-absorbing thing at Adelaide Oval in February 1932. Along the way Bradman's eagerness to reach 100 led to Australia's fourth batsman, Kippax, being run out without facing a ball. Trying to reach 300 with two runs off the last ball of an over, Don changed his mind on the second because of smart fielding. He signalled his last partner, Pud Thurlow, to go back but the Queenslander could not beat Viljoen's throw to wicketkeeper Cameron. Partners' falls by the wayside might have been little noticed by the public generally but watching players were more attentive.

You might say a batsman gifted with so much had no need always to push his barrow so hard that it could run over the toes of others. To expect a man to act against the dictates of his nature would be like telling a river not to run. Without a substantial element of self-interest in his make-up, how could a player have the drive and perseverance to win his way to the top?

Batting's VIP usually cruised ahead at 56 to his partners' 40. His scoring shots were more frequent and his management of the strike gave him more balls. Unlike batsmen's displeasure with jackmen who hog the bowling and do little with it, I did not hear partners complain about Don's control of the strike. They accepted it as the prerogative of the superstar of the radio pre-television era. When Bradman raced to a century against Middlesex in 75 minutes, Len Darling, though ever-eager to hit the ball, cheerfully acted as running partner, content with 37 to the master's 100. As Reg Duff left the room to open an innings with Victor Trumper in 1902 he said smilingly, 'Vic is taking me for a run around again.' Charles Barnett, the Englishman nearest to a Test 100 before lunch, said, 'For years I had to play second fiddle to a truly great batsman Wally Hammond. I was lucky if I had an average of two balls an over to make my runs but he never ran me out.'

A slow walker – little livelier than a stroll – Bradman conserved his energy for fast running between wickets and in the field. For rapid inter-ceptions and high-velocity throwing he was in the first flight of outfielders and mid-offs up to the second world war. His catching did not have the same confidence. Playing in 52 Tests, plus one as twelfth man, he held 33 catches, three-quarters of the chances he reached.

England was looking for bowlers to wind Bradman's speedo back. As directed by Douglas Jardine with a bodyline field, Harold Larwood did so without umpires invoking the dragnet law against unfair play. Besides dulling appetite, prolonged anxiety and tension can cause a run-down state though physicians find no specific illness; some call it stress sickness. Bradman's doctor ruled him unfit for the first bodyline Test.

The anguish bodyline caused Bradman was not lessened because other batsmen, too, were high on the list of targets for fright. Seeing him draw back and slash or skip to the off and hook, Larwood found the open stumps more magnetic than constant repetition of bouncers at him. When Don retreated outside his leg stump his bat – so often a flashing broadsword – had to be used more like a harpoon. If, instead of a bodyliner,

194

Larwood pitched one straight, Whaler Bradman had to trust that, should his slash miss, the ball would clear his forsaken stumps. Other batsmen were dismayed to learn of his asking to be lowered in the batting order: the terror whose fiery breath had scorched bowlers had been subdued by the lance of bodyline into a Reluctant Dragon. Above all a realist, Bradman could see no sense in getting himself knocked about in fruitless martyrdom. In the Tests Woodfull faced 201 more balls from the bodyline trio, McCabe 94 more. In heading the Australian averages with 56 Don pillaged a fair whack of his runs from Verity, Allen, Hammond and Mitchell – 230 of his total 396 (off 529 balls). The victorious Englishmen were content with halving his Test average, leaving it ready for some panel-beating.

Almost as hard to bear as the bruising blows others suffered in doggedly trying to outlast the bodyliners was the souring knowledge that their places in the team were questioned by some critics whose thesis was that Bradman alone had evolved a way to combat bodyline. Don could not be blamed for that. After the Tests he said that no matter what methods had been adopted he could not conceive that Larwood's attack could have been ineffective. Every good judge I knew thought so, too.

Though Larwood winged him once, a blow on the left forearm, the bruise had long faded while the nervous tension remained. The Australian Board had failed to get a clear-cut assurance that the 1934 team touring England would not be targets for a repetition of bodyline. Preparations for the tour coincided with South Australia luring Don from Sydney with a job on an Adelaide stockbroker's staff. In addition to passing the pre-tour medical check Bradman saw Adelaide specialists who, because of his run-down state, advised complete rest on the voyage to England. Now vice-captain, he wished to skip the first match, but Woodfull induced him to play. Despite 206 at Worcester, Don did not look like his cool self and three centuries in his first 15 games were below the usual Bradman quota.

Coupled with the absence of Jardine, Larwood and Voce from the English XI, I believe a significant augury helped lessen Don's misgivings. It was captain Wyatt's refusal to accede to Bowes's request for more than four leg fielders when the 194 cm (6 ft 4½ in) Yorkshireman was using bumpers fairly frequently. On his way to 304 in the Leeds Test the resurgent

195

runmaster made 271 in a day. Mates had to pull off his flannels and carry him to the massage table.

After London surgery for appendicitis he was unfit to travel home with the team and was convalescent for seven months. Unavailable to tour South Africa in 1935–36 he was appointed captain of SA and re-entered Shield cricket with 112. Bowlers soon found he had regained health, stamina and the triple-century touch.

Don was one of Australia's captains who tasted extremes of frustration and fulfilment. Trying to condense the causes and effects into a single chapter feels somewhat like writing 'Waltzing Matilda's' verses on a gumnut. When he became Australia's skipper at twenty-eight he discovered that captaincy brought more problems than he had observed in 134 first-class games, including 28 Tests. Least enthusiastic about his assumption of the captaincy in 1936 were leading Australian bowlers. Among other things, he wanted to alter field settings successfully used by experienced spinners O'Reilly and Grimmett, wizards unimpressed by a batsman's theories about their craft. A captain telling O'Reilly and Grimmett what to bowl was like an editor telling a cartoonist what to draw.

Old-timers stared at the first field he set for speedman Ernie McCormick. Chipperfield, McCabe and Sievers as slips and Fingleton at cover, certainly, but what was the side's most awkward fieldsman, 15-stone Bill O'Reilly, doing close to the bat at silly leg, a post demanding agility? Going to earth as Worthington mishooked the first ball for a catch by wicketkeeper Oldfield, O'Reilly lumbered across to point to speak to his skipper, who then drafted Robinson to suicide corner.

After fast balls rearing from rain-affected wickets at his chin got him for ducks in Brisbane and Sydney Bradman said he had no desire to be Randolph Turpinised by a cricket ball. Reading of his two blobs, bowlers wondered was he rejoining the human race.

Many people could hardly believe Englishmen had downed Australia on their merits in the first two Tests. 'My own father,' said Bradman 'told me those Tests must have been rigged to ensure better gate takings at the last three Tests. I told him you can't rig a game of cricket but I can't say I convinced him.'

196

A sharp instance of his near-electronic quickness of mind came when sticky turf put bowlers on top through a Melbourne Saturday full of drama. After England's recognised batsmen went down fighting, Bradman's concern was to save Australia having to bat again that evening on such a surface. He told his bowlers not to try to get the lower division out. Even so, the last man was in when close fieldsmen heard skipper Gubby Allen mutter, 'Chuck it, I've had it.' About half an hour remained if the light lasted and rain kept away. Bradman: 'Did Gubby tell you what he's doing?' Umpires Scott and Borwick: 'We take it he's declared.' Don: 'He didn't say so?' Borwick: 'I see what you mean. I'll go and confirm it.'

Going to the Englishmen's room, Borwick explained the position to Allen. 'The little blighter!' exclaimed Gubby, 'Of course I've declared.' The delay reduced time to bat by four minutes.

Astonished when he and O'Reilly were asked to go in first tailender Fleetwood-Smith asked why. Bradman: 'Chuck, the only way you can get out on this wicket is to hit the ball. You can't hit it on a good one, so you've no chance on this one.' Fleetwood-Smith survived the evening and was caught the first time a ball touched his bat on Monday. Four others batted while the pitch was improving before Bradman came in seventh to join Fingleton. Their record stand added 346. Playing his longest Test innings, seven hours 38 minutes, Don made 270, highest by a Test captain in Australia. A chase after 688 was too much for England.

Any time would have been bad enough, but officialdom could scarcely have chosen a less-appropriate moment for carpeting four Test players. Straight from the ground where a victory had just turned the tide, vice-captain McCabe, O'Reilly, Fleetwood-Smith and O'Brien were called to the Victorian Cricket Association rooms. Four Board men handed them cigarettes when chairman Dr Allen Robertson read them a long screed. In *Cricket Conquest* O'Reilly describes how the reading conveyed suggestions: someone was not 100 per cent loyal to the captain, some players were indulging in too many alcoholic beverages, others were not trying to keep themselves fit. When the players asked were they accused of such things they were told no charges were made against them. It puzzled them that the whole team had not been called together. Board men bound the players over

197

not to discuss the meeting with any of the press. 'Press!' exclaimed one. 'Why, reporters followed us here.' H.W. Hodgetts hurried to the window to see whether the watchdogs for the public were on view. Cricket supporters were left guessing at the whole truth. One of the indignant players, McCabe, asked Bradman had he anything to do with it. Don assured them he knew nothing of it until he heard they were going. Later Bradman was told Board men had not consulted him, as a procedure to protect him, but he immediately felt he was suspected of having made adverse reports on the players.

In the Adelaide Test Allen became the only cricketer of any nationality who talked Don Bradman out. After an hour for 26 the hard-core record-breaker covered up as he watched a couple of off-balls from Allen go by. Waiting by the pitch for the wicketkeeper to return the ball, Gubby jested, 'Why don't you have a go at 'em – they won't give you out!' Hooking at the next ball the taunted batsman snicked it into his sticks.

After century stands with McCabe and Ross Gregory in the second innings he plugged purposefully on to 212. England had a heavy contract, 392 to win. With an inspired touch on the sixth morning, as the skipper handed the ball to Fleetwood-Smith he told him the result of the Test was in his hands. Responding to this well-timed stimulus, the lighthearted googly left-hander in his first over drew Hammond forward to an out-curving off-break which screwed back to skittle England's champion. Strolling over to his gleeful skipper, Chuck asked, 'Was that what you wanted, Goldie?'

While their captain was holidaying before the final Test, England's batsmen resented bouncers for Victoria by footballer-cricketer Laurie Nash, who never played a Shield match for the state. The Englishmen's concern when Nash was chosen in thirteen for the Test caused a flap in Board circles. The Board called on the three selectors to reduce the list to twelve, believing that the bouncy newcomer would be the one squeezed out. Feeling it unfair to exclude any player at that stage, W.J. Johnson and E.A. Dwyer told the chairman they would rather resign. Up spoke Bradman (twenty-eight, ambitious, in his first year as captain-selector): 'And that goes for me, too.' Showdown successful.

Expressing English batsmen's uneasiness Allen suggested a truce restricting use of bumpers, saying: 'We don't want a bouncer war but if this starts we will really turn it on.'

Bradman: 'No, that won't happen.' Allen: 'Why not?' Bradman: 'Because my bowlers are faster than yours and can bowl nastier bumpers. You know my attitude on this. I have never favoured it and never encouraged it.' Peace reigned on a quiet track in hot weather and Australia's 604 clinched the rubber.

Bradman is the only skipper whose side has rallied to win a Test series after having been down two-nil. His 270, 212 and 169 in consecutive Tests in Australia's hours of trial quashed all misgivings about captaincy reducing his run capacity. The top-of-the-bill performer could double as stage manager and the box office had more customers than any Test series before or since.

Master of his fate, Bradman scored only one fewer century (14) as captain in 24 Tests than he did in 28 Tests before becoming skipper. Through 80 Test innings his average output was 36 an hour. Usually he and his partners exceeded a run a minute – scoring speed brought Australia wins where time-taking hundreds would have prevented a finish. I think the rapidity of this human dynamo's runmaking and his confident demoralisation of the bowling did as much to win matches as the magnitude of his scores.

Batsmen who play out time, waiting for the morrow, have failed to learn from his career that tired bowling is the easiest to hit. In his record for a day's Test batting in Australia (223 in five hours against West Indies) he scored most runs in the last session. In two other Tests he added more than 100 after tea. Yet, as captain in 1938 he buckled down to a shut-out innings to deny England a win at Trent Bridge by batting almost throughout the last day for the slowest century of his career. Partners outscored him and his 144 not out occupied 6 hours 5 minutes.

With his urge to make runs he combined a less-obvious resolve to guard against premature loss of his wicket. A partner in an interstate match, left-hander Alex Marks, trying to hook Aboriginal fast bowler Eddie Gilbert, snicked the ball against his head. Alex's cap lessened the force of the blow and deflected the ball past the wicketkeeper. Dazed, Marks was wandering about the crease when Bradman walked to him and said, 'You were lucky, Alex.' Marks: 'Yes, it could have been worse if it hadn't hit my cap.' Bradman: 'Yes, you were lucky. If it hadn't touched your cap you'd have been caught behind.'

The monarch of the crease appreciated public acclamation for performance on the field but away from the grounds felt the drawbacks of being a public figure. Renown haunted his steps. To come out the front door of the team's hotel was to risk being mobbed by hero-worshippers waiting for a glimpse of the record-breaker. He had to case the joint to find a side or back door. He was not one for chit-chat but I never knew him to be stand-offish.

When a lull (for him) was ended by a mighty score and an editor suggested an interview on how it felt to return to century-making, Don modestly dodged it, saying, 'Why, I might make a couple of blobs next time!' I never heard a boastful word or saw a swaggering step. One writer misread his slow walk in to bat as 'asking for applause'. Don was fully alert to the advantage of giving his eyes' pupils time to adjust to broad daylight on his way from the room.

He kept both his head and his Australian accent. His voice, on the upper side of neutral, had less pace yet more penetration than most balls bowled to him. I never knew him to explode into the coarse slang which is the franker *lingua franca* of locker-rooms. The only time I heard him tell a story with permissive tinge was to emphasise the importance of practice. He quoted the hard work of the great composer J.S. Bach, father of twenty-three, said by a schoolboy to have 'practised on an old spinster in the abbey'.

Left-arm swinger Bob Hynes and leg slip Ray Little were elated when they dismissed Don for 0 at Sydney but an onlooker accosted their captain Alan McGilvray, saying 'You've spoilt my day. I came here to see Bradman make 100. I'll never come to Sydney Cricket Ground again.'

Seven of his 16 ducks befell him in Tests. In all games bowlers got him first ball six times and second ball three times. Often he did not look as sure collecting his first 20 as Ponsford but once his bat cleared its throat it spoke volumes – volumes of *Wisden*, that is.

With rare exceptions it was only when they could make screwing balls rear from sticky turf that bowlers felt his wicket was up for grabs. In 14 innings when English bowlers bundled the side out under 200 Don was outscored by team-mates 11 times and himself passed 15 only three times. His average shed a couple of decimal points. He could treat each flop as an interlude, soon to be forgotten when he got on a wicket worth batting on. Time proved him a surer judge of posterity than some others. Bradman's angle on sticky-wicket responsibilities is the reverse of quixotic:

> *Sometimes personal considerations intrude. Many a captain has sacrificed his own wicket to the detriment of his side because he feared the stigma of not attempting to set an example to his men. It is all very well to be gallant and heroic, but the captain's job embodies the welfare of the team, and if his own personal success is an integral part of victory he should act accordingly ... On several occasions I was compelled to rearrange our batting order as a matter of tactics because of the state of the wicket. It almost invariably succeeded. Some were unkind enough to suggest that my purpose was to avoid batting on a wet wicket. Of course it was; but only because such avoidance was necessary in the interests of the team.*

When SA wicketkeeper Charlie Walker was hurt in Sydney in January 1938, Bradman surprised people by taking over behind the sticks for both innings. With a Test tour coming up I was one of those who thought he ran a needless risk, seeing that even practised international glovemen are liable to have fingers broken. When I asked Sir Donald whether, on reflection, he had been wise to keep wicket he waved the question aside as if it were a distant leg-bye.

Like Woodfull in 1934 he was one of three selectors of the side he took to Britain in 1938. The curtain stays down over whether co-selectors over-rode him about any players but the Englishmen were relieved to see the O'Reilly-Grimmett duo prematurely dissolved. Outstanding wicketkeeper Don Tallon was left behind, though other states' bowlers used to say they wished they had Queensland's gloved genius keeping to them. Coupled with inadequate pace support for speedman McCormick, those miscalculations doomed the side to struggle. England mainly held the initiative except for a win snatched at Leeds where O'Reilly and Fleetwood-Smith shared 17 wickets and Bradman made the only century. At the Oval a stumping at about 40 was the only chance Leonard Hutton gave in piling up 364 in 13 hours 20 minutes. When Hutton passed his 334 Don, fielding close, was first to shake the Yorkshireman's tiring hand. England's players thought Len looked more worn at each interval – but that was nothing to the state of O'Reilly and Fleetwood-Smith's fingers as Tiger ploughed through 85 overs and Chuck 87. After hours defending, deflecting and placing, Hutton hit a ball past the bowler. O'Reilly: 'Congratulations, son – I didn't know you had the strength.'

By amassing 903 for seven wickets the Englishmen pinned on Bradman the unwelcome badge of fielding captain with the highest Test total against him. Going down by an innings and 579 was the most crushing defeat any country ever suffered. Those reverses were two of the rare counter-weights opponents ever put on scales tilted by Don's unprecedented successes. It was a measure of respect for his run-potential that Hammond did not declare England's innings until after Bradman cracked an ankle bone, going over as he bowled from a foothole worn by O'Reilly. Two short because of Bradman's and Fingleton's leg injuries, the Australians had no chance. In batting they put pride second to sparing their overworked bowlers having to go on again, remembering the team still had six matches to play.

Though contracts since 1921 forbade the presence of wives on tour the 1938 team had requested the Board to permit wives to join the home-warding ship at Colombo. Don was finding the stresses of captaincy so excessive that manager Bill Jeanes cabled the Board to permit his wife Jessie to join Don in England after the last match. The Board's refusal led to a team meeting in Derbyshire asking Jeanes to cable: 'Captain's responsibilities colossal. Perhaps Board unaware players unanimously support request. No question embarrassment others.'

The refusal hurt Don so deeply that Jeanes cabled the chairman saying Bradman had prepared a public statement involving his retirement from international cricket. He had persuaded Don to withhold it pending the Board's consideration of the players' request. Wiser after the 1930 variation, the chairman held another vote on alternative proposals, as a result of which this cable settled the issue:

After careful consideration team's request Board of opinion no such

privilege be given Bradman which is not available to team as whole.
However Board agrees that wives of all members team may join
husbands in England after last match provided Board involved no cost
whatever as result.

Wives joined Bradman, McCabe, Fleetwood-Smith and manager Jeanes
after the last match. The drafted retirement did not come to light but Don
said English tour captaincy involved such exhausting pressures that he
resolved 'Never again.'

Cups of tea have always been his favourite drink at all hours. If poured
by him, they tend to be pale with milk. In his playing days liquid assets
interested him much more than bottled beverages. To unwind after a day's
exertions the reigning champion liked listening to music in his room In
Farewell to Cricket he says:

> *I was often accused of being unsociable because at the end of the day*
> *I did not think it my duty to breast the bar and engage in a beer-*
> *drinking contest. At least I made no attempt to interfere with the*
> *habits of others, and if I thought my most important need was a cup*
> *of tea I had as much right to complain of their late entry into the*
> *dining room as they had to complain of my absence from the bar.*

Use of the term 'beer-drinking contest' reveals how far his concept was
from the participants' idea of the nature of the evening gatherings, getting
to know each other in ways scarcely possible between fine leg and mid-off.
Its chief benefit was relaxation. (Relaxation was a state which I know he
appreciated in mellower years of life when, without over-indulgence, the
ex-abstainer became an authority on the red wines of South Australia.)

As red shoes took command of ballerina Moira Shearer in a fine film,
white boots generally led Don a dance at the wicket, as if they were in
charge. Swiftly-run threes seemed not to leave his 96 cm chest shortwinded.
On a 37°C afternoon in a Melbourne Test bowlers were used in two-over and
three-over spells. McCabe, around 50, told his skipper-partner, 'I'll have to
give it away.' Bradman asked him to hang on half an hour until tea. 'No more
running,' muttered Stan. The only scores for several overs were boundary
hits. About an hour after tea Stan gasped 'Braddles, I'm goosed – can't
stick it any longer.' He was caught for 112 of a 249 stand. When Bradman,

165 not out at stumps, slumped on to a seat others took his pads off.

When the Englishmen were persuaded to come out in 1946 for the first post-war Tests in Australia Bradman was still subject to twinges of fibrositis in the back that had caused his discharge from the Army physical training branch in 1941. Gastric troubles made him look older than his thirty-eight years and a strained leg muscle caused a recurring limp. Advised by his doctor not to overdo it, Don was not content to bat 3¼ hours at Brisbane for his customary century, with Australia well launched at 213 for two wickets. He went on two more hours to 187.

Having studied the Laws of Cricket to pass a Sydney examination for umpires, he had a thorough grasp of what those complex rules provide and permit. As Australia's innings continued into the third day the captain of the batting side had the say whether the pitch should be given its morning spruce-up with mower, broom and roller. On that Monday Bradman left it untouched, as was his legal right. After an hour or so England's batsmen became the main occupiers of a track unshaven since Friday. A changed rule now directs umpires to have the pitch cut every second day. On Ernie Toshack's first day on a sticky wicket the left-hander cheerfully accepted the role of looking a dunce in the crowd's eyes when his skipper took him to the Brisbane pitch and patted a spot to show how much farther to send the ball up.

Batsmen finding their strokes blocked acknowledged that Bradman made an exact science of field placing. His blockades were so effective that he seemed disinclined to disturb their working by posting more close fieldsmen. Googly left-hander George Tribe held discussions with him for a couple of minutes in a Sydney Test before he agreed to try a second slip for a while and a short mid-off later. Bradman gave more explicit directions than others to batsmen, especially when partnering them.

While Bradman was rattling off five 100s in six games against the Indians his mind and Amarnath's were shrewdly weighing the effects of an over-supply of new balls – an experimental rule still having harmful after-effects.

In his fresh start with a band of soon-famous cricketers Bradman acted to prevent any carry-over of pre-war misunderstandings. For instance, a quiet chat with each new player in his 1948 side went somewhat in this strain:

You've probably heard rumours about my relations with other players. I've been criticised a lot, but when I was a young boy from the country in a team of world-famous players they wouldn't speak to me. They seemed to resent me.

He appreciated leading a team whose respect for his knowledge of the game was as deep as their faith in his judgement.

Early in the 1948 tour news of his two-hour 187 and Australia's 721 in a day against Essex notified every Englishman that his team – the first to have seventeen players – bulged with strokesmen to play tunes on boundary pickets.

Above all, the bowling at Bradman's command was exceptionally formidable – probably the most overpowering force to cross the English coast since 1066. With red new balls plentiful enough to make a snooker table jealous, Lindwall, Miller and Bill Johnston formed a three-pronged fast attack that mostly left batsmen bereft of an answer. Relief bowlers aimed to keep runs down until the next new ball fell due – usually by 130 and twice before 90. To call in a new ball Bradman never hesitated to interrupt good spin bowling. In the course of getting 5 for 40 at Lord's Toshack was taken off twice, at 2 for 14 and 4 for 25. Including good all-rounders, his XI usually had six bowlers; wherever Don looked in the field he was likely to meet eager eyes of someone worthy of a turn. At least four of them thought him the greatest captain they had known. Field placing had a friendly air; if it were for Ian Johnson or Loxton he placed an arm on their shoulders. Metaphorically, he never 'put the arm' on Lindwall to bowl extra overs.

I never saw actions at the wicket show disapproval of an opposing side's tactics so plainly as Don's in the first innings at Trent Bridge. Three were out when Australia went ahead of England's meagre 165 and captain Norman Yardley in desperation resorted to leg theory. Bradman and Hassett would not attempt strokes at leg-side balls with the risk of being caught by six onside fielders. As balls passed six inches to a foot outside his legs Don often stood leaning on his bat with legs crossed, sometimes with hand on hip as if nothing had been bowled. I believe his attitudes were to direct onlookers' attention to the negative tactics but some of the crowd misread the message. Slow clapping was heard, reproachful cries of 'Come on Don' and a bye was greeted with derisive applause.

Jack Young, a good-looking left-hand spinner who sent along 11 consecutive scoreless overs, disliked having to bowl so tightly against his will. His discontent was eased by a laugh when he heard of a broadcaster's comment, 'That's the end of another Young maiden.' Playing that day were seven Englishmen who had been in the 1947 Adelaide Test when another fielding captain (guess who?) placed six fielders on the leg side for Toshack at a time when Australia was leading two-nil in the series. The dulling leg theory was much more flagrant at Trent Bridge, as it came from both ends and four bowlers figured in it. In neither city was it the sort of spectacle I like watching or the sort to induce crowds to feel that Test cricket is a game worth paying to watch.

In that Trent Bridge Test I blinked softheartedly as Lindwall, who had broken down with a strained groin, came in to bat when Australia was 200 ahead. Ray wouldn't have a runner, not liking one. Batting almost two hours, he doubled up in pain several times. The man needed as spearhead of Australia's attack would have been better off the field with physiotherapist Arthur James as partner. Ray recovered in time for the second Test, but it was touch and go. When I raised this with Sir Donald many years later he could not recollect the occurrence. These batsmen captains!

The power unit rolled on, with scarcely a flicker of the master-touch at the controls. One visible hitch was his attempt to induce Miller to bowl at Lord's when the all-rounder's side was sore from a strain at Sheffield. Miller handed the ball back and the skipper had to recall Bill Johnston from heading toward the boundary. Happening before a packed Saturday crowd, with the gates shut, caused a buzz not to be forgotten. For the first time Tests in England were lengthened to five days – an opening for Don's side to become the first to win four Tests on a tour of Britain.

With every city wanting to see him in 1948 he played in 25 of the 34 games, having less rest than anyone else. Usually turning out in Saturday games he took off midweek days, which were also more convenient for business.

His motto could have been 'Nothing succeeds except success'. It continued to crown his efforts into his last year. Experience saw him through many remarkable innings against post-war bowlers without his reproducing the batting that afflicted their predecessors when he was between twenty and thirty. With all respect to A.J. Liebling, the world waited twenty years in vain for a good big man to beat the good little man. The closest anyone came to fulfilling this was Alec Bedser with sharp new-ball indippers when Bradman was nearing forty.

Through most of his career he was head-and-shoulders above the next best, yet I think him too modest to claim that it was more than that. While bringing a glow to the scoreboard, his dominance sometimes cast shadows on fine players who, figuratively, came up to his armpits. Australia's sole century at the Oval in 1948, Arthur Morris's 196 run out, received discounted notice in the stir about Eric Hollies's unpicked wrong'un bowling Bradman for 0, second ball, in Don's last Test innings. The Oval crowd's all-the-way ovation and the grouped English XI's cheers by the wicket emotionally deepened Bradman's desire to play a farewell innings of his own standard. Imaginative scribes started a myth that the stirring reception brought tears to his eyes, blurring his sight of the ball. Sir Donald discounted that as a great exaggeration. As a witness, I recall his sighting Eric Hollies's first leg-break well enough to play it quietly to the off. He simply did not detect the next one was a wrong'un. It scraped his bat's inner edge on the way to the stumps to cause the most dramatic duck he ever made in England. Like a great actor struck dumb, he was applauded off. As he unbuckled his pads he exclaimed, 'Fancy doing that!'

Though it would have redressed the misfortunes of the squared 1938 rubber, to win the Test series on a successful tour of England was not enough. Amid the Australians' glee after their Leeds triumph settled the 1948 rubber, he warned them of the danger of a let-down. He earnestly urged them to make every effort to achieve the last of his ambitions: to lead his side through Britain unbeaten. As a fellow-traveller I felt that white-washing all opposition mattered much less in the overall glory than the plea-sure-giving progress around cities and towns still enduring a carry-over from wartime rationing. The stroke-rich batting excited feeling akin to the Australian people's relish of the West Indies twelve years later. The fielding was spectacular yet sure. Headed by Lindwall, Johnston and Miller the bowling at his command was awesome, making some opposing batsmen look awful. In war-weary Britain his team's cricket whipped up interest in the game as never before. The bright shield was only rarely streaked by a merciless glint, as when several bumpers were flung at a recovered batsman with a patched brow or a new ball was summoned in the finishing overs of an expiring game to uproot a Lancashire player on 99.

Success in four series out of five against England and India made his Test tally 15 wins, three losses, six unfinished. The nearest he came to losing a rubber was the level series in 1938.

Bradman's main share in 29 Test wins was top-score or equal top-score in 19 of them. Not counting his Oval disablement, his inability to top the score more than twice in 11 defeats confirms a common belief that batting for a losing side, like betting on losing horses, is harder going for various reasons. Don't assume that the contrast was as sharp as it sounds. Australian wins could have been losses without his dramatic 103 not out at Melbourne and his cat's-eye 103 in what Cardus called 'Leeds' unkindly light'. In five other Tests Australia trailed on the first innings before his second-innings hundreds swayed or saved the match.

Outsiders' suggestions that he was a disciplinarian completely miss his control of his players. His kitbag held no rod of iron. Players knew they were expected to turn out fit and anyone failing in this would jeopardise his Test place. None failed.

Opponents and critics who called him a ruthless captain, quoting instances, chose a word I think too harsh. Competitive to an extreme degree would be nearer the reality. He was no believer in other-cheekmanship. Adverse events left him implacable in vengeance, inexorable in pressing for every advantage existing laws permitted. He was relentless, striving for crushing victories to weaken enemy resistance for the series. Far from breaking new ground or ageing wickets, he was in most cases doing what he had seen others do. No bowlers who thought him stony-hearted and no batsmen harried by his speedmen were treated so pitilessly as Don and his co-players had been by the director of bodyline, the one who could justly be called ruthless. Bill Edrich and others thought Bradman callous when accusing him of laughing at their concern about bouncers from Lindwall and Miller. After an exchange of bouncers at Old Trafford in 1948 Edrich was rubbing a tender elbow when Bradman said, 'I'm sorry about this Bill, but when the boys get a bit wild they are hard to control.' Don spoke to Miller. His wells of compassion had not entirely dried out.

At a time when Australia had 645 on the board players noticed him chuckling in the room as a Brisbane thunderstorm doomed England to disaster on a sticky wicket. His frank explanation included:

> In my first Test match England, though leading by nearly 400, went in again and left us over 700 to attempt in our last innings, with two men out of action ... In my last pre-war Test England scored more than 900 before Hammond declared and I couldn't bat because I'd broken my ankle bowling. Now things have swung the other way do you blame me for being happy?

Never blasé, he was a keen appealer to the end. He was thirty-eight when an English batsman chipped him for appealing from gully for lbw; 'That was a pretty good appeal from your position.' (From the umpire's angle it was not out.) As one of the captains (not the first) accused of unfairly using the heavy roller to the disadvantage of opponents, he replied that if the laws clearly indicate what is allowable it is scarcely right to attack the captain for observing the law. One historic conqueror of most of the known world was revered by the Greeks as Alexander the Great. Those whose lands he ransacked called him The Vandal. It depends whose side you are on. When Englishmen heard of Bradman's retirement, the inimitable Robertson-Glasgow likened their relief to that of the Romans at news of the death of Hannibal.

A testimonial match in Melbourne yielded him £9342, easily a record for an Australian. Everything the Midas of batsmen had touched – except bat-handles – turned to lucre. The thousands of pounds he made when inflation was a backward infant started him on the millionaire train. They seemed like chickenfeed when Sir Donald read of soccer wizard Pele being Brazil's topmost taxpayer, Bruce Crampton pocketing more than a million dollars without being the world's No. 1 golfer. Don's worst enemy could not say he failed to give cricket a good run for his money.

On bats, books and scraps of paper, the most-sought Australian auto-graph remained neat, though his total of signatures probably exceeded his 28,067 runs. At a New Lambton school function young captain David Low was shyly pawing at his unruly hair when the honoured guest pulled out his comb and flattened it for him.

Cricket suffered a backwash from his retirement. The best players were now denied recognition they would have received in pre-Bradman days and scoring pace fell short of the exalted standards achieved by the only Australian Test cricketer honoured with a knighthood. Regulars became less regular, casuals more casual, strangers no longer asked their way to the grounds. Noting this, editors allowed less space. We should have expected this. Java has a proverb, 'Nothing grows in the shade of the amya tree.'

Grasping the bat raised an over-developed muscle between his right thumb and forefinger. It caused an unconventional grip at golf yet he got down to scratch for a while in 1959.

After Sir Donald made his pile (of runs, I mean) he captained Adelaide Stock Exchange XI in social games and appeared for a Taxation XI described as made up of taxation officials and taxpayers. His qualifications to represent the latter group were beyond challenge: stockbroker, investor, director of 16 companies. When his doctor advised him to reduce pressure of work he ceased broking – a drop in income rather than give up his cricket interests as a Test selector, committeeman and a Board member who had notable terms as chairman. Mutterings about selectors favouring some states could not be proved against SA's nominee. Of 119 Test players he led or sent into the field, 41 were Victorians, 34 New South Welshmen, 21 South Australians, 13 Queenslanders and 10 Western Australians.

The good fortune of the cricket field and business world did not extend to his family's health. At twenty-three, five years before he became captain, he married Jessie Menzies, a charming brunette, unfailingly gracious. Sadly their first boy lived only two days. Stricken at thirteen, their son John made such a fighting recovery from a polio frame that he set the state 120-yard hurdles record on Adelaide Oval. He became a lecturer in law at Adelaide University and had a property at Stirling in the hills. Complexes from living in the shadow of a father's fame led to John changing his surname at thirty-two to Bradsen. The Bradmans' daughter Shirley never enjoyed the health parents wish they could hand down. After a virus infection in 1970 a well-wisher said to Sir Donald, 'I believe you've not been too well.' Bradman: 'Don't believe a word of it – it's a story spread around by my undertaker and florist.'

When Billy Ibadulla, a Test century-maker for Pakistan, was coaching in Tasmania in 1969 he saw a 1934 film and was astonished by Bradman's balance while batting. No player of Ibadulla's day could match it. When Baron Learie Constantine said Bradman could still score 300 in a day, despite modern tactics, many young players believed that defensive field placing and bowling made cricket such a different game that it was no longer possible. When I discussed this with Sir Donald, he said:

> The only answer I can make is that some people were surprised when Barry Richards in Perth in 1970 proved that a batsman could still do so. At the time I was delighted, if only at proof that it could be done. But if a fielding side set out to place leg fields and bowl medium-pacers, making their first objective to restrict scoring, I'd say nobody could make 300 in a day.

As National Librarian, Sir Harold White rated Sir Robert Menzies and Sir Donald Bradman as the two Australians of his time who best succeeded in achieving their ambitions. It took all Sir Robert's eloquence to persuade Sir Donald to reappear at fifty-four as captain of the Prime Minister's XI against an English XI on Canberra's Manuka Oval. Knowing the 10,000 crowd wanted to see Bradman make runs, Brian Statham bowled with moderated menace. From a bottom corner of the bat a ball strayed between Bradman's boots. When it was heeled against the stumps bails fell. So did Statham's jaw.

After Sir Donald ceased representing stockbroking on the Adelaide Rotary Club they put him on the senior active list, so the tiny Rotarian wheel continued to appear on his lapel – a little wheel on a big wheel. He was made a Companion of the Order of Australia in 1979, and was the first male inducted in the Sport Australia Hall of Fame on 10 December 1985.

The NSW Government, coincidentally, had then just granted the first $100,000 to an Australian cricket museum named for the Don, set alongside the oval where he had begun his junior career six decades before. The opening of the first stage of the Bradman Museum on 14 October 1989 was the occasion for a rare public appearance by Sir Donald Bradman, who ruminated on the continuous flood of correspondence he received.

The knight told an appreciative audience:

There was one from a lad who said: 'My name is Terry White and I'm ten years of age and I've admired you ever since I was young.' The next one wasn't quite so pleasant. It said: 'I know this request comes rather late, but I should always regret if it became too late!' ... And I also referred to some letters indicating what the future calling of a boy might be. There was a potential insurance agent because the letter said: 'Don't be surprised if you get two letters from me. I posted two in case this one goes astray.'

Then there was the potential PM who finished up: 'PS – Keep this signature, it will be valuable one day.' But somebody must have heard that on air because not so very long afterwards I received a sequel when a chap wrote in similar fashion and said 'PS – Don't bother to keep this signature, it will never be worth anything.' That has me stumped, I don't know what his occupation is going to be.

Tour matches involving select XIs at Bradman Oval have become part of the Australian summer scene while Bradman Museum curator Richard Mulvaney has collected a fine range of exhibits across the full history of the game in this country. Mulvaney, a BA in pre-history from Canberra's Australian National University, also polices use and misuse of the Bradman name with zeal: the unauthorised manufacture of a Bradman Bitter Ale by Queensland's Power Brewing in 1993, for instance, was smartly quashed after discovery of an empty stubby during a match between a Bradman XI and South Africa. With the funds from a Channel 9 telethon on 29 May 1996, the completion of the $4.5 million museum was timed to coincide with the Don's 88th birthday.

Bradman's career could be called the boom before the bust that never came. All men may be born equal but some are more equal to an occasion than others. I always remember him as a man who made everyday events of what would in others have been delusions of grandeur. In fact, seeing a film showing Don walking away, a player said, 'Is that what his back looked like? I never saw it before.'

212

W.A. BROWN

24

A Touch of Class

To get the best out of a cello, musicians say, a cellist must live with the instrument. Something similar could be said of Bill Brown and his bat. This classical opening batsman did just about everything except sleep with it under his pillow. Bill and his bat were inseparable companions in long innings and in practice sessions but their attachment went beyond that. Behind dressing-room benches he would swing it gently, forever training it to keep to a straight and narrow path close to his legs. His bat was so well drilled that in matches it responded to the slightest pressure of caressing fingers. Crowds would often have liked to see much more pressure applied.

He adopted the adage that practice makes perfect for every shot. He played them all in text-book style – but only if satisfied that the oncoming ball was suitable. His choice of shot was well studied, like a golf champion choosing a club from his bag of 14. By their remarks, barrackers must have felt he was sometimes in a Brown study.

Brown is the only born Queenslander who has captained Australia, though a product of Sydney cricket who had entered Test ranks before being lured back to his birth-state.

William Alfred Brown's father, a Toowoomba farmer, moved the family to Sydney two years after his son's birth on 31 July 1912. From Canterbury district junior games on matting Bill moved up through Marrickville grades. In his seventh game for NSW he made 154 in Brisbane and in his 13th first-class match 205 against Victoria. To win a place as supporting opener to Woodfull and Ponsford in England in 1934 Brown had to outbid Jack Fingleton, a man of proven courage against bodyline, Keith Rigg, a Test century-maker against South Africa, and a South Australian left-hander Holmesdale Nitschke, owner of the 1973 Perth Cup winner Dayana. When the *Sun* printed the team Bradman would send, Don named Brown, twenty-one, for this place.

The first time Bill opened a Test innings his 105 showed his liking for the Lord's wicket. In using bowlers' pace for his shots rather than his own power, he reminded me of the carpenters' saying, 'Let the tools do the work.' He felt he was there to take the bowling, not to take it on. His batting was not fast but fastidious. From his Colt days he had no surging impulses to discipline. The pop tune I heard him croon most was *If There Were More than 24 Hours a Day.*

For artistry, Brown's leg-glancing could be mentioned in the same breath as Archie Jackson's. Delicate glides played a larger part in his run-making than they did for Jackson. I never doubted there were 90 degrees in the quarter of the field between square leg and the wicketkeeper's left boot until Brown made it look as if there must be more. His straight bat's welcoming blade would angle as if it had an inbuilt protractor.

Around middle height, about 176 cm (5 ft 9½ in), he stood easily erect. Unlike other Australian right-handers, he held an upright bat's face full to the bowler. As calm blue eyes in a pleasant boyish face scrutinised the bowling, his turned-up nose showed traces of long exposure to the sun. People say that with the leg-slip and leg-gully fieldsmen of the 1970s no man could glance so freely without being caught. No man except Bill Brown, perhaps. His forward-sloping bat mostly rolled the ball along the grass. Anything later than some glides off his toes would have involved chiropody. His deft touch could play cat-and-mouse with a fine-leg fieldsman placed to cut off a stream of strokes. If a moonbeam glide caused this man to be moved finer, a fraction more timber would deflect the ball wider past the exasperated fielder.

Not one of the hookless opening batsmen, he played the shot – in moderation. As a fast bowler delivered, Brown took his right foot back toward the off stump. Besides bringing him behind the ball this movement gave him a fraction longer to decide his shot. Cuts brought most of his off-side runs. When a half-volley approached on an acceptable line he would unwrap his cover drive, everything gracefully in place from the moment his front foot led into the stroke. You might have a long wait for it, but it was worth waiting for.

Brown was the most serene batsman I ever saw play for Australia. The only time his serenity was ripped asunder was late on an August afternoon in 1934 when fast left-hander Bill Voce hurled two overs of unashamed bodyline, packed leg field and all. Their ferocity made Bill forget his hook and duck his cap from several head-high bouncers while the Notts crowd, Larwood sympathisers, laughed derisively. Brown was not out overnight and it was not easy to sleep on the most feverish night a touring team in Britain has known. Discussions resulted in a protest closure at a total of three runs being averted by Notts officials keeping Voce off the field on the last day. Amid resentful onlookers' heckling, Brown gave an early slip-chance but settled down to make 100 not out in 2½ hours against an attack that could no longer apply a Voce-like grip.

They nicknamed Brown 'Nugget' after a shoe polish. He was always one of the better fielders in Test sides noted for their out-cricket. On or off the field he liked having everything just right. On tour his first action at the breakfast table was to adjust all the cutlery to the exact juxtaposition that would be required when the food arrived.

His partnership of 233 with Fingleton against South Africa at Cape Town in 1936 was the first double-century Test opening for Australia and one of this pair's three century stands in the series. Queensland Cricket Association lured the successful opener back north at twenty-four with an offer combining a job as a car salesman with £260 a year as coach. Later he founded a flourishing sportsgoods business.

On his second visit to Britain, the Lord's Test made him one of the stars of the first cricket match put to air for viewers – at that time, 1938, there were 17,000 television sets in the United Kingdom. Following Walter Hammond's grand, six-hour 240, Bill's 206 not out in six and a quarter hours did not cause smoke to rise from the back of those sets but the charm of his style gave viewers a favourable impression of Australian batsmanship. A Farnes bumper bruising him over the collar-bone had no visible effect on his coolness. His eighth partner, O'Reilly, explosively helped avert a follow-on. Aided by a let-off, Brown carried his bat through the innings of 422 off 121.4 overs. On the field from the start to 5 pm on the fourth day, he came through a prolonged trial of concentration. He held the record for

216

highest score by a player carrying his bat through a complete Test innings for 34 years until Glenn Turner's 223 not out against West Indies off 187.5 overs at Kingston in 1972.

Brown's highest score, 265 not out in six hours against Derbyshire at Chesterfield, came after he had twice been put down early. He earned a place in *Wisden's* Five Cricketers of the Year. Because of the ball's repeated jarring of the bat against his hand, Bill was one of the batsmen who complained of an ache in his right palm near the thumb. O'Reilly told him, 'There's one sure way to get rid of that.'

Brown: 'What is it, Tiger?'

O'Reilly: 'Get out sooner.'

Brown's 1057 runs in 11 innings in the 1938–39 Australian season included another bat-through achievement, 174 not out as Queensland captain against South Australia in Adelaide.

At twenty-eight he married Barbara Hart, a shipping company receptionist, on 7 December 1940, one year to the day before Japan's armed forces struck in Malaya on their southward drive to New Guinea and the Coral Sea. Bill took Barbara on a honeymoon trip to Queensland's Sydney match and a Melbourne game, Bradman's XI v. McCabe's XI. Her beauty was much admired in those cities but some Queensland officials looked at it differently and moved to add to his contract as state coach a clause forbidding taking his wife on a team's tour. By 1943 he was a pilot officer in the Royal Australian Air Force.

In the world's first post-war Test match Brown led Australia against NZ at Wellington in 1946. He lost the toss to Walter Hadlee, father-to-be of bowlers Dayle and Sir Richard, but three bowlers found enough moisture in the pitch to rout NZ for 42. The only partnership passing 32 in the match came when Barnes joined Brown in a resourceful stand of 109. Amid NZ's second slump, O'Reilly's left knee began to give way – an outcome of damage when a boot burst in Sydney. Seeing him having trouble reaching the wicket, Brown said to Australia's greatest bowler 'This might be it, Tiger. What do you wish to do? Stay on if you like.' O'Reilly struggled on until he had taken three for nine off seven overs, making his match figures eight for 33 and his total 144 wickets in 27 Tests.

Near the end Brown had to choose between two bowlers playing their first Test, leg-spinner Colin McCool and off-spinner Ian Johnson:

> I told them 'I want to be fair to both you fellas, so I'll toss a coin to decide.' Then I told Colin to have the next over from O'Reilly's end. By the time he got on, only one wicket was left and Col's second ball ended the match early on the second afternoon.

A broken thumb put Brown out of matches during England's first postwar tour of Australia. Bowling against an Australian XI in Sydney in 1947 Indian left-hander Vinoo Mankad stopped at the wicket and pointed to Brown's feet well outside the non-striker's crease. Two overs later Mankad stopped again and brought the ball down to knock the bails off. When Queensland played the Indians Mankad let Brown off with a warning. In a Sydney Test a few weeks later Bill was two feet out as the left-handed spinner brought his arm around and tipped the bails off. When umpire Andrew Barlow signalled Brown out for 18 the crowd applauded, as if commending the bowler for his vigilance. Bill sadly walked off like a man caught by the three-card trick a third time.

Controversial letters to newspapers accused Mankad of an unsporting act. Hearing that the bowler was upset, Bill telephoned him. Telling Vinoo not to worry, he said he was to blame. Putting Ken Archer behind the stumps, Brown and Tallon staged a burlesque in the last two overs of Queensland's next game at Adelaide Oval. With his first ball each of these irregular bowlers tried to run out a South Australian but neither Reg Craig nor Dick Niehuus had beaten the pistol.

In his third Lord's Test in 1948 Morris and Barnes opened the innings. Sent in sixth, Brown made 24 and 32 – his last Test. His total in 22 Tests was 1592, at almost 47 an innings. He was then close to thirty-six, a father of three sons. 'They were well spaced, like my centuries,' he remarked.

After his second tour of NZ as captain of an unbeaten side, Brown retired at thirty-seven with a career average of 51 for 13,838 runs in 189 first-class games. Of his 39 centuries, 23 were made abroad. On English turf he was rewarded with 100 for every six innings, compared with a ratio of 100 every ten innings in his own country.

For the first time since 1929 a born Queenslander had a voice in Test selections in 1952–53 when the Board appointed Brown with Ryder (Victoria) and South Australian captain Phil Ridings. A Test XI without a Queenslander underwent hostile demonstrations by Brisbane barrackers not yet aware that ill-health was affecting master-keeper Tallon. Angry protests were chalked on windows of Brown's sports-store in George Street. After helping choose the 1953 tour team he gave up Test selectorship with relief.

Brown still lives in Brisbane, enjoying a renown for his modest demeanour and skills as a raconteur. MCC officials thought so highly of his conversational flair when he attended the 1993 Lord's Test that they seated him beside Princess Anne: suitable company for a batsman who gave such courtly entertainment.

A.L. HASSETT

25

Puck in Flannels

The beauty of Ava Gardner was in full bloom when Stanley Kramer sent her to Melbourne to make the film *On the Beach*. Interviewed as her first impressions were forming, the glamorous American said of Melbourne, 'I have come here to make a movie about the end of the world. From what I've seen, it looks an appropriate place.' Nobody ever said anything to match that about Sydney, though Harry Secombe said, 'I must say Sydney will look nice when it is finished.' Other visitors could hardly echo Ava's opinion of Melbourne if they savoured the place in the sociable company of Lindsay Hassett, Ernie McCormick, George Schofield and their lunch mates in Young & Jackson's hotel.

In whatever wing of the heavenly studios the scenario was written casting Hassett as Test captain, deep thought must have been given to the part. Never before had a man been needed to take up leadership laid down by an identity so dominating international cricket as Sir Donald Bradman. The reaction of whoever would be named for the part could well be a resentful 'Why pick on me?' Suddenly cricket was like a room with the light switched off. The role would be an unwanted assignment like making the next speech after Sir Robert Menzies, playing the next set after Rod Laver or driving the next lap after Jack Brabham. People ceased giving so much attention, except to say or think the scoring rate had fallen away and the game needed personalities of the kind it used to have.

The heavenly script-writer must have decided that the only thing to do was allot the role to someone capable of seeing the funny side of even such an unwelcome part. Did such a man exist? We shall see.

Youngest of a Geelong real-estate agent's six sons, Arthur Lindsay Hassett was born on 28 August 1913, one day later on August's almanac than Bradman, six days later than Woodfull, three weeks later than Ryder. So far so good.

At Geelong College Lindsay was captain of cricket and football. At seventeen, still at college, Lindsay dashingly made 147, the only century of West Indies' game against Victorian Country at Geelong.

Lindsay's debut for his state at nineteen was against South Australia. Grimmett attended to that. The rising star was twenty-three before he held a regular place. Though only one century came from his bat in his first 20 matches his obvious class and consistency gained him selection at twenty-four to tour England. The little Victorian with an appetite for oysters and half-volleys soon proved himself the best of his country's new batsmen. On a Leeds track where 14 English and Australian wickets had tumbled cheaply that day, captain Bradman and vice-captain McCabe could not watch the tense finish. They sat in the room while word was passed from the balcony. Hassett blinked through the murky light and with pageboy aplomb lifted drives to race a gathering storm – and earn Bradman's praise as a masterful player in a crisis.

Rivalling Hassett's dependability in time of trouble was his name among cricketers for impishness. When a muddy goat's breathing and movement woke McCabe and O'Reilly in their room at Grindleford, the guilt for smuggling it in was never sheeted home, but Hassett's sending a suit to the cleaners was accepted as circumstantial evidence.

A self-winding wristwatch has finer parts of more precious metal than an eight-day clock. Hassett's batting ticked over with a jewelled movement. His quick-footed mastery of every stroke, plus text-book defence, gave his high-grip batting the stamp of greatness as well as producing figures to prove it.

With his other traits Hassett mixed fun to such a degree that a stranger might wonder if he knew when to stop. He did know when to stop: at the dressing-room door as he passed out, bat in hand. His long face would be solemnly set, his blue eyes rather downcast. Yet on the other side of the door team-mates would be gurgling at his parting jest or gesture. I think it was simply an unsparing sense of duty overpowering a sense of humour.

Imperturbable, he was more relaxed at the crease than most partners.

Chewing gum, Bradman's jaw would stop soon after a bowler began his run-up; Hassett would munch on calmly until the ball was in the air. He has been Australia's finest late-cutter since the war, the only one since McCabe with faith enough in the safety of the shot to play it as soon as he came in. He brought his bat down on the ball like the fall of an executioner's blade. He was the Ko-Ko of the crease steering the ball through the slips' shadows. His play was based on the balance of an Olympic gymnast. All these components produced the unexpected power that made one of his nicknames The Mighty Atom. To rising balls Hassett often went up on tiptoe. The extra inches of elevation could not save him in a Leeds Test when Dick Pollard suddenly made a ball jump lapel high; it chipped a shoulder off his bat and was caught at second slip.

Hassett facing O'Reilly – how unequal it seemed! In he would walk, casting little more shadow than his bat. Standing 190 cm (6 ft 3 in) the mighty leg-spinner towered 22 cm over him; it would have looked more apt for Lindsay to sell him a newspaper than contend with his varied bowling. Yet Hassett was the only one who handled the greatest bowler of the age with equanimity – plus a few taunts. No other batsman of any nationality made a century in each innings of a match against the Tiger.

At twenty-six Hassett became VX38843, one of 918,300 men in Australia's gross enlistment of 984,000 in the three armed forces. He was a gunner in the 2/2 Anti-Aircraft Regiment, sent to Egypt and Palestine in 1941.

When Prime Minister Curtin had their unit returned to Australia in 1942, Hassett's soldiering mate George Schofield was his best man when he married brunette Tessie Davis. George said Tessie had known Lindsay a long time, yet still accepted him as a husband at twenty-eight, before his unit was shipped to New Guinea.

Appointed captain of the Australian Services XI in 1945, Hassett resisted pressures to accept a commission. He led the side as a Warrant Officer II. His Services XI repopularised cricket after a six-year war that involved civil populations as never before. Five Victory Tests against England, with two wins each ... a close-fought series in India, billed as India v. Australia Tests ... six games against Australian states ... the homesick servicemen played 28 matches before three-quarters of a million people. Still on their Army or Air Force pay, they did not share in gate takings that brought thousands of pounds to British charities and thousands of rupees to Indian hospitals. Warrant Officer Hassett was paid 12 shillings a day.

As Blackpool celebrated the end of the war Hassett was called on to respond to the mayor's welcome. Looking down from the balcony, he began, 'Never in my life have I seen so many ugly men ...' Stray boos, until he went on, 'But never have I seen so many beautiful women.'

Carrying banners 'India for the Indians' a horde of National Congress demonstrators swarmed on to the Calcutta field to stop the Services' match against East Zone. Unconcernedly, Hassett asked the leader for a cigarette and a match. At the gate he sympathised with the leader's views, shook hands and wished him well. Anger dissolved, the mob withdrew. When Hafeez Kardar reached 100 for All-India Universities Hassett presented him with his cap. (The encouraging gesture was warmly remembered by Pakistanis touring Australia twenty-seven years later.)

There is something incongruous in the sight of husky bowlers going on and off at the behest of the smallest man on the ground and fielders trotting about at his direction. Without looking around, Lindsay would signal a man behind him to a different spot with an inconspicuous motion, as if brushing dust from his well-creased trousers. An exception was a match at Lahore where an all-rounder took a few wickets, became indisposed in the heat and retired from the field. After missing him in the hottest hours his team-mates saw him reappear later in the afternoon. Hassett ceremoniously waved him to the right, then a little to the left, then motioned him back-ward – until the fielder found he had been waved back out the gate. Team manager Keith Johnson told me, 'Lindsay was all fun, delighting in outraging pomposity and pretension. Yet he was as staunch as could be when it mattered. He could handle any crisis with a few words or a simple action.'

Venerable members of the Board of Control so little understood Hassett's qualities that he received only one vote out of 13 in the ballot for captaincy of the first post-war tour of New Zealand. In Victoria's batting order against Hammond's English team in 1947 Neil Harvey was listed to come in second drop, ahead of Lindsay. But the first two wickets tumbled for 24, and the score-posters had to take Harvey's name down from the board when Hassett came in himself. He made 126, and his partner Harvey's 69 set the eighteen-year-old left-hander's feet on the ladder to Test selection.

Before his fifth Test against England Lindsay turned thirty-three, so most of his international career was played beyond the ages at which Ponsford, Harvey and Benaud signed off. He looked conscious of this. Supporting Bradman in their third-wicket 276 at Brisbane he took 6½ hours to put 128 together against gifted leg-spinner Doug Wright, making top-spinners and wrong'uns bounce chest-high. Wright got him 12 times. Hassett is the only Australian who has scored ten Test centuries after turning thirty-three (nearest was Bradman with eight).

Crowds resented the over-dutiful change from the pre-war shot-player. At every appeal in an Adelaide Test barrackers implored umpires to 'Give him out!' Even when he swung a no-ball from Bedser for six, the Mound crowd's chief spokesman soon bawled 'Have a go Hassett!' After he was out and England's bowlers pinned Miller down, a wag brought the laugh of the day by calling 'Bring Hassett back!' Yet Lindsay still had the strokes to make 101 between lunch and tea against NSW. In his highest Test innings, 198 not out against India in 1948, his stroking charmed Adelaide into pardoning his labours against Wright and Bedser.

At one port in the Suez region the Australians saw an oil-rich Arab ruler attended by a retinue. They were told the sheik had 198 wives. An awed silence was broken by Lindsay saying, 'Hm, two more and he'd be entitled to a new ball.' At Aden wartime friends placed their cars at the disposal of Hassett's launch-load of companions. Lindsay allotted a glamorous model to travel in a two-seater with a dashing ex-airman. Hours later at reassembly point the last to appear were this couple. Eyeing them sternly Transport Officer Hassett said, 'Take that guilty look off your faces!'

In the second innings of the Lord's Test, 1948, he waited with the pads on while Barnes and Bradman put on 174. Lindsay was sitting in a row of players watching televised tennis. A wicket fell, Hassett walked in, mis-hit the first ball on to his leg peg, returned to the room and silently pushed a usurper from the seat he had left as if he had merely answered a call to the door.

Neat and nippy, he was one of Australia's finest covers and outfields. He was liable to give a running batsman a scare by throwing to the end he wasn't looking at. Yet when Lindwall knocked Compton's bat to the ground at the Oval and Denis fumbled for it instead of responding to Hutton's approach for a run, Hassett withheld his throw from gully until Denis was safely on his way.

Hassett's hands were so sure that he was thirty-five before I saw them spill a catch. Then two got away from them in one afternoon in front of the Old Trafford scoreboard – high hooks to long-leg by Washbrook off Lindwall. The little culprit took the helmet of a policeman patrolling the boundary and held it upside down in front of him to show what he needed. After a rain stoppage in the Notts Test, the man due to resume bowling could not find the ball until he remembered it was last seen in Hassett's possession as he passed a heap of sawdust.

No team could have a better deputy-skipper than he was to Bradman in England in 1948. *Wisden* named him one of the Five Cricketers of the Year. Only two Australians, Bradman and Ponsford, have surpassed Hassett's average of 74 for a tour. Yet in a telegraphic ballot to appoint a captain for the 1949–50 tour of South Africa I believe it took the last telegram to elect him and save the Board from an act of disgusting ingratitude. By then Sydney friends Stan McCabe and Edmund Dwyer had encouraged him to launch a sportsgoods shop in Melbourne – a successful venture.

Needing a deep breath and his thickest socks to reach 168 cm (5 ft 6½ in), Hassett was the shortest post-war Test captain until India's elfin Sunil Gavaskar led his country against Australia in 1979. Lindsay was off colour with tonsillitis when he came in at Johannesburg after both openers were out for ducks. With millilitres of penicillin in his bloodstream he made a rallying 112 (his first Test innings as captain) then put off an operation. Hassett and his bowlers' ruses on a rain-damaged Durban wicket gained breathing-space for the Australians when they should have gone down for the first time since the war. Though their first innings of 75 left them 236 behind South Africa they schemed and battled through to prevail with five wickets to spare – the most unlikely Test win any scorebook had contained since international cricket began. They ran out Jack Nel at a crucial time but Hassett told the umpire Bill Johnston's run-through might have obstructed Nel.

Captains scrap ordinary strategy on the sort of sticky Brisbane turf where 20 wickets tumbled on Monday after a washed-out Saturday in 1950. Although 160 behind, Brown declared at 68 for seven wickets, to wreck Australia's second innings while the pitch was treacherous. Once England had averted a follow-on, the closure did not surprise Hassett. When Bailey and Bedser fired out seven Australians for 32 Lindsay came out waving to close the innings. Brown, a ruddy giant of 187 cm (6 ft 2 in), looked down at him and asked, 'Well me old china, what happens now?' Hassett: 'It's your move now, my dear Brown.' Two closures in 79 minutes outdo other rare instances of two declarations in one Test day. The flurries resulted in the first of four wins straight by Australia.

Lindsay needed all his humour for the unprecedented experience of hearing Australian crowds barracking for England. Satiated by years of successes, barrackers sympathised with the underdogs and cheered on big-hearted Freddie. Victory had eluded England for 14 post-war Tests against Australia until Bedser's 10 wickets in Melbourne broke the sequence.

Hassett's ear was tuned to every watch-tick of tactics. He was the captain who allowed Miller and Lindwall to try the umbrella field in Test matches. He sent opponents in more often than any other captain in Australian first-class cricket in the decade after the second world war. He was rewarded by victory over the West Indies in Sydney but was denied it by an hour at Leeds in 1953.

In sacrificing his own batting interests by coming in earlier to stabilise his side Hassett exposed his sinewy flanks to a few malignant critics. In his last 20 Tests Australia's first wicket tumbled 26 times before the score reached 30 (13 of them between 0 and 8). Opening breakdowns caused Hassett, now nearing forty, to undertake the task of going in first. At the end of one trying over Lindsay pretended to spear Bedser's foot to the ground with his bat.

With his bandaged right arm almost useless, he opened the innings for 104 at Lord's, half of them pilfered with only the left hand gripping the bat. It was the tenth century among his 3073 runs in 43 Tests. He was the only

227

Australian captain who asked scorer-baggageman Bill Ferguson to join the players in meeting the Queen in front of Lord's pavilion.

Lindsay was often mistaken for Derby-winning jockey Charles Smirke. On such occasions he would divulge stable secrets of his own imagining.

In the Park Lane Hotel dining room a waiter happened to drop a splash of peach melba down Hassett's jacket. The embarrassed waiter took the coat to have it cleaned. Noticing a speck on his trousers, Lindsay called him back, climbed out of his pants, put them on the waiter's arm and resumed his meal in shirt, tie and underpants.

To ridicule averages, he conspired with other players to keep tailender Bill Johnston not out in 16 of his 17 innings in England in 1953. The moment Johnston (highest score 28) took his tour total to 102 Hassett vaulted the fence at Hastings to declare Australia's innings closed before the gangling left-hander could get out. When Johnston came in at Scarborough for his last innings Lindsay sent a note to the fielding skipper, Norman Yardley, explaining that if he scored 14 more runs not out he would beat Sir Donald Bradman's record tour average 115. Johnston did not have to face a ball, leaving him 0 not out and Bradman's record average to await some future challenger.

If many critics' plaudits for Hassett were faint for a captain who won 14 of his 24 Tests (one victory fewer than Bradman) the little Victorian was most appreciated by all who met the Australians personally. One High Commissioner wrote home to the Government that he had never seen a finer piece of ambassadorship. Keith Miller estimated that Lindsay had more genuine friends in all walks of life than any other cricketer. Cardus said Australia had sent no captain who shared Hassett's insight into English ways – without surrender of his Australianism. When Bailey, stalling, appealed against the light to prevent another over before lunch at Leeds, Hassett led the fieldsmen off, as if the point were beneath notice.

After four draws Hassett's fifth consecutive toss win was nullified by conditions suiting England's bowlers. On the day he lost the Ashes he bowled the last over but one. His congratulatory speech to Hutton on the Oval balcony was heard by millions over the air as well as by the crowd below. His lips parted comically as he said, 'England deserved to win, if not from the first ball at least from the second-last over.' (A gale of laughter.) English ex-captain Walter Robins enthused: 'Well done Lindsay, that was absolutely perfect.' Hassett: 'Not bad, considering that Tony Lock chucked half our side out.' In the privacy of the Australian room a wall clock was pelted to ruins with actions no umpire would have passed.

England's discerning Robertson-Glasgow wrote:

> *Hassett's greatest performances concern the heart of the game rather than its arithmetic. He conquered cricket's sourest and strongest enemy – win somehow; and he proved that Test matches, win or lose, can still be good fun as well as good finance.*

More people watched his team play than on Bradman's last tour and higher charges yielded the fattest profit any side had brought from England (£90,000).

The face that placed a thousand slips belongs to the sharpest wit who ever wrote a batting order. Passengers on liners thought he had misplaced his calling and should have been a successor to stage comedian Alfred Frith. Robed for a fancy-dress parade, he led a party of Arabs, chanting *The Desert Song*, into the dining room. Telling his entourage, 'Sheiks don't eat at tables,' he bade them squat cross-legged in a circle on deck. Diners tossed them rolls, chicken legs and a bottle of firewater.

He would wind up a late party by conducting a mirthful action song about the palace maid hanging out the clothes when 'Down Came a Blackbird'. His downbeat was flawless, especially in the silent repeat chorus amid fluttering handkerchiefs.

When Lindsay's lips parted in a piranha-like smile it was time to be on guard. The man who put the imp in impropriety had the art of saying the wrong thing in the right way. At a Nottingham civic party he asked the mayor, 'If I pull your chain will you flush?' His Worship related the story for months afterward as a source of countless laughs. Arriving late from golf at a blacktie party in Durban, Hassett broke the ice by slipping an ice-cube down the back of the hostess's dinner-gown. When she jumped up, another cube went down the front. The prankster apologised so graciously that the hostess became one of his keenest fans.

After the Queen awarded Hassett an MBE at Buckingham Palace she talked longer to him than to any other recipient of an honour that day. From a Sportsmen's Association function in Melbourne Town Hall national stations broadcast Hassett telling of two Marylebone Cricket Club members, used to etiquette at Lord's, placing bowler hats on their seats at Old Trafford while they went to the tea counter. Returning, they saw their hats on the ground and two Lancashire men in their seats. One member protested; 'I say, you chaps, we put our hats on those seats to keep them.' Lancashire man: 'Oop 'ere we keep seats with booms, not 'ats.'

Wisden's list of men with 50 or more hundreds ranks Hassett closest to Sir Donald Bradman among world batsmen for ratio of centuries, one for every five completed innings, ahead of Hammond, Hazare and Hutton. He had 59 centuries among his 16,890 runs at a career average of 58. His highest was 232. When cricket-loving Prime Minister Sir Robert Menzies presented him with a testimonial cheque Hassett responded, 'I am at a loss for words. I've had absolutely no practice at receiving cheques for £5000.'

When his turn came to go in for the Prime Minister's XI at Canberra he picked up the nearest bat, scored 18 and was surrounded by schoolchildren asking for his autograph. Sir Robert exclaimed, 'Isn't that characteristic of Lindsay – he's given a boy his bat.' Left-hander Arthur Morris: 'His bat – that's *my* bat!' In the pavilion Morris tried to look stern as he asked, 'Do you realise I'd used that bat only three times?' Hassett: 'What does it matter? You should have seen the look on the kid's face.'

On a cool Melbourne evening I was in a group with Hassett, fast bowler Ernie McCormick and friends in Young & Jackson's bar, where Australia's best-known nude, Chloe, looks down on drinkers. Glancing at the painting, Lindsay said, 'She looks a bit pale. They ought to send her to Surfers Paradise for a fortnight.' He would rather go fishing at Mallacoota.

Taken as toddlers to see their father bat, Margaret and Anne were puzzled by his instant dismissal for 0. One asked, 'Why is daddy coming back so soon? He never comes home early!'

Nephews have been keen cricketers with John Shaw, son of his sister Frances, most prominent. John headed South Melbourne's batting averages in five seasons. His 3000 runs for Victoria included centuries in Adelaide and Sydney and 94 against Trueman, Tyson and Loader in 1959. He made 120 run out against Auckland in his first innings in NZ in 1960.

Within three years of leaving the game to become a discerningly fair ABC broadcaster, Hassett perceived that he had erred in allowing a sense of responsibility to restrict his strokeplay. Warning Norman O'Neill against making the same mistake, he implied that he would not have done so again if given a chance to replay the last stretch of his career. Looking down from Lord's pressbox at a stubborn innings, he quipped, 'I'm glad I wasn't up here when I was down there.'

In his later years as a commentator watching triumph and disaster, Hassett was saddened by the inability of players to treat the two impostors just the same. He was last heard as broadcaster in 1981, retreating to Bateman's Bay on the New South Wales coast where he died on 16 June 1993. A day later, Michael Slater called his quick-footed strokeplay to mind in a Lord's Test.

Official minds did not find it easy to accept his puckish informality and his manly disinclination to salaam to authority. That counts for little beside the fact that wherever he went about the world Lindsay Hassett left people feeling warmer toward Australians than before.

A.R. MORRIS

26

Saying Hello
with Hundreds

Two things set Arthur Morris apart from other highly successful international batsmen. No other Test star has equalled this fair-haired left-hander in instant adaptability to strange conditions. No other post-war batsman has rivalled his smashing counter-attacks on bowling swift enough to give the toughest team the tremors. A menacing bouncer colliding with Morris's bat was like a rocky fist against an iron jaw.

Across the seven seas this chameleon of cricketers had the faculty of at once being in harmony with changes of background. Amid unfamiliar surroundings he attuned his play to local conditions with smoothness – a credit to alert observation as well as his adaptability and concentration. He is the only one who has introduced himself to four countries by making 100 runs or more. Contrasts in soils, mild light or glare, the ball's behaviour in different atmospheres and its varying bounce could not put his bat on the wrong track.

Arthur Robert Morris was born on 19 January 1922 at Bondi before bikinis decorated its beach. His schoolmaster father was a former Waverley club fast bowler. Arthur was only fourteen when promoted to first-grade Sydney cricket for St George as a slow left-handed over-the-wrist spinner. From last in, captain O'Reilly gradually lifted him to open the club's innings when he was fifteen.

A jockey who could bring off first-up coups on racetracks to parallel Morris's century-making would make a fortune for his backers. The compatible left-hander began it when he first stepped on Sydney Cricket Ground three weeks before he turned nineteen. With 148 and 111 against Queensland he made himself the first player in any country to score a century in each innings of his initial first-class match.

War prevented Morris from building on that inviting foundation until he was almost twenty-five. After Army service in New Guinea he was one of the last to emerge from jungle-green uniform. The first time he faced English bowling Morris made 115 for an Australian XI at Melbourne in 1946. On his first appearance on Adelaide Oval he scored 112 and 124 not out against England – giving him centuries in three consecutive Test innings of his first series. At his first sight of Indian bowling he ran up 162 for New South Wales in 1947.

Across the River Severn from Worcester Cathedral his first knock on the door of English cricket was 138. In his opening first-class match in South Africa he made 10 and 153 against Natal at Kingsmead. In drier heat he notified West Indians of his presence with 157 against Jamaica at Melbourne Park, Kingston. Each time he was opening the innings, while mates watched to see what the bowlers could get out of the wicket, if anything. Those globe-trotting entries formed part of a list of hundreds on first acquaintance with grounds. In his first innings at Perth West Australian fieldsmen chased his shots for 115. Sussex's first sight of the 175 cm (5 ft 9 in) left-hander lasted while he piled up 184 at Hove. Bristol marvelled as he went close to 300 in a day at Ashley Down. He capped his first match at Leeds with 182 to help win a Test. Besides Durban four other South African cities saw his first visit yield hundreds: Bulawayo 104, East London 106, Kimberley 50 and 102 not out, Port Elizabeth 157 in the final Test. Only Bradman (19), Sobers (10) and Greg Chappell (nine) made more centuries against England than Morris's eight in 24 Tests.

As his partner for four hours at Leeds Bradman doubted whether a more valuable innings was ever played than Morris's masterful 182 on a dusty fifth-day track in a stand of 301. Arthur is the only Australian who has hit 20 fours in reaching a Test 100 in England. He scored 33 boundaries in the day as Australia, against long odds, raised 404 in the last 5½ hours for a near-incredible win. On retirement Sir Donald rated Morris the best left-handed batsman he had seen.

Bristol fans predicted that tall off-spinner Tom Goddard, a 2900-wicket man, would bring the conquering Aussies down a peg on his home track. Morris often did not allow the ball to land on the pitch. Whoever heard of

17 boundary hits from one bat before lunch? Arthur hit them in his 102 before the interval. His score leapt to 231 before tea. When a fire started in a hedge by the pavilion an onlooker called 'Smoke him out!' Sweat trickling into Morris's eyes caused a few mis-hits before he was caught for 290 about 5.30 pm after hitting 42 fours and on-driving a six.

Within six months he stormed to another century before lunch in winning a Sydney match against Queensland on the third morning. In desperation fast-medium bowler Len Johnson began banging down bumpers, each one clapped by slipfielders. Morris hooked the bouncers high but safely scoring 108 not out in 82 minutes at five runs an over.

Unlike Harvey and Marsh, right-hand throwers, Morris is genuinely left-handed in everything from signing an autograph to knotting one of his fashionable ties. His fielding looked sure rather than spectacular because of his uncommon gift of anticipation.

Modest in manner and moderate in habits, Arthur did not smoke until he became an opening batsman in the Test atmosphere. When he buckled pads on, nervous tension revealed itself in his yawning, smiling sheepishly, lighting a last cigarette and silently sitting apart in a chair. He preferred his partner to take strike but once he got into action tension usually gave way to composure. He rarely watched from the dressing room. He was playing his phonograph records from *Annie Get Your Gun* when he heard of Hassett being bowled cheaply, so he whipped on 'My Defences Are Down' to welcome the skipper back to the room.

In his comfortable stance he faced an upright bat's blade full to the bowler. All he heard about the game's theories scarcely affected his doing what came naturally. Ian Johnson said his touch of unorthodoxy made it difficult to apply any set plan, for a bowler never knew just what to expect. Arthur's regulated back-lift took the bat outside the off stump. He based his batting on quick decision and ready foot-work to make position. His top hand guided and his bottom hand provided the thrust. Primarily a back-foot player, he put his 76 kg (12 stone) chiefly into hooks, pulls, sweeps and on-drives. Forearm strength powered his firm-wristed version of the cover-drive and he did not always get his front foot to the line. In a period when most batsmen eschewed lifting shots, confidence showed in his willingness to drive over the infield. In one period he admitted having become 'a bit on-side happy'. When he was struggling for form, a clever bowler restricting him to an on-the-line shot saw bat brought to ball like a housewife sweeping with a straw broom. A shuffle across to the off sometimes exposed his leg peg – it was seldom hit – and its worst effect was his playing at length balls outside the off stump.

Leaner days caught up with Morris, especially in periods when medium-pace genius Alec Bedser's mighty hand was getting more out of wickets than batsmen could answer. Fans found extra fascination in their repeated new-ball duels. The idea of a hoodoo caught on with the public so much that some thought Bedser had Morris hardly knowing whether he was Arthur or Martha. Their tussles formed as dramatic a tapestry as any international sport could produce yet rancour never intruded. Once in booked-out Sydney Morris harboured Alec and his twin Eric in his flat.

After dismissing his so-called bunny at Hobart on his twenty-ninth birthday Alec handed him a decorated parcel that evening, saying, 'I hope you'll like this birthday gift, Arthur. It may help you.' It was a textbook, *Better Cricket* by Lindsay Hassett and Ian Johnson, with a passage marked on batting. On the morning of his next Test innings the place allotted Morris for breakfast in an Adelaide hotel was at table 13. Momentarily he hesitated, then sat there. The left-hander batted all that day and half the next for a double century. That night Arthur handed the textbook back to Alec, with a cross marking hints on bowling. Bedser is the only bowler who dismissed one batsman 18 times in Tests – half the innings in which Morris faced him. In their 48 encounters in first-class games Alec took his wicket 22 times. While that was happening Morris was scoring 2600 runs, including ten centuries, eight of them in Tests. His longest trough without 100 in these games was 17 innings.

Team-mates admired and envied the indomitable left-hander's courage against the most hostile speedmen around. Hooking to the four winds and the white pickets, Arthur's bat seemed to have no top edge. Keith Miller's bouncers made nearly all the world's leading batsmen bend the knee, but never Morris. In his volatile twenties, Miller was bowling his second over against NSW at Sydney when Keith Carmody hit the first for three. Miller let fly a bumper at Morris, who stepped inside it and hooked it off his forelock to the fence. Keith exclaimed to near fieldsmen, 'Ever seen a whole over of bumpers?' The harder he bowled the harder Morris hooked. The over was plundered for 3, 4, 4, 4, 4, 3, 1 bye, 1 – easily the costliest Keith ever bowled.

The day Freddie Brown unmuzzled Frank Tyson against Australians at Northampton for the first time, waiting batsmen's concern was lessened by Morris's fearless hooking of short-pitched fliers in a stand of 175 with Harvey. That pair were the only two who managed Test centuries against 'Typhoon' Tyson's speed and bounce on harder Australian turf in the 1954–55 series. Rather than risk being caught at leg-slip off rising balls in a Brisbane Test, Morris took a number of unholy wallops on his hip, partly padded. He cracked hardy but when he walked with feigned unconcern his gait was as stiff as if he were a knight in heavy armour. At breakfast next morning I saw Arthur's hands were bruised and swollen. Yet he batted on two more hours to complete 153, made with 18 fours, two sixes and uncounted contusions. After that Test there was no stopping Tyson and Statham.

New South Wales had appointed Morris captain at twenty-five. Unostentatious in his handling of bowlers and fieldsmen, he had his players' goodwill. In one interstate match young fast left-hander Alan Walker had been toiling against a gale, so Morris gave him a chance with the wind before the innings ended. To enable this Lindwall, who had taken three wickets in five overs, was spelled, and objected, 'Don't take me off again when I'm getting wickets.' Morris resisted the provocation to get up on his hind legs to assert his authority. He waited until he could talk to the insubordinate bowler alone. Instead of an angry scene, this tact was rewarded with an apology and a firmer basis of friendship and respect.

Another time leg-spin bowler Doug Ring, who at times figured in tailend rallies, was batting for Victoria when Walker banged down a bumper. Morris told him quietly, 'No bumpers at tailenders, please Alan! Bowl them only to batsmen.' Years later at a lunch Ring recalled this. Morris: 'How many were you at the time?' Ring: 'Eighty-eight.'

Unselfishness that wins loyalty and trust was most evident when misunderstandings occurred between the wickets. Twice in Test matches Arthur ran through to sacrifice his wicket for partners when the mix-up was not his fault. Once he was 99. He never gave a fig for personal records. Though a last partner once suggested it, he scorned to boost his average by aiming to finish not out. Batting through in Adelaide for his highest Test innings he risked his wicket near the end trying to lift shots over deep-set fieldsmen rather than take singles more likely to leave him not out. He was last out for 206.

When he was called forward to the state-front of Test captaincy the footlights were on the blink. A trial at the nets found captain Hassett unfit with a hip injury so the intended twelfth man, Noblet, came in. When told of the ill-balanced team he would be leading – too few batsmen, too many pace bowlers – Morris, as he put it, was 'in a state of shock'. A shower prevented him from inspecting the wicket before tossing.

Opening the innings with Jim Burke, Morris found the city end of the pitch hard and the cathedral end soft, the covers having leaked. Batting on such a pitch was like having one foot on a moving train and the other on a banana skin. So 22 wickets tumbled in a day. It was the most unsparing slaughter on the first day of a Test in Australia for fifty years. Mowing the Australians down for 82, the West Indians were out for 105 by 5.15 pm, then took two more wickets. By reversing the order, Morris saved his five batsmen for Monday and Australia's second innings yielded 255. But the West Indians won. As Hassett's vice-captain in Britain, he packed the slips against Surrey, giving English onlookers their first view of the umbrella field.

A Sydney crowd's resentment of a slow-scoring NSW partnership led to official criticism of Morris for having put two cautious batsmen in together. Coming when attendances in Australia had ebbed, the discussion resulted in the appointment of Miller to captain the state with express directions to enliven the game.

The next time Morris had to step up as Australian skipper at Sydney in 1954, captain Johnson and vice-captain Miller were out with knee injuries. On winning the toss Arthur based his decision on his assessment of the pitch. No strip so grassy has been seen at Sydney since. Arthur told me he had two reasons for putting England in:

> I thought the pitch would be liveliest on the first day, giving us the best chance of getting England out for a low total. Then there was the

defensive consideration that Tyson and Statham gave England a more hostile attack than Australia could mount without Miller and with Lindwall lacking his sharpest edge because of a liver complaint.

Dismissal of England for 154 earned Morris congratulations on his reading of the pitch and his direction of Australia's quickest available bowlers. To keep England in the game Hutton tried every stratagem, so the crowd saw only a meagre 51.6 overs (85 balls an hour). Batsmen's only relief from incessant fast attack was seven medium-pace overs by Appleyard. Tyson's paralysing speed and Statham beating up into the wind swept England to victory by 38. So Morris was added to the list of Test captains who put the other side in yet finished on the losing side. More than two dozen skippers keep him company.

He and brunette showgirl Valerie Hudson were thirty-two when they married. Before his next tour of the West Indies ended she was stricken by a malignant malady, but did not tell him until his return. Instead of playing for Australia in England in 1956 Arthur commented on the Tests. Four months later cancer ended Valerie's life at thirty-four.

In 46 Tests his 3533 runs included 12 centuries. Among his 12,614 runs in 250 innings were 46 hundreds, with a career average of 54. He joined the Trust running the ground where centuries first put him into headlines. At forty-six he married attractive Judith Appleton, thirty-one, a shipping line secretary, a divorcee from Western Australia. He was public relations officer for Wormald International's security devices when the 1974 honours awarded him an MBE for services to sport, especially cricket.

Arthur and Judith Morris live in the New South Wales country town of Cessnock. Its trophy-lined den features a mug presented to him by former opening partner Ken Archer, featuring the pair going out to bat with the legend: 'Who's the old bloke next to KA?' The title of a belated biography by Jack McHarg published in February 1995 combines, like Morris himself, both aptness and understatement: 'An Elegant Genius'.

27

The Moody Earth

Except for players and ex-players, what happens on top of a wicket is everything, the whole box and dice. General public interest scarcely extends to the stretches of soil on which matches are played. Call them wicket, pitch, track, strip or worse, these 20 metres of seemingly inert earth dictate how a game will go. I know of no other skipper whose fortunes have been governed so much by Test wickets as Ian Johnson. His 17 Tests as captain were almost a study in extremes of ecology. If his batsmen were on good terms with the earth they could pile up 600 or 700. If they mistrusted the soil underfoot they could be put out for 84 while calling it something unprintable.

In addition to two series in England Johnson had the honour of being the first captain to lead Australia in Tests before West Indian, Pakistani and Indian crowds.

Ian William Johnson was born on 8 December 1918 in a sport-minded town. Ian was the elder son of North Melbourne wine-and-spirit grocer William Johnson, a slow bowler. South Melbourne chose Ian at sixteen, a Wesley College off-spinner. He was twenty-three days past seventeen at his debut for Victoria against Tasmania. Through his father's selectorship he came to know Don Bradman, an enduring friendship. In 1944 he was flying in a Beaufighter squadron, a married flight-lieutenant on the equivalent of two dollars a day.

After his Test debut at twenty-seven in Australia's first post-war Test in NZ he was in 12 of Bradman's last 15 sides. Tough enough to bowl without socks in Sydney's warmth, the 177 cm (5 ft 10 in) all-rounder signalled his presence with six English wickets for 42. To coax turn from firm Australian tracks he twisted the ball almost hard enough to screw a doorknob off.

No bowler with Johnson's high degree of flight is around today. West Indian and English batsmen visiting Australia and Springboks in South Africa had trouble judging just where the spinning ball would land as it dropped or drifted.

Next to versatile left-hander Bill Johnston Ian was Bradman's most used bowler in England in 1948 (4000 balls for 85 wickets in 22 games).

His regular removal of low-order players led to a teasing nickname 'Myxomatosis'. Jokes aside, Johnson's wickets among the top six outnumbered those in the bottom five by 44 to 41. They included master-batsman Hutton four times. Ian was Australia's only slow spinner until he was replaced in the last Test. Not holding his Test place on English tracks told against him in the next selection to tour five years later, when he was omitted.

When Ian came on to bowl in Bradman's benefit match Sid Barnes pulled a 12-inch toy bat from under his sweater and shaped up with it, for a laugh. Trevor Bailey insisted that Johnson threw every ball but said English umpires did not call bowlers who had not been no-balled in their own countries.

In a Brisbane Test he was heckled by Queenslanders angered by the omission of Tallon. Captain Lindsay Hassett sent him to field in the sun-scorched outfield nearest the noisiest barrackers. Asking them for a beer, and praising its quality, Ian entered the good graces of his tormentors. Johnson landed eight wickets in Hassett's testimonial match, even if Ian Craig and Keith Carmody pillaged 32 off one eight-ball over.

With an insight into newspaperdom through writing a column, Johnson was the first captain of Victoria to invite reporters into his team's room after a day's play, enabling uncertainties to be cleared up. He was the only bowler to exceed 30 Sheffield Shield wickets in the 1953–54 season.

He not only regained a Test place but, nearing thirty-six, was appointed captain before his 29th Test. It was only his 13th first-class game as skipper, but Hassett had stood down as captain of South Melbourne to give him additional experience.

Misreading the Brisbane turf, Hutton put Australia in to bat. Eleven spilt chances kept the Englishmen fielding until lunch on the third day and a total of 601 for eight brought an innings victory, Australia's only win.

A sensation occurred in a Melbourne heatwave. Shooters on the second day, once unthinkable on Melbourne shirtfronts, were less surprising because an outside wicket-maker had been hired to try to do better than the regular curator, hampered by soured soil. As evidence of illegal watering, players' boot-sprigs on Monday sank into softer turf, gaping cracks had narrowed. Hutton remarked, 'It helped us,' and Johnson said, 'It was like losing the toss twice over.'

Always at their best in adverse conditions, Johnson and wicketkeeper Len Maddocks made game stands but could not save Australia.

Looking beyond the series lost to England the recall of Johnson as captain was a tribute to his level-headedness. Ever a diplomat, he earned warm congratulations for his handling of what Board men feared would be a touchy assignment in the West Indies, after frictions there during the Englishmen's visit in 1954. Ian carried through the smooth diplomatic part of captaincy with inexhaustible urbanity.

As Australia's fieldsmen walked off after ending an innings at Sabina Park a bunch of barefoot boys ran to meet them. Instead of rushing past, Ian picked up a toddler and smilingly talked with him as he carried him off. Not used to this kind of thing at a Test, Jamaicans were delighted.

Bowling fast-medium swingers in a cross-wind Miller took two wickets in an over at Bridgetown. Johnson told him, 'I want some speed!' As they argued the skipper insisted, 'I'll say who bowls and what they bowl ... If I throw you the ball will you throw it back?' He replaced Miller with Lindwall, rather stiff in an evening breeze. As players filed off to the room Miller uttered enraged comments such as, 'You couldn't captain a team of schoolboys.' Under provocation Johnson spoke out as if his first name were Jack not Ian. 'If you want to go on like that why don't we go around the back and thrash it out?' Miller quietened and the pair travelled to the hotel in the same car.

That contentious bowling change turned out to be the costliest change in Test annals, as Denis Atkinson and Clairemont Depeiza batted all day without a wicket falling. They put on 347, the seventh-wicket Test record.

Strokeplayers regaled the islands' crowds with 21 Test centuries, a record

243

(Australia 12, West Indies 9). In putting his side two up, the skipper spun out seven West Indians in an innings, his biggest Test haul.

Ian persuaded a pilot on a Sunday flight to let him take the controls between Trinidad and the idyllic island of Tobago. When Board members heard of this, another 'Thou shalt not' was squeezed into players' contracts.

Scenic delights and hearty hospitality brought glowing praise from the captain every time he expressed his team's gratitude to hosts. Johnson was awarded an MBE in recognition of much more than a successful tour on the field.

Knowing when to take himself off as a bowler was a simpler decision than whether to take a curtain, amid acclaim, or remain on stage for a more difficult act. Many English strips on which he would bowl in 1956 differed as much from Australian and West Indian wickets as a green quince differs from a golden mango.

At the time Johnson took over as skipper against Hutton the Australian XI was running down, six years after the peak of 1948. Some eyes were blinded to this by the dazzle of record scoring on wickets of polished perfection in the Indies, against bowling much thinner than England had at call. When English interviewers challenged Johnson with Hutton's disbelief that batsmen as old as twenty-five could so change their habits, Ian replied, 'We will let you see and judge for yourselves.' Famous first words, I called them at the time.

Clinging to preconceived tactics helped to bring on defeat by Surrey – first Australian loss to a county for forty-four years. For the only time in his life Lindwall walked the field a whole day without being asked to bowl a ball. An attempt to convert left-hand paceman Davidson into a spinner pleased nobody, least of all the bowler. Not permitted to bowl at normal speed, Alan exclaimed to grinning century-maker Bernard Constable, 'I'd part your hair if I was allowed.' The nature of the defeat told more tales than Hoffmann. It gave Peter May an edge in strategy for the Tests. The reverse cast over the Australians' confidence a shadow shaped roughly like Laker. The shadow pursued them throughout the tour, except when temporarily banished at Lord's on the only seamers' strip of the series.

From that point history dealt Ian a rotten hand. Losing tosses doomed the weaker side to the worst of the wickets. Jim Laker's bowling was giving Australia the jimjams. One ball pitching about Lindwall's off stump at Manchester screwed past Ray's left ribs, going too wide for Evans to prevent byes.

With his slogan 'Guts and determination', Johnson had too much fibre to lose heart, even when on the ropes. After six Australians had tumbled for 81 one afternoon he tried pep-talk, but pushed it too far by asserting 'Here's where we make 500.' One of the not-out batsmen, Miller, looking up from unbuckling his pads, offered 'Six to four we don't'. Australia's innings yielded 143 and 140. They had their backs to the wall so often that the writing on it rubbed off on them. Eleven victims at Leeds whetted Laker's appetite for his main course, 19 out of 20 at Manchester.

At one point nine men were in bandages. The side won only nine of 31 first-class games, equalling the 1912 low.

When one of Laker's four short-legs, ex-guardsman Alan Oakman, had a bowl off four short steps Arthur Mailey murmured, 'Must have practised his run-up in his sentry-box.'

After the last mowing on the eve of the Test Bert Flack asked Walter Robins, 'Is there anything more I should do?' Robins: 'All I can suggest is that you get a packet of grass-seed.' Australia's fall for 84 was an all-out effort, literally, but not the kind Ian wanted.

Matching the saying that no man is a hero to his valet, baggage-man scorer Bill Ferguson said:

> Had Johnson been told by his friends in the press that he was, in fact, a passenger, he might have pondered on the advisability of standing down ... There could have been no disgrace for Ian in such a decision.

Treating his flight as if it were a dead bird dropping, venturesome Evans clumped 21 off one over at Manchester and 26 off an over at Scarborough. As one of the reporters whom Fergie accused of being full of excuses for defeat, I am impenitent. To have called those soon-powdery tracks Test wickets would have been somewhat like describing slagheaps as tulip beds.

Nothing conveyed as much to Australian readers as a photograph of the Old Trafford pitch being swept between innings, before rolling, by groundsmen resembling dim figures in a Sahara sandstorm.

Into each life some rain must fall but Ian had cause to believe he was copping it too copiously. For the first time since five-Test rubbers began no Australian made a century. Midfield actions revealed a deep sense of grievance: Burke's appeal against a glimmer of sunshine beside a stand ... Benaud's delays with 18 requests for block ... Johnson's appeal about sawdust blown forward from bowlers' footholes ('That's one Trevor Bailey didn't think of,' said Ian, still able to grin).

Had Johnson been a blend of Zhukov, Eisenhower and Montgomery his generalship could not have altered the inevitable, nor could any change in leadership. Lack of grass or lashings of rain had such effects that in ten Test innings the Australians batted on a good wicket only twice.

In a rain-delayed final Test the only laugh came when wicketkeeper Gilbert Langley's pants split and were closed with a safety-pin. Later stalling to deny England time to take more wickets, Johnson walked to the far end to give six pats to a ballmark his partner had already flattened. Sections of the crowd hooted when he walked around a mark at his end and knelt on the pitch to smooth it. From silly mid-on May told him with a wry smile, 'There's no need for you to try to tear your trousers.'

Time-wasting is indefensible, but Johnson and his team were reacting to a feeling that sub-standard wickets had given them a raw deal.

Better to remember that when a bat, which fuming Australians had returned unsigned to the Old Trafford groundsman, was brought back to the room by Trueman, Ian instantly agreed to Freddie's taking it to each player for autographing. Johnson deserved better of fate for his refusal to bow under the weight of sorrows.

Underlining the difference in off-spin methods, Laker, throughout his Test career, could average a wicket every 56 balls and 18 runs on home tracks while Johnson had to bowl 132 balls and pay 56 runs for each Test wicket on English soil. On harder tracks abroad Jim's cost went up to 28 runs a Test wicket, three more than Johnson's, and he had to bowl eight more balls than Ian for each.

Johnson, Lindwall and Lock were the only men who played Tests in the

1950s in all the leading cricket countries. Against Fazal Mahmood's bewildering cut from Karachi matting Ian's 1956 team fell four short of their Manchester 84. The resultant loss to Pakistan, a fledgling Test country, prompted Adelaide *News* cartoonist Norman Mitchell to suggest that island planters might scrape up a side to give the homewarding Australians a match. Prestige was salvaged by wins against India at Madras and Calcutta.

Johnson's 17 Tests as captain gave him a credit balance of seven wins to five losses. In the last of his 45 Tests he completed an all-round double, 109 wickets and 1000 runs. Only seven other Australians have passed those milestones. He held 30 Test catches. In 189 first-class games Ian took 619 wickets, average 23. His 4900 runs included centuries against Queensland and Somerset.

He dedicated his book *Cricket at the Crossroads* to his wife Lal, Test cricketer Dr Roy Park's slender blonde daughter. He was a RAAF pilot of twenty-four when he made her his nineteen-year-old bride. The Melbourne Cricket Club committee chose Johnson from 45 applicants for secretary in 1957. He was the third retired Test player to keep the great club abreast of changing times. He never smoked until he took to a pipe at the desk. During his twenty-five-year term managing the world's foremost cricket stadium its capacity grew from 105,000 to 125,000. Besides unequalled galleries of photographs arranged by Hans Ebeling, its pavilion houses Anthony Baer's unique collection.

Johnson served for twenty years on the Parole Board, and his MBE was later complemented by a OBE (1977) and a CBE (1983). He lives in Middle Park – rather too close for aural comfort to the Albert Park Lake where Victorian Premier Jeff Kennett staged the Australian Grand Prix in March 1996 – and retains many happy memories of the countries in which he played his cricket.

Though he has not been back to the West Indies in four decades, he still regularly visits Barbados: the Torquay holiday home he named for his favourite destination on tour in 1955.

247

R.R. LINDWALL

28

Guided Missiles

Ray Lindwall's fast bowling changed the look of international cricket and the expression on a thousand batsmen's faces. When this loose-flannelled genius of the crease entered the Test arena he was the only speedman in sight. Lindwall's example was as a spark to tinder. He had the distinction of restoring a neglected art to its place in the forefront of Test cricket's excitements. Before his career ended, four countries had bowlers too quick for batsmen's peace of mind.

In a spacecraft age we have grown used to speed, which is more than could be said of batsmen who faced Lindwall. None could ever say, paraphrasing *My Fair Lady*, that they had grown accustomed to his pace. Between the extremes of a fearsome bouncer and a late outswinger, he tried to keep batsmen guessing all the while. Hundreds guessed wrongly.

For a half-dozen years before Trueman trod a Test field Lindwall reigned as the world's No. 1 fast bowler. Before he passed his zenith he played in 36 Test matches, helped win 26 and was on the losing side only three times. Batsmen have since seen, if that is the word, the ball hurtle faster from the hands of Tyson, Hall, Lillee – fractionally yet frighteningly faster – but their awesome presence did not confer on their teams such redoubtability as the sides which had Lindwall from 1946 to 1952. With Miller sharing the new ball and Bradman making hundreds in six of those Tests, it was like a conjunction of Mars, Jupiter and Saturn.

As one who saw Lindwall take his first English Test wicket (Sir Leonard Hutton in 1946) his last (Roy Swetman in 1959) and most of those against six countries in between, watching him deliver thousands of balls etched his exemplary approach on my memory. The mind's eye sees a sandy-haired player of Swedish-Irish extraction almost 180 cm (5 ft 11 in) tall. His step is short, making the least possible call on muscle and sinew until all-out effort is needed.

Anxiously, the striker watches him move from two walking steps into the 13 running strides which form a model of accelerating approach. On the 12th stride a high-leading left arm sets the line for a side-on delivery, with his back arched. Body momentum tows his arm over and a flick of the wrist propels the ball on its destructive way. Lindwall's artistry might make it look almost effortless but his own lungs, limbs, groin and back told him differently. As he saw film of himself running up, he muttered rather surprised, 'I don't look tired!'

Lindwall gathered speed more gradually and took one stride fewer than Larwood. Instead of grounding his right boot parallel with the crease he pointed its plate-guarded toecap ahead. In his book, *Flying Stumps*, he tells how he tried to act on well-meant advice that he should bring his right arm over at a higher angle than his habitual one, about 30 degrees from perpendicular. It made a side-on body position uncomfortable so, after consulting the oracular O'Reilly, he stuck to his natural method. Batsmen felt Lindwall's bumper was boring at their throats. Hutton, who ranked him first among bowlers he faced, found him hardest of all to sight.

An inauspicious day for batsmen was 3 October 1921, birthday of Raymond Russell Lindwall at Mascot. At the Brothers' High School Darlinghurst, he became captain of cricket and football and was champion athlete. He would play in a boys' team on Saturday morning then pedal his bicycle breathlessly to play in a men's match after lunch. A few weeks after he turned twenty, NSW sent him to Brisbane for his first interstate match.

At twenty-four Lindwall emerged from Army service. Atebrin tablets gradually cleared up after-effects of tropical fevers. His 12th first-class match was a Test at Wellington in 1946. At Christchurch a bruised left-hander, Jack Smith, suggested photographing a batsman in a crash helmet and sending it on to the next city as a hint on how to play Lindwall. Ray quit his job in a Sydney engineer's office because he could not get time off to play and practise. When he said, 'Fast bowling is the toughest job in sport – tougher even than Rugby League,' Lindwall was speaking as an 80 kg (12 st 8 lb) full-back who had won state selection. Before each summer he ran roads like a training boxer. On Adelaide Oval he electrified 31,000 watchers by taking three wickets in four balls. Lindwall mowed down seven for 63 in the first innings of the next Test in Sydney. In between, he sent a bail flying 43 metres when he bowled Noblet of SA. In taking seven for 38 in India's second innings in Adelaide in 1948 he dealt out four ducks.

After the 1947 change sanctioning delivery with the back foot lifted, provided part of it was behind the line, a film showed that his right foot's drag across the crease carried him, sometimes, nearly a metre past the stumps. Before a battery of cameras at Worcester in 1948 Ray's take-off 45 cm (18 inches) behind the crease was passed by the umpires. Delivering the last ball before tea on greasy turf in his first Test in England Lindwall pulled a muscle in the right groin. It left him permanently susceptible to strains in this ticklish region.

Through post-war Britain Lindwall left a trail of shaken nerves and shattered stumps. The effect on dressing-room atmosphere can be judged from Yorkshire off-spinner Ellis Robinson's pantomime. Purporting to be the next man in, Ellis would begin pouring a drink of ale. 'Who's bowling, Ray Lindwall?' he would ask anxiously, his trembling hand rattling the bottle against the glass. 'What? Colin McCool ... ah!' and the rattling ceased as a steady hand finished the pouring.

But the rattling of stumps continued. Lindwall's most deadly spell was five wickets for eight in 49 balls after lunch in the Oval Test. Praising Bradman for his captaincy Ray said, 'Not once did Don keep me on for an extra over when I should have been given a rest.' His 27 wickets was then a record for an Australian fast bowler in England.

To prepare for Ray in 1949, some South Africa batsmen called in base-ball pitchers at practice. Running up at Port Elizabeth Lindwall twice stopped when he saw Eastern Province opening batsman Ray Connell standing forward from his crease. 'Anything wrong?' he asked. Connell: 'I always stand in front of the crease to fast bowling.' Lindwall: 'Not to me you don't!' Soon a forehead-high bumper knocked Connell unconscious over his stumps. Walking to his captain, Ray spoke to Hassett, who signalled to slipfielder Johnson to replace the bails. When Connell recovered he resumed his innings later in the day.

Still chary of imposing full-stretch strain on his groin, Lindwall, twenty-nine, was alongside the non-striker, Dr George Thoms, in a pause in play at Melbourne. Thoms happened to say, 'It is only a few years since I was sitting in the stand, watching you hurl them down at full speed.' An incautious remark, worth adding to the list of famous last words. Three balls later Thoms's stumps were scattered by a ball he scarcely saw. The departing Victorian's philosophic comment: 'As I walked away, it was no use yelling back that I hadn't meant it that way.'

Umpires took no action in Sydney when West Indians said they counted 25 bouncers in 40 balls by Lindwall to Everton Weekes. In six overs 10 got up shoulder-high or head-high, while an extra fielder reinforced the standard Australian quota of three leg fieldsmen for fast bowling. Lindwall always contended that, as Weekes continued trying to hook the fliers – against his captain's admonitions – he was justified in repeating them. O'Reilly believed the umpires should have intervened, although most of the offending balls flew over the middle and off stumps; the anti-intimidation law at that time specified balls 'at a batsman standing clear of his wicket'.

That match in 1952 and the Manchester instance in 1948 were the only times I saw Lindwall, in Tests, bounce three consecutive balls head-high to a batsman, but after surviving a fiery onslaught on a Sydney grasstop, Hassett, captaining Victoria, asked the umpire what was his definition of intimidation! Once Lindwall heard Hutton mutter, 'Remember lad, one day we'll have a fast bowler ...'

Twice bumpers struck batsmen full in the face: Gordon Woolmer, who attempted a hook while batting for The Rest of NSW in 1947, and opening batsman Jack Roberston, who tried to duck in Middlesex's second innings in 1948. Neither took any further part in the match. Ray told me afterwards, 'The sight of their injuries, bruised and swollen, upset me so much I could hardly sleep. On a later visit to England, Robertson asked me to broadcast with him and told listeners I was one of his greatest friends. I'm not sure Jack's wife has forgiven me, though.' The ball that gashed Compton between the eyes at Manchester glanced up from an attempted hook.

Occasionally he halted play in mid-over and waved deep fine-leg around 20 or 30 metres towards square, where a hook would often land. That made the striker think of a bumper, only to be taken aback by a yorker in his blockhole. Miller, known for picking up the bat with a masterful back-swing, came in to face him and, on a hunch, raised the bat-end only a foot from his boots. Along came a fast yorker but the bat came down just in time. Before he walked back for the next ball Lindwall called up the pitch, 'Can't you lift the bat now?'

Lindwall's £1300 fee for six months with Nelson in 1952 set a new high level for the Lancashire League. There he added an indipper to his armoury.

After Lindwall's first appearance before television cameras, a woman lip-reader wrote asking him to moderate his language on the field. She had seen him, so she said, make remarks after an umpire rejected his lbw appeal. In apologising, Ray added a rider that such vocabulary was unbecoming to a gentlewoman!

His response to calls on his stamina deepened admiration for his fitness and team-spirit. In a desperate attempt to prevent England regaining the Ashes he bowled 13 overs before lunch on the last day, 11 of them at the trot.

No fast bowler had lasted long enough in Test cricket to reach 100 wickets until he proved it could be done, at thirty-three in his 26th Test. Twenty months after his 100th victim, Lindwall's 52nd Test brought his 200th wicket.

In the West Indies Lindwall and Miller took 20 Test wickets each. I can still picture them toiling under a scorching sun, their lips blistered as its pitiless rays fried the sweat trickling down their faces. Lord Melody rounded off a calypso with these punch-lines:

Bawl, Lindwall, daun't be afraid!
Dem dat can't bat – break dey shaulder-blade!

Rather than disappoint a Grenada crowd, Lindwall bowled against Windward Islands in spite of a carbuncle on his right forefinger.

Visiting Brisbane to play in a match Ray met a blonde model, Peggy Robinson. At twenty-nine he married Peg, seventeen, the youngest bride cherished by any man to captain Australia.

After his third tour of England, in 1956, his seven Indian wickets for 43 helped bring a win at Madras. Lindwall was thirty-five when he captained his country in a Test at Bombay. Weakened by injuries and illness, it was a scratch side but you'd never have thought so, seeing the way they responded to his inspiringly aggressive captaincy in the heat. The Brabourne Stadium wicket was too good to permit a finish. Ray recalls:

The thing I remember most is being a captain without bowlers. Injuries kept Johnson, Miller and Archer out. Stomach trouble affected Davidson. Crawford strained a hip, Wilson pulled a muscle and a fever made Benaud too ill to bowl for part of the game. We had McDonald fielding as a substitute when he caught Ramchand for over 100. Burke and Harvey made centuries, enabling me to close with seven down and a good lead. Over 1000 runs were scored in the game but bowlers could not average five wickets a day.

As Queensland's skipper from 1955 to 1960 his out-cricket leadership was more assured than his direction of the batting.

The name Lindwall was missing from the Australian XI for two years. Determined not to accept eclipse, he pedalled a stationary training cycle on his lawn for half an hour each morning for three months. He nicknamed the bike 'Ching', because Peg, watching him pedalling without getting anywhere, sang 'Slow Boat to China'. When he almost lost heart, she encouraged him to train on. To correct a deviation from proper side-on delivery he rigged up a pulley to help exercises restore his left arm to the desired elevation.

As a veteran of thirty-seven with experience in 55 Tests, he was selected to play under a fourth captain, nine years his junior – Richie Benaud in his first season as skipper. Team-spirit enabled them to accept the situation with reciprocal grace. In a group discussing a day's play in Adelaide Benaud said, 'I couldn't do anything with Peter May.' Lindwall: 'You were instrumental in getting him out.' Richie, astonished: 'I was instrumental?' Ray: 'Yes, you made him over-confident.'

With his first ball of a Melbourne Test, Lindwall had Bailey caught by Davidson – at fourth slip, mind you. He bowled Bailey for 0 in England's second innings. That evening Bailey, looking at the menu, said, 'Roast duckling – that would be appropriate.' Passing his chair at that moment Lindwall put a hand on his shoulder and said, 'I didn't do it, Trevor – it must have hit something.'

Though he continued pace bowling until four months past thirty-eight, this did not dilute his career striking-rate past 60 balls a wicket. Lindwall's last four tests in Pakistan and India lifted his total to 228 wickets, taken with 13,666 balls in 61 Tests. Among the 228 were 145 in the first six of the batting order, 67 of them opening batsmen. He bowled 103 men in Test matches and skittled 14 Englishmen for 0. His expense rate was 38 runs per 100 balls. His 789 wickets in 224 games are the most by any Australian fast bowler for his country and state. An all-rounder, he topped 1500 runs in Tests and held 26 catches. His Melbourne 100 off English bowling in 1946 came in 113 minutes, aided by three chances. In Barbados he climbed out of a vinegar-and-water bath to raise 100 in 145 minutes

Lindwall's control of the ball at speed has yet to be equalled. To the end he usually completed an eight-ball over inside four minutes – a credit to himself and a reflection on others. He was awarded an MBE. His share from NSW's benefit fund and a testimonial with Miller and Morris was £1500. Ray was a Queensland selector for a dozen years. He partnered his wife as a florist in Fortitude Valley, Brisbane. For such a warrior on the cricket field, a life amid sheaves, posies and blooms may seem rather incongruous until you remember how often he cut down the flower of England's batting.

After some years of illness, Lindwall was a guest of the Tasmanian Cricket Association at the second Australia-Pakistan Test at Bellerive Oval in December 1995. He and his famous left-handed partner Alan Davidson were observed in a lengthy technical discussion with the Pakistani pair Waqar Younis and left-armer Wasim Akram.

It was his final public appearance. He suffered a stroke in Brisbane and died a few days later on 23 June 1996, leaving a wife, son and daughter.

In the procession of Australian captains an unpardonable gap would be left by skipping the part of Keith Miller, a dynamic all-rounder sidetracked by anxiety – other people's worrying. The nearest officialdom let him come was *de facto* leader, a vice-captain taking over Australia's first Test in Jamaica when a torn heel ligament on the second day put Ian Johnson off the field. With topscore 147 Miller had already helped put 515 runs on the board. The deputy skipper made the West Indies follow on and the Test was won by nine wickets.

A bouncer clash was the sort of thing the Australian Board had been praying wouldn't happen. The Board men were at the disadvantage of never having been within telescope range of the West Indies. For a year they had been alarmed by reports of crowd demonstrations against a touring English team. Yet an opponent, Garry Sobers, told the world later that Miller was the most popular cricketer who ever visited the Indies.

In a group talking with a Board member, Tasmanian solicitor Harold Bushby at Launceston, ex-captain Freddie Brown put the question, 'Why isn't Miller captain of Australia?' Bushby answered, 'He's too wild.' Baggageman Bill Ferguson said he knew some officials did not think Miller stable enough to captain a touring team but he thought that passing him over proved them out of touch with the modern scene.

Briefly, Keith Ross Miller, born 28 November 1919, had been under twenty when the second world war began. From the stresses and sophistication of the Air Force the strapping Mosquito fighter pilot emerged as the kind of cricketer every boy would like to be, the one who hit farthest and could bowl as fast as anyone.

He drove or swept 31 sixes in Tests. Taking the risk out of batting would be like taking the appetite out of eating or, as a wag said, the romance out of seduction.

As a magnetic personality, the crowd's favourite was a fusion of inconsistencies – impulsive, venturesome, wilful, variable, casual yet mettlesome, sensitive beneath his showmanship, open-handed, companionable, quick-tempered and as quickly calm again, vengeful yet easy-going. His traits revealed the debonair and devilish duality of his nature. Nettled, he could fling down savage bumpers yet Statham said Keith was like one of those chocolates, hard outside but with a soft centre.

Among the great matchwinners, Miller was the first to exceed 150 wickets and 2300 runs in Tests. Keith's 55 Tests yielded 170 wickets, 38 catches (some acrobatic) and 2958 runs, average 37. Among his 41 centuries five were made in Tests in which he was an opening bowler. As captain in some 35 first-class games Miller ad-libbed in ways no orthodox Test script would sanction.

The most damaging of his three losses was in an Adelaide game where

Phil Ridings sent NSW in first on a rain-affected track. As NSW fielded next day, a steward bringing out drinks was accompanied by Sid Barnes as twelfth man equipped for a stunt. The crowd laughed when Barnes brushed players' flannels, sprayed deodorant into their armpits, combed captain Miller's hair, and held up a mirror while a portable radio played. When the steward went off for more lemon squash but was officially prevented from returning, the crowd heckled Barnes for delaying play because there was too much equipment for him to carry off.

Miller later became a prominent ambassador for cricket. Viscount Cobham had him flown to New Zealand to play for his Governor's XI. Pakistanis gratefully remembered Keith turning up in Karachi to captain a side in a match for flood-relief funds in 1958, and English audiences were treated to a final sight of the great all-rounder the following year when he made 62, 102 not out and took two for 35 for Notts against Cambridge University. In November 1976, fifty-six-year-old Miller even undertook to captain an International XI against Pakistan in honour of the centenary of the country's founder Mohammed Ali Jinnah.

Cricket lovers who'd heard of his recent ill-health were delighted to see Miller holding court during the Fourth Test of the 1994–95 Ashes series at Adelaide Oval: the venue of his first Test hundred almost half a century earlier. Interviewing him in April 1996, Peter Fitzsimons noticed that the phone at Miller's Newport Beach home hardly stopped ringing.

Miller was the first of the skippers who led NSW to a record reign of nine years as top Sheffield Shield state. Without Miller's influence on Richie as a player and his vice-captain cricket would never have been blessed by the Benaud whose enlivening captaincy gave the game such a lift.

I.D. Craig

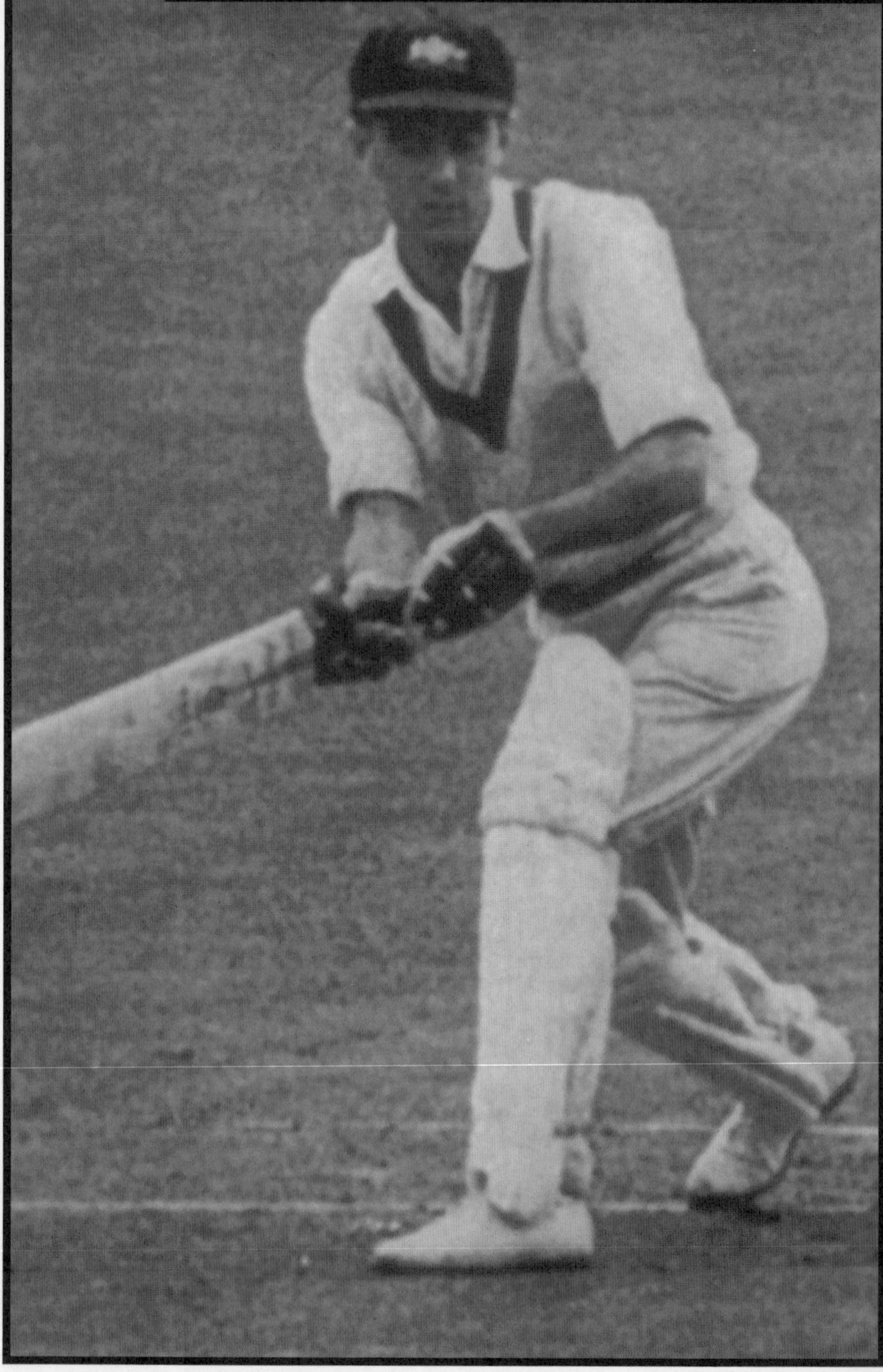

29

Youth at the Helm

The entrance of a young player quickens the interest of cricket-goers. His slightest success brings a ripple of encouragement. All young watchers are his allies and older men relive through his presence their own youthful ambitions. In his first Test match applause accompanied Ian Craig all the way to the middle at Melbourne. Many in the season's largest crowd, 47,000, had come especially to see the youngest cricketer ever to play in a Test match in Australia – seventeen years 239 days.

They saw a freckle-faced slip of a lad approach the wicket with quick, short steps, straight-backed as a pupil coming forward to receive a prize on speech night. The crowd's spokesmen shouted protests – 'Give the kid a fair go!' – when South African captain Jack Cheetham increased the tension by taking time to rearrange field placings. Cheetham had no ground for leniency because of the tender years of a batsman who had already had Springbok bowlers sweating in NSW. Counting every run as Ian neared 50, the crowd obviously hoped it would be the halfway mark toward making him the youngest century-maker in Test annals. A catch at cover off a new ball ended that wish at 53. By making topscore, 47, in the second innings Craig totalled a round 100, a debut raising the highest expectations .

Ian David Craig was born on 12 June 1935 at Yass, 112 kilometres closer to Sydney than Cootamundra, Bradman's birthplace. His father, banker John Craig, jokingly told friends, 'Australia's second Don Bradman has just been born.' As if to fulfil those words the boy showed unusual ball-sense. At thirteen he began playing in schoolboys' under-sixteen interstate baseball. For three years he was named in Australia's best schoolboy nine. Cricket was then running third behind baseball and rugby, yet at thirteen he played for Mosman in under-sixteen games. At North Sydney High School

Ian was rugby captain and cricket vice-captain to all-rounder Peter Philpott. Weighing less than 63 kg (10 stone) for his 173 cm (5 ft 8 in), Ian was the youngest cricketer ever to play for the state, sixteen years 249 days.

On his debut he was nine-tenths of the way toward 100 when South Australian left-arm spinner Jack Wilson trapped him lbw. In his ninth match he scored 213 not out, aided by luck when he fished for outswingers leaving his off stump. On 197 he started a couple of times for singles but was sent back by Miller, a crowd-conscious skipper who thought a better way to raise 200 would be a boundary hit. So Ian swept off-spinner Hugh Tayfield off his middle peg to the fence. By tea interval he had hit 22 fours and given two chances in 6¼ hours. When his captain told him he could take the pads off, the youngster said, 'Thank heaven for that.'

Ian was the youngest to score a double-century in a first-class match – seventeen years 207 days – 117 days younger than Hanif Mohammad had been for Pakistan against Bombay. Ian's double-century came in his 13th innings. Don had been five months past twenty and playing his 25th innings for his first 200. Craig's success prompted such headlines as ANOTHER BRADMAN and A NEW DON. Miller pointed out that linking Craig with Bradman put the lad in the unenviable position of having to make massive scores all the time. Once that label was hung on him, people looked for Bradman-like feats.

Ian's light frame and posture accentuated the neatness of his batting and the grace of his movements as the Bambi of the fielding side. He favoured on-shots and his play off his legs was especially attractive. Except for a down-the-handle grip lowering his back slightly, his stance was nicely poised. An unorthodox grip, with the back of the top hand almost toward point, tended to close the face of the bat. As if to correct this, as the bowler came to the crease Ian tilted his short handle away from his legs, then pulled it back – like a lever to open the gate of success. He had played only ten first-class games when he was chosen to tour England in 1953.

The most youthful cricketer Australia ever sent, six weeks short of eighteen, was fifteen months younger than Clem Hill had been in 1896. At a welcome Lord Justice Birkett predicted that as Ian left the pavilion to bat every mother in the land would pray for him and the prayer might be, 'May the Lord bless thy going in and thy coming out.'

The youngster was taking time by the forelock but not fortune. Setbacks made him uncertain what to expect from English tracks. The hairspring of confidence snapped. When teams were introduced to her in front of the Lord's pavilion, the Queen spoke longest to the freckled boy with greenish eyes. Among the things she said was, 'I understand this is your first visit to England?' Ian: 'Yes, your Majesty, and unless my batting improves it will be my last.'

The name Craig was missing from each Test and his highest score in 27 innings was 71 not out. His room-mate on most of the tour, Alan Davidson, did not once hear him complain. Instead of relaxing away from cricket when the roster gave him a day off, Ian went to Lord's daily to practise. He was unable to find an answer to incutters. He was trying to restore his own game to the touch he had attained in Australia rather than remake parts of his technique that English wickets showed to be inadequate. His back play was neither deep in the crease nor far enough across. In forward play his left shoulder was screwing out of line. Looking back years later Ian told me, 'You play strokes that come naturally. If you are not playing a shot well you restrict your use of it or eliminate it, as I did the hook when it got me out.'

Craig had to wait 13 months and 40 innings for his next century. It came in Hassett's testimonial match but in that lighthearted game four driven sixes in five balls from Ian Johnson confirmed little more than the power latent in his slim frame. On Australian turf googly left-handers Kline and Sincock worried him most. When Hutton's English XI toured Australia in 1954–55 Craig's pharmacy studies and Army national service kept him out of the picture.

He was the first cricketer sent to England twice before turning twenty-one. The 1956 team left him in a London hospital with food poisoning and the second Test was over before he got into his stride. His average was retreating as quickly as his hairline. When a Somerset wicketkeeper dropped a chance from his bat he said to slipfielder Colin McCool, 'That's the first time I've been let off in England.' McCool: 'Put your head down and make the most of it.' Craig made 62 and 100 not out – his first century in 38 innings in Britain. When Jim Laker had Australia grovelling on an infamous Old Trafford track Craig was Colin McDonald's most tenacious partner in an attempt to escape defeat by batting out the match. Spread over playable periods on four days Ian's dogged 38 kept out Laker and Lock for 4½ hours before the off-spinner had him lbw. The Manchester crowd applauded him all the way off. Such events get no reflection in the cold mirror of averages. This lists him at 19.8 for 18 innings in 11 Tests.

The only two Test wickets to batsmen's liking on the 1956 tour were at Lord's and Bombay – matches Ian missed.

Australian officials' collective thumb pulled up the youngest of the defeated brigade. New South Wales had Craig leading the state when he was twenty-one years 164 days. Soon the Board appointed Craig captain for a tour of New Zealand. Players date that 1957 trip as the start of Australia's climb back. Team harmony fostered by the callow skipper was better than for several seasons. Completing a three-year course at Sydney University brought a diploma in pharmacy. Before the next summer's visit to South Africa the Board consented to the newly fledged pharmacist having six months in England gaining experience. From London he joined the fourteen players Qantas had flown to Johannesburg.

Craig's personal qualities facilitated the experienced players' acceptance of a strange situation – having to be under the direction of a fledgling skipper nicknamed 'The Colt' who had led a side only 13 times and had only six Tests behind him. His sincere nature and unassuming manner obviated the risk of frictions. A good mixer, he was level-headed and tactful beyond his years. They knew he had not sought the position.

Unprecedented responsibilities were heaped on Ian's slender shoulders by an official's heart attack in Adelaide that left the team without a manager. Each morning before their coach left the Victoria Hotel, Johannesburg, their youthful skipper would pull out a diary and pass on to his players all he had been able to discover from helpful South Africans. They got by for a fortnight until the Board sent John Norton as manager. At crowded welcomes Craig's well-expressed speeches, flavoured with humour, held audiences' interest. Besides being the sort of son of whom any father could have been proud, he was an eligible bachelor to feminine eyes. When news came of

Ron Archer's engagement to Margaret Hutchinson in Brisbane, Ian sent a message saying all YWCA flags were being lowered to half mast.

Australia's youngest Test captain (twenty-two years 239 days) lost the toss at the Wanderers' ground in Johannesburg in the first match in South Africa to draw 100,000 spectators. Ian confessed later, 'Walking on as captain I felt I had the whole of Australia on my shoulders.' Within two days Craig was subjected to pressures too difficult for a skipper lacking depth of experience. Because Jackie McGlew profited from a few inaccurate balls to hit 13 off Benaud's second over, Ian took the leg-spinner off! When only three were down for 300 after lunch on the second day, Ian asked Davidson, 'What do we do now?' Instead of some shrugging-off remark like, 'As captain you should know', the so-far-wicketless bowler advised him to tighten up the game. Soon Davidson was pinning Waite and Endean down with an accurate line on the leg stump. On the fifth day, despite worn-wicket anxieties, Australia avoided defeat. Tensions turned Ian from a non-smoker into a player who took a last draw on a cigarette before he emerged through the dressing-room door.

As Adcock and Heine's hostility was humbling all on a spicy Durban strip Craig's plucky 52 helped Australia survive.

From a slim chest concealing a boyish heart came a voice as deep as Paul Robeson's, though lacking volume. Sometimes fieldsmen had to ask him to repeat a low-decibel rumble. After the first Test he realised it was better for Davidson to have first over with the glossy ball instead of Meckiff. On the first day of a Johannesburg Test his promotion of Benaud from seventh to fourth, diplomatically handled, was the most imaginative piece of captaincy of the season. It was rewarded with the fastest 100 of the rubber, giving the match momentum that clinched the series. Twice in the first four Tests Ian told the Springboks to follow on, though at Cape Town his players were divided about his decision.

After his 52 the Springbok bowlers prevented Craig from finding the right touch, like a guitarist who has lost his nail-scissors. They were helped because, in the side's interest, he often tried to quicken scoring as soon as he came in. Off-spinner Tayfield and others hit his stumps eight times in 17 innings on the tour, lowering his average to 36.9. The three completed

Tests were among his team's 11 wins in 20 first-class games. In naming Craig among Five Cricketers of the Year, all Australians, *South African Cricket Annual* editor Geoffrey Chettle took account of the way the youthful skipper coped with complexities. Much credit also belonged to players of greater capacity and deeper knowledge for the support they gave. Remember, it takes seven colours to make one rainbow.

Craig thought he had recovered fully from severe pre-season hepatitis until he was caught for 0 and 0 in his first two matches in November 1958. The second game was his only toss with Peter May before Ian dropped out for a season's rest. In Benaud's absence captaining Australia in Pakistan and India in 1959–60 Ian reappeared as NSW skipper and led a reserve Australian side on a brief tour of New Zealand. Of 48 games in three countries, teams he led through the gate won 27, tied one, lost two (both to Victoria) and 18 were not decided outright.

Putting his work first, he intended 1960–61 to be his last interstate season until he tapped a vein of form in first-wicket stands with Simpson. West Indian fieldsmen praised Craig's 83 for NSW as the best opening innings they saw against Wesley Hall on the tour of Australia. Sure on the back foot, he put away hip-high balls, rising awkwardly, with coolness that denied leg-side fielders the prospect of a catch. Wes went wicketless and paid out five runs an over.

On Craig's retirement for business reasons, three months short of twenty-seven, Benaud said his batting had the stamp of real maturity at a time for reaping benefits of his early experience. His playing of fiery Meckiff had been 'calm copybook stuff'. Ian's 7328 runs in 144 matches at an average of 37.9 included 15 centuries. Asked had he any regrets Craig said, 'No, I'd do it all over again.' If a selector today, would he load the responsibility of Test captaincy on a player only twenty-two?

> *I think it would depend a lot on the individual. Besides being a fine player, it is important that he should be well established in the side. At twenty-two I had only just got going ... The responsibility tended to make me go in thinking of what the position of the side called for, rather than going to the wicket simply as a batsman to settle down and build an innings. Bradman and others of great capacity have done both.*

At twenty-six Ian married an Adelaide accountant's daughter, Rosslyn Carroll, twenty-four, a brunette nursing sister. Succeeding Stan McCabe at thirty-three, Ian was the youngest trustee of Sydney Cricket Ground. He continued playing for Mosman until 1969 – an encounter with a 'raw but quick' Bankstown fast bowler called Jeff Thomson convinced him that his reactions might be slowing – and thereafter devoted himself full-time to his career as a pharmacist in Sydney.

In the 1980s Ian had the pleasure of watching another old boy of North Sydney High in Allan Border rise to the Australian captaincy, though by April 1994 he was an advocate of the succession of Mark Taylor. 'The way he (Border) has gone about the job with the minimum of hassle has always impressed me, especially considering the amount of cricket they play,' he said. 'But probably the time has come for change. I find it a little funny that it's match referees and the Board who've been maintaining discipline and not the captain. I think it's harder for Border to motivate himself than it was six to eight years ago. They are under such enormous pressure these days.' Ian was too self-effacing to add that he knew a little about pressure himself.

R. BENAUD

Come in Spinner!

amily trees branching from England, Scotland and Ireland have produced nearly all the foremost figures who have shaped Australia's cricket
history, yet the last four decades have brought special lustre to a name that
originated in France. At a Cricketers' Club dinner in Sydney celebrating a
record nine-year sequence of Sheffield Shield triumphs compere John Barnes
asked baritone Geoffrey Chard to sing 'The Road to the Isles' for
Sir Robert Menzies and 'Danny Boy' for ex-captains S.J. McCabe and
W.J. O'Reilly. Responding to a toast, reigning skipper Richie Benaud said,
'We've had requests for a Scottish song for the Prime Minister and an Irish
song for McCabe and O'Reilly but nobody asked for a French song for the
captain of the Australian XI.' Sir Robert led the laughter.

The Down Under branch of the Benaud family was founded by a man
who arrived in NSW by French sailing ship from La Rochelle. An assimilated
descendant, Louis Benaud bowled slow leg-breaks to take the whole 20
wickets in a match between Emu Plains and St Mary's. Lou was a cricket-
loving schoolteacher at Penrith when his elder son was born on 6 October
1930, christened Richard but never called it. At fifteen Richie began two
years' captaincy of Parramatta High School.

At ten his only sight of Grimmett in action started him thinking there's
no business like slow business. Though Richie's bowling was to mean most
for Australia, more was heard about his batting between his debut for
NSW at eighteen, his first Test at twenty-one and his fourth tour abroad at
twenty-six. At nineteen he lost a year after having been knocked out missing
a hook – necessitating a sinus operation to remove a piece of shattered
bone. A fractured thumb on his bowling hand and a broken finger seemed
only to deepen his determination.

As a bowler's son, Richie came into interstate cricket with habits that prevented him from reaching his full potential as a batsman. A grip well down the handle bowed the young six-footer's back. His bat's backswing was like a guide's finger pointing out the sights of the city. Noticing Miller's classic stance, Richie sought his advice. He raised his grip, ironed most of the stoop out of his spine and reduced the loop, but a flourish in the back-lift is hard to get rid of.

In his last innings of the 1953 tour of England a taunt made him re-remember his drive, the piston that made his batting work. He had been an hour playing himself in at Scarborough festival when Hutton teasingly remarked, 'What's matter, laad? Art playing for average?' Benaud's answer was 11 sixes, mostly drives. Once outfielder Bill Edrich playfully crossed the boundary and placed himself on a bank at the Trafalgar Square end. He re-entered the field before the next ball, only to see it land where he had stood. His 11 sixes remained a record for an Australian until Queenslander Andrew Symonds, playing for Gloucestershire in 1995, cleared the Abergavenny perimeter against Glamorgan 16 times.

At twenty-four in the West Indies Benaud's three Test wickets in four balls at Bourda attracted less notice than his buccaneering century in 78 minutes at Kingston – fastest Test 100 since the second world war. Lashing 20 off an over by fast bowler Frank King, Richie caused a Jamaican barracker to protest, 'Do it to England, mahn, not to us!'

The developing activist's most telling contribution on his second tour of England was 97 off 113 balls at Lord's – the only Test Australia won in 1956. As a gesture of resentment of inferior tracks in three Tests Benaud asked umpires to give him block 18 times in one innings. Those experiences imbued him with a resolve to beat England some day, somehow.

On his twenty-first birthday he had become engaged to pretty blonde Marcia Lavender. In a Sydney Test against South Africa a hard cut by Waite gashed his upper lip and smashed the gum. Before the Test was over Richie was in the field again. He took two wickets with leg breaks, despite the handicap of stitched lips sealed by plaster. At the wedding six days later he could only mumble and could only drink through a straw. Seven weeks later a Test tour of England took him away for 7½ months. A week after their first child, Gregory, was born Australia sent the young father to the West Indies for four months. Concern about fluctuating reports of his wife's health was reflected in the abandon with which he let fly at everything in his Kingston 121. Three months before their other son, Jeffrey, was born another Test tour took Richie to South Africa. Jeffrey was three months old before his father saw him. (After many strains on the marriage, Richie took the family on a tour of England before the breakup which resulted in his wife obtaining an uncontested divorce on the ground of desertion.)

His advance to a front-rank bowler owed much to guidelines he sought from O'Reilly: to cease overdoing so many sorts of balls in an over and to base his attack on leg-breaks. It took nine years to get the accuracy he sought. At his top from the ages of twenty-seven to thirty, Richie used the meanest cotton-pickin' fingers, aiming to keep his rate about 2½ runs an eight-ball over. He often succeeded in Tests, though his all-career outlay was nearer 2½. He was happiest twirling a leg-break and twisting the lion's tail. Benaud was the first Test player to couple 200 wickets with 2000 or more runs.

One step and five paces took him to the crease side-on. His delivery stride brought his arm over high with the wrist crooked. His shirt's plunging neckline revealed a bronzed chest, but his variations were well concealed. It was all done with an air of deliberation, conveying to the batsman that his downfall was only a matter of time. Commanding respect with length leg-breaks, he set batsmen up for his top-spinner. Pushed lower through the air his flipper usually caused them to play back and be trapped by its quicker nip. If pitches allowed enough grip for his wrong'un he posted a leg-slip.

Instead of promoting Benaud from vice-captain when Miller retired in 1956, NSW turned to Craig. When cricketers came to the Australian room in South Africa for a drink at the end of the day, Richie was among the welcoming hosts who would sit yarning with towels draped across their bare haunches. Mellowing of his off-field ways gradually changed official minds about his qualifications for leadership.

I estimate that he spun along more than 1000 balls in South Africa before the first game. My only doubt was whether his mastery of line and length would be at a cost of his spinning fingers becoming too raw. A mixture from a Timaru chemist in NZ (calamine and boracic acid) enabled

269

his corn-embossed fingers to flick along almost 6000 balls in first-class games. The Springboks thought no leg-spinner had a right to be so accurate. His 13 Natal wickets at Durban formed the biggest haul of his career.

As Jackie McGlew played a ball from Benaud in a long partnership with Waite at Kingsmead his bat slipped from his cautious grasp. Following through, the bowler picked up the bat. Before handing it to the batsman, Richie pretended to drive an imaginary ball, as if demonstrating how his bowling ought to be played. The crowd laughed. They had little to laugh about as the pair took almost 8½ hours to make 231 for the third wicket, averaging two runs an over. Patriotic applause was heard when the partnership added 100, more applause at 150. When the scoreboard showed 196, further applause surprised wicketkeeper Grout, who asked Waite, 'What's that for?' Waite: 'I suppose it's a record.' Grout: 'Must be an LP.'

By the time Australia had come through unbeaten Richie had 106 wickets in 18 first-class games, four centuries (two of them in Tests) and 23 catches. His triumphs afield were paralleled by the rounding-out of his personality. Benaud shares with Charles Turner the record of most wickets in a season anywhere outside England (Turner's 106 were in 12 matches in Australia in 1887–88).

Events in the three weeks before the first Test in 1958 did nothing to inspire confidence. Craig's second thoughts about his health left Australia without a captain. The selectors turned back to men the Board had bypassed for two years. Neil Harvey led an Australian XI in a Sydney game that ended in disaster on a boot-damaged pitch. About a week before the Test they switched to Benaud, hastily swallowing their preference for a batsman. Richie had led NSW only a couple of times in three years, his main experience in captaincy having been for Cumberland. As England's range of bowling looked the best that ever invaded Australia they were not surprised when Sir Donald Bradman told them, 'I only hope we can at least give you a good game.'

As Benaud was well aware of being third choice for want of another, the sequel showed the personal fibre of the man in addition to unexpected qualities of leadership. As one glimpse of a sunrise tells much, one ball told me Australia had fluked on the captain needed. As Alan Davidson bowled

270

it in Brisbane an edged catch was awaited by a U-field arc of slips and leg slips, except for O'Neill at cover and Kline at mid-on. Pitching on a grassy strip the first ball rose to hit left-hander Peter Richardson on the shoulder. Before a second ball Benaud brought mid-on a few yards from the batsman's hip. A field change before a ball touched a bat! We were witnessing the emergence of the No. 1 opportunist of all national cricket leaders. He never missed a chance to seize the initiative, trying to make things happen. The toecaps of his boots were always seeking a chance to get a foot in the door – either foot in any door his size 9½ boot could force ajar. Richie had the faculty of making snap decisions that did not snap back. Luck soon aided him when Bailey was not out in England's first innings. That caused May to send Bailey in earlier in the second dig, where for hours his encamping presence put better batsmen off their game. Superb fielding was making runs scarce anyhow. After a dreary stretch of 19 runs off 21 overs Ron Roberts asked the scorer, 'When did Bailey come in, George?' George Duckworth: 'Half past two.' Roberts: 'Yes, but which day?'

Richie spun out 43 Englishmen in seven matches. He was the only captain to take so many as 31 wickets until India's Bishan Bedi did so against Australia in 1977–78. (Pakistan's Imran Khan later took 40 Indian scalps as skipper in 1982–83.) Compared with three wickets a match in his first 32 Tests he averaged five victims a Test as bowler-captain.

Benaud's bubbling-over keenness was lapped up by his players. He ran to congratulate bowlers and catchers for each wicket but a little-noticed action in Melbourne revealed that his appreciation went far beyond highlights. After a false start for a dangerous run irrepressible Godfrey Evans slipped headlong and tried to poke his bat back. From backward point Colin McDonald's throw above the bails enabled Grout to run the venturer out. As the crowd noisily watched Evans depart and Lock came in Benaud ran from short leg to give an average fielder a passing pat for an orthodox throw.

Breaches of unemotional he-man tradition caused many older onlookers to say the next thing would be kissing and they found fervid embraces repugnant, as if bordering on homosexuality. From a practical standpoint I thought the only issue was whether rapture inspired bowlers and fieldsmen to do better. Don't tell me it didn't.

Ten years between Bradman's last Test and Benaud's 4-0 triumph against England had brought drastic changes. To his bowler's eye one ball's behaviour from the pitch told Richie as much as a blacktracker learns from a footprint. In a sense Richie was not so much a manager announcing decisions or an overseer issuing directions as a charge-hand, at the bench with his artisans, the most hard-working of them all. Harvey said Richie cultivated team morale better than any other captain he played with.

If he could contrive it, he liked closing innings to get a few overs at the other side at the fag-end of a day or before an interval. Besides asking to see any charts scorers made of batsmen's scoring strokes, he began a system of having a card of the bowlers' progress overs and runs at each interval.

Detonated by Cowdrey's bat, a blinding catch that knocked Benaud over backwards in the gully was the greatest ever seen at Lord's by Ian Peebles. Richie's 65 catches in 63 Tests included others almost as dramatic. In one series fielding brought almost two-thirds of England's wickets while the Englishmen caught, stumped or ran out fewer than half as many. He based his tactics on the knowledge that the more good balls a side bowled in a day the more wickets could fall.

His blue eyes gave nothing away. The surest pointer to any arousal was a drier tone of voice, uttered over a bottom lip like Maurice Chevalier's or Mel Torme's. Benaud would shoot straight from the lip. If events demanded firm correction, Richie's lower lip jutted farther out, like a tramcar's step. You could measure how well correctives were working by the way it retracted until a dragonfly could no longer have alighted on it. In the team-room he did not watch constantly but looked intently at anything he sensed could influence future tactics. He steered clear of politics, religion (his was cricket) and card games. He never smoked until he accepted cigarettes while sitting out official speeches on a successful tour of India when he was twenty-nine.

Top-level politics crossed his track in 1959 when US President Eisenhower on a visit to Pakistan was taken along to Karachi National Stadium to see a strange game everyone was talking about. Inside, surrounded by simmering thousands of Asians, he saw a cluster of eleven Australians calmly vying with the elect of the Islamic nation at cricket.

272

Seeing that the Pakistanis had arrayed Eisenhower in a blazer, the Australian captain said, 'I see you've joined the opposition, sir.' The President recovered neutrality by accepting Richie's cap. Benaud was the first visiting captain to win a series in Pakistan, and the last Australian.

At Madras admirers ran on to the field with a gift, an Indian-woven shawl. The crowd relished his pretence to run up to bowl with the shawl draped across his shoulders until an umpire intervened.

It was no fluke that English ex-captain Arthur Gilligan classed the 1960–61 West Indies series as the best cricket he ever saw. On Test eve Bradman told the Australians they could make it one of the game's greatest years by trying to play good cricket all the time, 'even to the point where the result becomes immaterial'. Neither side shrank from defeat in the delirious excitement that resulted in the first tied Test. Benaud and Frank Worrell each had the zealous loyalty – almost idolatry – of their players and handled public relations in ways that assured favourable images for their teams. Though the Australians could not rival the spectacular strokes of the West Indians, Benaud outdid Worrell in enterprising field settings. He would not place outfielders to deter Sobers, Kanhai and others from going for their shots. Instead, he showed faith in his bowlers' ability to get the stroke-players out. Apply that all through West Indies' innings and no wonder 90,800 packed into the Melbourne ground to set a world cricket record for one day.

In 1961 a surgeon disposed of Benaud's tonsils before his captaincy in England. Aboard the liner guidelines framed from lessons from previous visits even included a goodwill gesture – willingness to try walking out without waiting for umpires to rule on fine snicks to wicketkeepers. He gave no direction, leaving it to each individual (his countrymen generally have little faith in walking).

An obstinate tendon injury made his shoulder the most-discussed since the Venus de Milo's. For weeks the pain made him shave left-handed. The trouble failed to stop his developing exceptional team spirit, though his habits differed widely from Woodfull's ... late hours relaxing over a few beers, rising late to finish breakfast just in time to go to the ground. I recall inexplicable hunches that seemed to slip beyond a rational borderline

273

into the occult. The most uncanny occurred when Mike Smith came in at Edgbaston, his home ground. Benaud brought Lawry in to short gully, a new position for Mackay's medium-pace bowling. The Queenslander's second ball somehow flipped from Smith's pad to his bat then straight into Lawry's hands.

When Dexter's pace-setting bat was putting England on top in the decisive Manchester Test Benaud scorned to become defensive but took risks counter-attacking. Overnight he had consulted Lindwall, who agreed bowling around-the-wicket to spin from bootmarks would be worth trying but warned that every inaccurate ball missing the patch was likely to be banged to the boundary. A near-lost Test was rescued when Richie's legbreaks from the rough patch captured five for 13 in 25 balls. It was one of England's worst evenings since Philip Sassoon ordered a Union Jack lowered because its colours clashed with the sunset.

Though three of five tosses were lost, the 1961 team won the Wills prize for fastest scoring in each Test. His batsmen averaged 46.75 runs each 100 balls, nine runs more than the Englishmen. Crowds saw the Australians bowl almost 112 balls an hour, 14 an hour more than England's bowlers. Benaud was unrivalled in his consideration for touring players not needed in Tests. He saved them from pining as spare parts by making sure they were given opportunities against counties. His team was the first to have eight bowlers take 50 or more wickets each.

While playing to win, the spectators' best friend was alert to inject excitement into the game as well. At times when this looked like misfiring but didn't, players' feelings were summarised by English fast bowler Harold Rhodes: 'If you put your head in a bucket of slops, Benordy, you'd come up with a mouthful of diamonds.' In public relations to benefit the game Benaud was so far ahead of predecessors that raceglasses would have been needed to see who was at the head of the others. After the 1961 tour the Queen awarded him an OBE. First to bring a fully trained journalist's mind to bear on public relations, he understood newspapers and their reporters' needs. By forestalling misunderstandings he created goodwill worth thousands of pounds. The beneficence resulted in his team's go-ahead cricket being recognised and acclaimed by critics who would rather have seen

274

England win. No team left Britain after a closely-fought series amid such ringing praise as this side. These achievements, put on the scales with his skippership successes, lead me to rank him first among captains I have known. Reflecting over twenty years, noted umpire Charles Elliott said Richie was the best overseas captain.

Benaud was the first to lead Australia in 28 Tests. Against England, Pakistan, India, West Indies and South Africa his teams won 12, tied one, lost four and 11 were unfinished. He was the first Australian captain to put the other side in three times. Each time his judgement was borne out – against England in Melbourne, Pakistan at Dacca and the West Indies in Melbourne. He was an even worse tosser than Bradman, who lost 11 spins. Richie had to return to the room 17 times to tell his team the opposing skipper had the choice.

It could be said that he never lost a series but that was not his angle of approach. Though his bottom lip showed he was irked by others often using defensive field placing and bowling against his team, I recall only three instances of his forsaking his attacking line. When imaginative moves or injury to a leading bowler landed him in trouble his reverse action looked all the more drastic.

Unless other ruses were worth trying, he believed in making full use of his best bowlers. Several times he over-bowled fast left-hander Alan Davidson, allowing him insufficient rest. It was a study in psychology to see Richie persuading Alan to try another over. He would even help the left-hander peel off his sweater and take it to the umpire.

Davidson limping off Adelaide Oval with a torn thigh muscle early in England's first innings of the 1962–63 series put Benaud as near as he ever came to panicking. Irreparable loss of his top bowler affected him almost as much as Long John Silver would have been by amputation of his other leg. Next, Sydney's 'Horror Test' ended with a dwindling crowd hooting Australia's not out batsmen off the field. It wouldn't have done for the duke, sir. I mean the Duke of Norfolk, who as England's team manager was saddened by two defensive stalemates and pleaded for each Test to be played as a match to be won, instead of being treated as a segment in a series.

275

Chosen in a Combined XI for the South Africans' second match at Perth, the Australian captain said he preferred West Australian skipper Barry Shepherd to lead the side. But when Peter Pollock's bouncing speed daunted batsmen, Benaud asked could he go in first-drop in the second innings instead of seventh. The big Springbok fired a bumper at him. To say he hooked it for four would understate the shot; he clubbed it to the fence. Pollock took no more wickets and Benaud's 132 in a 237 stand with Simpson denied the South Africans a second win.

Benaud is the only Australian XI captain whom selectors sent into the field at high risk of losing a no-balled bowler and being left to fight out a Test, in effect one man short. At Brisbane umpire Colin Egar called fast left-hander Ian Meckiff four times in his only over against South Africa. Angry barrackers raged at Benaud for not switching the left-hander to the other end. To reporters' questions Benaud said:

I bowled Meckiff for hundreds of overs before umpires who approved his delivery and I accepted their decision. Now that an umpire does not accept Meckiff's delivery I accept that decision, too. I will not bowl him again.

After a telephoned threat to umpire Egar two detectives were at the ground. Benaud was sipping tea in the lunch-room when O'Neill told him masseur Jock Anderson was walking around muttering threats. Through a doorway a figure appeared, hat pulled down near sunglasses. The intruder displayed a *Sporting Globe* showing headlines asking why Benaud had not bowled Meckiff from the other end. 'Why didn't you?' rasped the semi-disguised Jock. Lifting the paper, he pointed a revolver at Benaud and fired. It was only a cap gun but at that moment, Richie said, his past life flashed before him.

Meckiff said that Richie, 'who is behind every player', had done the right thing on the day that ended his cricket career.

As a mocking paradox, the promoter of optimism was the mischievous adopter and spreader of a superstition about the number 87. Not only was it bad luck for a man to get out 13 short of 100, but the appearance of 87 anywhere on a scoreboard augured ill for someone (the equivalent of Englishmen calling 111 a Lord Nelson – one eye, one arm, one aspiration).

The sight of 87 made the team stir apprehensively. Batsmen risked their wickets with agitated strokes to get off the accursed number.

High-speed bowlers look more devastating but Richie got within four of having 300 Test batsmen in his net (17 of his 65 catches were off his own bowling).

Benaud was thirty-three when he gave his last emotional look at his name going off the Sydney scoreboard. In 259 games he had taken 945 wickets (average 24) and clung to about 250 catches. In 366 innings he totalled 11,801 runs (average 36). Highest of his 23 hundreds was 187 against Natal. In two Test series, 1956 and 1957–58, he hit more boundaries than any other player though once it was for a losing side.

Richie's brother John, taller, 13½ years younger and similarly dynamic, captained NSW for two years. In the second of his three Test matches John completed 100 by lifting an enormous six off Pakistan captain Intikhab Alam into the Melbourne crowd. Touring the West Indies in 1973 John replaced Keith Stackpole (broken finger) in the last Test. He later served as a Test selector.

Where some players end their career with precious little forethought, Richie's post-retirement career had never been in doubt. In 1953, after three years as a clerk at the John Fairfax Group, he successfully sought a transfer to news reporting from Sydney *Sun* editor Linsday Clinch. He learned valuable rudiments of the journalistic craft writing courts, industrial relations and police rounds.

Three books written while Australian captain – *Way of Cricket* (1961), *Tale of Two Tests* (1962) and *Spin Me a Spinner* (1963) – told Test cricket tensions from an informed inside source, and smoothed Benaud's path into the press box the moment he had discarded his last pair of boots.

In the hiatus between the 1956 tours of England and the sub-continent, Richie had also studied broadcasting techniques in a curriculum designed by the BBC's Head of Light Entertainment Tom Sloan. It stood him in good stead when he spent the winter of 1960 as a guest caller on the BBC of the England–South Africa series, and he was first invited to fill a seat for BBC TV in 1963.

Benaud's career since has straddled print and electronic media with the same *sang froid* that he radiated as a skipper. His journalism has been prodigious, while *Willow Patterns* (1968), *Benaud on Reflection* (1983) and *The Appeal of Cricket* (1995) contain incisive critiques that administrators would be advised to heed.

If that microphone maven John Arlott became renowned as 'The Voice of Cricket', too, Richie is now equally deserving of the epithet 'The Face of Cricket'. He has now commented on more than 50 cricket seasons in both hemispheres for the BBC and Channel Nine, mostly as anchorman and centre of gravity.

At thirty-six this wholehearted undoer of the English carried off blue-eyed Derbyshire brunette Daphne Surfleet, thirty. In Sydney she set up a public relations service, complementing her husband's television and newspaper activities.

At the recommendation of Ian Chappell, Kerry Packer called the pair at their Coogee apartment on 6 April 1977 and engaged D.E. Benaud & Associates to help launch World Series Cricket. Benaud saw it as a means to improving the players' lot and to broadening the game's appeal and although his role in the outlaw initiative would cost him many friends in cricket's *sanctum* was a whole-hearted supporter.

Many of the generation that has grown up with him as the public face of Channel Nine's Test match coverage since November 1979 have no idea that he did not lose a Test series as leader. Buttonholed by a twelve-year-old autograph hunter one evening at the SCG in December 1982, he was asked: 'Did you ever play cricket, Mr Benaud?'

He did. Rather well, too.

R.N. HARVEY

Pocket Dynamo

Since Neil Harvey's last stroke streaked to the pickets in 1963 no batsman anything like him has arisen. Probably, as with Bradman, we have no right to expect another. From time to time amid the upsurge of cricket interest Down Under newer stars give us reminders of his most scintillating hours: Ian Chappell's rousing century before lunch against Victoria in Adelaide, Doug Walters's 100 between tea and stumps in the 1974 Perth Test, Greg Chappell's 165 off 40 overs for Queensland against NZ on a grass-carpeted pitch where 30 wickets toppled in two days, Mark Waugh's exhilarating 138 on debut against England at Adelaide Oval on Australia Day 1991 . . . Taller players and right-handed batsmen.

In the all-time list of Australians in first-class cricket Neil Harvey's left-hand batting placed him fifth for runmaking. As a versatile fieldsman, this ball-hawk from baseball takes top place. He was famed for his catching, his unerring right-hand throws into wicketkeepers' gloves and his arrow-like pegging of an unattended wicket.

It takes a star of first magnitude to gleam in regions bedazzled by the record-breaking of Bradman. To the challenge of that situation Neil made himself the first cricketer to score Test centuries in 15 different cities. He was the first of any race able to top 20 centuries in a post-war period marked at times by substandard tracks that sent Test teams' totals in the 1950s dipping one-third below the average.

Had Michelangelo been a cricketer he would have batted like Harvey, with the touch that made chips of marble fly everywhere as he pressed on with the creation of a great piece of sculpture. No player today travels so far along the pitch to drive. Yet not one stumping occurred among his 127 dismissals in Tests.

Born on 3 October 1928 at Fitzroy, Robert Neil Harvey was fifth of six sons of Horace Harvey. Four of the brothers, Mervyn, Clarrie, Ray and Neil made centuries for states. Neil was always one of the smallest players on the field, standing about 171 cm (5 ft 7½ in) and 66.5 kg (10 st 7 lb).

The strength of his compact frame and the spirit animating his play made him a pocket dynamo. At seventeen his knocking at the door of the Victorian XI impelled me to write for the *Cricketer*, 'Harvey may have too far to go to reach the Test team next season but he'll get there sooner or later, sure enough.' He was eighteen, an apprentice fitter and turner, when his second game for Victoria in Tasmania brought him 154.

Neil was nineteen years eighteen weeks when he burst into Test cricket like a champagne cork. In his second Test he topped the score, 153 against India.

The Englishmen had hopes of making Australia follow on at Leeds when Harvey joined Miller, saying, 'What's going on out here? Let's get stuck into them, eh?' Taking risks against Laker he made 112 from 183 balls in his first Test in England.

Filling a key place in Australia's batting line-up made him consider his side's needs to make sure of high totals. He had to rein in impulses and be less free with shots involving a risk of getting out. Yet he still scored three-fifths of the runs made while he was in.

The Australians, out for 75 on a rain-soaked Durban track, seemed headed for defeat when the last six men were left to raise 240 on crumbling turf. With 151 not out in 5½ disciplined hours Harvey carried his team through to the most remarkable victory Test cricket had known. His 660 in eight innings set a record for a series in South Africa. Harvey's 1526 runs in 1949–50 are still the most for an Australian touring South Africa and he shares the record of eight centuries in one season there.

A Johannesburg optometrist testing the Australians found an impairment made Harvey's long sight the weakest. 'Who leads you out to bat?' he asked. Without spectacles Neil could not discern seam on the revolving ball and had difficulty telling 3 from 5 and 6 from 8 on the scoreboard. He was too shy to wear glasses until social games after he retired. Neil's chanceless 100 in 106 minutes against South Africa in Adelaide stands as the fastest Test century in Australia since the war.

Harvey was twenty-four when his 834 in five Tests against South Africans touring Australia displaced Bradman's 806 as the highest total in any series the Springboks played anywhere.

With two out for seven in reply to West Indies' 357 at Sabina Park in 1955 Harvey knuckled down to a double century. A planter offered ten shillings a run if he beat Hutton's Test record 364. Having put his side ahead, Neil had no desire to push his longest Test innings past seven hours six minutes for 204.

When Hutton said to Neil, 'You play and miss too many balls,' Harvey replied, 'I have a go at 'em, anyway.' Trevor Bailey asked, 'I wonder how many runs Harvey would make if he decided to stop playing strokes with an element of risk about them.'

He was the coolest receiver of bouncers I ever saw. No back-pedalling or ducking. Neil swayed his head across just enough to allow the rearing ball to hiss past his right shoulder.

Short-of-a-length bowling to him failed in its restrictive purpose. His speed in making position gave him time to deliver fence-bound square-cuts. Strokes penetrating every sector of the field left bowlers feeling ten fieldsmen were not enough to go around. An Indian scorer's chart of Harvey's chance-less 140 at Bombay showed his runs to have been impartially distributed past long-on, mid-wicket, square-leg, fine-leg, long-off, extra-cover, cover, backward point, gully and an occasional deflection past slip.

He was essentially practical, yet for a Test would choose flannels he had worn in successful innings.

In his second match as Victorian captain, NSW had three wickets left to get 16 to win. Characteristically, Neil called in Kline's two onside boundary riders and packed a close attacking field. Tempted to smack a wrong'un through the open space, Benaud, 63, snicked a slip catch. It paved the way for Victoria to avert defeat with one of only two ties in Shield history.

The day before Neil's fifth match as skipper the Board announced that Ian Craig would captain the Australian team in NZ with Harvey vice-captain. Ian said, 'Bad luck Nin. I thought you might have got it.' Though deeply hurt, Neil assured him he was behind him all the way. As Colin McDonald had broken his nose at practice, the resourceful left-hander opened the innings himself with Len Maddocks and made 209. In his candid book *My World of Cricket* Harvey tells:

> *My first double century for Victoria, coming on top of the captaincy issue, gave me as much pleasure as any innings I had ever played. My only disappointment was that I had succumbed to fatigue ... If I hadn't got out then I might have reached 300 the following day. I certainly had my mind set on such a score anyway.*

He never smoked and was a total abstainer until his late twenties, when he entered fully into after-play companionship.

The first time Harvey led an Australian side his drives caused Natal to place five men in a longfield arc to reduce shots to singles. From the Umgeni end of the Kingsmead ground a barracker began protesting, 'You're not *hitting* them, Harvey!' When Neil responded with deft glances and cuts the voice called reproachfully, 'You're only *touching* them, Harvey!' Later, in the hearing of the team, Neil rebuked two Australians for not having tried to score quicker when they knew he intended a closure to try to force a win. Coming from a senior player they admired, the reproof was heeded with respect.

A twice-broken finger snapped a thread of 48 consecutive Tests and gave Springbok bowlers some respite from his bat. A crippled girl and her companion who had been watching at Port Elizabeth were unable to get on packed buses. A passing car pulled in to give them a lift. The new passengers recognised the observant driver as Harvey.

Never a pause marked his acceptance of umpires' decisions ruling him out. When called into the slips he took no part in lbw appeals, leaving them to bowler and wicketkeeper. Chasing runs against the clock at Lahore, Harvey and right-hander Norman O'Neill realised that Pakistan's field-changing delays would deny them time to win. On 37 the left-hander allowed a ball to hit his wicket, enabling a right-handed pair to complete the chase. The team was the first to win a series in Pakistan.

Nearing thirty he looked around to secure his future better than selling sportsgoods. He moved to a Sydney glass and dining-ware firm.

An Australian XI he led against May's Englishmen in Sydney had no chance after pacemen's boots gouged out the worst hole I ever saw in an

Australian wicket. It could have held a meat dish. To judge anything from a heavy reverse in such a match would have been a travesty yet the selectors laid themselves open to suspicion of panic when they shied off Harvey as Craig's successor. Neil first heard when Benaud telephoned him, saying, 'Guess who's captain?' Harvey replied, 'You are.' Richie: 'That's right. I'm sorry, I thought you should have got it.' Benaud said Neil's simple assurance 'I'll be playing for you, Richie' was the vote of confidence he most wanted; it came from one who did most to make his job easy.

Captaining a Test side involves bringing together as many strands as there are in a Persian rug. When Harvey took over the post at Lord's in 1961 he was under the disadvantage of having a below-strength side. Benaud's painful shoulder tendons kept out the leading all-rounder. Davidson doubted whether his strained back would last out the match. Wicketkeeper Wally Grout had a black eye from a practice knock. I remember forecasting that to have a chance against England the Australians would have to catch like performing seals. When Harvey loss the toss to Cowdrey and a juggled gully chance went down, the windvane on Father Time's back was turned, as if a one-sided contest had no appeal to him.

As a thirty-two-year-old veteran of 70 Tests under half a dozen skippers Harvey had the tactical know-how to meet, even anticipate any twist in a complex game.

Saying, 'I'll try to pull out something special for you, Nin,' Davidson was aided by the ball's erratic behaviour from a ridge. Batsmen of both sides suffered so many blows on the gloves, thighs and ribs at the nursery end that it would have merited being renamed the surgery end. In the first-day skirmishes of the Battle of the Ridge 12 wickets fell. Harvey, his right arm bandaged, said, 'If it pitches on the up-side of the ridge the ball kicks, if on the down-side it shoots.' Blows he suffered while scoring made his gait look stiff. Thanks to Lawry's plucky 130, Australia led by 134.

In England's second innings Neil switched his newest bowler, Graham McKenzie, to attack the nursery end reasoning that the powerful youth's higher delivery would make the ball rear most from the ridge. Five cheap wickets rewarded the move. Harvey often placed himself in the spot where he judged a catch likeliest to come. Trying Simpson's over-the-wrist spin for the first time, he came close at silly leg for Illingworth. A bouncing wrong'un was popped to him.

Australia needed only 69 to win. Remembering past low-target slumps, Harvey advised his batsmen to play normally and hit the ball to avoid being made to struggle for runs. Trueman and Statham's salvoes broke through, confronting the last six with having to make 50 where the first four batsmen fell short of 20. After wicketkeeper John Murray caught him off Trueman, Harvey said as he passed incoming Burge, 'Keep playing your shots, Peter.' The Australians were relieved when a short-arm hook off Statham brought the winning boundary hit. Before the Test, co-selector Colin McDonald, captain of Victoria, had said, 'If I notice anything in the course of the game, Ninna, would you like me to mention it?' Harvey said he would appreciate that. Neil handled the side and the situations with such facility that McDonald remarked, 'There was never a need for me to mention anything.' Harvey handed control back to Benaud with Australia one-up.

Harvey's batting and fielding gave pleasure to more cricket-goers than any other Australian. His 67 centuries were spread around 35 fields in six countries, four of which never saw Bradman. More than half the entertaining left-hander's matches were representing Australia on nine tours abroad. His attractive play before home-ground crowds was excelled by his deeds overseas. Thirty-eight of his hundreds were overseas (nine more than in Australia). His 53.4 average abroad, compared with 48.7 at home, shows how much his adaptability meant.

For all their sparkle and frequency Harvey's centuries enthrone only part of his greatness. To me, the acid test is to succeed in conditions that enable bowlers to overwhelm others. This stood out in Neil's unconquered 92 as Tyson and Statham carved up his companions on a Sydney greentop. When last man Bill Johnston joined him Harvey asked, 'What do they think in the room?' Johnston: 'They reckon we're goosed.' Neil: 'Never mind, we'll give it a go.' In the city, crowds around radio shops blocked pavements not to miss a ball of his valiant innings until England won.

All strange to the Dacca mat, he made 96 against Fazal while seven partners were falling for 48. Harvey was the first Australian to pass the

285

half-century 45 times in Tests. Gripping sixties and seventies that leave many a century in the shade are remembered ... back-to-the-wall hours at Nottingham and Leeds when Laker and Lock had Australia down in the dumps ... dramatic defiance of Ghulam Ahmed on a Calcutta pitch treacherous after floods, and of Tayfield scenting victory on a quick-turning Durban strip. No man playing – not May, Cowdrey or Dexter – matched Harvey's resourceful touch in wresting 73 and 53 from the powder-puff pitch which scuttled the 1961 Leeds Test two days ahead of time.

On his first visit to South Africa Neil had met blonde Iris Greenish, daughter of a tramways superintendent. Iris came to Australia at twenty to marry Neil, twenty-five. Their first child, Robert, was born while Neil was at sea returning from the West Indies. Their daughter Anne was five days old when a tour took him to South Africa. Bruce was seven months old when the team flew to Pakistan. They parted after twenty years. At forty-seven Neil married blonde Barbara McGifford, forty-three, a bank teller.

Health and fitness enabled Harvey to play 79 Tests for Australia, a record of the time. He totalled 6149 runs, average 48.4 and made 62 catches. In 306 first class games he played 461 innings for 21,699 runs, a career average of 50, and brought off 228 catches. He was a young thirty-four when he left the game to build up Har-V-Sales Pty Ltd for Tupperware. How much he could have added to his great record can only be guessed from his having made centuries in two of his last three games and roped in six catches in his farewell Test. In his last state game the evergreen left-hander regaled a Sydney crowd with 231 not out against SA, the highest of his career. The session between lunch and tea yielded his durable bat 120 at a run a minute. The Queen made him an MBE at thirty-five.

Before Neil turned thirty-nine a Board ballot put him on the national selection committee. Among players introduced to Test cricket during his eleven years selectorship were high-speed bowler Jeff Thomson as partner of Dennis Lillee, folded-finger spinner John Gleeson, wicketkeeper Rodney Marsh, fast-medium bowler Max Walker, left-hander Gary Gilmour and batsmen Rick McCosker, Kim Hughes, Peter Toohey, Graham Yallop and Allan Border. He left the panel in 1979.

Harvey's place among the great can safely be left to an all-nation jury drawn from the elite of the bowlers he plundered: Laker and Lock, Trueman and Statham, Lindwall and Miller, Mankad and Fazal, Ramadhin and Valentine, Hall and Gibbs, Benaud and Tayfield, with Alec Bedser as foreman. Their verdict is sure of acclaim from those who packed the benches from Leeds to Trinidad, via Bombay.

R.B. SIMPSON

A Head for Heights

As a successful mountaineer never looks down, I suppose, a highly successful cricketer never looks back. That is, unless he wants recollection of some wrong to spur him on. Roped to nobody as he climbed, Bob Simpson had only his bat as an alpenstock. He had a head for heights but being left in the foothills for long waits retarded his chance to prove that he could keep above the snowline in the averages. Delays caused Simpson to modify his play and shed some of his dash to make sure of getting to the summit. He remade himself into a consistent opening batsman instead of a shot-playing middle-order man. His 311 against England at Old Trafford in 1964 was the highest innings by any Test captain until Graham Gooch scored 333 against India at Lord's in 1990.

Bob had natural ball-sense to a higher degree than any other sportsman I knew. Australia was fortunate that he stuck to cricket instead of being lured by an opportunity to become a professional golfer with the prospect of a larger pot of gold at the end of the rainbow than a cricket career could fill.

Excepting two wicketkeepers, Bob was the first Australian who brought off 100 catches in Test matches. Though such notable fielders as Harvey and Benaud played more Tests, none got within 40 of the total his hands closed on.

Robert Baddeley Simpson was the youngest of three sons of a Scottish couple, soccer-playing printer William Simpson and his wife Sarah. Bobby was born on 3 February 1936 in Marrickville. A week before turning seventeen he was batting impressively for NSW.

In his twelfth game for NSW he was 98 when a drizzle began and English captain Len Hutton took his team off. With partner Jim Burke, Simpson stayed while one of the umpires brought the Englishmen back. His concentration broken, the nineteen-year-old batsman swung wildly at left-hander Johnny Wardle and Evans stumped him, still two short of 100. Suspecting gamesmanship, Burke went to his defensive extreme to prevent the Englishmen getting another wicket. At last a barracker yelled, 'What do you think you are, Burke – a statue?' Farther around the Hill another voice chimed in, 'Yes – and wouldn't I like to be a pigeon!'

The missed-100 incident put the first pellet of iron into Simpson's soul. Before he turned twenty a jumping ball at practice broke his nose. Two operations were needed. No matter how a player tries to put such an injury out of mind, it cannot be completely forgotten.

To stake out an undeniable claim to a Test place he moved to a weaker state. Leaving home and his accountancy job on the Sydney Water Board he went 3700 kilometres west to write a sports column for the *Daily News*, Perth. He ended his stay on the bottom rung by winning selection at twenty-one to tour New Zealand. This helped him go with Craig's Test team to South Africa.

The trips came after he became engaged to Meg McCarthy, an attractive blue-eyed blonde with a dancer's figure and poise. Never co-operative with love, cricket separated them for ten months when he went to Perth and during Bob's half-year tour of South Africa. The forewarning of those partings helped Meg to be philosophic after they married when she was twenty and Bob twenty-two.

Dissatisfied with his batting in South Africa, despite a couple of centuries, he obtained guidance from Harvey which helped him become more side-on in style, especially in back-foot defence.

In two of a human's five senses, sight and touch, Simpson was exceptionally gifted. Chances his hands reached went down only in history. A lizard catching a passing fly is scarcely more unerring. There were no flies on Bob either; he did not let them land. The average man can only brush at an annoying fly. Bob caught them in mid-air with either right or left hand.

His well-fleshed fingers are about average length for a man 179 cm (5 ft 10½ in). He augmented natural talent by practice, getting a batsman about four metres away to hit balls firmly to him. 'Hit it harder!' he was always saying.

Simpson solved the old problem of the chest area, where a slip-fielder has difficulty cupping the hands properly with fingers pointing down or up. Letting the ball thud against his chest, he clasped it there. After he caught Barry Knight like this I saw O'Neill pull Bob's shirt open to look at the red mark on his flesh. It sounds painful and precarious, but helped make Bob the world's ace slip-catcher. 'Having spongy hands helps a lot,' Bob explained to me. 'Balls hitting the palm tend to rebound out, so I try to catch them at the base of my fingers.'

Australia's bowlers went through 11 Tests against England, Pakistan and India without him. Instead of brooding, Simpson became Accrington's professional for 1959 on £950 sterling. On Lancashire League wickets he continued eliminating risks from his technique. He headed the League batting with 1444 for Accrington (average 103) while Garry Sobers totalled 1454 (average 90) for Radcliffe in the Central Lancashire League. Before a Sunday game at Durham, former Services all-rounder Cecil Pepper told Bobby, 'They're saying here you are the best batsman in the Lancashire League but the Central League has a better bat in Sobers.' Simpson, lacing up his boots: 'Is that so?' Strolling to where the West Indian star was changing, Cecil said, 'They're saying here you are the finest batsman in the Central League but the best in the two Leagues is Simpson.' Sobers: 'They say that?' No more was said but the two batted together. Sobers slammed the bowling with powerful drives. What Simpson didn't cut he hooked with his old daring. In little more than half an hour each topped 70 with the most scintillating strokes Durham ever saw.

As an opening berth offered him better prospects than competing for a lower Test slot, Bob discarded long-handle 2 lb 3 oz bats to restrict his backswing with heavier short-handle ones. Going in first for WA, he commanded instant success: 98, 236 not out and 230 not out in the first three games. Over two consecutive matches he was on view eight days for every ball as batsman, bowler or fielder. Cartoonist Paul Rigby sketched Bob running along a deep trench his boots had worn between wicket and wicket.

His season on Lancashire tracks added a safety-pin, so to say, holding his reshaped technique securely together. In forward defence, while making 98 and 161 not out against Davidson and Benaud in Sydney, he kept his pad so close to his bat that powdered whiting coated the inner edge of the blade. I never noticed that on anyone else's bat. In five games for WA he totalled 902 at a record average of 300 for a season Down Under.

Reaching a Test rung as a regular perch had taken Bob almost eight years. Opening Australia's innings meant confronting the world's swiftest bowler, Wesley Hall. Simpson evolved an unorthodox way of dodging bouncers, swaying back from the waist like a physical jerk. He was bending over backwards to stay in and stay whole.

In Hobart I saw proof that the old Simpson spontaneity had not been drowned by science, only submerged. Opening for a Combined XI, Bob square-drove, hooked and cut four boundaries off Hall's first five balls. Bristling, the big Barbadian attempted five bouncers in an over but two did not rear from a slow pitch. Alf Valentine, the nearest fieldsman, called to non-striker Gerald Connor, 'Keep out of this, man – there's a war on!' Besides 19 fours in his 149, Simpson on-drove three sixes off Gibbs and Worrell. In an airline coach in Sydney, Wes Hall was speaking his mind about being the only fast bowler for a pending Test. He wound up with, 'Ah daunt mind having to do all the fast bawling if somebody will get one of the opening batsmen out.' From the seat in front, only his amused eyes visible, Worrell drawled, 'Such as Bahby Simpson?'

In the last innings of the rubber, prompted by his skipper, Bob cut the first ball to the fence, hooked a bumper to the opposite pickets, slashed 18 off Hall's opening over and 27 off 14 balls. Worrell withdrew Hall from the attack after only three overs – all credit to Simpson. After that series Bob could point to 445 runs, an average near 50 and only two blows higher than the thigh as vindication of his form of evasive action. He often said he had heard of batsmen who liked fast bowling but had never met any!

Russell Endean driving at Davidson in Port Elizabeth and Geoffrey Boycott facing Corling at Trent Bridge each edged a ball past second slip's left shin, untouched. Yet Simpson was flinging himself sideways to reach catches behind his team-mate. His certainty with ankle-high catches was admired by Ted Dexter who said, 'Bob bends only part-way, yet his hands get low in plenty of time.'

In the split second a slip-fielder has to sight a chance which players do not expect to be caught if the wicketkeeper flaps the ball to a difficult angle. As Simpson's hands were shaping for an edged shot off Davidson at Old Trafford, Grout's glove deflected it. At short range Bob's reflexes still picked up the ball's new course. The catch cost Peter May a century as he was 95. As a different sensation prompted Lady Kathleen Clarke to say of Lord Lambton, 'What jolly bad luck to be caught!' It was not the only ricochet among the catches Bob pouched off fast and medium pace bowlers. Off spinners, he finished a hat-trick for Lindsay Kline at Cape Town and three in four balls for Johnny Martin at Melbourne.

Being surer at picking turn in the air made him a better player of spin than even Harvey. At twenty-six he reached 1000 in a season Down Under before New Year. Only Ponsford had done so before him.

In his first game as NSW vice-captain Queensland piled up 613. The huge total created a situation in which Simpson could concentrate on a dual objective – in enabling his state to amass 661 he showed that if Australia wanted a captain who could make 359 runs in one innings, he was the man. He had played 23 Tests.

With his game and confidence in full bloom, he insisted that by application a player could drill himself into a winning habit. Scarcely conceding bowlers credit for producing balls too difficult, he blamed himself for each loss of his wicket.

Winning his first toss as Test skipper at New Year 1964, he did not shrink from putting South Africa in. When everyone expected him to start with his two quickest bowlers, Graham McKenzie and Alan Connolly, he used fast-medium swinger Neil Hawke opposite McKenzie. He had noticed that the wind in midfield was too strong for Connolly to plug into yet would enhance Hawke's swing.

A scriptural epistle enjoins the Corinthians that if the trumpet give an uncertain sound who shall prepare himself for battle. Nothing like that could be said about Simpson's captaincy. Once he made up his mind I doubt whether any persuasion could lure it back to cancel half a line. In field-placing bowlers found he was not deaf to their wishes but would not allow them to amend settings except through him. They appreciated

293

ruses suggested by their sharp-eyed capless skipper, an all-rounder whose wrong'un some West Indians found harder to spot than Benaud's.

One of the Fleet Street headlines heralding his 1964 team was, 'We can beat the pants off this lot.' His side was called the second-worst Australia had sent to England. Bob turned cheapjack comment to his own ends, unifying his side in resolve to prove detractors wrong.

When Freddie Titmus, running for a quick single, was knocked down by a collision with Hawke, the Trent Bridge crowd appreciated wicketkeeper Grout's sporting gesture of not trying to run him out. Bob approved but told Wally, 'Once is enough. There is a fair chance Freddie would not have made his ground if he had not been knocked over.' In a losing position at Leeds his message encouraging Burge to counter-attack, risking all, was rewarded by the Queenslander's valiant 160 and a one-up lead.

Simpson's strategy in the next Test was like a double-barrelled shotgun. By batting an hour into the third morning he ensured that one cartridge would kill any English hope of an equalising win. In the other barrel was a chance that if the pitch powdered his bowlers might get England out twice. His creep through the numbing nineties could only be explained by block-ages left in his mind by his having batted in 51 Test innings without a century. Manchester University students could have reflected that the first medicinal user of chloroform was named Simpson, too.

Through two days Bob's 265 were a fraction better than one run an over. Like a tortoise turned tiger overnight, he slogged at everything for 40 minutes on the third morning until he reached 311, the longest innings ever played against English bowling (12 hours 42 minutes). In reply to his closure at 656 for eight the Englishmen knuckled down to exceed 600 too, so five days contained only half a match.

With a mind no easier to change than a £100 note, he stuck to the same side except to use Cowper as stand-in; O'Neill was injured. Nothing like that had been seen for seventy years, but he was a firm believer in a settled side.

Traditional leg-breaks were out as he shaped his tactics on their soil to play the Englishmen at an English-style game. McKenzie, Hawke and Corling's swing and cut took 59 wickets, Veivers's off-spin 11. Bob's solitary wicket with his own leg-break on the last day was an ironic postscript.

From holding the Ashes in a mild climate his team had to saddle up for four Tests in Pakistan and India's heat. Recalling his non-selection in 1959, his 153 and 115 at Karachi gave him reason for personal satisfaction. Over-use left McKenzie at low ebb. Simpson's 1381 in 14 Tests set a record for a calendar year (in 1976 Vivian Richards incomparably pushed this record to 1710 in 11 Tests).

His captaincy coincided with the bizarre sixties, when Jean Shrimpton in a mini-skirt showed a Melbourne Cup throng a thing or two, and the Beatles' Liverpool sound was pitched to an opulent level.

Reappearing after a broken wrist and chickenpox, Simpson would not allow a gastric upset to interrupt his 225 against England at Adelaide Oval. Without breakfast or lunch on the second day, he had doses of physic sent out with the drinks. Seventh out after four squeamish hours he nibbled a chicken leg while his side was well along the way to squaring the rubber.

Mike Smith and Simpson kept the game moving in a well-fought rubber. Crowds saw both sides exceed 100 balls an hour but two washed-out days prevented the skippers' good intentions being fully recognised.

In his 201 at Bridgetown in 1965, he lifted the Australian opening record to 382 with Lawry. Yet on his last tours abroad he lost points as a national leader. It is hindsight to say that morale nose-dived because the team became obsessed with the menace of Griffith's bouncers and yorkers. Putting West Indies in first in the second Test was criticised as negative thinking, yet the players felt a more urgent psychological factor was involved. Simpson realised that, shaken on their nerve-roots by the blitz in the first Test, they needed above all a breathing space before being confronted with it again. When a group of Sydney fans air-freighted helmets to Trinidad he left them uncollected. Yet others concurred when one player said he was not 'too proud' to wear a helmet.

Later Griffith subjected Bob to five bouncers in six balls before an umpire warned him for intimidation. His resentment of Griffith's unpenalised bent-arm action and seldom-checked drag caused a bitter walking-off outburst to Sir Frank Worrell. 'Chucked out! How will that go down in the record book?' Yet he handed over the Worrell Trophy to Sobers with good grace. On South African tracks in 1966–67 Springbok bowlers held the aces. Proved Test campaigner Tom Veivers was starved of opportunities. And Benaud said the Australians virtually threw away a Durban Test by playing with half-an-eye on an umpire instead of both eyes on the ball.

Though as an irregular golfer Bob could drive greens which good players took two to reach, he disclaimed possessing power-strokes like O'Neill, Dexter and Burge. He was Simpson not Samson. Yet at thirty-one he could burst self-discipline's bonds to whip up 106 off 138 balls in a two-hour session between lunch and tea in his 277 against Queensland.

Simpson's 103 and 109 in consecutive Tests against the Indians in Australia made his tally 4131 in 92 innings in 52 Test matches. I have scarcely mentioned his googly bowling, but he took five Indian wickets at Sydney a few days before turning thirty-two. While out-swingers and in-duckers were veering about before his green-tinged hazel eyes, his mind's eye had spotted dollar signs looming in the background. He moved into public relations and management of Test men's sideline income.

His belief in the value of exchanging frequent singles with his opening partner was almost an addiction. Dozens of times I saw him risk being run out at the bowler's end – gambling on an inaccurate shy. In the end he ran himself out of big cricket (for the time being); Ian Brayshaw's throw from deep mid-on enabled bowler Tony Lock to knock all three stumps over.

Forthright condemnation of some bowlers' actions in his book *Captain's Story* resulted in fast left-hander Ian Meckiff suing him for libel damages. Veteran ex-president Sydney Smith said it was the first case of one Australian cricketer suing another. After five years the case was settled out of court, with an apology by Simpson and payment of an undisclosed amount, said to be $10,000. The publishers had withdrawn unsold copies.

Healthy and always fit, Bob did not need attention on a massage table, not even when he set a record at Old Trafford by being on the field as batsman, bowler or fieldsman throughout the five-day Test, except for a quarter-hour. By independent thought he evolved ways to save the stress of continuous concentration. While still interested in all movements by long-running pace bowlers, he trained himself to let peak concentration wait until their delivery stride. In his relaxed squat in slips, elbows on knees, he would not rise and concentrate until the ball left the bowler's hand. In a four-minute eight-ball over he reduced catch-alert concentration to about a dozen seconds. To give himself a break in a busy season he would occasionally have a half-hour's run-around at cover.

By trial and error (what error?) his originality set a new pattern for slip-fielding. In his first Test series he had begun standing wider than the customary fine slip spot, according to the pace and bounce the pitch was allowing the ball. I have seen him as far across as second slip, so that he, a companion slip and wicketkeeper were doing the work of four men – and doing it better than four men.

The bowlers' best friend is the only man who has grasped ten or more catches in a series four times – 13 in South Africa, 13 in Australia against the West Indies, 11 in the Indies and ten in England.

Compared with Simpson's 52½ Tests, Ian and Greg Chappell each took 69 Tests to reach their hundredth catches for Australia. Even treacle-eyed Garry Sobers, with fingers correspondingly sticky, took 81 Tests for his hundredth catch.

Australia's fielding continues to benefit from Simpson's amendments to slips' formation. Instead of standing in a row or arc as traditional as the Changing of the Guard, he made each man step forward to form almost a diagonal line from first slip to gully.

Western Suburbs Leagues Club induced him to reappear at thirty-five for the district's first-grade team. At forty he topped 1000 runs in a season a second time. It made him the first to head totals a fifth time, a year more than Victor Trumper.

When World Series Cricket created a challenging situation in 1977 the national selectors made an unprecedented move – appointing him captain for a whole home series before a ball had been bowled. All too conscious of his rookie team's immaturity, people were grateful. They were delighted that he was the first cricketer honoured with membership of the Order of Australia.

Even for a rustless run-getter, Nature's muscular marvel, it took courage to undertake the steep step to five-day Tests for his second coming after nine years. Meg, Kim and Debbie were happy to go along with the intrusion of captaincy into their family life.

Hurdling 1953 to 1978, Bob's experience in 250 first-class matches spanned twenty-six years. It began before ten of his team were born. Yet no generation gap was visible between them and their ever-fit 73 kg skipper.

Now a mid-order batsman, he set them examples in concentration, even if he used the pad against India's expert spinners often enough to have been born in Manchester, not Marrickville. By persisting through the longest hand of the series, 176 in 6½ hours, he became Australia's oldest century maker on a home wicket, forty-one years 286 days. The team room glowed with forty-two candles to mark his birthday.

When Melbourne scorer Walter Bright's chart revealed that 85 per cent of Mohinder Amarnath's strokes were leg-side, Simpson went to leg-slip and immediately pocketed a glance that had yielded several boundaries.

In the night before the Test ended a doctor was called at 3 am to fast bowler Ian Callen, playing his first Test, because an injection had caused fever and breathing difficulty. With a captain's slave-driver element, Simpson asked the wan bowler did he want Steve Rixon to stand over the stumps. Callen reacted with match-winning fire.

Bob scored most runs, 539, and was the only Australian who made two centuries. He held six catches out of nine, despite a broken little finger in the last two Tests.

To that attitude and application add the pluck to face the West Indies' unrivalled range of firepower and you have an idea of the courage demanded of him. No cash inducement was held out beyond Test and Sheffield Shield fees, about $13,000, the West Indies tour rate, $6900, captain's allowance and share in sponsors' prize money.

With his second hundred, 102 against Barbados, he reached the 60th century of his career, despite muscleman Wayne Daniel's intimidatory bouncers. Roberts, Croft and Garner carried off the first two Tests before the Windies' World Series' players pulled out. Best Australians Graeme Wood, 126, Craig Serjeant, 124, and Wayne Clark, eight wickets, were match-winners at Georgetown but Alvin Kallicharran's side made it three–one in Trinidad. After the crowd's bottle-throwing at Sabina Park an umpire would not allow the last 38 balls to be bowled on an extra day.

All joined in their captain's fitness exercises at 7 am but Bob could no longer shun the massage table. He ended the tour as his country's oldest regular skipper, until then Syd Gregory, forty-two in England. His 62 Tests yielded 4869 runs, average 46.8, 10 centuries and 27 half-centuries. His 111 catches included one as a substitute. Only Bradman and Harvey passed 20,000 before him. Besides totalling 21,029 in 436 innings in 284 games, average 58.9, he took 349 wickets and held 384 catches. In his ten Tests as comeback skipper four wins and five losses carried his totals to 12. Asked about his form, he replied: 'It's coming back to me better all the time.'

Bob trained in readiness to announce his availability for the 1978–79 Ashes series, and NSW was ready to reappoint him supremo but a majority of Board members and selectors acted otherwise. Showing no resentment, Bob joined Frank Tyson and Keith Miller in the ABC's telecasting group.

After a spell as a pressman for the *Sydney Morning Herald* and the *Age* using reporting ropes learned two decades earlier at the *Daily News,* Simpson was further renewed as state coach of NSW in 1984–85. When Sheffield Shield success was immediate, he placed himself first in line for the new role of national team coach delineated for Allan Border's side by the Australian Cricket Board.

Having excelled in both domains as a player, Simpson's dual emphases as coach were catching and running between wickets. What can be viewed as ancillary skills became central to the Australian effort when he undertook his first posting in the position in India, and openers David Boon and Geoff Marsh were chief among beneficiaries.

With Simpson a canny ringmaster, Border redoubled his lion-taming efforts. Within a year the pair had plotted a successful sub-continental campaign for the 1987 World Cup. 'More than anything I think I took a bit of the weight from Allan's shoulders,' Simpson said. 'I think Allan's basically a non-confrontational person and he appreciated the contribution I could make in those areas.'

The salaams for Simpson's appointment were muted a year later when he was pilloried along with Border and manager Col Egar for a fractious tour of Pakistan. When it almost ended in a team boycott, Simpson was widely criticised for overreacting to a string of adverse umpiring decisions and a favourably-prepared surface at Karachi's National Stadium.

The Pakistan political situation at the time was problematic. Its cricket-dotty dictator General Zia ul-Haq had just died in a plane crash, and various factions were manoeuvring in the vacuum. Yet the Australians, in turfing ten catches in three Tests, had contributed to their own poor showings as much if not more than corrupt officialdom.

Simpson scaled a second summit of ambition by coaching the Australians through their barnstorming 1989 Ashes tour. English critics praised the irreproachable orthodoxy of Australians' techniques, and Simpson's influence was so enviously eyed that Mike Turner approached him at tour's end offering a two-year county coaching contract to turn sow's ear Leicestershire into a silk purse.

This proved, as the saying advises, impossible. The job ended disappointingly in September 1991, with Leicestershire having retreated under Simpson's tutelage rather than advanced. The Australian was also attracting comment at home for shouldering selectorial duties in addition to his coaching position.

However he tried, Simpson could hardly avoid being a harbinger of bad tidings. Dean Jones said in his autobiography *Deano – My Call*:

> *Simmo naturally had the job of passing on a lot of selection decisions and that didn't always endear him to players who'd been left out of the side. Perhaps there was a tendency to shoot the messenger, but the set-up wasn't always healthy.*

Simpson's star waned further when Australia failed to make even the semi-finals of the 1992 World Cup in March 1992 but, after a second Ashes triumph during 1993, his coaching contract was renewed.

Undoubtedly the Australian feat that offered Simpson greatest satisfaction was coaching Mark Taylor's successful tourists in the Caribbean in April–May 1995. Beaten twice by the West Indies as captain in 1965 and 1978, and coach on an ill-fated 1991 campaign, he had this time to convalesce from a circulatory disorder.

To witness the visitors' fielding during that two-to-one series victory was like watching a troupe of Russian acrobats, testimony to the thousands of hours Simpson had spent hectoring them through hoops. In the decisive Fourth Test at Kingston, Taylor's team caught like carnivorous plants, and stopped and retrieved like inexhaustible blue heelers. At least a few bars of the Australian victory chant in the Sabina Park dressing chambers were howled in honour of the team's elder statesman.

On 17 May 1996, the ACB declined to extend Simpson's decade. Geoff Marsh, twenty-three years Simpson's junior, was anointed his successor. Born at a time when the most significant Simpson had been Wallis, who stole the heart of an English king, Bob had endured into an era when the most recognisable was Bart, a smart-mouth animation.

The sixty-year-old had been front or back in 155 Tests for Australia: 23 as player, 39 as captain, and the balance as off-field fulcrum. He had coached his country through 39 Test victories, 20 defeats, 36 draws and a tie, winning 14 series, losing eight and sharing half a dozen. Of 200 limited-overs internationals during his coaching career, Australia had won 125 and lost 71.

Although Simpson expressed disappointment at the ACB's decision, he could console himself that his influence was set to linger on the face on international cricket. A decade ago, a coach was something that shuttled teams to and from their fixtures. At the 1996 World Cup, all twelve countries included coaches in their squads.

33

Fine and Mild

The contention that golf is not good for batting – long blown out by Dexter, Graveney, Bradman, Hassett and others – does not seem to have been raised against hockey. Yet the curved-stick team game took a year out of one player's rise to Test cricket. When he was twenty-three Brian Booth's position as Australia's inside-left in the 1956 Olympic Games in Melbourne delayed his ascent to the Australian XI.

Lifting his hockey stick no higher than the shoulder developed forearm and wrist power. With a modified back-lift Booth appeared to stroke the ball rather than thump it the velocity to roll on to boundaries. The elegant strokeplayer looked taller than his 181 cm (5 ft 11½ in). A physical education teacher, he kept his spare frame to 66.5 kg (10 st 6 lb). The open angle of his shoulders turned his lean face square to the bowler, with his blue-grey eyes level. In unhurried back-play he moved thoroughly to the line of the ball. His effortless style owed much to unhesitating footwork right to the pitch of spin bowling. Besides a full range of graceful on-shots his cover drives and square drives were placed to advantage and he cut well.

Though a right-handed batsman, thrower and bowler, he writes left-handed. His left hand picks up a spoon, hammer, saw, paintbrush and pingpong racket – all single-handed actions.

Booth upheld a charming tradition of the batsmanship of Sydney, a city the sun kisses 342 days out of 365, giving out 2748 hours of sunshine a year, compared with London's 1466 hours. Brian has been one of the batsmen the sunshine loves. Besides flashing brightly from his hat, it made his flannels look creamier around his slender figure. It has given light and shade to the folds of his shirt, matching the light and shadow of his play – the sparkle of his shots and the depth of his defence. It always surprised me, if close enough when he came in, to see his face beaded with sweat, strands of brown hair sticking to his forehead, tiredness in his expression and his tread on the steps heavier than it had looked out in the middle.

Booth's bearing brought him an army of well-wishers. A kindly expression reflected an admirable disposition. The weather forecast terms of fine and mild fit his personality yet there is no lack of firmness in his living in accordance with staunch religious convictions.

A market gardener's son, Brian Charles Booth was born on 19 October 1933, at Perthville, six miles out of Bathurst, an old gold-mining area. After captaining Bathurst High School XI, Brian entered first-grade cricket for St George at nineteen when he began a four-year course at Sydney Teachers College. He was twelve weeks past twenty-one at his debut for New South Wales. Queenslanders added him to the long list of batsmen out for 0 on their debut and the return of Test players squeezed him out of the side.

One morning when NSW began a match against Hutton's English XI Booth was teaching at Hurlstone Agricultural College. Called from the classroom to a telephone, he was told injuries were keeping Morris and Watson out. By train and taxi he hurried to Sydney Cricket Ground. Bedser and Tyson had three out for 12 when he pushed open the door greeted by a call of 'Hurry up, you're in next!' The Englishmen had half the side out for 25 by the time he took guard with a borrowed bat. Amid the flurry Brian made 74 not out in a manner stamping him as a player with a future.

After his deviation to Olympic hockey, Booth raised his first century, 123, in his 15th match. With Norman O'Neill he made a fourth-wicket Sheffield Shield record of 325. In 1960 Brian won a place on a tour of New Zealand, going in first-drop after Craig and Simpson. His first venture there yielded 105 against Auckland.

Brian met Judith Williams when they were Teachers' College students. She could hardly bear to watch cricket, yet through interest in Brian she became a fan. They were twenty-four when they married on the only spare Saturday between Sydney's hockey and cricket seasons. Their first daughter was born a fortnight before he reached home from the 1961 tour. (In 1964 and 1965, tours of England, India and the West Indies took him away for 12 months out of 16.)

In a pre-tour game against Tasmania in 1961 Booth treated a Hobart crowd to 100 off 104 balls in an hour and a half. One of his sixes soared out of the ground. On the voyage to Britain he led the Australians' morning deck exercises. Their response was enthusiastic.

Brian is the only man I ever saw laugh on getting out at 99. In his twelfth innings in England he was one short of his third century there when Lancashire wicketkeeper Geoff Clayton appealed for a tickled catch. Booth began walking away before the umpire's finger came up. Instead of showing disappointment, he saw a comic side to losing his wicket at 99 to a bowler of the same name, Brian Booth, from Blackburn.

His Test debut at twenty-seven came on a day when the whole team could not pass 190 against Statham and Flavell on a green Old Trafford track. Struck in the body first ball, Brian walked gingerly around the stumps. Temperament and technique both came through a trial. Hooks, on-drives and square-cuts rolled well across a slow outfield. Booth made 46 of the day's best stand with Lawry. At the Oval in his second Test team-mates thought 100 would reward him. Unselfish concern about quickening Australia's run-rate caused him to try to lift Lock over the fielding cordon but Subba Row caught him for 71. The century had to wait until his third Test. In his 112 against England at Brisbane his round 100 came in the 37th over, better than two runs an over off his own beguiling bat. A rare semblance of annoyance was seen in the Melbourne Test when Dexter posted five leg fieldsmen and bowled outside the leg stick. As off-spinner Fred Titmus was bowling on the leg stump with five on-side fielders, earth's joys grew dim for everybody else present (about 70,000). In his Melbourne century leg theory restricted Brian to 103 off 73 overs.

Having to withstand five bouncers from Peter Pollock in early overs at Brisbane did not disturb Booth's fluent progress to his highest Test score, 169 off 81 overs. It was a tailored innings, fit to be put on display in a show-case and unrumpled by a single chance. To team-mates' congratulations on such innings his answers were always modest. 'I guess things went well for me,' he would say, or 'Glad to get them at any time.' The quality of his 169 brought a notable compliment from South African captain Trevor Goddard: 'We didn't mind the leather-chasing when he played so charmingly.' Though a broken finger put Brian out of one Test, five centuries were among his 1180 runs in the 1963–64 season and an expert panel voted him Australian Cricketer of the Year.

Booth scored 121 in 94 minutes between lunch and tea against Western Australia. His hook for six off a beamer from fast right-hander Desmond Hoare is one of the three longest hits to the roof of the Hill stand backing on to the Showground. The ball clanged on the iron at the back of the ridge. Congratulated on a hit so distant, Brian murmured characteristically, 'I think the ball slipped from Des's hand. I got a top edge, really.'

The nickname his father gave him as a toddler, Sam, stuck to him. In two consecutive Test series Down Under he made four of Australia's eight Test hundreds. As an Anglican parish councillor he belongs to a different sect from the paramartial Christian cohorts founded by General Booth but after one of his match-saving centuries Robert Gray spoke of him as 'Sam Booth, Australia's one-man salvation army'.

When leadership for the 1964 tour of England came up players felt the choice of Booth would be popular with the team, despite his brief experience handling a club side. Some doubted whether his disposition would allow him to be a sharp enough watchdog on issues affecting his side's interests or to be inexorable in pursuing victory. Yet on a showery Melbourne evening later he acted quickly and resolutely to cope with an unpleasant situation. The crowd heckled him because he showed the umpires a sodden ball hampering his bowlers. A rejected appeal infuriated NSW fieldsmen, positive that a Victorian batsman's attempted cut had edged a catch to their wicketkeeper. As they tramped into their room, simmering, Booth directed the doorkeeper to allow nobody else in for five minutes. He told the players, 'I know how you feel about the decision but as your skipper I am asking you not to say another word about it.' His firmness obviated recriminations and the team played better next day for not having nursed a grievance.

If a fine touch was caught he would walk out without waiting for a ruling (a procedure rarely followed by Australians, believing that errors made either way even up). With Booth the golden rule was threaded through the Laws of Cricket. After a partner's misjudgement ran him out for

16 at Northampton sympathising team-mates were choleric when he came in. All Brian said was, 'I'll have to run faster.'

Loose shots had no more place in his career than loose living. He responded to countless requests to address church and youth rallies. They ranged from appearing with an English opening batsman, the Rev. David Sheppard, in Sydney Town Hall to speaking from the pulpit of the Tranquillity Methodist Church, Port of Spain, before West Indian vice-captain Conrad Hunte preached. Amid coarse slang and ribaldry in locker rooms his quiet dignity contained no trace of a holier-than-thou attitude. He steadfastly tried to live up to scriptural tenets, with faith in their origin unshaken by sceptics calling the Ten Commandments a code devised for nomadic desert tribesmen. Because of his respect for Sunday observance he had no wish to play on Sundays in India or Pakistan on the way from Britain in 1964. Asked had he played four Sundays there out of courtesy for the custom of those countries Brian told me:

> When we left Australia for England the Indian dates had not been fixed. To be consistent I should not have played when it involved Sundays. Jack Potter was disabled and Norman O'Neill had been flown home ill so I felt that to withdraw would have been letting the side down.

Having number-plate BCB 777 on his car was the result of an idea by a St George team-mate, Vic Cristofani, brother of the former Services all-rounder. The first plate he arranged was BCB 000. When Brian heard this he said 'Steady on, Vic – I get enough of them without carrying them around.'

Before touring the West Indies at thirty-one he smilingly parried a question about Hall's and Griffith's bouncers by saying, 'Perhaps we could do with Ned Kelly's armour.' In Jamaica, he was fortunate that Hall's first souped-up bumper missed his head before he could stir. That day's ordeal drained all the colour from Brian's face. Team-mates admired his courage in the second innings for 56, Australia's top score. In the second Test he took several blows on the body while making 117 in a rallying stand with left-handed Bob Cowper's 143. His 117 was his most satisfying Test innings, he said, 'as they were on top of us at the time'.

I know of no other outfielder who on one Test day ran out two batsmen of the standard of Sobers and Butcher, as Brian did in Trinidad, when he was thirty-two years old. After his sinewy arm's second throw homed into Grout's gloves near the bails Brian continued running to congratulate the 'keeper: 'Well done, Wal – a beautiful take!' In the same innings he caught a hard sweep as if the ball was as soft as a brussels sprout.

As Simpson's vice-captain Booth had been skipper in 12 first-class games before he led Australia at Brisbane in Bob's absence with a broken wrist. With equal parts of example and tact, Brian led the side judiciously. He made Mike Smith's Englishmen follow on but after a Saturday washout no decision could be reached. When they saw Boycott's left glove paw Philpott's leg-break away, after a defensive shot, nearby fieldsmen told the Yorkshireman, 'Don't do that again, matey, or you'll be out.' When he verified from umpire Egar that he could have been out for handling the ball Geoffrey apologised. Asked for his view, Brian said:

When Boycott brushed the ball away with his hand we would have been justified in appealing but we did not want to see him lose his wicket that way. If the ball had been running back toward his stumps we might have appealed.

Two Tests later Booth was captain again (Simpson had chickenpox). No leader can look good while his followers are being routed by punitive hitting of the sort the bowlers suffered from Bob Barber. The marauding left-hander's bat allowed the ball about as much chance as a mushroom against a motor-mower. Except for a dropped leg-slip chance from Boycott, 12, the Australians could do nothing to interrupt England's best-ever start in Sydney, 234. Barber's 185 off 67 overs launched the Englishmen into a commanding position before 5 pm on the first day. They triumphed with an innings to spare.

From the eminence of captain Booth was dropped right out of Test cricket at thirty-two. Displaced by changes in a beaten side, he was not chosen again though he continued in first-class games until he was thirty-five. In 29 Tests his total 1773 (average 42) included five centuries. One more Test and he would have qualified for a retirement bonus from NSW's provident fund reward of $50 a Test to each man who played at least 30 Tests. Everybody felt sorry that the actuarial guillotine should have descended on the long neck of a model cricketer. The irony was more pungent because Booth played more often for NSW than anybody. After his last Test he had 21 more matches for NSW, making his total 92. Had he lived in Victoria his appearance would have qualified for more than $2000 from that state's fund. He headed a reserve Australian team's scoring as vice-captain to Leslie Favell in NZ in 1967. Booth's 1680 runs in 30 matches after his last Test included the top score of his career, 214 not out against Central Districts at Palmerston North.

A life member of the NSWCA, the MCC and St George Cricket Club, Booth published a delightful autobiography in 1983 called *Booth to Bat*. In his introduction, Sir Donald Bradman wrote that Brian's career was a model for any young cricketer: 'There was no flamboyance, no fuss and there were no tantrums – just a quiet responsible approach to the job at hand. Always he was the thorough gentleman and sportsman.' Though it received little publicity and had little of the celebrity appeal now deemed necessary for publishing success, Anzea Books reprinted *Booth to Bat* twice: first in 1987 and then in 1992. And if a prize were offered for fair-playmanship among Australia's post-war cricketers Brian Booth ought to win hands down, not only for deserving it but also because I feel other unblemished sportsmen would not accept a nomination against him.

W.M. LAWRY

34

He Did it His Way

As every viewer knows who sees televised weather charts of Australia, the weight of larger states has squeezed Victoria down into the south-east corner. The compression stops just short of forcing the state off the mainland to lessen the loneliness of apple-growing Tasmania. More than the roughness of Bass Strait prevents this. It is the toughness of Victoria's citizenry.

Victorians form about one-quarter of Australia's population, and are outnumbered by more than a million by NSW's people. They don't mind that and why should they? More Prime Ministers have been born in their confines than in any of the roomier states. In 1972 a German newspaper, *Frankfurter Rundschau*, praised Melbourne, adding, 'People there have a dream that Australia and perhaps the world revolve about their city.' In cricket this is no dream, as anybody can tell on Boxing Day of a Test tour.

The thirteenth Victorian Test captain, William Morris Lawry (born 11 February 1937) was named after one of the wiliest Prime Ministers, W.M. Hughes. In Thornbury, Lawry was the second son of a tobacco stripper but grew up not to smoke or drink liquor. Tending the family's pigeon lofts gave him a life-long interest in the racing birds. Baseball smartened his fielding. As a gawky left-hander from Preston Technical College he was in the Victorian Second XI at seventeen. Entraining for Adelaide, their captain Dick Maddocks noticed that Bill's magazines included *Phantom* comics. From that evening his nickname became 'The Phantom'.

The day before he turned nineteen Lawry made his debut for Victoria. A yearned-for century had to wait until Lawry's 23rd game.

The first time his long boots trod dry English turf Lawry introduced himself to London with 100 in three hours at the Oval. Surrey bowlers could not stop him scoring 101 between lunch and tea on his way to 165 in 4½ chanceless hours. A left-hander's hooks and sweeps brought a number of his 26 fours but most attention was commanded by shots thumped off the back foot through mid-wicket and confident front-foot drives past mid-off and extra-cover. It was a knock in which scoring was synonymous with batting.

In his first match at Lord's, Lawry made 104 and 84 not out against MCC. Next he was star batsman of a Test in which oft-bruised batsmen were fortunate to escape having fingers and ribs broken by balls kicking from a ridge. Lawry wrung his hand in pain and ripped his glove off counting his fingers to see how many Statham had left him. His height 187 cm (6 ft 2 in) helped but it was no more important than his heart. Twisting from another rearing ball he fell over backwards. Six hours he stuck it out for the only century of the Test. This resolute ridgemanship was the innings of Lawry's life.

London's air, wickets and light suited Lawry so well that he scored more runs than a costermonger's jacket has buttons, though perhaps not all so pearly. In seven games at Lord's and the Oval he made four centuries, the only Australian to have done so on his first trip. Among his 2117 runs were nine centuries, the most by any left-hander on a tour. No visitor from anywhere has since reached 2000 on a trip. In heading Australia's Test batting, he averaged a boundary every three overs. Yet the lanky left-hander who drove everything pacemen pitched up hardly ever left the crease to spinners, who mostly held him to a forward stretch.

Picture Lawry coming to the wicket behind a pink prow that makes his profile unmistakable. Gravity's pull keeps his head dutifully down. His wicket is as inviolate as a detective's daughter. Watching Lawry, as you have ample time to do, you sense that he loves batting. If he is not actually wedded to his art, everyone can see he's going steady.

Bill defended as if oppressed by realisation that loss of his wicket would mean ruin for his team. When Lawry's sense of responsibility got out of hand his stoop over his bat made me think of a camel's back looking for a last straw.

An Australia-wide broadside raked him for having laboured six hours for 133 for Victoria against the Englishmen in 1962. As Victoria

312

had been sent in on a moist track, I thought that in the first two hours Lawry deserved praise for sterling resistance where Statham and Coldwell could have broken the back of the innings before lunch. After the pitch quietened, his 35 off 30 overs between lunch and tea brought jeers. His anchor-chain showed no sign of rust.

Four hours for 45 made Lawry the chief target of curtain-call hooting at the end of Sydney's 'horror' Test in 1963. While faithfully fulfilling his captain's tea-interval injunction not to get out, he could not resist hitting two tempting balls for fours, then reverted to grim defence. After a while a barracker pleaded 'Come on Lightning, strike again!'

Only the team knew a contrasting side of Lawry. He and his comrade-in-mischief, fast bowler Frank Misson, were responsible for spoons belonging to the Queen Mother turning up in a pocket of a departing guest, manager Sydney Webb ... hotel breakfast plates wobbling eerily, rocked by a rubber puff-tube running under the table-cloth ... a stumble in the Oval dressing room splashing green ink over a group's shirts (the stain vanished in ten minutes) ... captain Richie Benaud's boots nailed to a floor.

Twice falls in the crease involved him in debates about hit-wicket. At four in a Melbourne Test against the South Africans he hooked a longhop from swing bowler Joe Partridge forward of square-leg. As he started to run his right boot skidded against the stumps. Umpire Lou Rowan's disallowance of appeals for hit-wicket was supported by photographs. For Victoria in 1965 Lawry was 100 when he stepped back to drag a slow offball from Titmus wide of mid-on. His left boot broke his wicket before he began running. A not-out ruling suggested that the umpire's eyes had followed ball from bat – and the Englishmen had to put up with Bill while he went on to 153. In his book *Run-Digger* he says that, having been the victim of bad decisions and enjoyed lucky decisions, he considers both part of the fortune of the game. He adds, 'I despise a player who claims he is a walker and then, when the pressure is on, refuses to walk when he knows he is out.' Barrackers more used to booing his caution cheered him in January 1964 for whipping up 102 in two hours after tea for Victoria against South Africa.

Lawry hooked at every bouncer Peter Pollock loosed at him in Australia in 1963–64. In South Africa he batted with bandages over ten stitches after a blow from Pollock. Most batsmen are never quite the same after a head injury but there was no sign of a shadow on the tough Victorian's courage. Significantly, when Peter picked a World XI he chose Lawry as opening batsman.

In 1964 not one of his five centuries was made in London. The most productive of all Australian opening pairs, he and Simpson made their country's first double century start against England. Griffith's and Hall's unnerving hostility rocked Australia's batting into ramshackle shape in 1965 before the Bridgetown Test. A Griffith bumper gashing Lawry's right cheekbone underlined the pluck needed for him and Simpson to fight back with Australia's tallest-ever opening stand of 382. Bill's 210 lasted nine hours. It was the highest of his 13 Test hundreds and is top score by an Australian in the Indies. He is the only player outside England's XI who has figured in 12 century opening partnerships in Tests. Simpson classed his faithful partner as 'just about the best opener I've seen'.

Not even Bradman had scored as many runs against an English side touring Australia as Lawry's 979 in 11 innings in 1965–66. They took 41½ hours. It seemed longer. In a Sydney Test Bill was averaging only one run an over when a scoreless stretch made a barracker complain, 'What's wrong with you Lawry? Have you taken the Pill?'

At Simpson's premature retirement, the selectors made Lawry skipper. He was nearing thirty-one, had a background of 42 Tests in six countries and had led teams in 44 first-class games. He began with two wins against the Indians in Australia.

Matching his batting outlook, determination to give nothing away was the spinal column of Lawry's captaincy. Used to handling a pace attack for Victoria, he assigned spin a minor part on true wickets. Johnny Gleeson the folded-finger flicker was the only spinner given long enough stretches to do himself justice. Lawry's decisions were based on his estimate of the wickets. In five Tests in India Bill put off-spinner Ashley Mallett on for 298 overs to take 29 wickets.

In a clairvoyant moment before the 1968 team's Qantas aircraft landed he pointed to the Tower of London, saying, 'That's where they'll want to

314

put me – on bread and water!' Bookmakers had England 5/4-on favourites when Lawry opened at Old Trafford and saw Snow remove two partners before lunch. His response dumbfounded those who had practically written him off as the hangnail of Test cricket. In the first over after the interval Lawry swung against the tide to attack off-spinner Pat Pocock. With two sixes and several fours Bill boldly seized the initiative, creating problems for Cowdrey in deployment of bowlers. I rank Lawry's 81 one of the three most telling knocks of his Test career. It set the tempo for Australia to pass 300 in the day and go on to win (a success that made them one up until England evened in the last Test).

Bill's 7½-hour 135 at the Oval was his side's only Test century in the series. A target far beyond reach in the fourth innings left a washout by storm the only hope of escape. Underwood's irresistible left hand brought an equalising win six minutes before time-up. Ralph Barker commented in *England v. Australia*, 'Had the Australians not shunned loitering, gardening and all other acts of gamesmanship England could never have won.' This is a credit to remember when later debits come home to roost in the Lawry loft.

Scores on the West Indians' visit in 1968–69 gave the impression that the Australians batted better. In fact they won three Tests to one by fielding better for their bowlers. There was no column to list 28 let-offs adding almost 1000 to the scores of Lawry and his men; their own fielding errors gave away about 300 runs but they clung to every chance from Sobers. When Graham McKenzie dismissed Garry with a shooter in Melbourne Bill patted him on the head. By rights he could have given the pitch a pat, too. Lawry was the only captain known to have disagreed with a batsman having a drink apart from the regular hourly drinks. Basil Butcher waited until a wicket fell, then ran off, leaving bat and gloves as a surety that he was not quitting the game in dry-throated disgust. Late one afternoon Sydney barrackers chided Bill for fiddling with field placings to deny Seymour Nurse a chance to complete 100 that evening.

Lawry's unrelaxed intensity led him into actions that sometimes annoyed others and stretched his own nerves taut. In *The Umpire's Story* Lou Rowan said Lawry was guilty of stifling his bowlers. To observe his antics and to

315

hear his comments whenever a batsman scored runs was nothing short of demoralising to the bowlers.

While he was batting, the sight of a partner's dangerous shot could make Bill slap his bat against his pad. The deadpan Buster Keaton of batting packed plenty of facial expression into appealing with melodramatic fervour in the field. His arms were often the first flung up. A tendency to fall out with crowds brought disconcerting results.

Some of Lawry's field demeanour in 1969 antagonised Indian crowds with whom the 1959–60 skipper (Benaud) had been popular. When he tried to fit in another over by McKenzie before lunch at Bombay the umpires ruled it was time for the interval. Thousands chattered at the sight of an Australian captain throwing his cap on the ground.

Only a couple of Indian wickets were left in the last hour of the fourth day when Alan Connolly caused Venkataraghavan to make a hurried stab at a ball. Dust rose and, hearing a noise as the ball went through to the wicketkeeper, three other fieldsmen appealed for a catch. It was a difficult decision, as the bat hit the pitch and I believe several of the Australians thought it touched the ground only. Given out, Venkat stood in dismay. The crowd heard a broadcaster say that in his view the bat had been nowhere near the ball. An angry protest demonstration rapidly worsened into a riot. Furious demonstrators hurled hundreds of bottles into the field. Smoke from fired awnings and smashed chairs billowed over the field. Like Hutton amid a less-frightening outburst at Georgetown, Lawry would not go off. Barrackers were shouting 'Aussies go home!' Seeing a mob of would-be invaders trying to push over a wiremesh barricade, the scared Australians were ready to bolt for the clubhouse if it gave way.

Apparently the crowd thought Lawry should have recalled Venkat. As the Australians knocked off runs to win on the last morning barrackers crowed gleefully when Surti bowled him. They hooted Bill off the field. Ex-captain Lala Amarnath said the public unnecessarily dragged Lawry into the controversy, as he had nothing to do with the umpiring decision. Indian left-hander Ajit Wadekar, who batted through the riot, says in his book, *My Cricketing Years*:

> *With a little graciousness, the unfortunate episode at the Brabourne*

Stadium could have been avoided. We had only one wicket left and there was a whole day to go. Yet, with a pall of smoke blowing across the field and the umpires unable to communicate with the scorers Lawry insisted on continuing the game. The riotous incidents of the last half-hour left their mark on the rest of the series.

After a midfield brush during a stoppage at Calcutta readers of most Indian newspapers read that Lawry had knocked a photographer down and struck him with his bat. In his later account in the *Sun*, Melbourne, Bill said that in trying to protect the wicket he pushed the man with his open hand. Stackpole recalled that in hunting the intrusive photographer away Bill prodded his backside with his bat, saying 'Now get off!' The man stumbled and fell. Whatever various versions said, Indian photographers wearing black armbands turned their backs on the Australians at the next game. To save being the only international side to be beaten by a zone team, Lawry and Gleeson tried every stratagem in the last hour at Bangalore. A woman in a colourful sari walking by a sightscreen gave Bill an excuse to step back from the wicket. An otherwise well-behaved Madras crowd booed and hissed Lawry as he faced the bowling and ceased when his partners had the strike. They had no way of knowing that, when sections of a disappointed Calcutta crowd bitterly abused India's captain, Lawry said to the Nawab of Pataudi, 'Come with us.' As escorts with bats, Bill and Stackpole walked either side of him to the dressing-room.

By squeezing tours of India and South Africa into one season the Board chose money and disregarded the interests of the players, who felt they had been given a raw deal. Most players were a stone underweight at the crossover. The gulf between slow spin-favouring tracks and grassy strips providing bounce was too wide for batsmen to bridge. No fault of Lawry's, nor was loss of the four Test tosses, leaving Australia faced in last innings by beyond-reach targets exceeding 450 each time. A Board attempt to add a fifth Test for an extra $200 each was effectively rejected by demanding $500. Earlier, Keith Miller, a dozen years out of the game, wondered whether he should offer the failing side his services, adding, 'At least I could break in Lawry's bat.'

When Barry Richards raced gloriously to 94 on the first morning of the

317

Durban Test Lawry used delaying subterfuges, then argued with an umpire that there was not time for another over. As partner Ali Bacher lost his wicket trying to give Richards the strike in that over Barry was denied the deserved honour of being the only Test century-maker before lunch in South Africa. Reporters criticised the Australian captain for petulant reactions to umpires' decisions. About 60 chances were spilt in 12 games. The season's trials failed to crush all wit from a homewarding Lawry. When an interviewer at Melbourne airport asked, 'Are you and Keith Miller good friends?' Bill replied, 'Keith who?' Besides stating team claims to a bonus from profits from India, Lawry's end-of-tour report contained criticisms that irked officials. So a power trail was laid for the World Series Cricket explosion.

Snow's incisive bowling and Boycott's consistent scoring gave Ray Illingworth's Englishmen an edge that Australia could not answer, especially in a Sydney Test won by 299 runs. As his side crumpled for 116, Lawry hung on for 60 not out off 57 overs. It was the second time he carried his unyielding bat through a Test innings. With Australia one down midway the selectors were looking for a more imaginative approach. After a fortunate lead of 101 in Melbourne lack of urgency in the next batting order left the fastest scorer of the match, Marsh, in the dressing-room. Bill's run rate in the series sagged to 13 an hour.

The axe came down before the final Test. A week short of thirty-four, the man who had held many a bridge for his country felt like not Horatius but Humpty Dumpty. He is the only regular Australian captain dumped in the course of a rubber.

Teams he led won nine Tests, lost eight and eight were unfinished. No trace of sourness has been heard in his radio or television comments. As a sidelight on his characteristic immersion in his job, Bill's wife heard him mutter a broadcasting phrase in his sleep.

Lawry first met Joy Barnes, a pleasant brunette secretary, at a church picture-night. He was twenty-five and Joy twenty-two when they married. He was in Brisbane playing for this state when their first child was born, six weeks before he left for a seven-month Test tour overseas.

When he left Test cricket, only Bradman and Harvey had scored more for Australia than Lawry's 5234 runs in 68 Tests. His average of 47 is on a high level for a batsman who opened against the menace of Hall, Griffith, Procter, Pollock, Trueman, Statham and Snow and countered the wiles of Titmus, Gibbs, Sobers, Prasanna and Bedi.

In 250 matches from 1956 to 1972 he totalled a Lawry-load of runs, 18,734 (average 50) and he made 50 hundreds. Only Dean Jones exceeds his 6615 runs for Victoria.

Though Lawry considered his cricket finished, cricket had not finished with him. Flushed from his loft by a telephone call from World Series Cricket organiser Austin Robertson in November 1977, Lawry joined a commentary panel for the embryonic enterprise led by his former skipper Richie Benaud.

Almost two decades later, he is a lynchpin of the Channel Nine team known for his regular ululation: 'Got 'im!' A generation of viewers who know his sunny voice have little idea of the pall he cast over opposition bowlers.

Because he was caught up in inexorable events that ended in his removal from the captaincy nobody should forget Lawry's essential attributes. Bowlers remember that getting him out was as difficult as picking a lock. He had the courage to stand by everything to the end, especially his wicket. Among those who remember his qualities are many whose protests about his run-rate never let him rest in peace.

35

To Those Who Wait

Of all players in team sports the ones most likely to find themselves in a queue are wicketkeepers. Batsmen aspiring to represent their country can aim at six places and bowlers four, leaving room for only one of the gloved fraternity. The margin of skill and luck between the foremost keeper and the next-in-line may be almost imperceptible yet it is enough to keep one in the spotlight and leave the other in shadows. As with a stage understudy, little or nothing is heard of a touring team's reserve keeper unless injury or illness puts the star out. He has difficulty keeping up to concert pitch.

Australia was fortunate to have both Barry Jarman and Wallace Grout when the national team was being rebuilt after the breakdown in 1956. Jarman is outstandingly the keenest component I ever saw in any spare-parts division. No doubt he was continuously aware that any day a mishap to the great Queenslander could bring him into the most important spot on the field, with the bowlers' success and the fate of a Test in his hands. Not only loyalty to his skipper and the side's interests kept him up to scratch.

When Barrington Noel Jarman was born at Hindmarsh on 17 February 1936, nature bestowed on him a double issue of enthusiasm. Neither injuries nor weeks of sitting around in dressing-rooms could diminish it. His keenness never went off the boil. The sight of his round face behind the stumps reassured bowlers who otherwise would have been lamenting the absence of the No. 1 keeper.

Barry's father Gordon Jarman was a market gardener. His grandfather Fred May, who had played against an English XI at Gawler, regularly took the boy to Adelaide Oval. As a fifteen-year-old schoolboy Barry rose to Woodville's A Grade District team. As a West Torrens footballer of seventeen he suffered a broken left shinbone and switched from playing to umpiring. In the same year 100 in 89 minutes won him a trophy for fastest century of the season. He was an apprentice fitter and turner when SA lifted him into first-class cricket at nineteen. Profiting by hints from Test keeper Gilbert Langley, Barry needed only seven games for his state to win selection at twenty as sole wicketkeeper for a tour of NZ. He returned with half his face numb from a knock in the nets.

He looked bulky for the post – only 171 cm tall (5 ft 7½ in) yet weighing 86 kg (13½ stone) – but was agile in moving to the line of the ball and in diving for snicks. Jarman squatted with his armpits close to his knees. His substantial hindquarters rocked a few times as he touched his knuckles to the grass then raised them, his brown eyes peering over his gloves at the approaching bowler. He was twenty-one and Grout thirty when they toured South Africa. Unable to decide who should keep in the first Test, selectors Craig, Harvey and Burge sought bowlers' opinions. The pacemen could not separate the pair. Leg-spinner Benaud had difficulty making up his mind before saying the older keeper might be surer up at the stumps. By that narrow margin Grout's nine-year reign of 51 Tests began.

Except for his first Test in 1959, at Kanpur when he was twenty-three years 296 days, Jarman was understudy for 27 Tests in six series. After an erratic ball broke Grout's jaw in 1962 Jarman's first chance against England came when he was twenty-six. A spectacular dive and skid on his right buttock enabled him to get one glove under the ball just above the grass to catch left-hander Geoff Pullar's leg glance. Oldtimers acclaimed it as the best in Melbourne since a historic catch by Hanson Carter fifteen years before Barry was born. I believe it takes another wicketkeeper to judge a wicket-keeper properly but bowlers, having much to gain or lose, are sharp-eyed observers. One of the greatest, Wesley Hall, who played against him for the West Indies and for Queensland, says in *Pace Like Fire*:

> *Barry Jarman, who deputised brilliantly for Grout in three Tests in 1965, was extremely unfortunate to be understudy to the best pair of hands in the business. Had Barry been born in England, I am sure he would have been an established Test player ... he has lightning reflexes and a 'nose' for anticipating the kick of the ball – hallmarks of all great wicketkeepers.*

A livewire in team fun, Barry missed no chance to reduce the altitude of the top brass, the 'big-noters'. His band of self-styled 'little-noters' excelled in getting their message across. On the same liner as one Test side a vice-regal family invited a select five to a party which began with drinks in the *Himalaya*'s poolside bar. When the captain, vice-captain and managers appeared immaculate in dinner jackets they found the uninvited other ranks holding a rival party in a corner of the bar with a couple of engineers. The 'little-noters' had left their jaws unshaven, were wearing their shaggiest pullovers and were dipping into a basket of chicken drumsticks.

Barry shone as vocalist for pianist Jim Burke's boogie-woogie numbers. Like Alan Kippax and Ray Flockton before him, he is a coiner of nick-names. As a result quiet off-spinner Ashley Mallett became 'Rowdy' and googly left-hander David Sincock was known as 'Evildick'. Slender opening batsman Ashley Woodcock was 'Splinter'. Barry is a partner in Rowe and Jarman's successful sportsgoods business.

As SA bowler John Beagley was about to bowl in Sydney forked lightning twice pierced rainclouds. He turned to begin his run but . . . no batsman! Only Jarman, sagging behind the sticks, laughingly incapable of speech. Billy Watson had bolted for the pavilion. Seeing him enter the room captain Richie Benaud, forefinger to bottom lip, asked, 'Blinks, why are you here?' Watson: 'When I saw the lightning flash my initials WW, I thought it time to go for cover.'

In one Sydney match Sobers batted superbly for SA against NSW, bowled fast-medium inswingers, switched to slow wrist-spin, then dived for a spectacular catch. When a fieldsman's throw knocked the bails off Sobers picked them up and rebuilt the wicket. Watching this wicketkeeper Barry Jarman quipped: 'What, are you an umpire, too?'

After 100 in the first innings against SA in Sydney, Norman O'Neill was 78 when Brian Hurn reminded him that 78 was 87 backwards. Two runs later O'Neill's cut at Neil Dansie's leg-break edged it into Jarman's gloves. 'Closest I've ever been to century in each innings,' the departing batsman said.

With feigned earnestness Barry told schoolmaster-broadcaster Frank Tyson, 'I like what you write, Frank, but why use all those long words? Don't forget us readers who only had a technical education. I only understand three long words – wheelbarrow, minestrone and mulligatawny.' As a batsman he attacked bowling as if it were a sausage-roll on a cold day. A rise in weight past 89 kg (14 st) caused Jarman to side-step lunch and begin smoking. He peeled off 9 kg. He applied his weight in 1961 at Scarborough to hit 26 off one over from off-spinner David Allen: 6, 6, 4, 4, 4, 2.

He had a podgy hand in ten NSW wickets at Adelaide in 1962 and sent back 45 batsmen in 11 matches in 1963–64. This seasonal record was lifted by West Australian star Rodney Marsh to 67 in 15 games in 1975–76. (Current incumbent Ian Healy enjoyed his best season in 1990–91, when he caught 47.)

Bombay watched Jarman catch four Indians and make his highest Test score, 78. Calcutta saw his first Test stumping. People used to say to Grout's deputy, 'Always the bridesmaid, never the bride – gee, you're unlucky.' Barry would say, 'Not unlucky, really. I'm fortunate to have been regarded as No. 2 keeper and to have enjoyed five overseas trips as Wal's stand-by.' After Grout's retirement with 187 Test scalps, Jarman had his first full series at thirty-one, four Tests against visiting Indians.

He stepped up to captain SA the day an ambulance took Les Favell to hospital. An edged hook at Grahame Corling gashed Favell's brow so deeply that flesh fell over his right eye. Lying on the bloodstained pitch while they brought a stretcher, the indomitable skipper said, 'You always said you'd make a good captain, Jarmo – now's your chance to prove it.'

England first saw Jarman's gloveplay in Tests as Lawry's vice-captain in 1968, his third visit. Though a ball from McKenzie at Lord's broke his right forefinger in three places, he gamely tried to bat until a fast ball from David Brown struck the damaged finger and put him out of the third Test. He reappeared at Leeds where both Lawry (broken finger) and Cowdrey (hamstring) were out with injuries. Team-mates had never seen the jolly keeper so quiet as in the two days before he walked out with Tom Graveney while cameras snapped the unique sight of two deputies tossing. When a first-innings lead of 13 had been increased to 250 by tea on the fourth day, people looked for a busy last session to leave a full day for the dismissal of England on a five-day-old pitch. Everything in his nature and his experience under Favell's enterprising captaincy raised expectations that he would have Australia pressing on in a bid for victory.

But after tea only 1½ runs an over crept on to the scoreboard and an appeal against fading light wasted half an hour. It was all as unlikely as a fleshy temptress by Norman Lindsay being awarded the Blake Prize for religious art. Yet Australia batted on into the last day, adding surplus runs at a sacrifice of time the bowlers would need to get England out and put Australia two up in the series. Beginning with a leeway of 325 to overtake in barely five hours England still had six wickets standing when time ran out. Benaud said the stark tragedy of it was that Jarman, the Australians and he could only assume Lawry, in the pavilion, threw away a wonderful chance to win the Test and go on to an unassailable lead in the series (squared when England equalised in the last Test).

When I asked Jarman how much do a regular captain's established policies allow for a deputising skipper to use his own initiative, Barry would not pass the buck.

Bill let me have my own head in the middle, though we did have the odd yarn in the breaks. I would say Bill wished it was my game and that's how we played it. We didn't have enough wickets to have a go.

As English spinners Illingworth and Underwood had 100 overs in the second innings, I asked about Benaud's criticism of Gleeson being given only 11 overs on the last day, when pace bowlers were mostly used on a boot-scraped wicket. Barry's angle on this:

I kept Connolly going for 24 overs on the trot because he was keeping the Englishmen below the quota they needed to win. Gleeson doesn't like bowling against the wind – that's why he had not many overs. The Englishmen still had time to win in the last session by having a go. If we had needed a win to square the series we would have given it a go. They had to win to get the Ashes. We didn't have to.

In his 19 Tests Jarman caught 50 and stumped four. On the all-time list of wicketkeepers in first-class matches he is one of the five Australians who have topped 500 wickets. In 191 games he helped bowlers to 560 wickets (431 caught, 129 stumped). Barry totalled 5615 lively runs (average 22) and the highest of his five centuries was 196 against NSW at Adelaide.

Of all the men who led Australia into the field Jarman had been the youngest bridegroom – twenty years nine months. His bride, pretty salesgirl Gaynor Goldfinch, was a month younger. He was playing in India when their first son Gavin was born and in England heard of the birth of a daughter. He was allowed to postpone his departure for the 1968 tour of England a week for the birth of their second son, Jason.

When Barry retired at thirty-three he praised Gaynor as the most understanding wife a cricketer ever had. In fourteen years' married life he had been home on only one New Year's Eve and she had reared three children in his absences. His Adelaide sporting goods store has been a popular port of call for many a touring cricketer.

I.M. CHAPPELL

36

The Houdini Touch

Tension during critical hours in big cricket can be so feverish that watching players dare not move from their seats, for fear of bringing disaster on the batsmen at the wicket. Just how their motionless vigil works has yet to be logically explained. One day in 1974 a state captain opened a sliding window in a Melbourne dressing-room. Soon afterward he closed it, not to keep cold air out but because a couple of wickets had been lost while it was open.

Keeping the psychological temperature of the dressing-room at tolerable level was one of the secrets underlying the success of Ian Chappell as Australia's Test captain. Winning half-lost matches is a stiff task calling for a resilient type of man.

Ian Michael Chappell was born in Adelaide on 29 September 1943. He is the eldest of three sons of baseballer-cricketer Martin Chappell. Through their mother, Jeanne, Ian, Gregory and Trevor are grandsons of Victor Richardson, Australia's 20th captain.

Coaching on Lyn Fuller's Glenelg backyard wicket prepared Ian for successes at Prince Alfred College at fourteen and for Glenelg Club on his way to the SA XI.

Playing under adventurous Les Favell helped shape the outlook of Ian and Greg Chappell. By example more than precept, Favell was just the man to encourage enterprise in the brothers who had inherited much of the confidence and ball-sense of their grandpa. At nineteen Ian had the nerve to make 149 against Davidson's and Benaud's bowling for NSW, then tried his luck in a year with Ramsbottom in the Lancashire League.

Ian became accustomed to seeing SA innings begun by the most challenging opener in the land who demolished a theory that a No. 1 batsman could succeed against opening bowlers only by cautiously trying to wear them down.

Favell was the skipper who lifted Ian Chappell from the middle division to No. 3 slot, swapping places with all-rounder Garry Sobers. Two games later Chappell justified his elevation by making 205 at Brisbane and was on his way to Test selection against Pakistan at twenty-one. The first time he touched a ball in a Test he caught Pakistan opener Abdul Kadir off McKenzie in Melbourne, one of four catches on his debut. He had to wait 13 months for his next Test chance.

Three errors by Indian fieldsmen at Melbourne helped him in his first Test century, 151, in his tenth Test.

Even in the dimness of a discotheque where they first met he could not fail to notice attractive blonde Kay Ingerson, daughter of a baker-store-keeper. Romance blossomed when both worked in a stockbroking office. He was twenty-three and Kay twenty when they married.

When the Australians assembled at Sydney airport to fly to England in 1968 one reposing player, twenty-four, had missed his connecting flight from Adelaide. You don't need an alarm-clock when you've a six-week baby in the room, at least that's what Ian and Kay had thought that morning. Another aircraft got him to the team on time, nerves steady. On the tour fighting spirit enabled him to put a padlock on his Test place on tracks where hundreds tended to stay hidden. By twenty-six he had developed a fully furnished batting style with wall-to-wall footwork. His boots became so sure in advancing to drive spinners that he was stumped only twice in more than 100 innings in Tests.

Around 180 cm (5 ft 11 in) and 78 kg (12 st 3 lb) Chappell entered the field with a toes-out walk. First he looked up at the sky, not beseeching Heaven's favour but to quicken his blue eyes' focus to outdoor light. His confidence was more than skin deep – he had onion-layers of it, enough to bring tears to bowlers' eyes. He gave no heed to anything the outgoing batsman said about the bowling or the pitch. As Sir Frank Worrell did, he preferred to find it all out for himself, with his wicket at stake. Never enmeshed in theories, his mind had no place for preconceived ideas, only the actualities out in the middle.

Between balls he restlessly rescraped his blockmark and hitched his invisible scrotal protector in a way noticed by sniggerers.

Bats weighing up to 2 lb 10 oz forced booming drives through a wide sector. Longitudinal sweeps and hooks sent the ball to a different latitude – and altitude if the bowler found the top edge of a hook not fully drilled in keeping down. He had what jet pilots call eyeball judgement. From a leg-stump guard he put his right foot back and across toward the off peg as pacemen delivered. Fronting around full-chested in back-foot defence left him a target for high-level hostility from John Snow in Australia. Dissatisfied with being made to bow and scrape, he resolved to switch from ducking to hooking. On a concrete wicket between seasons he and Greg took turns at hurling down simulated bouncers while the other prac-tised the hook. He had an American best-seller in mind when he joked, 'I guess you could call me the Happy Hooker.' As I see it, to have ceased hooking would have been a retreat from the match-swaying role that meant more to Australia than a higher slower-growing average.

In the first Test they played together Ian scored 50 before Greg (five years younger) made 108 on his debut against England at Perth. Captain Bill Lawry told the unmuzzled brothers, 'You're a couple of bandits but you can play.' In two months the senior brigand, twenty-seven, was promoted to take over as skipper. Ian had a background of 36 Tests in four countries and a batting average of 36. The selectors put him in charge when the barometer was set persistently low for Australia: five losses in the preceding nine Tests, unrelieved by a single win. The gap England was opening up was the widest for sixty years. Chappell had led sides in only ten first-class games. His thumb was not yet hardened by pinning up batting orders.

One day showed that the captaincy had passed to the right hands. Chappell would rather have had his ancestry back to Hereward the Wake than Ethelred the Unready. He had never told an opposing side to bat until his first Test toss. At first attempt he got England out under 200 at Sydney – the only time in the series. In deployment of bowlers, greater calls on spin and close support by fieldsmen there were touches recalling Benaud's first attempt. Let's call it move-in-manship. When a wicket fell near the end of the first day Ian came in himself, with two minutes to go.

Chappell's flair as a hunchman became visible when he brought on an unknown bowler, left-handed batsman Ken Eastwood, to have Keith Fletcher caught. When I asked why, Ian said, 'At my first sight of him at practice he bowled a couple of wrong'uns before I picked it and I thought English batsmen would do no better.'

After England's 62-run win, reporters found him a relaxed answerer, beer can in hand. The Australians' quota of three souvenir stumps came in as Eastwood – out cheaply in his only Test – was disappointedly packing his bag. Ian took one to him saying, 'I thought you might like this.' Unsuspected facets of banditry!

Thriving on responsibility, Chappell was the only batsman who made four 100s in Australia's series against Garry Sobers's World XI. Though the World XI won, two to one, the multiracial batsmen were the first to reel under the impact of Dennis Lillee as the world's swiftest bowler. Like a hawk among hens, the lean West Australian gave Chappell's attack the most demoralising element any Australian captain had since Lindwall, Miller and Johnston enfiladed opponents for Bradman.

In the neutral opinion of Barry Richards: 'Chappell is an easy captain to play under. He gives every player a chance to use his own judgement, without making too many demands.' The atmosphere in the Australian room was less charged with the tension that makes bowlers look harder to play. Ian usually took it easy with clusters of players relaxing over a few beers. On tour in England he had every player staying two hours after a day's play. The camaraderie welded new and old players, conventional and unorthodox freewheeling types into a unit.

Chappell's players were not the youngest side Australia sent abroad but to the eyes of England's youth they looked it from the zips of their mod gear to the ends of their Ringo-type moustaches. The jeans generation discovered Test cricket as a young man's game, worth watching from Lillee's staglike bound to Marsh's soaring sixes. What was good enough for Mick Jagger was good enough for them (as since reflected in the make-up of Australian crowds).

Answering Arnold's, Snow's and Greig's seam bowling on a responsive Manchester pitch was beyond the Australians, soon one down. Ever

331

seeking something different, and having no left-handed paceman, Chappell encouraged Bob Massie to experiment bowling around-the-wicket. The reward was that, switching from side to side at Lord's, the either-way swinger captured 16 wickets – first man to land more than 12 at his Test debut. The success broke a sequence of 15 Tests without a win.

After a heavy disguise of fungus made the shorn Leeds strip unrecognisable as a Test wicket, Chappell's team was down two-one. They dealt the Ashes mentality the hardest uppercut it ever received. Crammed with action, the final Test attracted such crowds that the Oval's gates were shut on full houses three days running and the match brought in record takings. In a crucial recovery Ian and Greg provided an unprecedented sight: brothers scoring hundreds in the same Test innings. A casual smoker, Ian puffed through a few cigars before the Sheahan-Marsh stand got his side in, halving the rubber. Four finishes out of five: something English onlookers had seen only once before, on Bradman's last tour. People paid £261,283 sterling, then the highest sum ever from one Test series. Much-travelled manager Ray Steele wrote in a foreword to Chappell's *Tigers Among the Lions* that it was the least average-conscious team with which he had toured and Ian must be credited for that.

Nerve counts as much as know-how, sometimes more. In two Tests against Pakistan the Australians were in losing positions yet would not bow to inevitability. Chappell's unorthodox closure at 441 for five wickets on the second morning against Pakistan in Melbourne worked on the match like yeast.

When the Pakistanis looked like romping in with a day to spare in Sydney, Australian players booked out of their motel. Pakistan needed only 159 for victory. Snatching one of the most preposterous wins in modern Test annals, Chappell and his men trooped off the field like Houdinis freed from a padlocked chest submerged in a river.

Once ABC broadcaster Alan McGilvray asked Ian, 'Suppose trying from the start for a win misfires where safety-first play might not?' Chappell: 'If you suffer a loss or two it's not the end of the world. If you can win a few by setting out to do so, it's worth while.'

When injuries, illness and time take away half a side yet a captain moulds the replacements into a successful team he has to be admitted to company where no lesser light may shine. With Lillee and Massie out of action Chappell used a second-string attack, Walker and Hammond, to get front-line results in the West Indies in 1973.

A born athlete's strength and stamina carried the cricketing Houdini through a sequence of 71 Tests without a break, though it took exceptional toughness for him to appear in a Trinidad Test on a sprained ankle. Anchored by pain, the disabled skipper could not use his normal free foot-work as the world's top off-spinner, Lance Gibbs, made the ball screw from powdering turf at deceptive heights while two fielders waited around the corner. Hobbling with his heels near the stumps, Chappell played ball after ball down, leaving the legtrap men empty-handed. Fellow batsmen would not have believed he could last that crease-bound way, yet he stuck it out almost four hours for 97, keeping his side's chance alive.

By lunch on the last day the West Indians were on the threshold of victory. To get 66 more runs they had five wickets left, including that fine left-hander Alvin Kallicharran needing nine more for 100. Trinidadians were betting about how many wickets would still be standing when the winning run came. In a sweltering dressing-room Chappell uttered a few sentences of commonsense appraisal, nothing like an exhorting type of pep-talk:

We've been playing like a bunch of genitals. Before we came off we were beginning to whinge a bit about things not going our way. Remember our old principles of line and length and concentrate 100 per cent on the job and we'll still have a chance.

Walker's first ball after the interval deviated enough for Kallicharran to touch it into Marsh's gloves. Chappell told me:

As often happens, especially on a five-day-old pitch, once you get a breakthrough things seem to fall into place. Tangles Walker, who keeps at it and at it, was the ideal bowler and O'Keeffe did his part. The boys kept up the pressure in the field.

Houdini the Second talking, so matter-of-fact that you'd never guess it. In the last hour his side grabbed five wickets for 21. Their win by 44 was an affront to the laws of probability. Before the last man fell the outerground crowd at Queen's Park Oval began chanting, 'A-a-men, A-a-men, Amen!'

During the series West Indian listeners heard these broadcast comments from Reds Perreira and Andy Ganteaume:

We see the Aussies smile in the field, a friendly team playing good cricket which appeals to the crowd ... Ian Chappell's team are a fighting unit who never give up, no matter how the match is heading ... These Australian batsmen are not just prodding around waiting for the bad ball to score but are playing fine cricket. Something is happening all the time.

Room attendants found them the most likable visiting side since Johnson's convivial crew in 1955.

Declaring a ballot voting him Australia's Cricketer of 1973, Arthur Morris complimented Chappell on building up one of the finest-ever sides. When Alan Davidson complimented him on the team spirit, Ian mentioned how Massie, who lost his place through illness as the tour began, was seen at the nets trying to teach the man who displaced him, Walker, how to bowl an out-swinger to add to his inswinger and leg-cutter. In the conversational tone of his speechmaking Chappell said, 'I have been fortunate to be made captain at a time when Australia's selectors picked a side able to play good cricket. They give me no pats on the back – or the reverse when things go wrong.'

At Wellington in 1974 Ian and Greg made themselves the first brothers who scored centuries in each innings of a Test. Because scoreboard name plates showed them as Chappell I and Chappell G, one of his nicknames is Chappelli.

In his 69th Test he joined Simpson as a catcher of 100 and went on to 105 in 75 Tests. Among a dozen men who have caught six in a Test Richardson was the only reigning skipper until his grandson helped bowlers to take six New Zealand wickets at Adelaide in 1974. Ian's twenty-seven catches in 1968–69 are the most in an Australian summer, excepting wicketkeepers. (Graeme Hole is next, having taken 26 in 1952–53.) Manning catching positions often leaves nobody at deep third man to back up the slip cordon. When edged balls streaked between slip-fielders Chappell was quickest to chase after them. As reserve wicketkeeper in NZ he borrowed Marsh's gloves to catch three Otago batsmen off Greg at Carisbrook.

Against a stack of credits in Chappell's captaincy the chief offset is his expecting too much of fast bowlers. If Dennis Lillee's speed slackened, Ian would spur him on with such exhortations as, 'If I'd wanted a slow bowler I'd have called on Jenner.' When Lillee walked off a Sydney Test against Pakistan to have a painful back examined it was believed he was out of the match. Yet after one rest day a rally by tail-end team-mates induced him to offer to have a go. Through 11 three-quarter-pace overs on the fourth evening and 12 more on the trot in the last 2¼ hours I could not have been the only one watching with awe, admiration and anxiety. Three stretch fractures in the lumbar region put him out of first-class cricket for almost two years before his belligerent reappearance. After a long bowl in Melbourne against New Zealand Doug Walters made a mock protest to his skipper at dinner: 'You burnt out Lillee in 1972, you busted up Hammond in '73 – Who'll be sore in '74? Me!'

From the far edge of the generation gap came criticism of Chappell's informality and unfenced range of expression. One ex-player called Ian's white towel hat out of place in a Test match, without explaining why. Dig below the surface and you find volcanic depth in his nature. It emitted sulphuric fumes which caused some New Zealanders to choke with indignation at Lancaster Park in the Christchurch Test, 1974. Temper's topsoil had been worn thin by a stretch of five series as Australian captain in not much more than two years, with scant rest since he set out for England in 1972. A leg shot by Brian Hastings bounced into the boundary but was signalled a six. Chappell ran from slip to ask umpire Monteith to revise his decision. Remarks by non-striker Glenn Turner brought a short sharp outburst from Chappell, reportedly containing a couple of four-letter words which, in the lower levels of invective, are ascribed symbolism different from their anatomic meanings. When NZ captain Bevan Congdon demanded an apology, Chappell declined, saying happenings on the field should be kept there.

This self-daubed smudge on Chappell's image was one evidence of the most complex character of my time. It looked uglier to older generations.

He never minced words, only bowlers. Players of their vintage have no aversion to biological verbs and nouns from Anglo-Saxon village vernacular long ostracised by refined society.

Ian captained Australia through a period when change broke into a gallop and the old folk at home saw once-revered standards being dismissed by some as illusions. In Bradman's day Sydney editors banned any reference to Lysistrata; by Chappell's time families could see Diane Cilento playing in Aristophanes's comedy on television. Aborigines put up a symbolic tent embassy on Canberra lawns opposite Parliament House. A young man and woman amused 52,000 at Randwick racecourse by streaking past the winning post. A Tasmanian Premier tossed the penny in Australia's first legal two-up school since the game was outlawed in 1912. Olympic champion Shane Gould stepped along in a city march supporting a request by women surfers to be allowed to become members of surf clubs. On the day Ian was reappointed skipper for the 1974–75 Tests against England an unwed mother, Helen Morgan, twenty-two (Miss United Kingdom), was selected as Miss World.

Australia's XI looked up to Chappell as captain, with more conventional players not concerned about his free use of expletives. Without starch or frills, his manner encouraged a relaxed atmosphere in the room. Pre-play discussion was tersely relevant. Anxiety and theorising were out. Once he saw what bowlers were getting out of the pitch close scrutiny eased. Chappell preferred to talk to players about other topics. Coupled with this, he reinforced the confidence of his players by treating each as an expert in his own part of the game, knowing what to do.

He held such sway over them they are sure he must rank with the greatest Test skippers of all time. They wonder whether Benaud could have been superior. He had the same priorities when he said, 'To win a Test one thing you must do is take 20 wickets. Our aim is to score fast enough to give our bowlers time to get the opposition out twice.' He commanded the confidence of his players as completely as Richie did. In a crisis each was unsurpassed at summoning forth the utmost players can give. Each put initiative before uniformity, pressure before percentage play. Ian's fieldsmen never just hung around. They were on their toes under his assured direction.

336

He always had a finger on the pulse of the game. Like a jiujitsu expert knowing vulnerable nerve-centres he was foremost in using fielding pressure to squeeze batsmen into error. Bowlers could not hope for better backing than his close field settings. Chappell pushed move-in-manship degrees beyond even Benaud's standard. At times he went from slip to close point to confront the striker not far from handshaking distance. To pack six catchers in the slips and gully region in the 1974 Perth Test he left the on-side field in front of the wicket bereft of fieldsmen, a strange sight; to Lillee's two leg slips it looked as bare as Mother Hubbard's cupboard.

Jeff Thomson partnering Lillee gave Chappell the most daunting high-speed battery to deepen batsmen's concern since Hall and Griffith. He lacked Benaud's self-control under heckling and, though unable to approach Richie's achieved aim of a high daily quota of balls, he was an activist whose tactics stimulated interest.

In 1975 Bradman said, 'Choosing between them was a photo-finish: a slight edge in flair and initiative got Richie my vote.'

Forecasting that history would see Chappell as the maker of modern cricket, Bob Simpson said he gave the game a new image which youth could react to, though in the process he made enemies in high places. Tony Greig said that, becoming leader when Australian cricket was on its knees, Ian prompted an astonishing transformation until he led a bunch of players who would die for him in the field, the strongest side in the world.

As No. 3 batsman Chappell did more than was in all-rounder Benaud's power to shape Australia's innings whether an opener's dismissal called him forth in the first over or a prosperous start enabled him to have his 2 lb 10 oz bat handy. Australia needed his batting as much as a dowager needs a girdle. In his 30 Tests as skipper the opening pair only twice tamed the bowling for 100 runs. In 29 innings the total was fewer than 20 when he came in to face confident new-ball bowlers as trouble-shooter. Pakistan had a wicket in the first over in Adelaide when he began batting for his highest Test score, 196 off 57 overs. Sweeps and pulls for three sixes helped him plunder 21 off one over from captain Intikhab Alam. On a day 18 wickets tumbled at Auckland tall left-hander Richard Collinge could hardly have looked more difficult on a pig of a pitch if his pace bowling had sprouted tusks. For most of the first hour Chappell made sure he was at the nasty end, his own wicket at risk every ball. He topped 5000 runs in his 68th Test.

In the fourth over of the Brisbane Test, 1974, he came in amid a shaky start on an uncertain track. The strokesman capable of a run a minute suppressed his hook until he patiently put the innings on an even keel. When a top-edge hook off Willis ballooned a catch to Greig, Chappell's 90 was his only dismissal in the nineties in 54 innings as Test skipper.

Questioners at the National Press Club, Canberra, asked would Test results have been altered if his batsmen had to face Thomson and Lillee as a combination instead of singly in state sides. Chappell's reply:

> I think the Englishmen played into our hands a little by allowing us to place so many slips and by seldom attempting shots in front of the wicket. I think Australian players would have hit more balls down the ground. We might have failed a couple of times more disastrously but in a couple of Tests we might have forced Thomson and Lillee out of the attack.

Ian is a director of a firm he formed to co-ordinate activities in sales promotion, advertising and journalism. Tapes airmailed from overseas and interstate provided contents for his books, *Tiger Among the Lions*, *My World of Cricket* and *Passing Tests*.

As he coped with varying situations I saw him as the most resourceful batsman in the game. After 4½ years of off-field and on-field pressures he stepped back into the ranks at thirty-two. Ian was the first to lead Australia in 30 Tests, the second to win 15. Ten were unfinished. His side made an all-out bid against the West Indies in the first World Cup final at Lord's, hailed as the best one-day game ever played.

Originality counted. Ian was the first touring skipper to let his vice-captain handle the side in lesser games while himself playing for match practice – a novel idea easier because the vice-captain was his brother Greg, heir presumptive. He was the first captain to air players' views to Board meetings, on the initiative of Ray Steele and 1974 chairman Tim Caldwell. His players were the first to have an allowance of $200 a Test – doubled in 1975, plus bonuses of $200 a Test in 1975 and $400 in 1976. They were the first listed for credits in a Board retirement benefit fund drafted by Robert

Parish and Leonard Maddocks. With awards from advertising sponsors, time given to cricket could at last bring a regular Test player round $8000 in a big season, still short of their idea of a standard.

When Lillee's and Marsh's dissatisfaction gave Kerry Packer an opening to launch World Series Cricket, Chappell hand-picked twenty-seven players for enticing contracts. With Ian's guidance in the governing group, Packer took only two years to overcome the establishment and carry off sole rights for Channel Nine to televise big cricket (to the regret of thousands who had appreciated the ABC's service). Packer called his deal an absolute bonanza.

In addition to being the outstanding captain in WSC, Chappell had brought his players to the finest pitch of fitness I ever saw in an Australian side. Ian's average of 40 in 14 Supertests was a great achievement against such incisive fast bowling by Roberts, Holding, Garner, Croft and Daniel. Even he realised it would be foolhardy not to protect his skull.

After an infuriated mob invaded the Bourda pavilion in cricket's most frightening riot a team vote on whether to quit Georgetown was tied. Acting with courage and responsibility, Chappell said:

I am not asking any player to walk out on the field if he does not want to. I am not asking any player to put his life on the line. But I feel we have to go back there just to show them we will not allow mob rule to stop us playing. Before each day I will go to the ground and ensure that there is adequate security for the players.

In the West Indies he was partly responsible for the Players' Association court which imposed 15 fines, including $100 on David Hookes for smashing down his stumps when he was given out. In Australia captain Mike Brearley found most of his actions, even those hardest to accept, stemmed from strongly held convictions about how the game should be played.

Yet inability to control a cross-grained element in his nature resulted in the ignominy of a Georgetown court fining him for having assaulted a Guyanese official in the Bourda pavilion. In his last season at thirty-six he was involved in midfield oral brushes. Asked about controversies, he said that he regretted only two incidents during his career, both involving umpires. He added: 'I did not invent sledging – there were plenty of on-field

339

clashes before I came into the game. I was pretty ordinary in the games-manship stakes.'

Three Tests after his comeback took him to 105 catches in 75 Tests and 5347 runs in 142 innings, average 40, with 14 centuries. In 14 Supertests he scored 893, with one century. In 259 first-class games he totalled 19,663, average 42, with 59 hundreds, sharing sixth place with Hassett. Of his 176 wickets 20 were in Tests.

On Chappell's final West Indies tour was WSC employee Barbara-Anne Loois, who became Chappell's second wife three years later. By that time, Chappell was a fixture in Channel Nine's commentary cabal nestling between his friend Richie Benaud, predecessor Bill Lawry and former nemesis Tony Greig.

Chappell packed his kit on his final day of first-class cricket and never reopened it. Unlike his brother, he eschews celebratory and testimonial games. And unlike Houdini, lured fatally into one last feat, Chappell is content to rest on laurels as plenteous as any among Australian Test captains.

G.S. CHAPPELL

37

A Mind of His Own

Players differ from each other much as trees do, elm from oak, bluegum from stringybark. Cricket's equivalent of arborists need no scoreboard to identify one international batsman from another. Build, gait, bearing and mannerisms are distinctive. To me, Greg Chappell was the game's poplar, upright in growth with little spread.

In his walk to the wicket, the erectness of his tall figure conveyed confidence. His straight back had no ramrod stiffness. His steps look short for a man of his height: 185 cm (6 ft 1 in).

What gave Greg Chappell's batting its slender elegance? Crowds relished his way of leaning into strokes like a poplar in wind. Drives rattled the base of the sightscreen or skimmed by mid-on and mid-wicket. He finished strokes standing taller than most others of his time. Except when balls tended to prop, he played fluently right through them; long-armed follow-through added to the eye-appeal. Frequently the bat finished pointing to the sky – a pointed hint to his average. His kind of average knows how to take a hint. It has a python-like capacity for digesting heavy meals. Greg's 380 runs in two courses that NZ chefs served at Wellington when he was twenty-five were then the tallest total by anybody in one Test match. He and Allan Border alone have twice made a hundred in each innings of a Test.

Martin and Jeanne Chappell's second son Gregory Stephen was born on 7 August 1948. Martin told me, 'Even as a kid Greg had the shot he whips away off his left hip instead of turning the ball as others do.' His build was in the Chappell mould, fairly solid, until at fifteen he began shooting up past 6 ft while at Prince Alfred College. His spare frame took ten more years to reach 76 kg (12 st).

Ian was touring South Africa when Adelaide Oval scoreboard used his nameplate for Greg's first match for SA at eighteen. The youth's 53 and 62 not out gave him 115 for one dismissal.

Chappell first trod on a Sydney wicket after removal of tons of a midfield hump had lowered it by 45 cm (18 in). While the pitch was convalescent after major surgery batsmen's scores were low, too. No visitor could get near 100 on it. Coming in fifth as SA sagged against Test bowlers Corling, Gleeson and Philpott, Greg topped the score, 68 not out. Impressed by his talent and temperament, I sought him out to discover more about a potential Test player and wish him well on his way to add lustre to the family name. A week later Greg scored 104 at Brisbane, his first state century in his seventh game at eighteen.

A second Chappell nameplate was painted when Greg, nineteen, and Ian appeared in the South Australian XI in 1967. Ability in crises continued to show up. Garth McKenzie had four wickets for 18 before Greg made 154 without a chance against WA. A batsman with new sideburns down his cheeks was learning the password to gain admittance to the upper circle of Test batsmen.

On the way, two seasons with Somerset advanced his game. Scoring 2500 runs on county tracks tightened his defence against balls deviating off the seam.

As the John Player League's bottom club, Somerset looked least likely to have the first century-maker in these 40-overs-a-side games. League leaders Surrey had one Somerset wicket for five when Chappell walked in to rip 100 off 35 overs in 88 minutes. Off 38 overs he lashed 128 not out.

In SA's second innings against NSW in the next season, Greg was not feeling well. As he went in with two out for 39 his parting remark was, 'There'll be a few shots played.' Fifteen of those shots pounded the pickets as Chappell ran away with 100 in 92 minutes.

With a recently dislocated thumb strapped, Greg Chappell made 129 and 156 not out against Queensland in Brisbane five months after turning twenty-one.

After examination disclosed an enlarged spleen and glandular fever I felt Sir Donald Bradman thought it better not to subject him to a heavy tour of

India and South Africa. Instead, Greg exceeded 500 runs in seven games for another Australian team in NZ.

Chappell can stay expressionless throughout any spoof. On their first overseas trip, practical jokers initiated fast bowlers Dennis Lillee and Alan Thomson into off-field jocularities. Word went around that something of Graeme Watson's was missing and that Greg might be a kleptomaniac. Chappell acted in ways to deepen suspicion. Manager Frank Bryant, well in the joke, told players, 'If it is proved, Greg will have to go home.' To end uncertainty Chappell's room was informally searched for missing articles. Watching this, Lillee and Thomson were concerned lest something incriminating be found, until Kerry O'Keeffe's splutter of laughter exposed the conspiracy.

In SA's second innings against the Englishmen in 1970 Greg smote 102 off 100 balls in 118 minutes. Given a place at Perth in the second Test, he saw John Snow and Peter Lever get five out for 107 before he joined Ian Redpath in a double-century stand. One of the largest prime-viewing-hour audiences watched Chappell approaching 100. Suddenly the WACA ground was replaced on the screen by the 7 o'clock news. The switch-away from Chappell on 98 provoked the fattest bagful of protesting letters of the year. A century in his first Test innings at twenty-two prompted him to say, 'Maybe I'll be Greg Chappell from now on, not Ian's young brother or Victor Richardson's grandson.'

When Snow's bouncer felled Terry Jenner at Sydney, the ball rebounded from his skull to cover-point. His hair matted with congealed blood, Jenner heard room-mate Greg say, 'There was a single in it,' in a tone regretting a lost opportunity.

As winners at Old Trafford in 1972, England shaped for another victory at Lord's by grabbing Australia's first two wickets for seven. Through six chanceless hours Greg kept out 301 balls, ever conscious of his side's dependence on his intact wicket, yet picking the right balls to hit 14 fours in 131. English praise was headed by Trevor Bailey calling his 131 the outstanding innings of the series. It was one of the best innings in any batsman's career.

In the final Test at the Oval, Arnold and Snow shot the openers out for 34 yet Greg tackled them with assurance. By contrast with Lord's, 14 shots rapped the boundaries in only three hours on his way to 100 in 190 minutes. He hit 17 fours in 113, again chanceless, of a 201 stand with Ian, the first instance of brothers making hundreds in the same Test.

Watching the first live telecast of a Test via satellite, Australians saw Greg play forward to a ball that rose abruptly to his throat. He dropped his bat and walked yards away. (To my questions later he replied, 'It didn't make me feel sick but it was hard to breathe for a while.') Batting on such a track was like Russian roulette. Scoreless overs made televiewers anxiously wonder whether the struggling Australians could get another run. To break the shackles, Chappell quick-stepped forward to lift Underwood over vacant mid-off to the fence.

For songs in the team's coach Greg and Paul Sheahan composed topical verses to well-known tunes, always laughable if sometimes licentious. Each player was given a stanza in a parody on *The Quartermaster's Store*, such as 'Stack, Stack needs a sauna front and back on the Aussie England tour'.

Greg's dry wit was enjoyed by the Australian Cricket Society's Newcastle branch. As guest speaker he began by recalling that, after a similar club night, one man told him it was the worst after-dinner speech he had ever heard. Told of this, the club president said soothingly, 'Don't worry, Greg – he's not worth bothering about. He just goes around saying what everyone else says.'

Sydney barrackers calling for Walters to bowl against Pakistan instead of Greg began chanting, 'Off, off, off!' In mid-over Chappell veered across and pretended to hand the ball to Doug.

First Australian to score 1000 in the West Indies, Chappell totalled 1110 in 17 innings in 10 games.

Greg was nearing twenty-five when Channel 0 director Ronald Archer and other go-ahead Queenslanders lured him to Brisbane with an offer said to be worth at least $15,000 a year. Chappell made state captaincy an essential and wicketkeeper John Maclean, a friend from their NZ tour, made way for him.

As a revelation of batting genius under difficulties, give me Greg's feat on Brisbane's grassiest strip where Queensland's match against NZ was ended in two days by Tony Dell (12 wickets), Geoff Dymock, Dayle Hadlee and

Bryan Andrews. The pacemen had outgoing batsmen almost blocking the gangway. After NZ slumped for 100 and Queensland wickets tumbled, survival was Chappell's sole aim for half an hour. Next day he surged on to 165 off 40 overs and NZ went down by an innings. Bowlers got the other 29 wickets at a give-away average, 11 each. I doubt whether a hunt through the careers of star batsmen would find anything to surpass or even equal it.

No man totalled 1000 in a season for Queensland until his 1178 in nine games, 1013 of them in eight Sheffield Shield matches.

A cricketer's hours in public view are less than one third of his day. Pressures in the other two-thirds can be greater than tense stretches on the field. In the most demanding of Greg's first eight years in first-class cricket, 1973–74, he underwent patchy health, floods fouling their Kenmore home, his wife losing her baby – it says much for his ability to apply his mind to the job in hand that he created a world Test record.

In a fraternal run-fiesta at Wellington, the Chappells became the only brothers with a hundred each in both innings of a Test. Ian 145 and 121, Greg 247 not out and 133: the most runs scored in a Test match until Graham Gooch's grand double of 333 and 123 at Lord's against India in 1990. The Chappells' 646 topped even Ponsford's and Bradman's tallest united efforts, 625 at the Oval in 1934.

Greg's 247 spurted from his bat at 40 runs an hour, imperious hours spangled with a six and 30 fours. His first 100 came off 160 balls, 47 balls fewer than Ian's 100. Passing Ken Barrington's 1763 Down Under in 1963, Greg set a record for an Australian with 1880 in 17 matches in both countries. He shares with Bradman the Australian record of a century in each innings of four matches.

Throat and lung troubles required treatment throughout the 1974–75 series against England, yet as the straightest player in either side he scored most runs in the season, 1484, and made most catches in the Tests, 14. Ian would not call on him to bowl and Greg left early after each day's play to rest. Surgery to his tonsils threw him out of normal training. During a bad trot, his seven Test innings in England in 1975 totalled 106, about as many runs as people expected of him in one day before tea interval.

Coming in as prospective third victim in a hat-trick is scarcely a moment to begin a rapid century. Glamorgan left-hander Malcolm Nash sent back Alan Turner and Ian Chappell with two balls before Greg entered at Swansea. Yet Chappell made 100 off 77 balls. The 100 leapt on to the board in 66 minutes, seven minutes quicker than Bradman's fastest one in England.

Autographs had led to Greg meeting an office equipment supplier's daughter in a Sydney suburb, Bexley. Judy Donaldson's sister Elizabeth wrote to Adelaide for signatures. Next time SA played in Sydney, tickets were given to the Donaldsons. Imagine the effect when Greg found Judy to be an exquisite green-eyed beauty contest winner. At twenty-three he travelled to Bexley to wed Judy, twenty-one, in 1971.

After tours of England and West Indies, he was batting for Queensland in Sydney when he could not see her in the stand and learned that his wife was in hospital, having lost their first baby. She had not wanted him to know until the match was over. World Cup matches took him to England again three weeks before the birth of their first son. Stephen was three months old before his father saw him.

At the wicket, Chappell's only departure from upright line was his stance. From boyhood habit he leaned over his bat. His early pick-up was fairly high yet controlled. Wrists took it as straight back as orthodoxy decrees. His left boot crept in a few inches and the right came up alongside. This unorthodox shuffle was his way to avoid committing himself to a forward movement before he had judged the length of the ball. Before he moved to leg-stump block his shuffle often exposed this peg behind his legs.

Greg's hands swung one of the three heaviest bats in the Australian XI, 2 lb 12 oz (1.25 kg). His high grip made more use than the others of a short-handle bat's leverage.

Greg was a bowler's dream of a fieldsman. The hands at the ends of his long arms were so sure and his confidence in them so complete that the ball usually seemed to fasten to them. His upward reach brought down every-thing except perhaps a homewarding angel. Batsmen thought the way he picked up ankle-low slip chances was devilish. Seven catches against England in a Perth Test made him first to bring off so many in one Test.

After his mid-twenties, Greg gleamed as one of the brightest stars in cricket's Milky Way.

Selecting his best team from Australians since the second world war Sir Donald Bradman named 12 in the *Sydney Morning Herald* and Adelaide *News*: Simpson, Morris, Bradman, Harvey, Ian and Greg Chappell, Miller, Benaud, Davidson, Lindwall, Tallon, Hassett.

I was discussing this batting order with Greg when he commented: 'Ian is a more powerful player. A couple of times he's been dubbed The Butcher for the way he has savaged bowling. He can savage bowlers more than I have.' He agreed that he hit the ball in the air in front of the wicket more, whereas Ian did so more behind square leg, hooking and sweeping. Ian flayed Victoria's bowlers for 125 before lunch (110 minutes) on Adelaide Oval, within ten runs of Bradman's fastest pre-lunch score in Australia on the same oval against Tasmania in 1936. Ian followed his 125 with 97 in an afternoon session in the second innings. I never knew Greg's brother to have two such inflammable knocks in one match. When runs were needed in a hurry both sometimes started along the track before the bowler delivered.

Greg had a forthright, positive approach to the game, as to everything else. Steady blue eyes seemed to welcome a challenging situation. Greg's mind is ever-active in waking hours. Nature balances this by making him a long sleeper. His unbending will-to-win and confident example lifted Queensland players' self-reliance, and Jeff Thomson's move from Sydney daunted opponents.

When the national selectors named him Test captain at twenty-seven he had played in 34 Tests in four countries. Nine hundreds were among his 2507 Test runs and he had caught 46 batsmen in addition to having taken 24 wickets as a medium-pace seamer who bowls better than a batsman should. As vice-captain in England he directed the Australians in five out of 14 games; his brother twice let him run the side in the field while Ian himself fielded.

Greg lost his first toss to Clive Lloyd six months after the 190 cm (6 ft 3 in) Guyanese led West Indies through India and Pakistan with success. Lloyd had won acclaim for his match-winning part in the World Cup final, putting Australia down by 17 runs.

The ultimate in boyhood daydreams was fulfilled by the outstanding part Greg played in his first-up win as captain. Only two Australians before him had reached 100 the first time they batted as Test skippers, Noble in 1903 and Hassett in 1949. As partner watching him play Gibbs and googly left-hander Inshan Ali when Australia needed 219 on a worn Brisbane track, his brother saw him cope with their turn for 2½ hours. With frequent singles in his 74 not out Ian gave him two-thirds of the strike. Greg's respect for awkward turning balls was matched by power and placing of his strokes in his chanceless 109 not out off 172 balls. A panel voted him Man of the Match, first incoming Test captain to score a century in each innings.

Incoming batsmen invariably found him crowding them with close field-smen in the Benaud-Chappell manner. The sight of bold shots crossing untenanted outfields did not bustle him into switching infielders back from catching positions. Preferring to let batsmen try to hit over the top, he was rewarded with some prized wickets.

A 1902 penny, a two-up relic given Greg by Ray McRae of Seppelt's Vineyard, fell wrongly for his opponent in the last five tosses, whether Lloyd called tails or heads. In Adelaide Clive rumbled, 'Oh no, you're not using that ugly thing again!' Greg is the only Australian toss-winner who has won four Tests by sending opponents in. Two were in succession against the West Indies. No one else has sent opponents in six times.

Watching Rod Marsh carefully taping his fingers before going out to take Lillee and Thomson, Greg asked, 'When do you get into the ring with Tony Mundine, Bacchus?'

The first time Greg captained Australia in Adelaide was a 40-overs game a few days after his team had been thrashed by an innings in the Perth Test. Without Thomson, Australia dismissed the World Cup conquerors for 224 in 37.6 overs in Adelaide then made 225 for five wickets off 31.5 overs. The effect of the reverse on the one-day champions became plainer when Australia avenged the Perth hiding by winning the next Test in Melbourne.

England's captain Tony Greig knew what to look for in sizing up a future opponent. He said:

> There comes a time when every captain has to prove to his players that he is a good leader. Greg Chappell did so in Melbourne by decision and example, though it couldn't have been easy after humiliating defeat in Perth. His 182 not out in Sydney was the finest crisis innings

I have seen by a captain. For a side in trouble, with possible defeat ahead, he responded with confidence and dedication.

For all their similarities Greg's dynamism was less positive than Ian's. He said: 'I think I'll be a bit tougher but I can't see myself cracking the whip.' Having a mind of his own showed up in several variations mattering enough to influence prospects. After a couple of Tests, Greg began amending field-settings that had served Australia well. 'West Indians are not like Englishmen standing there trying to exist,' he said. 'They are playing shots at our best balls. Rather than wait in slips for catches to come, we will have to use more strategy.' Among variations we saw a deepish point as well as gully to counter Fredericks's back-foot square-drive, and adjustment of leg outfielders brought three Test-swaying catches in Sydney.

To move Ian from first slip would have seemed sacrilegious until Greg swapped places. For Queensland, he found it easier to size up positions. Greg ran from slip to make suggestions to his bowlers more than any predecessor. We soon had evidence of readiness to scrap regular tactics.

After Gilmour's blazing 95 in Adelaide the West Indians began batting five minutes before lunch. Instead of Lillee with the breeze Chappell gave the ball to Gary to bowl into it, though he was limping. Greg chose the left-hander because his shorter run gave a possibility of starting another over. Gilmour's fifth-ball trapping of Fredericks crowned the move. In the second innings, rather than bat on to increase Australia's lead beyond 489, he declared with seven out because he wanted to get half an hour's bowling before lunch. Initiative was again rewarded when Lillee got Fredericks in his third over.

Confidence in his own judgement reached a peak when Greg reshaped the pace attack which had been the dominant element in Australia's climb to the top through 1972 to 1976. For 23 Tests before and after Lillee overcame back injury Ian always gave Dennis first use of the new ball, downwind. After pleurisy kept Lillee out of the Sydney Test, Greg bowled Gilmour and Thomson for ten overs in Adelaide before calling on him. In the final Melbourne Test Thomson handled the ball first each time and in the second innings Lillee was first change into the breeze for the eighth over. It was rather like a Prime Minister being ushered into a secondary seat.

Lillee missed a fresh ball's extra life but it did not show up in the averages. Compared with Thomson's 29 wickets in six Tests Lillee's 27 in five Tests fell to a quicker striking-rate, 39 balls to 42.

The captain was one of eight Test players who pedalled bicycles to the Melbourne ground past long queues on the day 85,596 watched a Test open. The ride was arranged by Lillee in his new job as promotions manager for Eurocars. Those wondering whether the captain should have taken part have little concept of the rally-around mateship that gives the Australians' team spirit such reality.

After Brisbane radio 4IP's ten-year contract for $633,000 made Jeff Thomson cricket history's highest-paid speedman, newsmen asked how the team felt about one player receiving so much. Greg, grinning: 'Well, on our trip from Brisbane Thommo borrowed ten cents to buy a newspaper – and hasn't paid me back.' Early in 1976 the Chappells were appointed directors of Living Insurance Pty Ltd, consultants for Eagle Star in SA.

Since they first met him captaining Queensland, the West Indians had to contend with him for almost 22 hours, in which he totalled 747 runs at 35 an hour. He hit 72 fours and a six off their bowlers, who did not take his wicket in five out of 13 innings. Their worst setback – and his richest luck – was a hard low slip chance off Roberts when he was 11 in the Sydney Test. The let-off cost West Indies their chance to equalise the rubber. Greg's masterly 182 not out guided Australia along the victory trail – their third success in the first series to result in five wins to one.

His 702 in six Tests lifted the Australian record for a series against the Indies from Walters's 699 in four Tests. He was the only player to be voted Man of the Match twice.

Chappell's third consecutive 1000-a-season in Australia yielded 1547 runs in 15 matches at 85.94. Only Bradman, Harvey and Walter Hammond have made more. Greg's Queenslanders carried off the 1976 Gillette Cup. His closing gesture was to smite 28 off an over from Mallett.

He incurred well-founded criticism for not having told Marsh and Cosier to go for a win when the wicketkeeper's and all-rounder's failure to attempt 56 in the last 15 overs let the Adelaide crowd and television viewers down. Benaud winced. The let-off allowed Pakistan to square the rubber when Imran Khan carved off 12 wickets in Sydney.

In the Melbourne Centenary Test umpire Tom Brooks gave Derek Randall out at 161. From the bowler's end it looked as if a snick carried to Marsh's gloves. When Derek, departing, did not hear Rod's call that it was no catch Greg called him back. The win by 45 was Chappell's eighth victory in 12 Tests.

Greg was the 1977 Ashes side's only scorer of 1000 runs. His 112 at Old Trafford, third of his five centuries, was his fourteenth in 48 Tests. After he played Derek Underwood on, the side looked like a dismasted yacht, as it often seemed while England won three consecutive Tests. Lawry's 1968 side had been the only other Australians not to have a player named in *Wisden's* Five Cricketers of the Year, whereas England had Willis, Hendrick and Botham. The Englishmen decisively outcaught the Australians. In the first four Tests 19 dropped catches cost close to 500, nearly double the cost of England's 12 misses.

Chappell's image with cricket followers suffered when they heard he had been bound to secrecy when he signed a tough contract to play World Series Cricket for a private promoter, Kerry Packer, who launched it as a lever to prise sole television rights from an unwilling Australian Cricket Board. Insiders were aware that Greg weighed his decision so long that he was the last Australian to join.

He was dismayed when news of the contracts came out in May instead of after the tour. 'WSC was foreign to all I had known about cricket,' he said. 'I understand how people were shocked, because that's how I felt at first. For people to whom cricket was almost a religion we were heretics.' Two factors swayed him. One was the standover attitude arising from the Board's monopoly. The other was that Packer's contracts came at a moment when he was finding it difficult to justify the time he was giving to cricket without being rewarded with security.

He wrote to Sir Donald Bradman and Board chairman Bob Parish on behalf of the players to explain why they joined WSC, to put their case before the Board decided how to react. No reply came. When Parish arrived for International Cricket Council discussions he stayed in the team's hotel, the Waldorf. When their paths crossed in the foyer nothing was said. Finally Greg went to Parish and said he would like to talk with him. Parish told him: 'I don't think we have anything to talk about.'

Travelling with the Australians it was curious to observe cross-currents of propaganda fired at cricket-goers uneasy about the future of their game.

Inescapably, when twelve Packer signees were in a coach discussing prospects they would drop the subject if joined by others not involved. I noticed a tendency for similar groupings at meals. My impression was that repeated media references created more hubbub outside and around the team than a division within the side. Nevertheless, I felt Craig Serjeant was unlucky to miss three Tests.

Some odd statements I read looked even stranger in the light of the first-hand assessment by Geoffrey Boycott:

> I guess they may have been conscious of the Packer business but it didn't seem to affect the spirit in the field. I can say without a shadow of doubt that I have never played against an Australian side that tried harder. Throughout the game when the Australians were bowling and fielding all the players were encouraging each other and egging each other on, particularly Chappell and vice-captain Marsh. They could not have done more to keep the spirit going.

On return from the tour Chappell reiterated his belief that World Series would have benefits for cricket, in addition to having brought bigger rewards for players. The ruthless reality of commercialism took only two years to land Packer a hand-over of his TV prize. As well, the Board gave him promotional rights for ten years, estimated to yield vastly more than his $4 million outlay.

Greg had summoned up extraordinary resolution to begin the achievements that made him the outstanding Australian batsman in WSC's last year. To relieve constant jarring of a strained right forearm in a Perth Supertest he frequently had to play shots one-handed. He defied the World XI attack for 5¾ hours in making 174. As acting captain at VFL Park he was 246 not out when he closed the innings at six for 538.

When palsy caused by an ear virus paralysed his right eyelid he was ruled unfit until a flicker allowed him to tour the West Indies. Primarily a front-foot player, he had not noticed that the battery headed by Roberts and Holding had driven him onto the back foot in Australia. Extra bowling by Lillee after practice did not uncover the cause of a lean sequence. Finally he realised that he had fallen into a compromise shuffle neither forward nor back. Detection of the flaw and his eyelid's recovery enabled Greg to score 90 at Bridgetown in the second Supertest, 150 at Port of Spain, 113 at Georgetown and finish with 104 and 85 in Antigua.

Because of the blistering firepower faced, that cluster stands out as the greatest sequence of his career. One of the last to wear a helmet, he felt he had regained his surest touch and concentration. His 1416 in 14 Supertests, average 54, more than doubled the total of the nearest Australian (Ian 693).

He re-entered traditional Tests with 74 and 124 against the West Indies at Brisbane and wound up a twin-series with 114 and 40 not out against England at Melbourne. He attributed Australia's reversal of the 1977 losses in England to the experience his side had gained. Mike Brearley gave much of the credit to Greg when he said England had no complaint about the Australians' behaviour.

Pakistan's superior spinners then won a Karachi Test before two draws. After seven hours lost by rain at Faisalabad a refusal to play on the rest day caused Chappell to say his side would bat on for practice. His part in a record total, 617, was 235 not out (23 fours). It took over the record between the countries from Ian's 196 at Adelaide. Greg batted 7 hours 23 minutes, his longest Test innings.

Chappell's tally was 11 wins to six losses with another seven unfinished including the English Centenary Test. He is the only one since four-ball overs ended in 1884 who has used 11 bowlers in a Test innings.

Stephen was five and Linda three when Judy bore their third child, Jonathan, in April 1980.

The first lasting blot on Chappell's escutcheon was made in the dying fall of a one-day final against New Zealand at the MCG on 1 February 1981. Craving for a lay-day from the toil of an unremitting schedule, Greg instructed his brother Trevor to deliver the last ball of the match to New Zealander Brian McKechnie underarm.

Critics, including Richie Benaud and brother Ian, denounced his

354

temporary loss of perspective. Yet there was a sorry inevitability about such an infringement of cricket's spirit. *Wisden Cricket Monthly*'s astute editor David Frith had foreseen the precise same scenario 20 months earlier: 'I have been waiting with trepidation for the moment when, with six runs needed off the final ball and a lot of money at stake, the bowler informs the umpire of a change of action and rolls the ball along the ground.'

It was simply ironic that Chappell, whose rectitude had hardly been in doubt throughout his career, should have been the man who finally buckled before the pitiless programming of modern cricket tours. Chappell made further mute protest about the heavy demands on his contemporaries when, preferring to reacquaint himself with his young family, he absented himself from the 1981 Ashes tour.

There was cruel comeuppance for Greg Chappell when he resumed the top job six months later. After a poised double-century against Pakistan at the Gabba, his form slumped with the ruinous completeness of the Dow-Jones Industrial Average in October 1929.

Four ducks came in 11 days, and for six weeks Chappell languished in Tin Pan Alley: brother, could you spare him a run? The circuit-breaker was a conversation in the SCG nets during the Second Test against the West Indies in February 1982 with the West Indian doctor Rudi Webster.

Webster, whose *Winning Ways* is at many batsmen's bedsides, offered mildly: 'I don't want to get on the bandwagon, but I just wondered if you had thought about whether you were watching the ball.' Chappell scoffed, but later appreciated that Webster had put a finger on his batting's fading pulse.

A tour of New Zealand shortly after threatened to be a briar patch, but Greg found it a bed of roses when his batting touch surged back. He made 108 in the first of three one-day internationals, then dominated the Third Test at Christchurch with a magisterial 176 that underwrote a handsome victory.

Chappell, moreover, rehabilitated himself in the eyes of those across the Tasman by making light of potential controversies and calming a few of his more extrovert personalities. Dennis Lillee thought that his skipper's anaemic batting streak had enhanced him as a leader of men: 'Almost overnight he became a more understanding captain.'

Given the sad circumstances of his 1977 Ashes visit, Chappell regarded the 1982–83 series against Bob Willis's Englishmen as the opportunity to complete unfinished business. His Test centuries at Perth and Adelaide – his first at a ground whose long straight boundaries had always denied him high scores – had a reprimanding quality. Clean-shaven for the first time in more than a decade, Greg showed crowds his clean-cut good looks as well as his clean-hit good strokes during a 2-1 series victory.

Having reclaimed the Ashes, Chappell devoted his final summer to the pursuit of Sir Donald Bradman's Test run-scoring record. While Kim Hughes led Australia against Pakistan, his elder statesman crept up on Bradman's 6996 runs and finally cornered it at the SCG on 3 January 1984.

Chappell had already designated the Test his last, and Bradman's own fate in his ultimate Test innings crossed his mind when he came out to bat under heavy skies at 12.24 pm. Luck was on his side. Greg was dropped by Abdul Qadir at 47, and at 65 was presented with the record gift-wrapped in the form of overthrows from Mohsin Khan.

He was 79 not out at stumps and, chaperoned by Allan Border the following day, pushed boldly past a 24th Test century. A pilgrim from the Hill scampered across the field to genuflect before Chappell, kissing his glove, and was allowed to make his exit unimpeded. The batsman's 182 from 400 deliveries took less than nine hours and included 17 boundaries.

Sydney cricket lovers had scarcely finished their hosannahs when Chappell, having requested a relocation from first to second slip, clutched Mohsin's edge in front of his face. Bowler Lawson was the first to congratulate him on a record 121st Test catch, and Marsh second. 'I would have broken it weeks ago if you hadn't poached so many,' Chappell quipped to the keeper. Cricket can scarcely have enjoyed such a mortgage on newspaper front pages as it did for the duration of that match, which also saw the retirement of Dennis Lillee and Rod Marsh.

Chappell was one of the selectors who, during the following season, appointed Allan Border as Australia's 38th captain. He had high hopes of Border, having lured him to Queensland in April 1980, and fully expected the left-hander to topple him from his exalted position in the ranks of Australia's Test runmakers.

Dissatisfied with the homogeneity and bureaucracy of the Australian

Cricket Board, Chappell stood down at the end of the 1987–88 season for the less onerous task of commentary. Viewers were exposed to a sense of humour hitherto unexpected.

One of the satisfactory elements of the ACB's decision to fabricate an 'Australia A' team in the 1994–95 season was a reunion between Chappell and the game to which he had been such an ornament. Chappell was appointed coach and, a shrewd counsellor to his pack of prodigies, suggested the faculty for communication he developed during his captaincy career had not grown dormant.

G.N. YALLOP

Colours Dipped

38

International cricket was in turmoil when the spring of 1977 demanded drastic changes. Three states had to find captains in refilling their ranks after more than twenty of Australia's best players moved into higher taxation brackets by signing contracts to play World Series Cricket.

Amid this unprecedented upheaval Victoria turned to an untried skipper, Graham Neil Yallop, to pick up the reins dropped by the defection of wicketkeeper-batsman Richie Robinson.

Turmoil and upheaval had never disturbed the life of this graceful left-hand batsman, who was born on 7 October 1952. He was only fifteen when he rose to the first eleven of Carey Baptist Grammar School where Frank Tyson was coach. After his debut for Victoria at twenty he was not called on at twenty-one for anything higher than the Colts XI.

On three visits to England he broadened his batting technique. Playing for Northamptonshire Seconds at Cardiff in 1975, he met Helen Perkins, a tall, slim brunette; he made 3000 runs for Walsall in the Birmingham League. After marrying Helen at twenty-three in his school chapel Graham took her back to see her parents in 1976 and played for Glamorgan Seconds. She had never seen a cricket match until he took her but soon became fond of the game. Her pile of newspaper clippings mentioning him rose rapidly when Victoria appointed him captain in 1977.

Two years before the WSC commotion he had won promotion to the Test side at a time when the selectors' omission of Rick McCosker displeased the Australian XI. Graham felt the backwash when he tried to locate his locker. Entrusted with the No. 3 berth against the high-speed West Indians, he came through three Tests in the hot seat with a creditable average, 44. After early-season rain prevented him from starting the next season well, missing 14 Tests, including the 1977 tour of England, his confidence diminished.

Though plentiful evidence showed him to be Australia's most accomplished player of spin, the selectors did not choose him against India's pre-eminent spinners until the last Test, when he was made vice-captain to Simpson. He made a century.

At his father's APY Castings foundry, Kensington, Graham was making slip-catching cradles until he became agent for Duncan Fearnley's sports-goods. His reserved nature led to an impression that his disposition made him likely to react to events, not to meet them head-on.

Polished batting had brought him 1149 runs in 21 matches, including four centuries. Without ostentation, he had made himself Victoria's best batsman since Ian Redpath. When he scored 105 and 114 not out in Sydney he was the first Victorian to make twin centuries in a match in four years since Alan Sieler's 157 and 105 at Brisbane.

The family name, from Norfolk, inevitably prompted the nickname 'Wallop', not the nature of his batting, never unruly. Keith Stackpole classed him as the best-equipped batsman playing traditional cricket, having emerged from a casual approach that held him back for a year or two.

About 182 cm (close to 6 ft) and 76 kg (12 st), Yallop's brown eyes stayed level above a slightly open stance, feet together. He raised the bat early. Glides along the pitch did much to give him command over spin bowling. Drives too fast for fieldsmen to intercept were not smashed with the force of O'Neill or Dexter, nor punched as Bradman and Weekes used to. His polished strokes were nearer the velvet touch of Stollmeyer or Kippax.

At twenty-three Graham made 16 on his Test debut against the West Indies. His reactions to a fiery over from Holding caused the West Indians to test him with a larger quota of bouncers than they tried against others. It looked as if they, like Ian Chappell, had reservations about his ability against real speed.

Only two captains had led Australia younger than Graham, twenty-six. They were William Murdoch, twenty-four, and Ian Craig, twenty-two. Fans in other states noticed Victorian opinions that the unassuming cricketer lacked the on-field aggression of Ian Chappell, Benaud and Bradman.

As a candid soothsayer, Chappell wrote:

I believe him to be on the negative side and he will have to lead by example from the front. If he accepts the responsibilities the job brings he will do well to retain the position for the full season and to have given England a tough fight. If he can bring off victory and the return of the Ashes it will be the greatest performance since Houdini and Yallop will deserve any medal they can find to pin on him.

As events unfolded, Ian had no reason to wish that, unlike the sequel to Omar Khayyam's moving finger, tears could wash out one word of it.

A heaped plateful of problems began to form within two hours of Graham's winning the toss on a Brisbane pitch that gladdened the eyes of England's unsurpassed seam bowlers. Not long after they had bundled Australia out for 116 Derek Randall edged a wicket-worthy ball from Rodney Hogg to an awkward height. Yallop tried to clasp it to his body but it got away as he fell. Loss of confidence caused him to leave first slip.

Urgency was not apparent from the first day in Brisbane. It should have been imperative to confront England's batsmen with leg-spinner Jim Higgs at the earliest logical opportunity. Yet he did not call on Jim until the 63rd over. Keith Miller said it took a dropped catch by Higgs to remind his captain a leg-spinner was on the field. The least effective change was use of medium-pacer Trevor Laughlin, which postponed leg-spin for half an hour.

In Melbourne Higgs bowled with one slip, to Botham and Miller, to the relief of the Englishmen who thought he should have had three or four men around the bat. The margin of Australia's probable win was shrinking while Yallop took 51 overs to bring the key bowlers to the ends where rough patches would aid them. Within 17 balls from the north end Higgs's leg-break and wrong'un had Botham and Miller caught. With his 23rd ball from the south end Geoff Dymock ringbarked the innings by trapping Gower lbw.

In their second-innings rally in Sydney in the fourth Test England's top-half batsmen must have relished having no close leg fieldsmen to worry about when they faced Higgs's bouncy wrong'un.

A more experienced captain would not have given Bruce Yardley, turning the ball to the on, five fieldsmen on the off side and expected him to bowl without a mid-wicket for some time.

As on-field consultations with bowlers had caused uncertainty in the team, a sign that Yallop was planning things with them before each day was welcomed. Pre-adjusted settings for each batsman were beneficial but his marshalling of the attack continued to be uninspiring.

Lack of an understanding relationship with Rodney Hogg resulted in heated words when the temperamental paceman cut short stretches of bowling because of breathing difficulties in heat. In Adelaide, where a new ball was due, the captain followed Hogg off to the room and wrote later: 'At one stage Hogg suggested we survey the back of the Adelaide Oval – and I don't think he had tennis in mind.'

Yallop should have realised that Hogg was not going to get results bowling long spells and had worked it out that in five spells he could get through 17 eight-ball overs in a day. For his 41 English wickets he bowled more overs, 217.4, than anyone else in the series. Rod admitted he was probably fairly hard to control but said he was not the only one who felt that Yallop was intolerant and non-understanding.

No other Australian captain I have known has been such an introvert. Asked whether Graham was difficult to live with when cricket crises emerged, Helen said: 'No – never. I talk to him more about the game than he does. You have to winkle everything out of him.' But the tone of some clippings in the mounting pile caused Victorian president Ray Steele to say: 'Yallop has been thrown into the post perhaps a little before his time but I hope some of the English critics will get off his back.'

The spark that sets great captains apart from the general run has little to do with education or manners or whether they have more than the average eight cubic inches of brain. It has a parallel in the personality that distinguishes an ace cartoonist from a competent artist.

English captain Mike Brearley said each of the first five Tests could have gone either way on the last day. Manager Doug Insole's summing-up:

Fortune rather than the lack of skill played an important part in Australia's defeat. We could easily have lost in Sydney and Adelaide and, had we done that, the series would have been open until the last match. It was a great deal closer than the 5-1 result implied. Our feeling is that a much-maligned Australian side played against a very good English side.

Umpiring decisions are the shakiest ground for opinion, yet a reprieve, second ball, spared Derek Randall when he would have been willing to walk, lbw to Dymock, in Sydney, instead of going on to the largest and longest score of the rubber, 150. Neither was it any fault of Graham's that six spilt chances in the second innings enabled Brearley's patient ringcraft to succeed.

Australia's slump for 111 in the 50th over of line and length was the worst instance of an innings gurgling down the plughole. It eroded the players' confidence. By then the Englishmen were marching into the field like an army of occupation.

Yallop's own nerve as a batsman was proven in desperate situations. After loss of two wickets for two runs in the first nine balls of the second innings at Brisbane Graham's 102 did much to rally the side.

While his team sagged toward defeat in the second Sydney Test Yallop played the most distinguished innings of his career. Brearley had never seen his range of attack against spin surpassed. Graham's footwork brought him close enough to the pitch of off-spinners Miller and Emburey to be sure of lifting on-drives safely. His first 100 came off fewest balls in the rubber. After a chanceless century, his 121 formed two-thirds of the runs scored while he was in. His memorable achievement won him the prize for player of the match. He alone scored two hundreds in the series, making his tally three in 14 Tests.

Australia's 143 in Melbourne was the ninth prang under 200, completing loss of the rubber, 5-1. Yallop felt frustrated when batsmen got out to shots that the seasoned Englishmen would not allow themselves to play.

Against Pakistan Yallop's calamitous run out on the last day in Melbourne – Australia's 13th in seven Tests – preceded the breakthrough in which Sarfraz Nawaz, nine for 86, captured seven for one in 35 balls.

Yallop was never able to take a firm grasp of a parcel that kept falling to pieces. A torn calf muscle kept him out of the last Test, ending his captaincy. Though at state level he captained Victoria to the Sheffield Shield it was

363

beyond him to bring to the national team the unified effort for which Australians were looking. They felt like thumbing prayer-books for the name of the patron saint of born losers. While playing in the Centenary Test at Lord's in 1980, Yallop learned that he had been relieved even as Victoria's captain.

The title of Yallop's ghosted book, *Lambs to the Slaughter*, was part of a statement that he was the fall guy for the downfall to talented opposition that was expected to whitewash Australia anyway. An attempt in the Victorian Supreme Court to enable him to amend part of the text ended in a settlement out of court.

Yallop was recalled to the colours in February 1980 when Australia's selectors guessed rightly that his sweet skills against spin would stand him in good stead on a tour of Pakistan. His 172 at Faisalabad included a stand of 217 with Greg Chappell, still a fourth-wicket record for Tests between the two nations.

The Victorian was next asked to augment Kim Hughes's 1981 team in Chappell's absence and, although his returns were inconsistent against the incisive pace bowling of England's Bob Willis, Yallop made 114 in the second innings of the Fifth Test at Old Trafford. He mocked the tense circumstances of the game by taking a smooth three hours.

Two years and 18 Tests elapsed before Yallop's 34th Test cap was occasioned by a rich vein of Sheffield Shield form and a pressing need for left-handers to neutralise Pakistan's prehensile wrist-spinner Abdul Qadir. Yallop's comeback innings, a sparkling 141 at Perth, showed his skills undimmed.

In the Boxing Day Test at the MCG, he took full advantage of a benign pitch to record what was then the third-longest Test innings by an Australian. Yallop's 716-minute 268 contained 29 boundaries, and enabled him to eclipse the Australian record for runs in calendar year held for fifty-four years by Bradman.

Yallop had 10 days only to savour this satisfaction. On 8 January 1984 he scratched himself from the rest of the summer by sustaining a knee injury sliding into a fence during a World Series Cup match against West Indies. It eliminated him from contention for Australia's forthcoming tour of the Caribbean and, while this had a beneficial short-term effect on his insurance premiums, cost him further glory.

Yallop played only one further Test – where he appeared an apprehensive target for the likes of Holding, Garner and Marshall on a treacherous WACA wicket – and sensed that, in spite of his 2756 Test runs at 41.13, this time his banishment would be permanent. Accepting the handsome rewards dangled by agents of South African cricket in April 1985 and joining Kim Hughes's ersatz Australian XI, he saw out the balance of his career on the veldt.

Yallop's 30th and last first-class century was an unbeaten 182 in a score of 332 against a South African Invitation XI at East London's Jan Smuts Oval on 10 January 1987. It was an innings in keeping with the Victorian's career, which was dotted by days of serene command against indifferent opposition. Despite 11,615 first-class runs at a handsome 45.90, he left behind sense of a talent never completely fulfilled.

39

Beginner's Luck

Though he had never captained a team in a first-class match, nobody thought it strange when Kim Hughes was appointed to lead Australia in 1979. Appearance and personality were so much on his side that cricket folk accepted him in the face of broken precedents.

No West Australian had a chance of captaining his country until such unforeseen events as the split between World Series Cricket and the traditional set-up. The least experienced skipper in 102 years of Test history would not have been needed until it was found four days before the match that an injury would compel Graham Yallop to withdraw. As captain of North Perth, Kim's qualifications had been limited to one win in 10 games.

Kimberley John Hughes, born on 26 January 1954, is the eldest son of a headmaster who made a name in Australian Rules football for Subiaco. At fifteen Kim became the youngest to make a first-grade century. The Floreat Park boy's 112 for Subiaco against Midland-Guildford impressed Norman O'Neill, Keith Slater and Tony Mann. In his second senior season he topped WACA aggregates. He played for WA Colts at eighteen and twenty then mystified fellow-players by moving from Perth's true wickets to Adelaide for half a season.

At Graylands Teachers' College Kim trained as a physical education teacher. Possibly his nickname 'Clag' had some connection with the classroom. He played club cricket in Scotland in 1976.

At twenty-one he scored 119 and 60 against New South Wales, fifth West Australian to make a century on his first-class debut. In his fourth game he scored 101 against the West Indians and in his 14th, 117 not out against the Pakistanis. A month after he married Jenny Davidson, his charming sweetheart from schooldays, he was touring England with the team led by Greg Chappell that was riven by World Series Cricket's disclosure.

Though the defection of so many senior players seemed to offer Hughes a fistful of opportunities, a mercurial temperament meant that he did not immediately grasp them. In his maiden Test innings at the Oval he laboured 37 tense minutes over a single.

At his first sight of Indian bowling, including Prasanna, Chandrasekhar and Venkataraghavan, Kim's scintillating 99 for WA won him a Test place. He hit an enormous six to an upper deck in Sydney but that was no consolation for his ardour helping Indian captain Bishan Bedi outwit him in three of his four Test innings. Two operations for appendicitis kept him out of the running in the West Indies. In those frustrating years he was never given two consecutive Tests.

There were never any doubts of Hughes's precocious promise. His stance was upright, side-on with eyes level, his grip nearly as high as Greg Chappell's, his back lift as controlled as his follow-through was generous. In defence he moved well behind the ball. Scope for his superb gully cuts and forcing shots off the back foot was reduced by his inbuilt habit of playing forward too much.

Kim had an almost continuous wrestle trying to curb impetuosity, an element in his effervescent personality. Barry Richards put his finger on a trait that led Kim into shots that jeopardised his wicket. 'Barry told me not to premeditate innings,' he said. (Blunt team-mates called it 'playing by numbers'.) The ball he attacked was not always of the type he had decided to play. His shot selection was most flawed at the outset of innings: an anxious starter, he tended to creep across the crease with a nondescript movement which increased the liability to be trapped lbw.

His background was 69 runs in six innings when he walked in at Brisbane in December 1978 with the scoreboard dismally showing three out and Australia still 151 behind England. Knowing there were several contenders for his place, he was well aware that it could be his last Test innings for some time.

Keeping his head over the ball, he added discipline to dexterity. A six off Bob Willis to the dogtrack behind square-leg rewarded a perfect hook.

After Mike Brearley posted a second outfielder Hughes steadfastly declined other temptations to hook, and took six chanceless hours for 100.

Off his 315th ball Kim drove off-spinner Geoff Miller straight for six. When Brearley dropped Chris Old back to the boundary he did not try to repeat the shot off the remaining 94 balls. His 170 stand with Yallop was the highest for the fourth wicket at Woolloongabba Oval. Lasting four minutes short of eight hours, the innings was Australia's slowest century against England until 1981.

Hughes's acceptance of responsibility impressed Brearley, who described his 129 as the batting of the match. Giving the bowlers much of the credit for his single-mindedness, Kim said: 'They bowled so well I had to keep my mind on the job.'

Though he could do that at twenty-three, Hughes kept fans waiting a further eight Tests before he batted with similar concentration. When the Englishmen held him on 38 for 35 minutes in Melbourne the volatile element in his nature rebelled. To the first ball of a Botham over he danced along the track and Gower caught a mis-hit at cover. Another rush of blood to the eyelashes stymied in his next Test innings in Sydney.

After six losses in seven Tests an injury to Yallop caused the selectors to call on Hughes at short notice. Having the kind of personality that generates enthusiasm, Kim achieved a dramatic transformation. He escorted players from Perth airport to a motel, where he chaired a meeting with a pep-talk. He renewed team spirit by such innovations as switching the least-acquainted players to share rooms. He had them travelling between motel and ground as a unit to warm up together. He rekindled will-to-win in a side shaken by having been bundled out under 200 in 10 of their 14 innings against England and Pakistan. In three days his foresight and drive recharged the atmosphere in the practice nets and dressing room. Televiewers heard vice-captain Andrew Hilditch tell of the players' enthusiastic response to their new leader.

It helped that Kim was the most prepossessing of Australia's captains, with even features on an oval face beneath curly hair as fair as a field of corn. As a fieldsman 182 cm tall (almost 6 ft) and 78 kg (12 st 4 lb) he set an agile lead.

Winning the toss, Hughes sent Pakistan in. His preparation gave the side such uplift that it surprised the Pakistanis, who had been riding high after undefeated success against India and New Zealand. After an ankle injury on the third day kept him off the field his influence was still inspiring and Australia squared the two-Test series.

In England his out-of-practice side had no chance in the 1979 World Cup. His comments to interviewers were frank admissions of why they lost, without straining after excuses. As captain on an 11-match tour of India starting in September 1979 Hughes said that the pending return of WSC stars offered a challenging incentive to players to prove themselves worthy to hold places. His cheerful refusal to be panicked by an uneasy atmosphere enabled the Australians to open their tour at Srinagar in Kashmir. Behind lines of colourfully clad girls and a flute-and-drum band the players saw an unbroken wall of brown uniforms. The Kashmiri Government drafted 8000 police, many armed, to the Amar Singh ground after reported threats from a Liberation Front. The Australian Board relented after the unperturbed players made a plea for the game to go on.

With his first century outside Australia, Kim partnered left-hander Allan Border, 162, in a third-wicket record of 222 in the opening Test at Madras, but bowling problems arose at once when Rodney Hogg had to leave the field after each of his early short spells. Rod was no-balled 42 times in the first two Tests. A spate of 14 no-balls caused a Bangalore crowd to shout and hurl oranges at him. Hogg called his captain over to show where his boot had landed, then kicked out the middle stump toward Umpire Ramaswamy. After an overhead full toss was called 'wide' Hughes sent the agitated bowler from the field, as much for his own protection as for disciplinary reasons. Both apologised to the umpire.

Illness prevented Rick Darling opening the second innings at Bangalore and Border was lowered because of influenza. Characteristically frank, Hughes admitted his side had been lucky not to lose the first two Tests. Next a back injury caused fast bowler Alan Hurst to be flown home. Team spirit showed through at Nagpur when left-arm seamer Geoff Dymock took 12 wickets, his most ever, and Hogg came to light with five. All-rounder Bruce

Yardley had a toe broken in the Third Test defeat at Nagpur and had to be omitted from the fourth Test at Delhi.

In the Sixth Test at Bombay a third-wicket stand of 132 by Hughes, 80, and Border, 61, could not prevent the unbeaten Indians scoring their second win, this time by an innings. The captain's 594 runs in six Tests, average 59, are easily a record for an Australian in India. Nearest have been Keith Stackpole, 368, and Ian Chappell, 324, who averaged 46 in five Tests in 1969.

Hughes became Greg Chappell's vice-captain in 1979–80 when the World Series Cricketers were reassimilated into the national team, and the pair were seen at harmony at once in the First Test at Brisbane against the West Indies. Though he began awkwardly, struggling to acclimatise to grassier surfaces with both feet on the crease, Kim soon rediscovered touch in his skipper's company.

Against Roberts, Holding, Garner and Croft, Hughes (130 not out) added 118 in 171 minutes with Chappell (124). Hughes had evidently attained a standard of maturity: he hooked only if no leg fieldsman was deep, took painful knocks from Roberts and Croft rather than risk his wicket, and saw his self-discipline rewarded. In the course of hitting 17 fours off 346 balls in 379 minutes, Hughes passed 1000 runs in his 15th Test. Though he was under pressure an hour and half less than in his first Test hundred his form caused him to rank this innings higher.

As Greg Chappell's vice-captain for the Centenary Test at Lord's in 1980, Hughes laid his strongest claims to greatness with scores of 117 and 84. His delightful batting, spangled with five sixes, made him an unrivalled man of the match. The century was his first in England. Kim's nature, it seemed, required a spark of challenge to ignite his greatest batting.

The contrast could not have been more marked than in 1980–81 when, appointed West Australia's captain, he was out under 20 in a stretch of 13 out of 14 innings in first-class matches. Yet in the fifth of the season's Tests he charmed Adelaide cricket-goers and television viewers with 213 and 53 not out, the latter on his twenty-seventh birthday. As at Lord's, he was Man of the Match.

Hughes's double-century, gloriously gathered from 301 balls, lifted the Australian individual record against India from Greg Chappell (whose 204

371

in the preceding Test had just usurped Don Bradman's 201 in 1948). It came fifteen days after the birth of his twin sons Sean and Simon. He was 85 not out on the first evening when he received a telegram from them saying: 'Well done Dad – keep it going – Sean and Simon.' Kim said later 'I had to get 100 each for the boys. I feel as if I'm doing something worthwhile for the time I've been away.'

Hughes's captaincy career resumed in March 1981 when Greg Chappell stood aside from the forthcoming Ashes tour. Kim was entrusted with a sixteen-man squad whose strength lay in his state's elder statesmen Lillee and Marsh, and in the bonny Allan Border.

Underestimated by English critics, Hughes's team played spirited cricket against a team led by Ian Botham to seize the Texaco Trophy one-day series 2-1. It then won a dramatic, low-scoring First Test at Trent Bridge in light that would not have been entertained in a late-night card school.

After a drawn Second Test at Lord's England called up as captain the gnomic Mike Brearley. Rejuvenated by Brearley's subtle influence, Botham dominated the balance of the series with a sequence of leonine performances. When England were down and out in Leeds and Birmingham, the all-rounder spoke volumes with bat and ball.

At Headingley the home team in their second innings were still 92 in arrears of Australia when Botham rallied tail-end colleagues round him during an innings of 149 not out.

'Beefy' carved out sufficient advantage for Bob Willis to roar down the slope from the Kirkstall Lane end and earn for his side only the second Test victory after following on (Jack Blackham had similarly seen the tables turned on him at Sydney in 1894–95).

Further calamity befell Hughes's men at Edgbaston, where Botham delivered England victory with five wickets at the cost of a single in 28 destructive deliveries. Hughes earned high marks from his counterpart by appearing at a benefit function for Willis straight after the defeat, and Brearley was a sympathetic ear for his plaintive meditation: 'Reckon mum'll talk to me when I get home. And dad. And me wife. But who else?'

Worse was to follow at Old Trafford, where Botham wrested the Fifth Test from Australia's grasp with an innings of 118. The old ball left his bat hard, the new ball harder, and Hughes stood hapless throughout the mayhem like a tired child unable to enjoy a carnival.

The worst of Hughes's suffering was that his own batting form was wretched. Seven times in a dozen dismissals he was adjudged lbw feeling round his front fender. Had he rediscovered at any stage his Centenary Test sparkle, Hughes would have found it easier dealing with friction in touring ranks. WSC alumni Marsh and Lillee, in particular, nursed resentment about Hughes's speedy rise to the captaincy of WA.

Hard graft in the WACA Ground nets on Hughes's return to Australia cured a crooked pick-up and, under the returned Chappell, the West Australian played what Richie Benaud deemed his most memorable Test innings. During the Boxing Day Test against the West Indies, with Australia's rigging shot away at four for 26, Hughes dived into the melee for four hours 20 minutes, wielding his bat like a cutlass.

Though he was 71 when No. 11 Terry Alderman joined him at nine for 155, Hughes so skilfully commandeered the strike for the next half-hour that Australia's last line of resistance added 43. With his 11th four – a square cut to the point boundary from Garner that left fielders rooted to their positions – he pirated a hundred out of 175 runs off the bat made during his time at the crease.

As the pitch played tricks cruel and crueller on dumbfounded batsman, Hughes's runs were as rubies to the Australian treasury. He was Man of the Match in the victory: one of only three against the West Indies during the 1980s.

Saddled with the leadership of Australia again by Chappell's absence during an ill-starred tour of Pakistan in September 1982, Kim saw Australia whitewashed in three Tests against Imran Khan's XI, twisted round the wrist of Abdul Qadir (22 wickets).

He restored his stocks by batting with elan as Chappell's vice-captain during Australia's series against England in 1982–83, but then led Australia through a demoralising World Cup campaign that began with defeat at the hands of Zimbabwe and ended with thrashings from the West Indies and India. Senior colleagues looked askance when he took an early flight home. Many thought Marsh a better leadership option, and David Hookes spoke their mind when interviewed on Adelaide's 5DN by Ken Cunningham. A wounded Hughes commented: 'It's nice to know the Australian captain is getting the support of his vice-captain.' Australian Cricket Board manager Bob Merriman docked Hookes $1200 – almost a quarter of his World Cup tour fee.

Hughes then faced a stern examination from Greg Chappell, who had withdrawn his candidature for captaincy, when they roomed together in August 1983 at Melbourne's Hilton Hotel for a meeting of the ACB players' sub-committee. Over breakfast, the older man spent half an hour trying to persuade Hughes to stand down in favour of Marsh.

Hughes went within an ace of doing so. Merriman flew to Perth to draft a resignation statement but, by the time the manager had returned to his Geelong home, Hughes had telephoned to rescind the decision. Kim retained the job at an ACB vote, if only by a narrow majority.

The last year of his Test career was full of false dawns and thwarted hopes. With Chappell, Lillee and Marsh available as players, he finally won a series as captain just before his thirtieth birthday by beating Pakistan in the First Test at Perth and the Fifth Test at Sydney.

In between times, Hughes made an exquisite 106 in four and half hours at Adelaide Oval. Describing elegant minuets on a turning pitch, he confounded the cunning Qadir with 10 fours and a single sweetly swept six. It was his ninth Test century, and his Test record had swelled by the end of the series to 4119 runs at 41.

Kim also won respect from his men by organising opposition to ACB 'key player' contracts that would have restricted signatories to 'authorised or approved matches' for the next two years; transparently an insurance policy against Australians following English, West Indian and Sri Lankan XIs to South Africa.

When a team vote favoured protest, Hughes took the lead. At 7.30 am on 8 February 1984 – the day of the first World Series Cup Final against the West Indies at the SCG – grievances were aired to ACB chairman Fred Bennett and legal adviser Gerry Raftesath. Recalled Geoff Lawson:

I could sense the blood rising in Rod Hogg as the lawyer told us how fortunate we were to have the ACB as our bosses. At the phrase 'fair and proper', he ... launched into a tirade on the ACB's treatment of the players over the years. Hoggy accentuated the word 'fair' in a loud voice, and further emphasised his point with a carefully-chosen expletive.

Tiered contracts devised by Hughes's counsel Stephen Owen-Conway and Lawson's counsel Terry Buddin were eventually accepted.

But the seeds of Hughes's downfall were sown by the retirements of the Chappell-Lillee-Marsh triumvirate at the SCG, with a tour of the West Indies imminent. Even with the reassurance of the great trio's 12,000 Test runs, 400 Test wickets and 500 dismissals, Australia would have faced a tall task in the Caribbean. Robbed of it, the trip was like tackling the Hindu Kush in T-shirts and trackshoes.

Hughes first blotted his copybook on tour with impromptu civil disobedience during the tour match at Guaracara Park when, protesting against an unimaginative declaration by Trinidad's Ranjie Nanan, he deadbatted the longest of long-hops for an hour while his partner Wayne Phillips lounged on the ground at the non-strikers' end. A fine of $400 was levied by manager Col Egar and senior players Border and Lawson.

When Australia's luck ran out after two drawn Tests, Hughes then found it impossible to rouse an inexperienced squad. Players observed his patriotic call to don green baggies during the Third Test at Bridgetown, but slumped for 97 on a pitch on which the home team had just made 509. Tests at Antigua and Kingston lasted little more than seven days in toto, and the West Indies did not lose a second innings wicket for the entire series.

Though the captaincy had turned from holy grail to poison chalice, Hughes was able to derive some lessons from the 3-0 defeat. The hyper-fitness and professional regimentation of the West Indies, drilled by their trainer Dennis 'Sluggo' Waight, left Australia's captain urging that Australia's physiotherapist in the Caribbean, Cronulla practitioner Errol Alcott, be made a permanent adjunct to the team. The personable Geelong industrial relations advocate Bob Merriman was made a full-time team manager and, in August 1984, Hughes led an Australian team on its first visit to Canberra's Australian Institute of Sport. Fourteen players were lectured on motivation, professionalism and attitude by sport psychologist Dr Dick Telford and former Australian soccer coach Jim Shoulder.

Team-mates were impressed and the short-term reward was a successful tour of India celebrating the Golden Jubilee of the Ranji Trophy. Australia won the three one-day internationals played to a finish. Mike Coward acclaimed the result in the Adelaide *Advertiser*: 'To a man the Australian players care about Hughes and his future in the game. They believe he is the right man to lead Australia and plan to give him their unconditional support.'

Australian composure, however, soon frayed under West Indian interrogation. Hughes's XI reduced Clive Lloyd's side to five for 104 after inserting them in the First Test at the WACA Ground, but eight dropped chances relieved the pressure like eight punctures in a bicycle tyre. In reply to 416, Australia was routed for 76 and 228 (59 of them added for the last wicket by Geoff Lawson and Terry Alderman).

Australian critics were unforgiving, Ian Chappell so damning on Channel Nine that Hughes refused to respond to his questions in pre-match interviews. Bill Lawry, mauled by the press fifteen years earlier, spoke out on Hughes's behalf at a Rotary luncheon on the eve of the Second Test at the Gabba, saying that the captain was being 'dragged down like a dingo in the pack' and 'devoured by his own from within and without'.

English observers were more understanding. Lloyd's men had just inflicted a 5-0 'blackwash' on England and the sight of Australia sinking by an innings and 112 runs provoked feelings of fraternity from the Oldest Enemy. 'Australia were murdered, just as we were murdered, Test in, Test out, all last summer,' wrote the urbane Ian Wooldridge of the *Daily Mail*. 'It was like finding an old mate in the next bed in intensive care.'

The Second Test ran according to the recent script: Hughes failed with the bat, torpedoed by a shooter for 4 in the second innings, and reprieved Richie Richardson on 42 as the Antiguan made 138. The epilogue, though, was unanticipated. The West Indies were on the verge of their 10th consecutive Test victory at 8.30 am on 26 November when Greg Chappell's telephone rang at home: it was Bob Merriman asking him to come to meet Hughes at the ground in half an hour. Captain and ex-captain composed a resignation statement in a QCA office, written out in Hughes's exact hand. Despite the dissuasive efforts of deputy Allan Border, the skipper read it out haltingly at the post-match press conference until tears confounded him.

Hughes lasted two Tests in Border's team, and just a dozen deliveries. When finally spelled, he had compiled a woebegone 296 runs in his preceding 18 Test innings. Hughes was a sad, diminished figure during the World Championship of Cricket and the Rothmans Trophy in Sharjah in March–April 1985, and his 26 runs in four innings were nowhere near sufficient to earn him a sixth trip to England.

It was in the Emirates that Hughes first considered a date with clandestiny. He had been approached by former NSW Test opener Bruce Francis about joining a secret 'rebel' touring team to visit South Africa during a McDonald's Cup match for Western Australia against NSW at the SCG in December 1982. An English team sponsored by South African Breweries and led by Graham Gooch had just toured the veldt, followed by Sri Lankan side and West Indian ensembles.

Hughes's name was not among those named when the *Australian* and the Adelaide *Advertiser* published the inchoate Australian 'rebel' team on 13 April 1985, but Francis passed on intelligence to his South African Cricket Union superiors Ali Bacher, Joe Pamensky and Geoff Dakin that the ex-captain was open to offers.

Hughes himself contacted Bacher on 26 April and he was furtively ferried to Johannesburg via Hong Kong and Mauritius three weeks later. When he held a press conference at the Perth Sheraton explaining his decision to lead the 'rebels', Channel Nine broadcast it live.

Though Hughes's impiety was widely deplored by politicians, he actually attracted public support far stronger than any he had enjoyed as national captain. Opinion polls showed a strong majority in favour of Hughes's decision to take advantage of his free trade as a sportsman. Bill O'Reilly was one who rushed to his defence:

> As a thoughtful, ambitious, well-educated family man, Hughes had exercised the right which every Australian considered to be his right from birth. He has made his decision to take advantage of an unparalleled offer to set his family – a wife and three kids – up for life. In case you haven't guessed, I'm entirely on Hughes's side and to hell with the Weeping Willies sinking much too slowly under crocodile tears.

377

Expensive court actions were fought between the South African Cricket Union and the Australian Cricket Board over players' contractual obligations, while Hughes himself successfully challenged an indefinite WACA ban on his participation in grade cricket with fellow *personae non grata* Terry Alderman, Tom Hogan and Greg Shipperd.

The unauthorised unit that crystallised cast the four West Australians alongside Victorians Yallop, Rod McCurdy and Mick Taylor, NSW opening pair John Dyson and Steve Smith and keeper Steve Rixon, South Australians Hogg and batting colt Mike Haysman, plus Queenslanders Carl Rackemann, John Maguire and Trevor Hohns. Last to sign was Tasmanian all-rounder Peter Faulkner.

All parties involved strove to imbue the trip with the aura of an official visit. As they were feted in November 1985 at a $72-a-plate dinner for 600 beneath the chandeliers in Johannesburg's Carlton Hotel, Hughes presented his Australian blazer to Springbok captain Clive Rice with the quip: 'I must also add that this is the last present Clive will be getting from us this season.'

For the seasons of 1985–86 and 1986–87 (when they were augmented by the erstwhile Australian Kepler Wessels), the 'rebel' Australians provided teams led by Rice and Peter Kirsten with spirited opposition. Hughes himself averaged 43.7 from 27 completed innings, including centuries against Boland and Orange Free State, and was lauded by Ali Bacher as 'a credit to the Australian people'.

Yet, while infinitely consoling to South Africa's cricket community at the time, the residual effect of the rebel tours was minimal. And in Hughes's case they made him – at least in the eyes of his national and state control boards – the Richard Nixon of Australian cricket.

Kim made a concerted effort to re-establish himself in his home town, moving into a house in City Beach while wife Jenny was pregnant with their fourth child. Having earlier been a promotions officer at the City Building Society, he took a job with a member firm on the floor of the Perth Stock Exchange. Gleefully accepting an invitation from the WACA to rejoin its Sheffield Shield practice squad, he made a century in three hours for Subiaco-Floreat in his first club outing in 1987.

Kim's younger brother Glen Arthur Hughes, born in Gommalling on 23 November 1959 and educated at City Beach High School, had kept the family flag flying in the Sheffield Shield by making a successful debut for Tasmania in 1986–87. Having played for Bayswater-Morley in the Perth grades and Kearsley Cricket Club in England as a teenager, Glen now began to blossom before Kim's eyes with 147 and 95 against Victoria in November 1987. The innings spurred his older sibling to declare: 'I feel I've got another five or six or seven good years left in me ... My enthusiasm for the game is as great as it has ever been.'

Kim's comeback a fortnight later at home for WA against NSW augured well. His four-hour 76 out of 154 as an opener from 171 balls underpinned an innings victory for his state. But, to paraphrase F. Scott Fitzgerald's remark about American lives, there are few second acts in Australian cricket. Hughes lost his place after scrounging 115 runs in his next seven innings. While Glen was Tasmania's highest-scoring batsman during 1988–89, Kim was allowed only four innings for 5, 26, 14 and 10. He sensed, probably rightly, that his state would have no further use for him.

The Hughes brothers headed for South Africa in 1989–90, Glen accepting a contract to play for Orange Free State in the Castle Currie Cup while the last days of Kim's career were played out as skipper of Natal. He led the province 14 times to little effect and, having scored a threadbare 432 runs in 25 completed innings, was deposed in favour of the Zimbabwean all-rounder Peter Rawson in February 1991.

Reconsidering his earlier optimism on the basis of four first-class half-centuries in four seasons, the thirty-seven-year-old Hughes returned to Perth. 'Looking back I suppose it all caught up with me,' he told Norm Tasker of *Inside Edge* magazine. 'All those years of facing the West Indies quicks had me thinking about the short ball.'

Hughes's record from fifteen years' in first-class cricket leaves him somewhat short of the front rank. His average after 216 matches for 12,711 runs is 36.5, and on only 26 of the 95 occasions that he passed fifty did he attain three figures. Yet at his breeziest Kim Hughes was as enchanting as any batsman seen since the war, and his aura is of a man more sinned against than sinning.

A.R. BORDER

40

Occupation: Cricketer

Like nature, Australian cricket abhors a vacuum. Allan Border filled a host of them during two decades in his country's game, assiduously acquiring a record collection of Test caps, runs and catches. His careworn feats were a comfort and consolation to Australians during a period barren of cricket success, then a symbol of faith rewarded when fortunes grew more favourable.

Faith in his own instinct did not come easily to one who confessed to finding 'the fear of failure' most compelling among motivations. Border's demeanour was of a man wont to worry whether he had left his back door unbolted, despite finding it secure whenever he checked. But perseverance was his motif. No batsman was beset by more crises or faced greater physical danger than Border, yet no-one's technique and temperament remained such a glass of fashion and mould of form. No previous Australian was as candid about his misgivings on taking the top job, yet no-one held it longer and few have surrendered it less willingly.

Born in Cremorne on 27 July 1955, a day that England's adhesive Trevor Bailey spent two hours making eight runs against South Africa, Border might be said to have been born under the sign of the last ditch. And though his childhood hero was the West Indian one-man-team Garry Sobers, a left-hander who made it appear that it was the rest of the world that batted the 'wrong way round', he found stoicism his natural vein.

Border's father was a wool-classer named John, his mother a shop-keeper named Sheila, and his cosily conservative upbringing in the 50s and 60s had all the features mocked by suburban satirists like Barry Humphries and jeered by intellectuals like Ronald Conway and Craig McGregor. *Chez* Border was a red-brick Federation shack called 'Omaha' with a Kingswood station wagon in the fibro garage when it wasn't shuttling the three boys to and from their weekend sporting engagements.

Young Allan didn't have to go far to be inducted in the game: 'Omaha' neighboured the playing field of Mosman-Middle Harbour Cricket Club. It was there that Border as a pint-sized left-hander first asserted his naked talent with a century at age eleven – a year younger than Bradman when first he achieved that landmark – and he was initiated into first grade in his seventeenth year, batting number nine perchance to bowl his left-arm spin.

Adolescent distractions and perhaps a streak of self-doubt almost saw Border drift from the game. There were sore enticements on nearby Balmoral Beach and, had it not been for the perseverance of a patron in Mosman captain-coach Barry Knight, Border might have remained a lowly clerk in the film library at BP handy for inter-office cricket challenges.

In the winter of 1975 as Australia played its first World Cup in England, Knight cajoled Border to undertake a spell of one-on-one tuition at the indoor cricket school that the former English all-rounder ran in Sydney's Kent Street. Infected with Knight's zeal from a quarter-century of cricket, Border lifted his horizons. Despite only intermittent first grade appearances in 1974–75, Border became a circuit star in 1975–76 deserving of his first taste of representative honours in NSW Colts.

Unlike another alumnus of North Sydney High, Ian Craig, Allan did not arrive on the scene in January 1977 amid a company of heralds. When he first filled a vacuum as an anonymous reservist in a NSW Sheffield Shield team depleted by a national call, his abbreviated season passed largely unremarked. News was first of the celebrations of 100 years of Test cricket in the Centenary Test, then of the party-crashing by businessman Kerry Packer.

But there was no mistaking Border's bold tread. After visiting England as a village cricketer in 1977 and as a Lancashire League professional in 1978, he listed his occupation on the annual NSWCA registration form as 'professional cricketer'. His personal life was designed to accommodate his cricket. The girlfriend he took on those trips, Jane Hiscox, had been raised to understand the cricket-smitten: Jane's father John was a Mosman committee man so dotty about the game that his Daimler had the number-plate HOWZAT.

Test caps have hardly been cheaper than in those hazy, crazy, *laissez-faire* days when Australia's cricket talent served rival bosses. Barely six weeks after Border had registered his maiden first-class hundred before 934 spectators at the WACA Ground, he was taking guard in a Test match against England before an MCG crowd of 35,000. Heartened by the applause of Melburnians echoing round its concrete catacombs, Border made a composed 29.

The gravity of Test cricket at once became him: stocky, stern, spare with strokes and statements, he had a grim mien in grim times. Though the flourish of his powers could be seen when he leaned into a favourite cover-drive, native introspection meant that he curbed himself to play comfortably within the frontiers of his ability. Border's footwork against spin was poised, his patience against pace monastic and, at 177 cm (5 ft 9 in) and 80 kg (12 st 8 lb), he fitted everyone's identikit of the underdog.

Despite enduring seven Test defeats in the calendar year 1979, Border salvaged more than 1000 Test runs including centuries against Pakistan and India at first brush. There was also 115 in his second outing with the reunited Australian Test team, on a WACA tarmac where the batsman's gashed eye from a Graeme Dilley bouncer left him resembling Tony Mundine after a torrid 15 rounds. Studying Allan's squat features, droll wrist-spinner Jim Higgs at once christened him Pugsley, after the homunculus of the TV parody *The Addams Family*.

Australia's physiotherapist Errol Alcott later described Border as 'the gutsiest little player I've come across', capable of taking the field when almost mummified by bandages. Save for one thumb, every finger of Border's hands would be broken at least once during his career. Yet the longest absence he tolerated from Australian ranks was a stretch of four one-day matches resting a wounded hamstring.

Border was the most self-sufficient Australian player since Bradman. Score, circumstances, state of pitch, climate and competition perturbed him no more than an inauspicious horoscope. His unguarded moments were few, his unforced errors almost unnaturally infrequent.

Though England's acts of escapology cruelled Australia's 1981 Ashes tour, Border's batting provided inordinate redemption. Ten hours' work first underwrote the only Australian victory at Trent Bridge, in light more suitable for bats winged than bats wooden, then guaranteed that Australia would not suffer Test defeat at Lord's for more than half a century.

In spite of a broken finger in the last two Tests, Border batted 15 hours and 738 deliveries for 123 not out, 106 not out and 84 without a scintilla of error. Never dismayed by the company of tail-end colleagues, cool self-denial and careful husbandry of the strike prolonged each innings.

England's captain Mike Brearley, perched close enough to Border to study the stalwart's stubble while he batted, later diarised: 'He drove Willis for two, but when he came back to take strike he was muttering to himself under his breath: "Bad shot, bad shot. Too wide. Concentrate."' Such private admonitions would be incanted over and over again in Border's career, like a yogi's mantra.

Uncomfortable about his financial security after marrying Jane in Sydney's Blessed Sacrament Church on 12 April 1980, Border decided to accept a lucrative contract to play his cricket for Queensland under Greg Chappell. The older man would become one of Border's most eloquent advocates, convinced that his uncommon sense made him an ideal leader.

Chappell's most stubborn dissenter in that judgement was Border himself. Eyewitness experience of the pressures under which his skippers Chappell and Hughes operated made Border sublimate any designs on the captaincy. 'Captains cop so much flak,' he said during the 1981–82 season. 'I am not a diplomat like Kim Hughes or Greg Chappell. It's terribly difficult to do the right thing . . . If I had to do that I suspect it might end up in a free-for-all.' When six months later Chappell broached the topic in a round at the Royal Queensland Golf Club, Border was even more direct: 'I don't want to know about it.'

In spite of his remonstrances, Border's batting form was making an unambiguous case for recognition. When adversity threatened, opponents found him as hard to remove as quick-drying cement. Australia lost at Adelaide Oval to the West Indies in January 1982, though it took the tourists 10 hours to unfasten Border for 78 and 126. Australia lost at the MCG to England in December 1982, too, but not before Border had squired Jeff Thomson through a last wicket stand of 71 that reduced the margin to a paltry three runs. The left-hander's calendar 1983 then yielded 584 Test runs at 97, and he continued to catch at second slip like a Venus fly-trap.

The tide came in Border's affairs when the Chappell-Lillee-Marsh triumvirate bowed out in the Sydney Test against Pakistan in January 1984. With a season of the Queensland captaincy behind him, Border accepted the mantle of Hughes's vice-captain on the subsequent Caribbean tour.

The left-hander was a lonely island of excellence in an abject series for Australia. Withstanding the fast bowling was like playing chicken between the lanes of a city expressway. Sideswiped constantly by Garner, Marshall, Daniel, Holding and Baptiste, Border clocked up 521 runs at 74.

His finest feat of resuscitation was in the Second Test at Port-of-Spain. Taking block in sultry heat at three for 16, Border breathed 98 not out into the lifeless Australian innings. Against the skyscraping Joel Garner, Border granted 30 centimetres in airspace but no quarter. His runs came mostly through cross-batted cuts and pulls from an abbreviated backswing, leavened with a cover drive like a boxer's left jab.

Garner prevented Border transiting to a century after 349 minutes and 254 balls by cornering last man Terry Alderman. But the swing bowler redeemed himself in the second innings by standing the watch with Border for the last 105 minutes of the game, enabling him to achieve three figures from 281 balls.

When Kim Hughes stood down from the captaincy seven months later, Border stood alone as a potential successor. Clairvoyant Queensland comrades pinned a plastic sheriff's badge on him when he led them at Launceston four days after Hughes's exit, and that was where Greg Chappell (now a selector) pulled him aside and made him Australian captain.

These were dog days for Australian cricket. The national team was struggling to recompose itself. So many answers were posited to its dilemmas that the original questions were forgotten. Players were turned over like the drummers of the mock-rock group Spinal Tap.

West Indies, New Zealand, England, India, Pakistan were queueing for the opportunity to avenge past indignities. Feelings among players and administrators were further wounded when it emerged that Hughes and fourteen colleagues had been beguiled into a contraband cricket campaign in South Africa.

Border regarded the task lugubriously. A diffident orator, he asked Sir Donald Bradman to deliver the pre-Test address at Adelaide's Hilton International before he led Australia for the first time against West Indies. Observers were surprised when, on the game's first morning practice, manager Bob Merriman was deputised to hit outfield catches. On the field, Australia's 38th skipper looked unsure or unwilling to enforce discipline, and impoverished of ideas. It was said eventually that the only place Allan Border declared was at airport customs.

Reluctant as a skipper, Border nonetheless sustained irreproachable standards of batsmanship. With the aid of a new blade from the Worcester bat craftsman Duncan Fearnley, he began the 1985 Ashes tour by scoring 106, 135 and 125. Aware that mischievous keeper Wayne Phillips had wagered against the chance he would emulate Charlie Macartney by registering a fourth consecutive century, Border added a round 100 against Derbyshire with sadistic glee.

His self-control defied every artifice opponents devised to disturb it. On one occasion the cheeky Englishman Allan Lamb sought to unsettle Border by donning a plastic duck's bill while fielding at short-leg. The Australian made a century.

Border never hid his own competitiveness under a bushel. Fast bowler Dave Gilbert told of a one-day match where he inadvertently impeded two returns to the bowler's end, and was twice hit painfully in the back. Instead of receiving an expression of sympathy from his captain, he heard Border grouse: 'Oh for Chrissake, Lizard, get out of the way!'

But in his native introspection, Border resembled a tragedian soliloquising in a big, empty theatre. He watched with a martyred air as pace bowlers yielded half-volleys, fielders fluffed catches and batsmen crumbled repeatedly. Often the only clue to his thinking was his pose, arms akimbo, in moments of particular dejection. It became universally known as the 'teapot'.

On only one occasion could Border translate personal success into team triumph. The Second Test at Lord's in 1985 was the ultimate DIY victory: Border bore Australia to a match-winning position with 196 out of 425, then resumed the burden when a last-day run chase was flagging with 41 not out.

Otherwise Border's bat was pressed into service for stalemates alone. He saved Australia by a doleful day's dead-batting at Old Trafford for 146 not out. In the subsequent home summer he stymied an Indian victory thrust at the MCG with a calculating seven-hour 163, then confounded the Kiwis with twin centuries at Lancaster Park.

'Allan Robert Border is Australian cricket circa 1985,' avowed Mile Coward in the *Sydney Morning Herald*. 'He, and he alone, has given the Australian cricket lover something to hope for.' In his own way, in fact, the grizzled left-hander was as indispensable to Australian endeavour as Bradman half a century earlier. While the intelligence 'Bradman's out' acknowledged that victory might be elusive, bulletins of Border's dismissal contained the sense that defeat was now unavoidable.

It was a gruelling responsibility, the strains of which became tangible in March 1986 as Australia played a one-day series against New Zealand after the indignity of surrendering the Tests to Jeremy Coney's combative combination. A mortified media corps, attending what they expected to be a routine conference, listened in deferential silence as Border wore his heart on his track-suit sleeve.

'They're going to have to show me whether they really want to play for Australia and whether they really want to play under me,' he lamented. 'I'll find out over the next three games and my decision will be made after that.' The confession that Border's patience knew bounds stunned authorities, players and critics. He sounded like a man in need of pastoral care.

The short-term impact was that performances did improve, the longer-term consequence a seminal decision that the Australian captain's burden would henceforward be lightened by a coach. The first appointment to this new position, and for ten years its only incumbent, was Bob Simpson.

Simpson had known Border since their teams – Western Suburbs and Mosman – had clashed in Sydney first grade more than a decade before. He had led Border in the Sheffield Shield during his second innings as Australian leader in 1977–78, then studied his captaincy at close quarters as a journalist and commentator.

After accompanying the Australians to New Zealand as an assistant manager Simpson damned their disorganisation in a report to the ACB.

Although transformation was not instantaneous when he became coach of Border's Australians in India in 1986, observers at once noticed advances. The tourists were demonstrably purposeful in preparation, improving especially in the areas on which Simpson harped: fielding and running between wickets.

Border found that he shouldered his responsibilities with greater equanimity. In the airless enclosure of Chepauk during the First Test, he became a confessor for Dean Jones during the young Victorian's death-before-dishonour double-century. When Jones conceded that he was wilting after eight hours in the concrete crucible, Border goaded him on with the words: 'OK, we'll send for someone with a big ticker ... a Queenslander' (Greg Ritchie was the next man in).

Border banked his own 106 in the match, but by far his greatest contribution to the contest was his dare to declare on the final morning setting the home side 348 to win. Like Richie Benaud's decision to chase the runs in the Gabba Test of 1960, the decision was a blue-sky investment that bore ample reward.

A teasing day's cricket unfolded where runs often seemed to be seeping uncomfortably. Border persevered with spinners Greg Matthews and Ray Bright when prudence might have suggested otherwise, and Australia finally broke through in the last session. In the decisive final over that blessed Test match cricket with its second tie in 110 years, the Australian skipper talked Matthews through the ordeal with the aplomb Frank Worrell had shown a quarter-century before.

Early overconfidence and eccentric selections undermined Australia's bid to reclaim the Ashes at home in 1986–87, but the seventh consecutive series that Border had either lost or drawn proved a darkness before the dawn for the team's new management. Almost imperceptibly, Border had surrounded himself with the raw material for a most competitive ensemble: openers David Boon and Geoff Marsh, all-rounder Steve Waugh, fast bowlers Craig McDermott and Bruce Reid. When Australia returned to the sub-continent in September 1987 for the fourth World Cup, Border reaped the rewards of his forbearance.

Local pundits like Zaheer Abbas publicly branded the Australians as pushovers. But, ignoring odds of 16-1 against success, Border and Simpson schemed a campaign that devolved duties to individuals. While vice-captain Marsh anchored Australia's efforts, Boon was mandated to play his strokes and Jones's electric running encouraged. Fielding was rehearsed with zeal, and the economy and acumen of Waugh and McDermott harnessed in the closing overs.

Strangely, Border was rarely an outstanding one-day batsman. A captive of its format in the middle-order, he rarely had the scope to found an innings of any duration. But he was a student of its strategies and, with short-range fielding skills honed by his years as a junior baseballer, was worth his weight in bullion as a short mid-wicket fielder.

Border would recall the celebration after Australia's one-run victory against India at Chepauk in their first match as one of his headiest moments. Players seemed suffused with a quiet confidence, while the lobby of the Taj Coromandel Hotel in Madras suddenly became full of familiar accents as expatriates, tourists and business travellers 'just seemed to lob and mingle'. The captain saw it as a 'springboard of a spirit in a team that until that day had been painted as a team of losers'.

Zimbabwe and New Zealand were each twice overthrown, and the canny Kiwis John Wright and Ewen Chatfield intuited that their cousins from the southern hemisphere were the team to beat when they saw the Australians at an improvised lay-day fielding practice on a hotel lawn in Chandigarh.

Promoters' prayers were for a sub-continental derby in the final at Eden Gardens, but the two oldest Test nations rained on their parade in the semi-finals: Australia bested Pakistan, and England accounted for India. Adopted by Calcuttans as an ersatz favourite, Australia won a well-contested final by seven runs with a last display of disciplined cricket. Border accepted the handsome diamond-studded World Cup with reverence, like a pilgrim glimpsing the ark of the covenant.

Australian journalists swelled with patriotic pride, and English scribes did not begrudge them. Wrote Scyld Berry in his admirable *Cricket Odyssey*:

The more I reflected on Australia's winning, the more pleased I felt.

Border received the Reliance World Cup, held it high, and did nothing vulgar like kiss it or stick the lid on his head. The Australians did a victory lap and were most generously applauded, but only I suspect because they were asked to do so: most seemed too abashed and pink behind the ears to have thought of such an act of self-aggrandise-ment. And my heart was warmed when Border was lifted respectfully onto the shoulders of two of his players ... No more deserving current Test skipper could have taken hold of the fourth World Cup.

Even the English players joined in the celebrations. Discovering in the dressing-room that the cricket ball adorning the handsome trophy was detachable, the teams spontaneously re-enacted some of the action from the middle.

When Border led Australia to a 1-0 Test series victory against New Zealand at home, its first under his leadership, the captain seemed to have added a cubit to his span. With his batting in full flower, he became Australia's greatest Test run-scorer on a pluperfect Adelaide Oval pitch in December 1987. Cutting and polishing his first Test double-century in 10 hours, the skipper displayed the craftsmanship of fastidious lapidary.

But Border queered his own pitch in Pakistan in September 1988 when, like many a touring captain before him, he bridled at the first hint of partisan umpiring and surface preparation. With coach Bob Simpson and manager Col Egar amplifying his complaints, Border threatened impetu-ously to withdraw from the series after heavy defeat in the Karachi Test: 'Somebody has to make a stand. The situation is unacceptable and damaging to international cricket, yet nothing seems to be done.'

The Australians were not complaining from a position of strength. They had fielded poorly, and batted fatalistically. Although the team played with pluck to draw the last two Tests – Border making the only century, 113 not out at Faisalabad – the tour was a a blow to Australian prestige.

Further setbacks were forthcoming in Australia when a West Indian team, captained with minatory intent by Vivian Richards, ran roughshod over Australia in the first three Tests of the home summer. Though Garner had retired, twenty-five-year-old Antiguan Curtly Ambrose was his body-double – telescopic arms and a yorker like Lee Harvey Oswald's bullet.

The Third Test at the MCG was Border's 100th, and the crowd before whom he'd been baptised in Test cricket a decade earlier flocked in hope of an appropriate memorial. Silence attended the Ambrose delivery that hit the base of Border's stumps fifth ball. It was his first cipher in 89 starts.

The Test devolved into one of the ugliest ever witnessed in Australia. On a disintegrating pitch, Ambrose and Patterson lived up to their taunt: 'If you wanna drive, buy a Peugeot.' Feeling like a coconut in a fairground shy, Border made the top score of 20 in 167 minutes. He said afterward: 'I get absolutely no joy or satisfaction from Test cricket as it has been in this match ... I don't think I've ever seen blokes hit so much. It's just not enjoyable.'

Border even departed from his post-match social custom of joining his opponents in a drink. When West Indians deplored this departure from protocol, Dean Jones explained: 'They talk about us not having a beer with them but it's a bit hard to come up to them afterwards and say: "Look, well-bowled. I enjoyed that one in the stomach."'

In the four years to the end of 1988, Border's record as Test captain showed little improvement on Kim Hughes's melancholy read-out: six wins and 13 defeats. Ian Chappell had become a vehement critic of the Queenslander's regime: 'When things go wrong Border withdraws into his shell like a beleaguered tortoise.' Yet, with the bruises and abrasions of Melbourne barely faded, Border led an Australian rally at the SCG that merits a larger memorial.

With Sydney's reputation as a surface for spinners, Richards seized first innings on winning the toss and saw his batsmen rattle up one for 144. Then Border's men pressed the ball into their captain's hand. The West Indian batting melted away. Twenty-six overs later Border was leaving his old stamping ground blinking at figures of seven for 46. A telegram from Barry Knight was waiting: 'Well done. Still don't think you can bowl.'

As Boon compiled his seventh and best Test century, Border formed a devoted escort: the skipper's inelastic 75 in 6¼ hours contained the most protracted Australian Test half-century (262 deliveries). The prize was worth the waiting: Australia's third first-innings lead over West Indies in a decade.

The tourists' Barbadian bulwark, Desmond Haynes, laid down a brilliant second innings holding action. But when Border ended his 11th Test century, en route to a further bag of four for 50, a witty headline writer described the visitors as victims of 'Borderline'. By scoring the winning runs in his 16 not out, the Australian captain completed what *Wisden* described as 'an all-round performance seldom surpassed by a captain in Test cricket'.

1989 would become Allan Border's *annus mirabilis*. With a steel previously kept in his scabbard he led Australia to its most thorough Ashes conquest since Bradman's last tour.

The campaign plans had Border's fingerprints all over them. Invited to the selection table, he sought and was granted sixteen cricketers of a feather: players he liked, respected, and who could take care of themselves. He plotted with the benefit of two successful winters in county cricket with Essex, surmising that the subtle variations of Westralian swing bowler Terry Alderman and the sagacity of Sydney speedster Geoff Lawson would be the best way to unsettle the home team's flashy but fragile batting.

Border and Simpson also persevered with the daring move of separating the established opening pair of Boon and Marsh by inserting untried left-handed opener Mark Taylor. And both thought highly enough of the tranquil but tough Steve Waugh to draft him as a senior batsman, in spite of his 23 Tests without a century.

Above all, Border demanded of himself and his team a more overt toughness. Upset that Ian Chappell had criticised him for his cordiality toward English peers and pals like David Gower and Ian Botham, Border sought to radiate bustle, bristle and business on the field.

In the First Test at Headingley, all these stratagems were applied and endorsed. When Gower won the toss and inserted the visitors in a portentous gloom, the Australian skipper struck the sparks which ignited effort with a muscular 66. Maiden Test centuries ensued for Taylor and Waugh, underwriting the highest Test total seen at Leeds, before Alderman and Lawson took eight wickets between them and left England 200 in arrears.

Growing in confidence by the hour, Border set England a target of 402 in 83 overs on the fifth morning. The listless home team, with only stalemate to play for, folded to Alderman for a fretful 191, and Australia had won its first Test at Headingley in a quarter of a century. It was a victory and a vindication, condign for captain and coach.

English players were shocked by the conviction of Australia's cricket. Accustomed to finding Border a jolly swagman skipper, Gower was startled to find him a born-again bushranger. 'He was mean to the opposition, the press and indeed his own players,' Gower wrote later. 'He sledged pretty fiercely too, which is something which doesn't normally bother me ... although on this tour it was hyper-unfriendly.'

As a hapless home team was scuttled 4-0, it was clear that Australia's ascendancy stemmed from the top. 'Gower's main problem is that he has not captained well,' wrote the insightful Lawson in his tour diary.

> *He seems to have had one plan out on the field and, when that hasn't worked, he's been stuck ... That's the main difference between him and AB. AB didn't really want the job ... and struggled to come to terms with it. But he's a smart bloke who, when he sets himself to do something, works at it until he's improved enough to satisfy himself. AB has learned to be a good captain, Gower does not appear to be too interested in learning.*

Border's pride in his 'good dressing-room' was transparent. Its characters were diverse, its desire united. The captain was touched when David Boon offered him the chance to score the winning runs in the series at Old Trafford but insisted that the Tasmanian deserved the privilege as much.

The statistical skeleton of the series reads graphically. While the host selectors staged a cricket cotillion with twenty-nine dancers on the card, Australia relied on a disciplined dozen. While only one English player averaged more than 40 during the series, Waugh, Taylor, Border and Jones all averaged in excess of 70, Boon 55. The best local bowler took a dozen wickets at 35, while Alderman and Lawson claimed 70 wickets between them. Such was Australia's pitiless command that an unfortunate Nottingham man committed suicide at the end of the series.

The 1989 Ashes series can now be regarded as foreseeable, like one of those juvenile thrillers that climaxes: 'With one bound, he was free.' England had been 'blackwashed' 4-0 by the West Indies a year earlier. The team was a house divided against itself because of clandestine plans by a group of the home team for a rebel tour of South Africa. And, although Australia had won only one series in England since 1964, Border marshalled a team *mutas mutandis* of abundant raw talent.

But there had been no sense of predestiny when Australia arrived. And those at home, who had watched the series unfold in disbelieving rapture, treated Border's men to a ticker-tape parade through the streets of Sydney and a thanksgiving lap of honour at the AFL Grand Final. The captain himself was awarded the Order of Australia and nominated Australian of the Year by the Australia Day Council in 1990. Newly knighted New Zealander Sir Richard Hadlee commented: 'It's a crying shame that Australia no longer offers knighthoods because Allan Border deserves it.'

Emerging from its cocoon of confusion, the second four years of Border's captaincy regime would yield sixteen victories and only three defeats. So refreshing was the change of fortune that, despite the West Indies' decades of dominance there, Australians were cautiously optimistic about the team's prospects in the Caribbean in March–April 1991.

After having the better of a draw at Sabina Park, however, Australia was mauled *mano e mano* at Bourda where there were more expletives exchanged than in a Sydney cop car. The nadir of the Test was when Dean Jones, deaf to the call of 'no ball' accompanying the ball that had bowled him, was run out by Carl Hooper from the rebound.

While Border stomped at the non-striker's end, Simpson was turning to page 1244 of a 1990 *Wisden* that he had borrowed from the press box for confirmation that umpire Clyde Cumberbatch's decision was in contravention of Law 38.2. The Guyanese would demonstrate their sympathy by burning Cumberbatch in effigy from a noose.

It was a predicament for any touring captain to see the pieties of the game so offended, but Border addressed the incident with calm and candour. He admitted that he had not known the law personally, and refused to claim outright that an Australian would not have taken advantage of the same infringement. 'We accept it as one of those freak things that happen,' Border said mildly. 'It was such a horrendous set of circumstances. So stupid.' His was an underrated act of diplomacy in a tour not thick with examples.

As the tour continued to sour, Border began to brood. His batting plumbed new depths of introversion, his 275 series runs taking a tortured 18 hours. A desire to tough out the West Indies pace attack by occupation seemed to rob the captain of offensive strokes and to cloud his judgement. After a two-hour 29 at Bridgetown was ended by a ball from Marshall that broke his left thumb, Border insisted stubbornly on taking his second-wicket spot in the next dig. Dismissal after five balls of scoreless agony in lengthening shadow on the fourth evening suggested that he should have saved himself for another day.

Border's continued commitment finally received reward at Antigua. As Australia raised a bold five for 355 on the first day from 87 overs, the platform for a glittering stand by Jones and newcomer Mark Waugh was erected by tenacious batting from Taylor and Border.

At times the captain's self-possession seemed unearthly. When he was struck in the back of the helmet by Courtney Walsh, Border's head must have rung like the Liberty Bell; yet his prime concern was for the rebounding ball, and he moved protectively over the stumps.

Border wore a seraphic smile on the last day when his left-arm spin claimed the crucial wicket: Viv Richards, before his faithful for the last time, caught for two at backward square-leg by Alderman, as Australia gained a consoling victory by 157 runs.

Border's first playing alias, Pugsley, had now been supplemented by the nickname AB. It was suitably elemental. His players had known no other captain. Teenage cricket fans could not conceive of cricket without him. But when writer Adrian McGregor profiled Border for *Good Weekend* magazine, the skipper was delivered of a new epithet: 'Captain Grumpy'.

It stuck. Border's combustible temper, founded on unswerving loyalty to his charges, could leave powder-marks on dressing-room walls. In only his second Test as skipper, he was furious to discover that Geoff Lawson had been unilaterally fined $500 for 'conduct unbecoming' by the ACB. Protesting that umpires Peter McConnell and Steve Randell themselves had filed no official complaint against the fast bowler, Border insisted that the fine be taken from the team kitty.

On another occasion, according to Mark Ray's *Border & Beyond*, the

Australian captain refused to toss in a World Series Cup match because some of his players had been docked for wearing 'non-authorised clothing' in a poster photograph. Long-suffering media manager Ian McDonald had to call in ACB chairman Malcolm Gray to conciliate before Border would consent to playing.

Border's most protracted and infamous tantrum came on the last day of Australia's Adelaide Oval Test against India in January 1992. It was announced before play that the selectors, after long rumination, had finally retrenched out-of-form vice-captain Geoff Marsh. So highly did Border esteem his fifth and firmest deputy that he refused to take the field for the first 20 minutes while he harangued chairman of selectors Lawrie Sawle on the telephone. Nor did he accompany the team to Perth at the end of the day, travelling 24 hours later when some of his anger had subsided.

On the one hand, Border's behaviour demonstrated his supererogatory loyalty. Sawle did not take offence, saying later that Border's loyalty was to his 'everlasting credit'. But the pique was hardly encouraging to Marsh's replacement, the Victorian opener Wayne Phillips. Given a hostile reception by Marsh's home crowd, he failed twice in what proved his only Test.

Ten months later Border committed another indiscretion. When umpires Steve Randell and Terry Prue reported him for dissent in the last session of a tense draw with the West Indies at the Gabba, Border became the first player proscribed by an International Cricket Council referee. Brooding that a victory chance had gone awry, the Australian captain did not appear at the post-match disciplinary hearing.

Though his eminence as a player was something to which Border was largely indifferent, this was one occasion on which it was advantageous. ICC referee Raman Subba Row was understandably reluctant to suspend Test cricket's most-capped player, and decided to levy only a fine of $2000. Border later conceded that he had been lucky.

The 1992–93 rubber against Richie Richardson's West Indians proved, ultimately, Border's most frustrating. Beaten so often by teams from the islands, Border's team took a 1-0 series lead into the Fourth Test at Adelaide Oval and, in oppressive humidity on a ticklish track, stood within two runs of reclaiming the Frank Worrell Trophy as 6 pm approached on 26 January 1993.

While Border had fondled what team-mates regarded as his 'worry ball' in the dressing-room and patriots in the crowd were chorusing 'Waltzing Matilda', last pair Tim May and Craig McDermott had negotiated the bowling nervelessly for an hour and a half. And when McDermott turned the third ball of Walsh's 19th over off his pads, it seemed for a nanosecond that the series was Australia's.

Short-leg fielder Haynes dropped a hand on the ball to keep the Australians at home; exultations died on local lips. And when two deliveries later a short ball appeared to brush McDermott's helmet, umpire Darrell Hair upheld an appeal for a catch at the wicket that left the series ajar and expelled expectancy from the home rooms. Border hurled his worry ball into the floor with such force that it rebounded into the ceiling.

Because the West Australian Cricket Association had decreed a 'result wicket' for the Fifth Test, Border's men found another untamed surface awaiting them three days later. Border's 31st Test against the West Indies was the nastiest, most brutish and shortest: his bat was halfway to nowhere in the first innings when Ambrose grazed its outside edge, and groping sightlessly in the second when a ball from Ian Bishop ricocheted from the inside. Border's first 'pair' delayed by only four deliveries an innings defeat of seven sessions duration. 'I wanted to beat these blokes,' Border lamented, more in sorrow than anger. 'This was definitely my last chance. But it just wasn't meant to be.'

The last twelvemonth of Border's Test captaincy was faithful to the preceding eight. It began with personal landmark on 26 February 1993: an innings of 88 against New Zealand in which, with an improvised swat against spinner Dipak Patel, he became Test cricket's tallest scorer.

It saddened Border that he'd not been able to surpass Sunil Gavaskar's 10,122 run tally before a home crowd but, for a cricketer who'd risen to the Test occasion from Kingston to Kandy, an audience of 3100 damp Christchurchgoers in a game uncovered by Channel Nine was curiously apposite. For Border, publicity and the possibility of acclaim had always been secondary to the simple motivation of playing for Australia.

Border revelled more in his team's continued advances. Augmented by the prodigious leg-spinner Shane Warne, who harvested wickets at will, Australia retained the Ashes in England in 1993 by the margin of 4-0.

The series was Border's most comprehensively capable as skipper: the stoic corporal of 1985 and the strict commandant of 1989 had become a subtle conductor. He applied his spinners artfully. When injuries to McDermott and Julian deprived him of two keen strikers, the captain cajoled greater and greater efforts from the unswerving Merv Hughes. Gratified that there had never been less call for his batting, he was always present when called to account. His double-hundred at Headingley was as deliberate as the passing of a mandatory sentence.

There was spontaneous adoration for Border when, awarded a testimonial by the ACB for the 1993–94 home summer, he was the self-effacing recipient of numerous tributes. Only Bradman can have stirred greater reverence during his international career than Border, although the allegiances they inspired were as different as the individuals. Where the Don's deeds evoked awe by transcending ordinary understanding, Border's batathons when odds were insurmountable occasioned admiration leavened with affection and affinity.

A benefit match at the Gabba was sold out, and a century there against New Zealand in his 150th Test was received like a papal blessing. Border was moved to receive lengthy salaams from 50,000 Sydneysiders after he had led Australia to victory in the World Series Cup. When Australia then visited South Africa at summer's end, its heroic healer Nelson Mandela had no doubt which Australian hand he most wanted to shake. As teams were presented in the opening tour match, Mandela insisted: 'Where is Allan Border?'

Disappointments there were, as well. The loss of Border's wicket in the Second Test against South Africa at the SCG, bowled without essaying a shot, was the turning point of a fluctuating match. The captain, endlessly rotating his worry ball in silent self-condemnation, watched as Australia ebbed to defeat by a mere six runs.

There was controversy when Australia lost again to South Africa at Wanderers six weeks later. Having stranded first Mark Waugh then himself with misjudged calls, Border cut a crestfallen and uncommunicative figure when he led Australia into the field. He did not come to the aid of the party until Shane Warne earned a rebuke from umpire David Shepherd for sending victim Andrew Hudson packing with an unseemly volley of abuse. When Warne and Merv Hughes were both fined for behavioural misdemeanours, Border was pilloried for abdicating his disciplinary duties.

In both series, Australia achieved parity. It was the first time that the national team under Border had come from behind to restore equality, and testified to the analeptic powers it had learned from its leader. In what proved Border's final Test innings, he steered Australia once more to a safe anchorage with a 225-minute innings of 42 not out. 'No way am I getting out here,' Border averred to partner Mark Waugh, 'it might be my last dig.'

There remained no formal adieu; Border the batsman never thought further than the next ball. He was acutely aware of the expectation he would quit, but contrarily harboured private thoughts that he might continue.

Feeling his hand forced when the ACB convened in his absence a meeting of senior players on 9 and 10 May 1994, Allan finally confirmed in a television interview that he would retire from Test cricket. It was typical of the man. In his headstrong but heartfelt way, he confirmed the magnitude and meaning to him of the job he'd never felt quite up to.

Border mellowed over his last two seasons in first-class cricket, in the first of which he underwrote Queensland's maiden Sheffield Shield victory, and passed gently from the game. Before a crowd at the MCG on 26 March 1996 not much larger than the one before which he'd begun his first-class career, Border was caught at deep fine-leg for 34 in 146 minutes by Victorian substitute fielder Brad Stacey, almost seventeen years his junior. Border's first-class run account closed on 27,131 at 51.4, just 936 short of Bradman's record tally, with 70 centuries from 385 matches.

The self-imposed austerity of Border's batsmanship may prevent its full appreciation. It may be that, in years to come, critics of Allan Border will echo baseballer Danny Ozark's observation of a colleague: 'His limitations were limitless.'

Certainly, he is hard to bracket with the Don. Where Bradman was a player of cause, Border drew satisfaction primarily from effect. Asked to nominate his best Test innings, Bradman has always volunteered his 254 at Lord's in 1930: its freedom from the faintest error appealed to the knight's technical passions. Posed the same question, Border has recalled his two abstinent epics at Port-of-Spain in 1984: innings whose greatest merit was denying victory to a remorseless West Indian side.

But Border's day-in-day-out durability stands out from *Wisden* as though in copperplate. His record in unfamiliar conditions is without compeer: nobody has scored more Test runs away from their native heath and Border's batting average away from home is 11 runs higher than his average on Australian soil.

Border's cricket must also be read in terms of his era. The 1980s, when he outscored all contemporaries, was a period of unprecedented congestion in cricket's calendar. In as many active summers as Bradman, Border played three times as many Tests as the Don. No-one approaches his 29 tours. He learned to pack his passport alongside his pads, and spent almost as long in departure lounges as dressing-rooms. The man who usurps Border at the top of the Test run-scoring tables will have logged a lot of frequent flier miles.

Border's place in the pantheon of captains is not ultimately conspicuous. His record of 31 wins and 21 losses hardly places him in the Benaud/ Chappell league, and the teams he commanded had a flair for fumbling in the clinches that was often remarked on (Border played in six of the 20 closest Test finishes and never won).

Again, though, any assessment should have regard to the status of the job in his years as a player. In the years 1977 to 1984, no fewer than a dozen players captained Australian teams official and unofficial: in addition to Ian and Greg Chappell, Bob Simpson, Graham Yallop and Kim Hughes as described in this book, teams were led by Rod Marsh, Doug Walters, Kerry O'Keeffe, Richie Robinson, Ross Edwards, Jeff Thomson and Andrew Hilditch.

Observing the way the captaincy alternated between Greg Chappell and Kim Hughes in the early eighties, the Australian cricket lover would have been forgiven for wondering whether this was another of those jobs that could be mechanised, computerised or run by a committee.

Allan Border restored the captaincy's dignity. He proved that the man in charge was material, and the role was a fine thing worth fighting for. When he swayed beneath his burden, it was because command carried responsibilities not borne lightly.

The early years of Border's captaincy can be seen – to borrow a phrase made familiar by Treasurer Paul Keating – as 'the recession we had to have'. Australian cricket hadn't known loss as sudden and profound as that of the simultaneous retirements of Greg Chappell, Dennis Lillee and Rod Marsh since Benaud, Neil Harvey, Alan Davidson and Ken Mackay had bowed out in quick succession two decades earlier. Having joined the Australian team in an autumnal stage, Border had to withstand the full blast of winter before the joys of spring. In the summer the country's cricket now enjoys, his work should not be overlooked.

M.A. TAYLOR

41

In Safe Hands

Cricket is said to accommodate two kinds of madmen: fast bowlers, whose hyperkinetic exertions suggest minds unhinged; and opening batsmen, who to face them must by implication be a few deliveries shy of the full over. International cricket since the mid-1970s has required of openers a masochism ever more pronounced. As the West Indies and Pakistan in particular have thrown up a profusion of pacemen who maim as they claim, opening batsmanship has become a profession as fraught as steeplejacking and deep-sea diving.

Mark Anthony Taylor, however, gives no sense of an unsound mind as he goes about his risky work. Patient, practical and sure of his footing outside off-stump, Taylor makes his mark with a soldier-settler's resolution. Australia's sixth-highest Test run scorer with 5502 runs at 46 from 72 Tests has 'done that' whenever he's 'been there' in international cricket. He is the first Australian to secure centuries on the full sextet of home Test grounds. Like a man proud of the firm grip of his handshake, he is never shy making first impressions: he made Test centuries at first brush with England, South Africa, Sri Lanka and Pakistan.

When he succeeded Allan Border as Australia's captain in May 1994, there were some who mistook Mark's self-sufficiency for self-absorption. They wondered aloud whether he had the great skippers' knack for instilling confidence and allegiance in others. By retaining the Ashes, recapturing the long-lost Frank Worrell Trophy and almost appropriating the World Cup within his first two years' tenure, Taylor disabused doubters.

Australians in general have taken to the earnest, animated way with which their 39th captain expresses ideas, commanding respect without demanding it. And, in an era where sport is increasingly the preserve of bionic sylphs, Taylor cuts an almost reassuring figure: his physique is more suggestive of channel-surfing than body-surfing, and his head turns to the nickname 'Tubby'.

Taylor undertakes the rigours of modern cricket tours with equanimity, possibly the result of an itinerant upbringing in the Riverina and Sunraysia districts of New South Wales and Victoria. Father Tony was a valuer with the Rural Bank of NSW, and regular relocations meant that, while Mark was born in Leeton on 27 October 1964, he was a pre-schooler in Mildura, began primary school in West Wyalong and finished it in Wagga Wagga.

When Mark first showed sporting prowess as an eight-year-old at South Wagga Primary, it was in the unlikely field of Australian Rules football. The Victorian oval ball game usually loses something in the translation the further north one travels, but back-pocket Taylor's physique and phlegmatism would in time arouse interest from Victorian Football League talent scouts.

Mark, though, had begun learning the rudiments of cricket from his father, a club player with Maitland thirds. Tony Taylor drilled his son in the tenets of sound technique during hours with a cork 'compo' cricket ball in the concrete confines of the family garage. Cricket's claims on the boy were redoubled when, as a ten-year-old on a family Christmas holiday at Bondi, he attended his first Test. Mark was an excited face on the SCG Hill (elevated by his father's Esky), cheering Australia against England on the opening day of the Fourth Test of the 1974–75 series.

Turnstiles counted 52,461 entrants that day as Australia compiled four for 251, and Mark's brush with history was propitious. This was the Test match in which Ian Chappell's Australians reclaimed the Ashes, the trophy which was to play such an important role in Taylor's later life.

He soon after joined Wagga's Lake Albert Cricket Club, a stern establishment with a crowded honour board and a distinctive puritanism: it scorns batting or bowling average trophies, preferring to elect an annual 'Clubman of the Year' distinguished by his on- and off-field contribution to the club's betterment.

Mark's spanking 116 in an under-fourteen game at Bolton Park notified locals of a humming cricket talent, and had a further auspicious element: an impressed guest square-leg umpire was Geoff Lawson, a lanky LACC old boy from the Riverina who had just achieved a state cap, and who would later be an Australian team-mate, state captain and finally coach.

With father Tony, mother Judy and sisters Tina and Lisa, Mark moved to a bank house at Lindfield in northern Sydney in 1978. Spotted playing for the local under-sixteen side by former Gordon players Laurie Blackman and Ken Walker, he was guided toward the Northern Districts Grade Cricket Club when his family shifted to Epping.

It was at Northern Districts that the youngster attracted another handy patron: former NSW all-rounder Neil Marks. One look at the sixteen-year-old South Chatswood High School boy Mark Taylor, solid in defence and nerveless in attack, convinced Marks that he had an embryonic Test talent on his hands. Taylor was drafted at once into the third-grade side, and within three seasons was playing first-grade under former NSW batsman Ross Turner.

Marks promoted his precocious opener avidly. At Epping Oval one Saturday Marks sidled up to Bankstown's Len Pascoe and advised him *sotto voce* that Northern Districts had a player 'who's gonna belt the ears off ya'. The Australian fast bowler snarled a reply, unaccustomed to such irreverence, but the prediction was borne out: Taylor hooked him for six, clean out of the arena, to win the match for his side.

When the canny Marks stationed Taylor alongside keeper Tim Ebbeck, regular runs were complemented by copious catches. Blessed with an acute judgement of angles, Mark seemed even as a teenager to have fly-paper palms.

Unlike contemporaries Border, McDermott, Healy and the Waughs, Taylor approached a prospective sporting career with the cautious fore-knowledge that many are called, few chosen. He elected to establish a profession before considering the hazards of a livelihood from cricket, enrolling in 1982 to study surveying at the University of NSW.

Mark played for NSW in the Barclays under-nineteen championship in January 1984 – Steve Waugh's 386 runs just edging out Taylor's 334 runs as best aggregate – then in the national under-19s against Sri Lanka a month later, but persisted methodically with his degree until graduation in 1987.

Tolerant lecturers deferred examinations when playing commitments impinged.

The little fortune that no cricket career can do without came Taylor's way in May 1985 as a result of Kim Hughes's sanction-busting South African tours. Among defectors were NSW's opening pair John Dyson and Steve Smith. Refabrication of Dirk Wellham's state side would entail a completely new opening combination. After Taylor made an unbeaten 185 against Mosman in October 1985, and a century for the state 2nd XI against Victoria's 2nd XI just 24 hours before the first selection meeting, he was selected to fill the breach with Mark Waugh, Steve's twenty-year-old twin.

Taylor turned twenty-one during his first Sheffield Shield match at the Hobart's TCA Ground, and by summer's end had come of age as a cricketer. From 20 innings his average was almost 50, placing him eighth on the national ladder, including two centuries at South Australia's expense. The harmonious combination he formed with journeyman left-hander Steve Small was like water and fire: where Small wreaked havoc with a 3-pound blunderbat, Taylor was baptised 'Stodge' for his stoical approach. *Wisden* considered them the key factor in NSW's successful Sheffield Shield campaign.

After Taylor confirmed favourable impressions in his second season with 765 further runs at 40, many wise judges were prepared to advocate his elevation to Test status. And for about three hours in January 1987, Mark laboured under the delusion that their calls had been answered.

Having consented in advance to appear on Channel Nine's *Today* program if he was called up for the Fifth Test at the SCG, Taylor was woken at 6 am by a producer at Channel Nine's Artarmon studios with the news that he had been so blessed. Emerging from the shower 20 minutes later, he received a second call asking if NSW had a 'P. Taylor'. When Mark confirmed that off-spinner Peter Taylor was indeed a colleague, for both NSW and Northern Districts, he suspected a case of mistaken identity and returned to bed.

Taylor was further confused by hearing on the 7 am news the composition of the team, which included only one opener. Perhaps they *did* mean him. It wasn't until Wellham rang at 9.15 am that Mark stood down from baggy green alert.

After an indifferent third season, winter work as a professional in the Bolton League with Greenmount revived Mark's game like a pinch of snuff. There were runs aplenty (a record 1300 at an average of 70) a league championship at the end (Greenmount's first), and an enjoyable exposure to seniority. Taylor told author Jack Egan:

> The first two weeks I was a bit nervous about it, and then there was a training session a week or so later that was going rather poorly; everyone was sort of doing their own thing and one bloke walked past me and said: 'This is an absolute shambles.'
>
> I thought: 'It's time for me to step in here.' So I said: 'Right, you, you and you bowl, you pad up, you bat, and the rest of you over here with me.'
>
> From there it went well, because they could see I was starting to get serious about it ... The more they could see I was serious about it and wasn't just using them as a holiday, the more they started to put in and the better the association I made with everyone.

When Taylor returned to NSW, his captain Lawson noticed the stiffened sinews in Taylor's strokeplay. The left-hander had learned to hit his cut, rather than simply to place it. His drives punctured rather than perforated the covers. A hook, neglected, was rediscovered. It wasn't long before team-mates had revised Taylor's nickname to 'Slogger'.

Mark enjoyed his new streak of assertiveness and, returning from a match at Newcastle against WA where he scored 28 and 83 on a difficult pitch from an attack including four Test bowlers, matter-of-factly told his fiancee Judi Matthews that he was 'ready' if a Test call now came. He was finally selected for the Fourth Test of the season against West Indies (although, recalling the farce a few years earlier, inquired first of those who passed him the news: 'Are you sure it's me?'). Having put a foot in the airliner door to England for the winter, he wrote his own tickets by compiling twin centuries against Western Australia in the last Sheffield Shield match of the season.

Mark's marriage to Judi and his selection for the 1989 Ashes tour came in a heady rush, although his place was still far from assured for the First Test at Headingley. There were widespread misgivings about a de-merger of the successful firm of David Boon and Geoff Marsh. It was only a belief shared by captain Allan Border and coach Bob Simpson in the efficacy of left-hand/right-hand opening partnerships that saw Taylor accommodated and Boon reinvented to appear at the fall of the first wicket.

Rarely can a cricket investment have borne such a handsome coupon. At the end of the first day's play at Leeds – after Australia had been inserted beneath an ominous vault of cloud – Taylor had underwritten a score of 3-207 with a cool, resourceful 96 not out.

Accepting that England's four fast bowlers were likely to enjoy the odd moral victory in the gloaming, Taylor was untroubled when his edge was beaten. He set himself simply to miss nothing astray, and waited to have the last word when England's pacemen began to tire in the last half hour. A meal with his parents and a sound slumber later, Taylor turned Derek Pringle to the fine-leg boundary to register a maiden Test century.

Australia's victory in the First Test reversed all the rubber's portents, and Border would classify Taylor's six-and-a-half-hour 136 as 'the critical innings of the series'. Simpson added: 'We wanted a left-hander at the top, but not just any left-hander. We waited until we felt we had the right one.'

Taylor emerged as Australia's sternest sentinel. With a classically light bat (2 pounds 8 ounces) coming down as straight as his surveyors' plumb-line, he batted almost 38 hours over the duration of the rubber. And, though Englishmen came to cherish Mark's wicket ahead of any other, they claimed it only 10 times in 1868 deliveries.

The summit of his series came at Nottingham, where he liaised with Marsh in a first-wicket Ashes record. The pair raised 301 on the first day, tormenting England's captain David Gower with their swift turnover of strike. Where some batsmen are inclined to bolt abruptly, like commuters starting after a departing bus, Taylor always runs between wickets with the intent of one on a serious errand. The partners' patriotic *esprit de corps* was evident at stumps when photographers arrived to memorialise their feat: having batted all day in helmets, Taylor and Marsh fished out their baggy caps for the gaze of posterity.

So desperate did Gower become for a wicket on the second morning that he jokingly sent his 12th man Greg Thomas to the press box to poll the resident sages on how to break the openers' concentration. When the teams lunched on the second day, after Marsh had finally succumbed to tiredness at 329, Gower was seen sipping a glass of champagne. The hard-pressed local skipper explained to Lawson: 'I'm celebrating our wicket, Henry.' Gower's champagne was well and truly flat by the time Taylor made his first mistake, having batted more than nine hours for 219: the highest Ashes score since 1966.

Taylor received a congratulatory letter after the innings from Arthur Morris, the cultured left-hand opener from New South Wales whose 1948 aggregate of 696 runs he had surpassed. And Taylor's final return during Australia's most successful northern summer for forty-one years was 839 runs at 83.9: an Ashes aggregate that only Bradman among Australians has exceeded.

Back on his home pitches in 1989–90, Taylor paraded his new accomplishments with 1403 first-class runs at 70 including four centuries in five Tests against Sri Lanka and Pakistan. In a low-scoring Boxing Day Test on a treacherous MCG pitch against Pakistan, Taylor grafted 52 and 101 from 384 deliveries in totals of 207 and 8-312.

Man of the Match Wasim Akram, who walks back ten paces and fires like a quick-draw duellist, found in the Australian a marksman worthy of his mettle. He beat Taylor frequently with his wicked left-arm swing, but was unable to include him in his 11-wicket harvest.

By the time Taylor's average had swelled to an exalted 70 after 14 Tests, he had a fine gallery of flatterers. Asked whom he considered capable of surpassing his Test record score of 365 not out, Sir Garfield Sobers replied: 'I fancy Mark Taylor, the Australian opener ... because he has tremendous concentration, great ability and can score at the required rate.'

Greg Chappell judged Taylor's batting an index of his personality, and proposed that he might be the stuff of which leaders are made:

> I see a special quality in Mark Taylor. Richie Benaud, Sir Donald Bradman and Ian Chappell all had a hard, calculating edge to their character, and it's obvious from the way Taylor bats that he has the steely heart necessary in a successful Australian captain.

Most importantly, Allan Border was of a mind. 'He's a very astute young man,' Border said in February 1990. 'He gets on very well in a group situation but he's also the sort of bloke who can come down hard now and then, as all captains need to do. His tactics on the field are impressive. He thinks about it and knows what's going on.'

While Taylor had to that stage led only Northern Districts in a few matches during 1987–88, he provided supporting evidence for the Chappell-Border hypothesis when the injured Lawson withdrew from the Sheffield Shield final against Queensland only half an hour before choice of innings on 23 March 1990.

Neil Marks, now a NSW selector, asked only two things of Taylor: 'Win the toss and score a century.' His former charge overachieved: 127 and 100 from almost 11 hours' duty against an able XI including Border, Healy, McDermott, Rackemann and Ritchie underpinned NSW's 40th Shield victory.

Taylor might have displaced Bradman as the national cricket yardstick had his upward arc been sustained, and it was no surprise to the New South Welshman when his subsequent seasons featured as many snakes as ladders. 'Really, it was ridiculous, jumping straight from obscurity to being compared with Bradman,' he told journalist Terry Smith in 1990. 'I don't think you can put it down to luck because I like to think I'm a good player, but I did go through a hot streak. I know I'm going to have some bad times, so I try to be philosophical.'

Graham Gooch's Englishmen were first to check Mark's advance at the end of that year, unsettling him by bowling round the wicket. Taylor adjusted his guard from two legs to middle, but lost for a time his almost supernatural awareness of the whereabouts of off-stump.

Pinned down by bombardment from Curtley Ambrose, Courtney Walsh, Patrick Patterson and Malcolm Marshall, Taylor's first exploration of the Caribbean in March–April 1991 began slowly. Sporting more protective gear than a riot policeman keeping the peace in Ulster, Taylor struggled initially to balance occupation with activity. Coach Simpson's gimlet eye detected a creeping ailment in Taylor's batting after the Second Test, suggesting that the opener might be falling across to off-stump, and his last three innings of the rubber were spread over 15½ hours (76, 59 and 144).

The runs came in handy for, as Mark and Judi Taylor holidayed in Vanuatu with Dean Jones and Merv Hughes afterward, Australia's selectors were considering their options to succeed Allan Border. They decided to trial Taylor for a fortnight as a skipper for an Australia B team touring Zimbabwe in September 1991 – a squad vice-captained by Steve Waugh and including future Testmen Shane Warne, Stuart Law, Peter McIntyre and Paul Reiffel – and received rosy reports from team manager and Australian selector John Benaud.

During the 1991–92 Australian season, however, the left-hander found a particularly slippery snake. Critics alleged that he was overweight and unworthy of a regular position in Australia's first-choice limited-overs XI. Australia's selectors implied their own lack of conviction by including him in only two of the season's 18 short-haul matches.

Acknowledging that insecurity of one-day tenure might queer his leadership pitch, Taylor followed his compadre Steve Small to the Penrith gymnasium run by physiotherapist and past NSW player Kevin Chevell. Chevell's circuit routines were so exacting that the opener shed 10 kilograms of fat and added five kilograms of muscle, fining down in the process to the 87 kilograms that Mark considers his optimum displacement. Taylor's investment of energy impressed selectors state and national: he was appointed to succeed Geoff Lawson as NSW captain and inked in to replace Geoff Marsh as Border's deputy for Australia's tour of Sri Lanka.

Seniority was not without its drawbacks. Though he and Judi became parents on 16 May 1992, Mark had to acknowledge that he was now a likely absentee for most of son William's formative years.

When the new Australian vice-captain made a commiseratory call to his predecessor, Michelle Marsh answered the telephone. 'Oh, congratulations,' she said. 'But you've got my husband's job.' Taylor recalled: 'She was right: I did, and I really felt that I had stolen it from him.'

The 1992–93 season duly provided mixed blessings for Australia's new second-in-command. Having successfully stood in as skipper for an injured Border during four limited-overs matches (three wins and a tie), Taylor briefly lost his Test spot for the Fifth Test against the West Indies at the WACA Ground after 16 innings without a fifty. Like a cavalryman whose horse had colic before Balaclava, Taylor had picked the right engagement to miss: Australia was routed in 14 hours' playing time by an innings and 25 runs. When Taylor resumed acquaintance with English pitches, the left-hander's touch returned fast in the company of a new opening partner from an old stamping ground.

Twenty-three-year-old Michael Slater, born in Wagga and following Lawson to the University of NSW, had bubbled up from the NSW Second XI in a matter of six months. With his snap and dash and strength-through-joy strokes, Slater at once suggested a complementarity with Taylor. Although they had opened together for their state but once, Taylor and Slater had by the end of the 1993 Ashes series forged a fruitful professional and fraternal bond. English tabloids referred to them as the 'Wagga Wagga Floggers' after their alliances averaged a ripe 80 over the six Tests, and Taylor was a VIP guest at Slater's Wagga wedding to Stephanie Blackett on 18 September 1993.

Alert to conjecture that he might shortly be captain-elect, Taylor bided his time during Border's 1993–94 testimonial season. He became an unobtrusively diplomatic deputy who soothed ruffled feathers and often mediated between Border and junior team members.

Mark's pacific temperament was conspicuous by its absence when he missed the First Test against South Africa at the Wanderers in February 1994 with a stomach upset. There was a distinct shortage of cool heads as Shane Warne and Merv Hughes were fined for misconduct, rising to the bait of a hostile crowd.

Taylor pointedly counselled leg-spinning prodigy Warne when leading Australia during the subsequent match against Boland. The New South Welshman had led Warne on his first overseas senior tour (to Zimbabwe with Australia B), and knew better than most the pressures exerted by a hasty rise to prominence. 'I don't think I gave Warney a rev,' Taylor later remembered. 'We just had a chat about where he was going in Test cricket. I was merely pointing out that I didn't think he was enjoying his cricket as much as before and I was trying to find out why.'

Where Australia's first captain Dave Gregory was appointed by his men on the day of the First Test, Australia's most recent skipper had an elongated and elaborate initiation. Media speculation about Border's successor reached a deafening din when Australia returned from Sharjah in April 1994. Front-runners Taylor, Healy, Boon and Steve Waugh were hemmed in by TV cameras as they attended debriefings on 9 and 10 May at the ACB's Jolimont Street HQ in Melbourne. Their virtues were extensively debated in the press.

Taylor was seeking some solitude on the Gurley farm of his old stunt double Peter Taylor nine days later when he received the mobile telephone call confirming his mandate from ACB media manager Ian McDonald. Ensuring against possible confusion about the relevant Taylor, McDonald advised: 'Tubby, it's you.'

McDonald met his 6 am flight from Moree at Mascot next day, and ferried him to the NSWCA's Druitt Street offices for conferences with print and electronic journalists. A Channel Nine limousine was idling outside throughout, stocked with champagne and a *Sports Sunday* reporter and crew. The limo conveyed Taylor to Willoughby to face *A Current Affair's* cricket-fancying anchorman Ray Martin. After an SCG photo session and a meeting with the ACB at Paddington's Lord Nelson Hotel, Taylor was flying back to Moree as television news bulletins went to air announcing his promotion.

To deal with his new responsibilities toward the media Mark appointed a manager: John Fordham, whose Fordham Communications also handles the accounts of radio guru John Laws and rugby star Ricky Stuart. Taylor endorsed an ACB decision to hone his players' personal presentation skills by retaining Rogen Australia, a consultancy run by former *Auckland Star* journalist Neil Flett that had just primed Sydney's pitch for the 2000 Olympics. And when a team meeting followed at the Australian Institute of Sport in Adelaide, involving lectures from nutritionist Lorna Garden and sport psychologist Graham Winter, players also heard from Channel Nine sports director Gary Burns on the subject of the network's policies for live coverage.

Though Dave Gregory would hardly have recognised the trappings of the office he first occupied, he would have endorsed Taylor's captaincy charter. Foremost among tasks Taylor foresaw was restoring some of cricket's civility. 'I'm not a big sledger myself, so I'm not a huge supporter of sledging,' he said. 'I think, from a batsman's point of view, it only makes you play better. It's up to me to keep our players as cool as I can on the field. I think I'll be trying to stamp it out for sure.'

Taylor also felt fortunate in the timing and circumstances of his appointment, as might an investment manager inheriting a portfolio of bonds just short of maturity, for Australia was blessed with a core of players quietly crystallising. At the end of the Australia-South Africa series Taylor, David Boon, Craig McDermott, Ian Healy and the Waughs had 364 Test caps between them, and only Boon had enjoyed a thirtieth birthday. In Warne, Slater, the apprentice batsman Michael Bevan and paceman Glenn McGrath were the first fruits of the Australian Institute of Sport's cricket academy, which promised a well of talent for summers ahead.

Nonetheless, Taylor's first assignment promised to be arduous: three Tests in Pakistan and up to 10 one-day internationals there and in Sri Lanka. Apprehension now attends virtually every meeting between cricket's east and west. Recent Australian cricketers touring the sub-continent have felt as welcome as someone reading *The Satanic Verses* aloud in a Karachi bazaar.

The new skipper certainly felt the pressure. His catching became fallible, and his batting contribution leading Australia in the First Test at Karachi was 11 scoreless deliveries. Mark was then a thwarted spectator while Inzamam-ul-Haq and Mushtaq Ahmed added 57 toward only the seventh one-wicket victory in 1268 Tests.

Taylor's immediate sensation on making his first pair was despondent: 'Oh well, at least I've captained Australia for one Test.' His notes after the defeat began: 'I'm in my room, the captain who lost his first Test. But I don't know how.' Within a short time, however, Taylor had rationalised defeat: 'I have experienced the worst, bring out the best.' He had also digested a lesson: 'It took a pair in the First Test to make me realise that I've got to make sure I look after my own batting. I was putting in the hours in the nets, so there was nothing wrong with my preparation, but when I was actually out there I wasn't quite focusing on my job as an opening batsman. I was still too busy thinking about everyone else and the team and what have you.'

The problems didn't end there. In Peshawar, there was an earthquake. In Gujranwala, a riot. Steve Waugh, Healy and McDermott were invalided out of the tour, while Boon, Warne and Slater suffered frights if not injuries when hit by crowd jetsam in a one-day international against South Africa. There was agitation in the touring camp over what Warne, Mark Waugh and Tim May alleged were inducements to fail from Pakistan's captain Salim Malik. Taylor turned thirty on tour, but may have felt considerably older at its end.

Mark managed, however, both to contain Australian consternation and to delineate his role in detail. Where Border had devolved to Simpson the task of pre-play talks, Taylor undertook the duty with some relish. He commissioned a team newsletter, 'No Whinge, No Wine', which respected no authority and buoyed morale.

The Australians' on-field behaviour earned a citation for sportsmanship from ICC referee John Reid. Having had the better of drawn Tests at Rawalpindi and Lahore while winning the triangular Wills one-day series in Pakistan, Taylor returned home to contest the Ashes snugly settled in his new role.

Mark grew in his job daily against Mike Atherton's Englishmen. His attitude from the outset was positive, his public remarks refreshingly free of artifice and false modesty. When journalists solicited Taylor's slant on the ACB's innovation of an Australia A team in the four-sided one-day World Series Cup, the captain hid none of his reservations: 'It does take away from the game a bit. I was brought up on one country, one team. Having two teams does devalue that.' After a sparkling 150 from 234 deliveries in the tour match at Newcastle Sports Ground in November 1994, Taylor assessed the series without coyness: 'If we play to our potential we should have no trouble retaining the Ashes.'

Taylor's preparedness as skipper to be his own man was apparent from the First Test at the Gabba. Having gainsaid the wisdom that a follow-on should always be enforced and elected to bat again after securing a first-innings lead of 259, Mark did not resile from his decision when England's Graeme Hick and Graham Thorpe combined in a worthwhile delaying action. As England crumbled on the last day, he saw one of his own dicta

415

validated: 'The essence of captaincy is making a decision and then sticking by it. Indecision is no way to win a Test match.'

Taylor took the Second Test handily also, then showed in the Third at the SCG his reluctance to let sleeping matches lie. Boldly jeopardising his series lead, he instructed his men to chase an unlikely total of 449 in four sessions.

When England's opening bowlers Devon Malcolm and Darren Gough set out to make inroads in Australia's second innings just before tea on the fourth day, Taylor and Slater met them with coruscating strokes. Where there was a hint of reckless abandon to the younger man's play, Taylor displayed the intrepid calm of a riveter aloft on a high-rise girder.

Brows in the English press corps were furrowed when the pair prolonged their partnership to 208 in four and three-quarter hours on the final day (Taylor a chanceless 113 in 248 deliveries) and only an untimely interference from the elements and tightening out-cricket from the tourists prevented a historic victory.

On-field success allowed Taylor to deepen his impression on the landscape. He encouraged as a general policy the easing of state commitments on overworked internationals and discouraged cards, books and walkmen in the dressing-room. 'It's important to watch even when you're not playing,' Taylor said. 'It's amazing what you can learn watching.'

When England unexpectedly won the Fourth Test at Adelaide Oval over the 1995 Australia Day weekend, Taylor took his solitary summer setback with aplomb. After calm observations about the general distribution of luck during the Test, Taylor flew to Sydney to attend the birth of his second child.

As critics debated the significance of Australia's setback in fevered terms, Taylor was sharing a bed at home with his son William. The following morning – not without a certain squeamishness – he was by his wife's side during an emergency caesarean that delivered them a second son, Jack, named for Judi's grandfather.

Taylor said later that chatting cheerily of his new offspring to well-wishers all the way back across the continent to the Fifth Test at the WACA recalibrated his sense of normality. He presided over a sweeping 329-run home victory, pausing only to order three cheers each for tourists Graham Gooch and Mike Gatting, who were playing in their last Tests.

Although the 3-1 Ashes victory fostered hopes of a feisty Australian challenge to the West Indies in April 1995, there was no underestimation of the task at hand. Many sides had travelled hopefully to the Caribbean over the preceding twenty-two years, but all had returned empty-handed. The Frank Worrell Trophy had become such a fixture in the islands since its confiscation in 1978 that it had actually been mislaid for a time (another Bermuda Triangle mystery was only ruled out when it turned up in a forgotten cabinet at the home of former West Indian manager Wes Hall).

Yet, having emerged during the twilight of the strongest West Indian sides, Taylor did not feel intimidated at the prospect of visiting them in their lair. Where his predecessor Allan Border had enjoyed only five victories and three centuries in his 31 Tests against the West Indies, Taylor had played in 10 Tests against them for three wins, four draws and three defeats and averaged almost 50 on Caribbean soil.

The famous 2-1 victory displayed, in due course, a resourcefulness and trust in his players that Taylor shared with the last Test captain to beat the West Indies at home: Ian Chappell. Just as Chappell took the 1972–73 series despite losing his two top pacemen Dennis Lillee and Bob Massie, Taylor won while manipulating an attack minus Craig McDermott and Damien Fleming that had few pretensions but deep discipline. Just as Chappell encouraged his batsmen to attack at all times, Taylor set a spirited example by unsheathing his hook shot at every opportunity. Where Chappell had made only two forced changes to his Test side during the series, Taylor stuck to the same XI throughout.

Chappell's side went within an ace of defeat at Trinidad and Taylor's team were beaten there on a pitch trickier than a riverboat gambler, yet both surged back to supremacy. Mark, in particular, radiated positive thoughts even in adversity, asserting amid the grief of the Queen's Park loss that Australia should still win the decisive Sabina Park match. They did so overwhelmingly. Fittingly it was Taylor who threw the ball toward the ionosphere after taking the catch that clinched the game by an innings and 53 runs.

Like Chappell, who wrote *Passing Tests* after his 1973 sojourn, Taylor also had a work in progress throughout the trip. On a pocket tape recorder, he daily confided the impressions that made up his *Taylor Made*. The sentiments therein were, like the man himself, unvarnished. After a bruising skirmish with West Indian speed during the Second Test at Antigua, for instance, Taylor made no bones of his distaste for the home team's methods:

It wasn't cricket. Honestly, I don't think the people over here know what cricket is half the time. All they want to see is short balls and blokes either ducking or hooking – or getting hit. That's what they seem to think cricket is all about. And it's a damned shame because there's a hell of a lot more to cricket than that.

Despite the reek of a burning Test rubber, however, Taylor fulfilled a professed desire to clear the air of on-field belligerence. Compared to Australia's R-rated 1991 Caribbean tour, voices were raised solely in appeal during Australia's Worrell Trophy win.

Homecoming reception was rapturous. At a Sydney ticker-tape parade, the Trophy was caressed as covetously as a new bride. 'We'd like to hang onto this for a while yet,' Taylor told Australians, 'and make them suffer like we did.' Among the honours forthcoming for the captain was, at a luncheon at the Menzies Hotel on 25 August, the title of NSW Father of the Year (suggesting that Taylor is supreme practitioner of the concept of 'quality time').

Amid the euphoria, Taylor and Steve Waugh took to the ACB proposals for a substantial increase in international match fees and retainers. It was also at their instigation that on 21 September 1995 plans were mooted for a Cricket Players Association of Australia: a collective bargaining body long advocated by the new NSW team coach Geoff Lawson.

Taylor earned all his pay packet during a second home summer where he was required to exercise more diplomacy than Lord Casey. Disclosure of the bribes apparently offered Shane Warne, Mark Waugh and Tim May lent a unsavoury odour to Australia's 1995–96 series against Pakistan, especially when alleged intermediary Salim Malik was unexpectedly included in Wasim Akram's team. Between them, Taylor and Akram ensured that bottled animosity did not ooze onto the field during Australia's 2-1 victory.

418

Geoff Lawson, reporting for *Cricketer International*, praised the teams for their 'total absence of malice'.

Having kicked off the season with a shrewd 126 for NSW against Victoria, there was also an exemplary extroversion to Taylor's cricket. His 338 runs at 67 included a 14th Test century at Bellerive, carrying away the individual award in 155-run victory, while Mark also pocketed his 100th Test catch in only his 70th Test.

Further strife beckoned in Australia's three-match rubber against Arjuna Ranatunga's Sri Lankans. Tempers were strained when the tourists were first accused of and exonerated from ball-tampering, then saw their top Test wicket-taker Muttiah Muralitharan judged guilty of throwing by three umpires.

Taylor maintained a bystander's innocence as his XI swept the series clean and, by summer's end, had secured a reputation for lateral thought. When Mark turned to Greg Blewett at Bellerive because of an injury to Warne, the anodyne medium-pacer picked up two wickets in two overs that redirected the course of the match. When thoughts were all of Warne in the MCG Boxing Day Test against the Sri Lankans, Mark allocated four overs to twenty-one-year-old newcomer Ricky Ponting. The Tasmanian does not so much spin the ball as gently rotate it, but he induced the edge from a circumspect Asanka Gurusinha that began the visitors' subsidence toward following on.

In a summer that careered from one crisis to the next, the captain's composure was ruffled only at the presentation ceremony after the last World Series Cup final. Some rum umpiring and petulance on both sides had fanned ill-feeling, and only Ranatunga and the young quick Ravindra Pushpakumara accepted Taylor's proffered hand. Australia's captain had produced his most consistent streak of one-day form in leading Australia to the trophy (423 runs in 10 completed innings at a hasty 67 per hundred balls), but in a candid press conference at the end of the last Test at Adelaide Oval expressed regret that he'd not addressed discontent sooner: 'I wish I'd taken the Australian team into our opponents' dressing rooms for a drink three weeks ago and not left it until the last Test.'

After a fractious summer several Australian players, including Warne and

419

McDermott, nursed reservations about playing the opening match of their campaign for the 1996 World Cup at Sri Lanka's Premadasa Stadium. Some had received threatening correspondence and telephone calls. So when a terrorist bomb planted by the revolutionary Tamil Tigers detonated in Colombo on 31 January, killing 80 and injuring 1000, the seismic emanations shook foundations at Jolimont Street. Chief executive Graham Halbish's board convened a special session resulting in the forfeiture of the first match.

That international cricket should have been foiled by fanatics was widely deplored, although the phenomenon was older than Test cricket itself. As long ago as 1789, a tour of France mooted by the Duke of Dorset was called off on account of revolution. While Taylor admitted relief about side-stepping Sri Lanka, he insisted: 'There was no lobbying by the players: the board took a unanimous decision which took it out of our hands.'

When the West Indies Cricket Board of Control struck a similar stance, and another explosive device was found a mile from Premadasa two days before the tournament began, Australians' concerns appeared to have been legitimated. But, as they formed a ragged file of striped blazers to gape at the $2 million Gianfranco Lunetta *son et lumiere* show, Taylor's men were not among the most popular guests for the Cup's Calcutta grand opening. Their retinue was swelled at once by two Special Forces bodyguards, expert in martial arts.

Determined to rehabilitate his team in hearts and minds, Taylor was happy to admit large audiences to practices at the Bombay Gymkhana Club Ground. Warne was observed hitting catches to children, and Healy coaching a member's wicketkeeping son. Management and players began distributing 10,000 team photos to eager autograph hunters.

When the Australians moved on to the Taj Residency Hotel at the Indian port city of Visakhapatnam, Taylor began directing wandering minds toward the task of lifting the Cup. Having seen Australia undermined by stereotyped strategies in 1992, he was intent on spicing Australian efforts with variety. His most obvious gambit was unpicking his opening partnership with Michael Slater so that he could deploy Mark Waugh at No. 1. Benching Slater was an astonishing display of Australian cricket affluence – like lighting a cigar with a $100 note – but the skipper sensed that Waugh's *savoir faire* and skills of placement suited the first 15 overs of a one-day innings.

The Marks had opened together in their maiden first-class match just over a decade earlier, and went back to the future in style. Waugh's three tournament centuries were unstoppable and unprecedented. A listless outing cost Australia its match at Jaipur against the West Indies, but the disposal of Kenya and the overthrow of India guaranteed that Australia would make the quarter-final cut.

Taylor then tinkered with the mechanism to engineer Australia's avenue into the final. Faced beneath the lights at Bombay by New Zealand's tallest one-day tally, Mark elevated Shane Warne as a pinch-hitter. The leg-spinner kicked the chocks from under Australia's wheels with 24 in 14 deliveries. Taylor's team rolled past 287 with six wickets and more than two overs in hand.

Set back by losing its four choicest wickets for 15 runs against the West Indies at Chandigarh, Australia could scrounge only eight for 207. By the time Shivnarine Chanderpaul and Richie Richardson had steered their team to two for 165 in the 41st over, it appeared that excess baggage would be the Australians' next worry. Taylor, however, had harried his opponents all night. Running the gamut of his attacking alternatives, he had even prevailed on his eighth bowler Stuart Law to improvise a variety of wrist-spin. As a result, Australia entered the match's final throes with overs in hand from its most dangerous bowlers.

Glenn McGrath, augmented by Warne and supported by a solid gold ring of fielders, rounded up the remaining West Indians for the addition of 36. Tears were shed in the post-match mid-pitch huddle, from which Taylor emerged with a fair comment: 'It was a great game and the West Indies should have won. They won 95 per cent of it and we won the last five per cent.'

National euphoria was such that the ACB would have been entitled to clear cabinet space for the Cup. The *Australian* newspaper before the Cup final gloated prematurely by spreading an exuberant Shane Warne across its front page beneath the headline: 'World Cup victory jig – one match away.'

Yet Australia's escapology had been deluding and, while rated a 1-3 shoo-in for the final at Lahore's Gaddafi Stadium on 17 March, it faced Sri Lankan opponents to whom victory meant rather more than an ornament for the sideboard.

Grievances that Sri Lankans felt after their team's Australian tour had been deepened by the ACB's forfeiture of its match there. While Taylor tried sobering speech the day before the final to the effect that the contest was no more than a cricket match, Ranatunga's rhetoric demonstrated that his 66-1 Cup outsiders still felt seriously slighted and regarded it as something greater. Professional pragmatism ultimately came second to depth of determination. Though Taylor comforted those at home with an uninhibited 74 out of 137 from 83 deliveries – passing 3000 one-day runs in the process – his middle order slid into a restless slumber against Sri Lanka's spinners.

The Sri Lankans pursued Australia's middling seven for 241 with poise and panache and, when Warne found purchase impossible because of the dewfall in Pakistan's first floodlit match, Aravinda de Silva and Ranatunga combined in a crusading, unbeaten, match-winning stand of 97. Fortunately the match's vehemence did not spill over beyond the boundary. Man of the Match de Silva was magnanimous in victory: 'It's not about sweet revenge. But it will boost the game back home. It's a day I shall never forget.' While his disappointment was evident as he addressed the press after the match, Taylor took his conciliatory cue. 'There's always an atmosphere of friendliness between the two sides as far as I'm concerned,' he said. 'We were outplayed – there is no doubt Sri Lanka were a better side today.'

Australian victory in the World Cup would have made a fine coda for this narrative, but its defeat is also a suitable epiphany: the latest twist to the changing challenges that Australia's captains have met over 120 years, at home and abroad, for richer for poorer, in sickness and in health. Sri Lanka, a team that twenty years ago was being commended for its pluck in defeat against Australia, has established itself as a worthy rival. In India, Sachin Tendulkar and Anil Kumble omnipotent reign. Pakistan maintains an enviable record, especially at home, while South Africa has surged back into Test cricket as a formidable competitor.

England and the West Indies, traditionally Australia's most vigorous opponents, might be in eclipse, but both won their second last Tests against us. Flower-powered Zimbabwe are improving all the while and few will be surprised if Kenya has crystallised into a Test nation by the turn of the century. Never in cricket's history, in fact, have so many legitimately contended for the title of 'World Champion'.

One element is a constant, however, and Sri Lanka's World Cup victory verifies it. While resources add a cubit to a country's span, the quality of raw human *materiel* will continue to be the ultimate determinant of cricket supremacy: the 'flesh and blood' referred to in this book's opening chapter. Mark Taylor's successors will probably anchor pay-TV talk shows and have sites on the World Wide Web but, like their predecessors, they will need character and conviction first and foremost to defend Australian cricket's traditions.

THE CAPTAINS' TABLE

SEASON	WHERE PLAYED	AUST CAPT	OPP CAPT	WON	LOST	DRAWN	TIED
1867–77	Australia	D.W. Gregory	J. Lillywhite (E)	1	1	0	0
1878–79	Australia	D.W. Gregory	Lord Harris (E)	1	0	1	0
1880	England	W.L. Murdoch	Lord Harris	0	1	0	0
1881–82	Australia	W.L. Murdoch	A. Shaw (E)	2	0	2	0
1882	England	W.L. Murdoch	A.N. Hornby	1	0	0	0
1882–83	Australia	W.L. Murdoch	Hon. Ivo Bligh (E)	2	2	0	0
1884	England	W.L. Murdoch	A.N. Hornby (1)	0	1	2	0
			Lord Harris (2)				
1884–85	Australia	T.P. Horan (2)	A. Shrewsbury (E)	2	3	0	0
		W.L. Murdoch (1)					
		H.H. Massie (1)					
		J.M. Blackham (1)					
1886	England	H.J.H. Scott	A.G. Steel	0	3	0	0
1886–87	Australia	P.S. McDonnell	A. Shrewsbury (E)	0	2	0	0
1887–88	Australia	P.S. McDonnell	W.W. Read (E)	0	1	0	0
1888	England	P.S. McDonnell	W.G. Grace (2)	1	2	0	0
			A.G. Steel (1)				
1890	England	W.L. Murdoch	W.G. Grace	0	2	0	0
1891–92	Australia	J.M. Blackham	W.G. Grace (E)	2	1	0	0
1893	England	J.M. Blackham	A.E. Stoddart (1)	0	1	2	0
			W.G. Grace (2)				

SEASON	WHERE PLAYED	AUST CAPT	OPP CAPT	WON	LOST	DRAWN	TIED
1894–95	Australia	J.M. Blackham (1) / G. Giffen (4)	A.E. Stoddart (E)	2	3	0	0
1896	England	G.H.S. Trott	W.G. Grace	1	2	0	0
1897–98	Australia	G.H.S. Trott	A.C. MacLaren (2) / A.E. Stoddart (4) (E)	4	1	0	0
1899	England	J. Darling	A.C. MacLaren (1) (E) / W.G. Grace (1)	1	0	4	0
1901–02	Australia	J. Darling (3) / H. Trumble (2)	A.C. MacLaren (4)	4	1	0	0
1902	England	J. Darling	A.C. MacLaren (E)	2	1	2	0
1902–03	South Africa	J. Darling	A.C. MacLaren / H.M. Taberer (1) / J.H. Anderson (1) / A.E. Halliwell (1)	2	1	0	0
1903–04	Australia	M.A. Noble	P.F. Warner (E)	2	3	0	0
1905	England	J. Darling	Hon. F.S. Jackson	0	2	3	0
1907–08	Australia	M.A. Noble	A.O. Jones (2) (E) / F.L. Fane (3) (E)	4	1	0	0
1909	England	M.A. Noble	A.C. MacLaren	2	1	2	0
1910–11	Australia	C. Hill	P.W. Sherwell (SA)	4	1	0	0
1911–12	Australia	C. Hill	J.W.H.T. Douglas (E)	1	4	0	0
1912	England	S.E. Gregory	C.B. Fry	0	1	2	0
1912	England	S.E. Gregory	F. Mitchell (2) (SA) / L.J. Tancred (1) (SA)	2	0	1	0
1920–21	Australia	W.W. Armstrong	J.W.H.T. Douglas (E)	5	0	0	0

SEASON	WHERE PLAYED	AUST CAPT	OPP CAPT	WON	LOST	DRAWN	TIED
1921	England	W.W. Armstrong	J.W.H.T. Douglas (2) / Hon. L. Tennyson (3)	3	0	2	0
1921–22	South Africa	H.L. Collins	H.W. Taylor	1	0	2	0
1924–25	Australia	H.L. Collins	A.E.R. Gilligan (E)	4	1	0	0
1926	England	H.L. Collins (3) / W. Bardsley (2)	A.W. Carr (4) / A.P.F. Chapman (1)	0	1	4	0
1928–29	Australia	J. Ryder	A.P.F. Chapman (4) (E) / J.C. White (1) (E)	1	4	0	0
1930	England	W.M. Woodfull	A.P.F. Chapman (4) / R.E.S. Wyatt (1)	2	1	2	0
1930–31	Australia	W.M. Woodfull	G.C. Grant (WI)	4	1	0	0
1931–32	Australia	W.M. Woodfull	H.B. Cameron (SA)	5	0	0	0
1932–33	Australia	W.M. Woodfull	D.R. Jardine (E)	1	4	0	0
1934	England	W.M. Woodfull	C.F. Walters (1) / R.E.S. Wyatt (4)	2	1	2	0
1935–36	South Africa	V. Richardson	H.F. Wade	4	0	1	0
1936–37	Australia	D.G. Bradman	G.O. Allen (E)	3	2	0	0
1938	England	D.G. Bradman	W.R. Hammond	1	1	2	0
1945–46	New Zealand	W.A. Brown	W.A. Hadlee	1	0	0	0
1946–47	Australia	D.G. Bradman	W.R. Hammond (4) (E) / N.W.D. Yardley (1) (E)	3	0	2	0
1947–48	Australia	D.G. Bradman	L. Amarnath (I)	4	0	1	0
1948	England	D.G. Bradman	N.W.D. Yardley	4	0	1	0
1949–50	South Africa	A.L. Hassett	A.D. Nourse	4	0	1	0
1950–51	Australia	A.L. Hassett	F.R. Brown (E)	4	1	0	0

SEASON	WHERE PLAYED	AUST CAPT	OPP CAPT	WON	LOST	DRAWN	TIED
1951–52	Australia	A.L. Hassett (4)	J. Goddard (4) (WI)	4	1	0	0
		A.R. Morris (1)	J. Stollmeyer (1) (WI)				0
1952–53	Australia	A.L. Hassett	J. Cheetham (SA)	2	2	1	0
1953	England	A.L. Hassett	L. Hutton	0	1	4	0
1954–55	Australia	I.W. Johnson (4)	L. Hutton (E)	1	3	1	0
		A.R. Morris (1)					
1954–55	West Indies	I.W. Johnson	D. Atkinson (3)	3	0	2	0
			J. Stollmeyer (2)				
1956	England	I.W. Johnson	P.B.H. May	1	2	2	0
1956–57	Pakistan	I.W. Johnson	A.H. Kardar	0	1	0	0
1956–57	India	I.W. Johnson (2)	P. Umrigar	2	0	1	0
		R.R. Lindwall (1)					
1957–58	South Africa	I.D. Craig	J. McGlew (1)	3	0	2	0
			C. van Ryneveld (4)				
1958–59	Australia	R. Benaud	P.B.H. May (E)	4	0	1	0
1959–60	Pakistan	R. Benaud	Fazal Mahmood (2)	2	0	1	0
			Imtiaz Ahmed (1)				
1959–60	India	R. Benaud	G.S. Ramchand	3	1	1	0
1960–61	Australia	R. Benaud (4)	F.M. Worrell (WI)	2	1	1	1
1961	England	R. Benaud (4)	M.C. Cowdrey (2)	2	1	2	0
		R.N. Harvey (1)	P.B.H. May (3)				
1962–63	Australia	R. Benaud	E.R. Dexter (E)	1	1	3	0
1963–64	Australia	R. Benaud (1)	T.L. Goddard (SA)	1	1	3	0
		R.B. Simpson (4)					
1964	England	R.B. Simpson	E.R. Dexter	1	0	4	0

SEASON	WHERE PLAYED	AUST CAPT	OPP CAPT	WON	LOST	DRAWN	TIED
1964–65	India	R.B. Simpson	Nawab of Pataudi	1	1	1	0
1964–65	Pakistan	R.B. Simpson	Hanif Mohammad	0	0	1	0
1964–65	Australia	R.B. Simpson	Hanif Mohammad (P)	0	0	1	0
1965	West Indies	R.B. Simpson	G.S. Sobers	1	2	2	0
1965–66	Australia	B.C. Booth (2)	M.J.K. Smith (E)	1	1	3	0
		R.B. Simpson (3)					
1966–67	South Africa	R.B. Simpson	P. van der Merwe	1	3	1	0
1967–68	Australia	R.B. Simpson (2)	C. Borde (1) (I)	4	0	0	0
		W.M. Lawry (2)	Nawab of Pataudi (3) (I)				
1968	England	W.M. Lawry (4)	M.C. Cowdrey (4)	1	1	3	0
		B.N. Jarman (1)	T.W. Graveney (1)				
1968–69	Australia	W.M. Lawry	G.S. Sobers (WI)	3	1	1	0
1969–70	India	W.M. Lawry	Nawab of Pataudi	3	1	1	0
1969–70	South Africa	W.M. Lawry	A. Bacher	0	4	0	0
1970–71	Australia	W.M. Lawry (5)	R. Illingworth (E)	0	2	4	0
		I.M. Chappell (1)					
1972	England	I.M. Chappell	R. Illingworth	2	2	1	0
1972–73	Australia	I.M. Chappell	Intikhab Alam (P)	3	0	0	0
1972–73	West Indies	I.M. Chappell	Rohan Kanhai	2	0	3	0
1973–74	Australia	I.M. Chappell	B.E. Congdon (NZ)	2	0	1	0
1974	New Zealand	I.M. Chappell	B.E. Congdon	1	1	1	0
1974–75	Australia	I.M. Chappell	M.H. Denness (5) (E)	4	1	1	0
			J.H. Edrich (1) (E)				
1975	England	I.M. Chappell	M.H. Denness (1)	1	0	3	0
			A.W. Greig (3)				

SEASON	WHERE PLAYED	AUST CAPT	OPP CAPT	WON	LOST	DRAWN	TIED
1975–76	Australia	G.S. Chappell	C.H. Lloyd (WI)	5	1	0	0
1976–77	Australia	G.S. Chappell	Mushtaq Mohammad (P)	1	1	1	0
1976–77	New Zealand	G.S. Chappell	G. Turner	1	0	1	0
1976–77	Australia	G.S. Chappell	A.W. Greig (E)	1	0	0	0
1977	England	G.S. Chappell	J.M. Brearley	0	3	2	0
1977–78	Australia	R.B. Simpson	B.S. Bedi (I)	3	2	0	0
1977–78	West Indies	R.B. Simpson	C.H. Lloyd (2)	1	3	1	0
			A. Kallicharran (3)				
1978–79	Australia	G.N. Yallop	J.M. Brearley (E)	1	5	0	0
1978–79	Australia	G.N. Yallop (1)	Mushtaq Mohammad (P)	1	1	0	0
		K.J. Hughes (1)					
1979	India	K.J. Hughes	S. Gavaskar	0	2	4	0
1979–80	Australia	G.S. Chappell	C.H. Lloyd (WI)	0	2	4	0
1979–80	Australia	G.S. Chappell	J.M. Brearley (P)	3	0	0	0
1979–80	Pakistan	G.S. Chappell	Javed Miandad	0	1	2	0
1980	England	G.S. Chappell	I. Botham	0	0	1	0
1980–81	Australia	G.S. Chappell	G.P. Howarth (2) (NZ)	2	0	1	0
			M.G. Burgess (1) (NZ)				
1980–81	Australia	G.S. Chappell	S.M. Gavaskar (I)	1	1	1	0
1981	England	K.J. Hughes	J.M. Brearley (4)	1	3	2	0
			I.T. Botham (2)				
1981–82	Australia	G.S. Chappell	C.H. Lloyd (WI)	1	1	1	0
1981–82	Australia	G.S. Chappell	Javed Miandad (P)	2	1	0	0
1981–82	New Zealand	G.S. Chappell	G.P. Howarth (NZ)	1	1	1	0
1982–83	Australia	G.S. Chappell	R.D.G. Willis (E)	2	1	2	0

SEASON	WHERE PLAYED	AUST CAPT	OPP CAPT	WON	LOST	DRAWN	TIED
1983	Pakistan	K.J. Hughes	Imran Khan	0	3	0	0
1983	Sri Lanka	G.S. Chappell	L.R.D. Mendis	1	0	0	0
1983–84	Australia	K.J. Hughes	Imran Khan (2) (P) Zaheer Abbas (3) (P)	2	0	3	0
1983–84	West Indies	K.J. Hughes	C.H. Lloyd (4)	0	3	2	0
1984–5	Australia	A.R. Border (3) K.J. Hughes (2)	I.V.A. Richards (1) C.H. Lloyd (WI)	1	3	1	0
1985	England	A.R. Border	D.I. Gower	1	3	2	0
1985–86	Australia	A.R. Border	J.V. Coney (NZ)	1	2	0	0
1985–86	Australia	A.R. Border	Kapil Dev (I)	0	0	3	0
1985–86	New Zealand	A.R. Border	J.V. Coney	0	1	2	0
1986–87	India	A.R. Border	Kapil Dev	0	0	2	1
1986–87	Australia	A.R. Border	M.W. Gatting (E)	1	2	2	0
1987–88	Australia	A.R. Border	J.J. Crowe (NZ)	1	0	2	0
1987–88	Australia	A.R. Border	M.W. Gatting (E)	0	0	1	0
1987–88	Australia	A.R. Border	R.S. Madugalle (SL)	1	0	0	0
1988–89	Pakistan	A.R. Border	Javed Miandad	0	1	2	0
1988–89	Australia	A.R. Border	I.V.A. Richards (WI)	1	3	1	0
1989	England	A.R. Border	D.I. Gower	4	0	2	0
1989–90	Australia	A.R. Border	J.G. Wright (NZ)	0	0	1	0
1989–90	Australia	A.R. Border	A. Ranatunga (SL)	1	0	1	0
1989–90	Australia	A.R. Border	Imran Khan (P)	1	0	2	0
1989–90	New Zealand	A.R. Border	J.G. Wright	0	1	0	0

SEASON	WHERE PLAYED	AUST CAPT	OPP CAPT	WON	LOST	DRAWN	TIED
1990–91	Australia	A.R. Border	G.A. Gooch (4) (E) A.J. Lamb (1) (E)	3	0	2	0
1990–91	West Indies	A.R. Border	I.V.A. Richards	1	2	2	0
1991–92	Australia	A.R. Border	M. Azharuddin (I)	4	0	1	0
1992–93	Sri Lanka	A.R. Border	A. Ranatunga	1	0	2	0
1992–93	Australia	A.R. Border	R.B. Richardson (WI)	1	2	2	0
1992–93	New Zealand	A.R. Border	M.D. Crowe	1	1	1	0
1993	England	A.R. Border	G.A. Gooch (4) M.A. Atherton (2)	4	1	1	0
1993–94	Australia	A.R. Border	M.D. Crowe (1) (NZ) K.R. Rutherford (2) (NZ)	2	0	1	0
1993–94	Australia	A.R. Border	K.C. Wessels (2) (SA) W.J. Cronje (1) (SA)	1	1	1	0
1993–94	South Africa	A.R. Border	K.C. Wessels	1	1	1	0
1994–95	Pakistan	M.A. Taylor	Salim Malik	0	1	2	0
1994–95	Australia	M.A. Taylor	M.A. Atherton (E)	3	1	1	0
1994–95	West Indies	M.A. Taylor	R.B. Richardson	2	1	1	0
1995–96	Australia	M.A. Taylor	Wasim Akram (P)	2	1	0	0
1995–96	Australia	M.A. Taylor	A. Ranatunga (SL)	3	0	0	0

BOOKS CONSULTED

Prime resources for this book include *With Bat and Ball* by George Giffen, Ward Lock, London, 1898; *Giants of the Game* by C.B. Fry, Ward Lock and E.P. Publishing, London; *33 Years of Cricket* by Frank Iredale, Beatty Richardson, Sydney, 1920; *Test Tussles On and Off the Field* by D.K. Darling, Hobart, 1970; *The Golden Age of Cricket* by Robert Trumble, Melbourne, 1968; *An Australian Cricketer on Tour* by Frank Laver, Bell & Sons, London; *Mr. Cricket* by W.H. Ferguson, Nicholas Kaye, London, 1957; *Farewell to Cricket* by Sir Donald Bradman, Hodder & Stoughton, London, 1950; *More Cricket Prints* by R.C. Robertson-Glasgow, Werner Laurie, London, 1948; *The Paddock That Grew* by Keith Dunstan, Cassell Australia, Melbourne, 1975; *The Victor Richardson Story* by Richardson, Rigby, Adelaide, 1966; *The Great All-rounders* and *The Great Bowlers* edited by John Arlott, Pelham, London 1968 and 1969; *Way of Cricket* and *Willow Patterns* by Richie Benaud, Hodder & Stoughton, London, 1961 and 1969; *My World of Cricket* by Neil Harvey, Hodder & Stoughton, London, 1963; *Allan Border: The Autobiography* by Allan Border, Methuen, Sydney, 1985; *Beyond 10,000* by Allan Border, Swan Publishing, Sydney, 1993; *The Border Years* by Gideon Haigh, Text Publishing, Melbourne, 1994; *Taylor Made* by Mark Taylor, Pan MacMillan, Sydney, 1995.

Other books and publications consulted are the *Australian Encyclopaedia*, Grolier, Sydney; *The Greatest of My Time* by Trevor Bailey, Eyre & Spottiswoode, London, 1968; *England v. Australia* by Ralph Barker and Irving Rosenwater, Heinemann, Melbourne, 1969; *Our Cricket Story* by Alec and Eric Bedser, Evans, London, 1949; *The Appeal of Cricket: The Modern Game* by Richie Benaud, Hodder & Stoughton, London, 1995; *Ashes Glory* by Allan Border, Swan Publishing, Sydney, 1989; *The Ashes Retained* by Mike Brearley, Hodder & Stoughton, London, 1979; *Phoenix from the Ashes* by Mike Brearley, Hodder & Stoughton, London, 1982; *Australian Summer* by Sir Neville Cardus, Collins, London, 1973; *The Ashes '77* by Greg Chappell and David Frith, Angus & Robertson, Sydney, 1977; *Tigers Among the Lions* by Ian Chappell, Investigator,

Adelaide, 1972; *My World of Cricket* by Ian Chappell, Pollard, Sydney, 1974; *Chappelli* by Ian Chappell, Hutchinson, Melbourne, 1976; *End of an Innings* by Denis Compton, Oldbourne, London, 1958; *The Incomparable Game* by Colin Cowdrey, Hodder & Stoughton, London, 1970; *Fifteen Paces* by Alan Davidson, Souvenir, London, 1963; *100 Not Out* by Sydney Downer, Rigby, Adelaide, 1972; *Runs in the Family* by John Edrich, Stanley Paul, London, 1972; *Extra Cover* by Jack Egan, ABC Books, Sydney, 1989; *By Hook or by Cut* by Les Favell, Investigator, Adelaide, 1970; *Fingleton on Cricket* by Jack Fingleton, Collins, London, 1972; *The Wisden Book of Test Cricket* Vol 1 by Bill Frindall, Macdonald & Jane, London, 1978; *The Wisden Book of Test Cricket* Vol 2 by Bill Frindall, MacDonald & Jane, London, 1995; *My Dear Victorious Stod* by David Frith, London, 1970; *Waugh Declared* by Mark Gateley, Ironbark Press, Sydney, 1992; *Leading from the Front* by Mike Gatting (with Angela Patmore), Queen Anne Press, London, 1988; *Gower: The Autobiography* by David Gower (with Martin Johnson), Collins Willow, London, 1993; *My Country's Keeper* by Wallace Grout, Pelham, London, 1965; *The Cricket War* by Gideon Haigh, Text Publishing, Melbourne, 1993; *One Summer, Every Summer* by Gideon Haigh, Text Publishing, Melbourne, 1995; *Pace Like Fire* by Wes Hall, Pelham, London, 1965; *Cricket Rebels* by Chris Harte and Warwick Hadfield, QB Books, Sydney, 1985; *Two Tours and Pollock* by Chris Harte, Sports Marketing (Australia), Adelaide, 1988; *Hookesy* by David Hookes (with Alan Shiell), ABC Books, Sydney, 1993; *Cricket at the Crossroads* by Ian Johnson, Cassell, London, 1957; *Kangaroo Invasion* by Brunell Jones, Trinidad, 1973; *Deano – My Call* by Dean Jones (with Terry Brindle), Swan Publishing, Sydney, 1994; *Over to Me* by Jim Laker, Frederick Muller, London, 1960; *The Larwood Story* by Harold Larwood with Kevin Perkins, W.H. Allen, London, 1965, *Run-digger* by Bill Lawry, Souvenir, London, 1966; *Diary of the Ashes* by Geoff Lawson (with Mark Ray), Ironbark Press, Sydney, 1989; *Henry* by Geoff Lawson, Ironbark Press, Sydney, 1992; *Back to the Mark* by Dennis Lillee, Hutchinson, Australia, 1974; *My Life in Cricket* by Dennis Lillee, Methuen, Sydney, 1985; *Strike Bowler* by Craig McDermott (with Phil Derriman), ABC Books, Sydney, 1992; *Greg Chappell* by Adrian McGregor, Williams Collins, Sydney, 1985; *Slasher Opens Up* by Ken Mackay, Pelham, London, 1964; *10 for 66 and All That* by Arthur Mailey, Phoenix; *Rowdy* by Ashley Mallett, Lynton, Adelaide, 1973; *Games People Played* by W.F. Mandle, Historical Studies,

Melbourne University; *The Inside Edge* by Rod Marsh, Swan Publishing, Sydney, 1983; *Cricket Crossfire* by Keith Miller, Oldbourne, London, 1957; *Australian Cricket, A History* by A.G. Moyes, Angus & Robertson, Sydney, 1959; *The Game's the Thing* by M.A. Noble, Cassell, London, 1926; *Cricket Conquest* by W.J. O'Reilly, Werner Laurie, London, 1950; *A History of Tasmanian Cricket* by Roger Page, Government Printer, Hobart, 1957; *Six and Out* edited by Jack Pollard, Lansdowne, Melbourne, 1964; *Border and Beyond* by Mark Ray, ABC Books, Sydney, 1995; *The Umpire's Story* by Lou Rowan, Jack Pollard, Sydney, 1972; *Captain's Story* by Bobby Simpson, Stanley Paul, London, 1966; *Simmo* by Bob Simpson, Hutchinson, Melbourne, 1979; *With the 15th Australian XI* by Sydney Smith, 1922; *The Bedside Book of Cricket Centuries* by Terry Smith, Angus & Robertson, Sydney, 1991; *Cricket Crusader* by Sir Garry Sobers, Pelham, London, 1966; *Not Just for Openers* by Keith Stackpole and Alan Trengove, Stockwell, Melbourne, 1974; *A Spell at the Top* by Brian Statham, Souvenir, London, 1969; *David Gower: A Man Out of Time* by Rob Steen, Victor Gollancz, London, 1995; *Sort of a Cricket Person* by E.W. Swanton, Collins, London, 1973; *David Boon: In The Firing Line* by Mark Thomas, Sun Books, Melbourne, 1993; *Captains on a See-saw* by Phil Tresidder, Souvenir, London, 1969; *A Typhoon Called Tyson* by Frank Tyson, Phoenix; *My Cricketing Years* by Ajit Wadekar, Vikas, Delhi, 1973; *Bradman the Great* by B.J. Wakley, Nicholas Kaye, London, 1959; *Looking for Runs* by Doug Walters, Pelham, London, 1971; *Ashes Diary* by Steve Waugh, Ironbark Press, Sydney, 1993; *South African Tour Diary* by Steve Waugh, Ironbark Press, Sydney, 1994; *West Indies Tour Diary* by Steve Waugh, HarperCollins, Sydney, 1995; *Solid Knocks and Second Thoughts* by Dirk Wellham (with Howard Rich), Reed Books, Sydney, 1988; *Quick Whit* by Mike Whitney, Ironbark Press, Sydney, 1994; *Whiticisms* by Mike Whitney, Ironbark Press, Sydney, 1995; *Lambs to the Slaughter* by Graham Yallop, Outback Books, Melbourne, 1979; *Wisden's Cricketers' Almanack*; *Pelham Cricket Year*; *Benson & Hedges Cricket Year*; *Association of Cricket Statisticians Yearbooks*; *Playfair Cricket Annual*; *ABC Cricket Book*; *The Cricketer International*; *Wisden Cricket Monthly*; *Cricketer*; *Australian Cricket*; *World of Cricket Monthly*; *Sportsweek*; *Inside Edge*; *Inside Sport*; *Sports Weekly*; *Pakistan Cricketer*; *South African Cricket Action*; *Cricket Society Journal*; *Pavilion* and *Extra Cover*; NSW Cricket Association Year Books.

INDEX

This index is arranged alphabetically, word for word.

In general, the use of a person's initials, usually with his given or familiar name in brackets, indicates a Test player. All the indexed Pakistani cricketers, and Kapil Dev (India) and Inshan Ali (West Indies) are also Test players, but other indexed people without initials are not.

Bold page numbers indicate where sections relating to the captain begin.

and Alan Davidson 275
and Clarrie Grimmett 267
and Wally Grout 99, 322
and Neil Harvey 272, 282, 284, 287
and Barry Jarman 325
and Ray Lindwall 254, 274
and Keith Miller 257, 268
and Bill O'Reilly 269
and public relations 274
and Bob Simpson 276, 296
and underarm delivery 354
and World Series Cricket 319
and Frank Worrell 273
as all-rounder 61, 64 269
as bowler
    statistics 64
    strike rate 138
as commentator 319, 340
as fielder
    in gully 272
birth 267
divorce 269
family 267
fast scoring 268
marriage
    to Marcia Lavener 268
retirement 225, 401
statistics 275, 277
    11 sixes in innings 268
    Test 269
technique 269
Bennett, Fred 374
Berry, Scyld 389
betting 142
    allegations 415, 418
Bevan, M.G. (Michael) 414
Bishop, I.R. (Ian) 397
Blackett, Stephanie *see* Slater, Stephanie
Blackham, J. McC. (Jack) 5, 12, **41**, 43,
    54, 372
    1893 tour of England 45
    aid to captains 43
    and John Conway 41
    and George Giffen 41, 43, 45, 62
    and W.G. Grace 43–5
    and Syd Gregory 46, 130
    and Clem Hill 116
    and Tom Horan 28
    and Will Murdoch 42
    and Fred Spofforth 41

appeals by 44
appearance 42
as a batsman 44
assessment 44
attributes 45
background 41
death 47
injuries 42
later life 46–7
nervousness 45–6
statistics 46
technique 41–2
Blackie, D.D. (Don) 166
Blackman, Laurie 405
Blewett, G.S. (Greg) 419
Bligh, Florence Rose (nee Morphy) 23
Bligh, I.F.W. (Hon. Ivo) 23
Blunden, Edward 137
Blythe, C. 82
Board of Control *see also* Australian
        Cricket Board
    1912 dispute 109–10, 113–14
    and Ian Chappell 338
    and Lindsay Hassett 224
    and profit sharing 107, 109
    appointment of manager 110
    constitution 105, 107
bodyline 174–5, 177, 184, 195
    and Board of Control 195
    and Don Bradman 194
    and umpires 194
    and Bill Voce (in 1934) 176, 216
    and Bill Woodfull 177
Bonnor, G.J. (George) 34, 37, 44
    1880 tour of England 19
    1886 tour of England 50
        as hitter 54
        fast scoring 119
Boon, D.C. (David) 68, 299, 388, 391, 393,
        408, 413–15
Booth, B.C. (Brian) **303**
    1961 tour of England 305
    and Bob Cowper 307
    and Bill Lawry 305
    and Norm O'Neill 304
    and Bob Simpson 308
    as fielder 307
    as hockey player 303
    birth 304
    fast scoring 305–6

437

marriage 304
occupation 303
slow scoring 305
statistics 308
technique 303
Booth, Brian 305
Booth, Judith (nee Williams) 304
Border, A.R. (Allan) 2, 111, 134, 287, **381**,
405, 410–11
1978–79 tour of India 370–1
1981 tour of England 383
1984 tour of West Indies 375, 385, 400
1985 tour of England 386
1986 tour of New Zealand 387
1988 tour of Pakistan 390
1989 tour of England 392
1991 tour of West Indies 394–5
1993 tour of England 398
1993–94 tour of South Africa 398
and Australian Cricket Board 399
and Don Bradman 386
and Mike Brearley 384
and captaincy 384, 400–1
and Greg Chappell 356, 384
and Ian Chappell 391–2
and Ian Craig 265
and discipline 399
and David Gower 393
and Kim Hughes 370, 376
and injuries 383
and Geoff Lawson 395
and Geoff Marsh 396
and on-field dissent 396
and Bob Simpson 299, 387–8, 415
and sledging 393
and Garry Sobers 381
and Mark Taylor 408–9
and West Indians 391, 417
as all-rounder 392
as bowler 391
marriage 384
move to Queensland 384
nicknames 395
'pair' 397
statistics 381
aggregates 125
away from home 400
centuries
in England 160
in each innings 342

four successive 386
first-class 399
most Test runs 397
technique 383
testimonial 398
tours of England 85–6
Border Cricket Union 3
Border, Jane (nee Hiscox) 384
Bosanquet, B.J.T. 138
Botham, I.T. (Ian) 352, 361, 369, 372, 392
and Bob Taylor 99
as fielder 99
statistics 101
bouncers 143, 199
and Greg Chappell 330
and Ian Chappell 330
and Neil Harvey 282
and Bill Lawry 313
and Ray Lindwall 252
and Keith Miller 256
and Bob Simpson 292, 295
and Graham Yallop 360
Bowes, W.E. (Bill) 195
Boycott, G. (Geoffrey) 292, 308, 318
1974–75 tour of Australia 158
1977 tour of England 353
Boyle, H.F. (Harry) 12, 21, 22
and Henry (Tup) Scott 49
Boyle, H.S. (Harry)
in England 13
Bradley, W.M. 132
Bradman, D.G. (Sir Donald) **188**, 360
1930 tour of England 183, 189, 400
1934 tour of England 195
selector 176
1938 tour of England 199, 222
as selector 201
1948 tour of England 141, 205, 225
and abstinence 203
and Gubby Allen 198, 199
and Alec Bedser 207
and Richie Benaud 337
and Board of Control 114, 199, 202
and Allan Border 386
and bouncers 199, 208
and bowlers 196
and Bill Brown 215
and Greg Chappell 343, 352
and Ian Chappell 337
and discipline 208

449

statistics
  double centuries 22, 24
  triple century 21
  young Test captain, 55, 360
Murray, J.T. (John) 285
Musgrove, Harry 72
Mushtaq Ahmed 414

Nanan, Ranjie 375
Nash, Laurie 198
Nash, Malcolm 347
Nel, J.D. (Jack) 227
Newland, Josephine (nee Ferguson) 120
Newland, Phillip 120
Niehuus, Dick 218
Nitschke, H.C. (Holmesdale or 'Slinger')
  184, 214
Noble, Ellen (nee Ferguson) 102
Noble, M.A. (Monty or Alf) **98**, 113, 349
  1899 tour of England 97
  1905 tour of England 100
  1909 tour of England 100, 137
  and Warwick Armstrong 100, 102
  and Warren Bardsley 101
  and Charles Fry 101
  and 'Stork' Hendry 101
  and Jim Kelly 99
  and Frank Laver 100, 101
  and SCG Trust 103
  and Hugh Trumble 91–2, 98
  and substitutes 101
  appearance 96
  as all-rounder 61, 96
  as bowler 96, 98
    technique 97
  as commentator 172
  as disciplinarian 101
  as fielder 99
  as tactician 142
  birth 96
  death 103
  marriage 102
  names known by 96
  occupation 97, 102
  statistics 61–2, 101
    averages 98
  technique 98
    as bowler 97
  winning the toss 101
Noblet, G. 238, 251

North Sydney High 382
Norton, John 262
Nurse, S.M. (Seymour) 315

Oakman, A.S.M. (Alan) 245
O'Brien, L.P.J. 197
O'Donnell, Aileen see Armstrong, Aileen
Ogilvie, A.D. (David) 134
O'Keeffe, K.J. (Kerry) 134, 333, 344, 400
Old, C.M. (Chris) 369
Oldfield, W.A. (Bert) 196
  1921 tour of England 141, 143
  and Warren Bardsley 157
  and Herby Collins 151–2
  and Clarrie Grimmett 99
  and Harold Larwood 175
  and Bill Woodfull 178
  appeals by 44
  in AIF 148
O'Neill, N.C. (Norman) 134, 271, 276,
  283, 291, 294, 307, 323
  and Brian Booth 304
  and Kim Hughes 367
  and Bob Simpson 296
  and strokeplay 231
O'Reilly, W.J. (Bill) 62, 197, 267
  1934 tour of England 176
  1938 tour of England 201, 216
  and Board of Control 197
  and Don Bradman 196
  and Bill Brown 217
  and double leg trap 186
  and Clarrie Grimmett 186, 201
  and Lindsay Hassett 223
  and Kim Hughes 377
  and Jack Massie 39
  and Arthur Morris 233
  and Vic Richardson 185
  and Bill Woodfull 175, 177–8
  as fielder 196
  last Test 217
  wicket-taking in England 93

Packer, Kerry 278, 339, 352–3, 382
Paine, Marjorie see Collins, Marjorie
Palmer, G.E. (George) 21–2
  and Percy McDonnell 53
  and Fred Spofforth 44
Pamensky, Joe 377
Pardon, Sydney 50, 156

455

Stacey, Brad 399
Stackpole, K.R. (Keith) 35, 54, 68, 111,
        277, 317, 371
    and Jack Ryder 168
    and Graham Yallop 360
Statham, J.B. (Brian) 211, 237, 256, 305,
        312–13, 319
    and Fred Trueman 285, 287
    and Frank Tyson 239
Steel, A.G. 36, 50
Steele, Ray 332, 338, 362
Stewart, A.J. (Alec) 129
Stewart, M.J. (Mickey) 129
Stoddart, A.E. (Andrew) 5, 44, 46, 63,
        71–2, 130
Stollmeyer, J.B. (Jeffrey) 4, 360
Storer, W. (William) 73, 132
Strudwick, H. 150
Subba Row, R. (Raman) 305, 396
substitutes 29
Sullivan, Maria *see* Gregory, Maria
Surti, R.F. 316
Sutcliffe, H. (Herbert)
    and Jack Hobbs 151, 154, 166
Swetman, R. (Roy) 249
Sydney Church of England Grammar
        School 39
Symonds, Andrew 268

Tallon, Bill 165
Tallon, D. (Don) 202, 218–19
    and Don Bradman 348
Tasker, Norm 379
Tate, F.W. (Fred) 83, 93
Tate, M.W. (Maurice) 151
    and Warren Bardsley 158
    and Harold Larwood 166
Tayfield, H.J. (Hugh) 260, 263, 286–7
Taylor, J.M. (Johnny) 141, 143–4, 152
Taylor, Judi (nee Matthews) 407, 416
Taylor, M.A. (Mark) 2, 5, 111, **403**, 404–5
    1989 tour of England 392–3, 407
    1991 tour of West Indies 395, 410
    1991 tour of Zimbabwe 411
    1993–94 tour of South Africa 412
    1994 tour of Pakistan and Sri Lanka 414
    1995 tour of West Indies 417
    and 'Australia A' 415
    and Bolton League 407
    and Allan Border 408

and Greg Chappell 409
and Ian Craig 265
and John Fordham 413
and Geoff Lawson 407
and Geoff Marsh 408, 411
and Arthur Morris 409
and player payments 418
and Peter Taylor 406, 413
and Bob Simpson 300, 408, 410, 415
and Michael Slater 412, 416
and sledging 413
and Steve Small 406
and Mark Waugh 406, 420–1
appointment 413
as author 418
as fielder 405, 419
birth 404
marriage 407
occupation 405
statistics 403
    centuries in each innings 410
technique 410
Taylor, Mick 378
Taylor, P.L. (Peter) 406, 413
Taylor, R.W. (Bob) 99
Telford, Dick 375
Tennyson, L.H. 143
Thomas, G.R. (Grahame) 134
Thomas, Greg 408
Thoms, George (Dr) 252
Thomson, A.L. (Alan) 344
Thomson, J.R. (Jeff) 62, 134, 265, 286,
        338, 348–9, 400
    and Dennis Lillee 337
    and Rod Marsh 99
Thorpe, G.P. (Graham) 415
Thurlow, H.M. ('Pud') 193
Thwaites, Colin 165
Titmus, F.J. (Freddie) 294, 305, 313, 319
Toohey, P.M. (Peter) 286
Toshack, E.R.H. (Ernie) 134, 204–6
Travers, Basil 39
Tribe, G.E. (George) 204
Trimble, Sam 134
Trott, A.E. (Albert) 61, 69
    and Monty Noble 97
    suicide 74
Trott, G.H.S. (Harry) 4, 45, 61, **67**
    and baseball 72
    and George Giffen 64, 67

and Syd Gregory 70, 131
and Tom Horan 73
and Fred Spofforth 71
and Bill Woodfull 172
appearance 67
as all-rounder 68
as point fieldsman 68
as tactician 142
assessment 73
attitude to game 70
birth 67
death 73
fast scoring 68
insanity 73
later life 73
marriage 68
statistics 69
technique 67
tours of England 68
Trott, Violet (nee Hodson) 68
Trueman, F.S. (Fred) 246, 249, 285,
      287, 319
Trumble, Florence (nee Christian) 92
Trumble, H. (Hugh) 61, **89**, 132
1890 tour of England 90
1896 tour of England 91
1899 tour of England 92
1902 tour of England 82–4, 93
and alcohol 90
and Jack Blackham 45
and Joe Darling 82, 93
and Johnny Douglas 92
and English pitches 91
and C.B. Fry 89
and George Giffen 45, 63
and Clem Hill 117
and Tom Horan 32
and F.S. Jackson 91
and Jim Kelly 71
and Melbourne Cricket Club 94
and Monty Noble 91, 98
and Wilfred Rhodes 93
and Jack Ryder 94
and Sir Pelham Warner 92
appearance 89
as all-rounder 92
  in England 145
as bowler 93
as fielder 92–3
  in slips 91

birth 89
later life 94
marriage 93
occupation 94
return from retirement 93
success in England 93
statistics
  12 wickets twice in Tests 93
  hat-tricks 89
    first 92
    second 93
  wicket-takers 61
technique 91
Trumble, J.W. (John) 90
Trumble, Robert 121
Trumper, Ann (nee Briggs) 120
Trumper, V.T. (Victor) 120, 297
1899 selection 79
1902 tour of England 83
1905 tour of England 109
1911–12 series 123
1912 dispute 111
and Warren Bardsley 158
and Board of Control 123
and Joe Darling 77, 79, 83
and Reg Duff 194
and Clem Hill 119
and Peter McAlister 124
and Wilfred Rhodes 77
and team spirit 158
fast scoring 35, 54, 83, 119
marriage 120
superstition 83
Tunks, Bill 9
Turner, A. (Alan) 347
Turner, C.T.B. (Charles) 55–6, 61, 90, 270
  wicket-taking in England 91
Turner, G.M. (Glenn) 217, 335
Turner, Mike 300
Turner, Ross 405
Tyldesley, E. (Ernest) 143, 149
Tyldesley, J.T. (Johnny) 80–1
Tyson, F.H. (Frank) 237, 239, 249, 285,
      299, 304, 323, 359

Ulyett, G. (George) 11, 22, 24, 29
umbrella field 227, 238
underarm delivery 354
Underwood, D.L. (Derek) 315, 325, 352